Study Guide for use with

Fundamentals of Corporate Finance

second

canadian

edition

Richard A. Brealey
Bank of England and London Business School

Stewart C. Myers
Sloan School of Management
Massachusetts Institute of Technology

Alan J. Marcus
Wallace E. Carroll School of Management
Boston College

Elizabeth M. Maynes
Schulich School of Business
York University—Toronto

Devashis Mitra
University of New Brunswick—Fredericton

Prepared by

Matthew Will
Johns Hopkins University

Keith Cheung
University of Windsor

 **McGraw-Hill**
Ryerson

Toronto Montréal Boston Burr Ridge, IL Dubuque, IA Madison, WI New York San Francisco St. Louis Bangkok
Bogotá Caracas Kuala Lumpur Lisbon London Madrid Mexico City Milan New Delhi Santiago Seoul
Singapore Sydney Taipei

Study Guide
for use with
Fundamentals of Corporate Finance
Second Canadian Edition

Copyright © 2003 by McGraw-Hill Ryerson Limited, a Subsidiary of The McGraw-Hill Companies. All rights reserved. No part of this publication may be reproduced or transmitted in any form or by any means, or stored in a data base or retrieval system, without the prior written permission of McGraw-Hill Ryerson Limited, or in the case of photocopying or other reprographic copying, a license from The Canadian Copyright Licensing Agency (Access Copyright). For an Access Copyright licence, visit www.accesscopyright.ca or call toll free to 1-800-893-5777.

ISBN: 0-07-0898685

1 2 3 4 5 6 7 8 9 10 CP 0 9 8 7 6 5 4 3

Printed and bound in Canada

Care has been taken to trace ownership of copyright material contained in this text; however, the publisher will welcome any information that enables them to rectify any reference or credit for subsequent editions.

Vice President, Editorial and Media Technology: Patrick Ferrier
Executive Sponsoring Editor: Lynn Fisher
Developmental Editor: Daphne Scriabin
Production Coordinator: Paula Brown
Printer: Canadian Printco

TABLE OF CONTENTS

CHAPTER		PAGE

Preface

The book you are using, <u>Fundamentals of Corporate Finance</u>, is by far one of the best textbooks you will encounter as a student of finance. The authors represent some of the top minds in finance. While each has a depth and specialty that sets them apart from their peers, a more important trait may be the breadth of the knowledge each has in the field of finance. As a student of finance you are less concerned with the minutia of specific topics, than you are with the broad aspects encountered as a practitioner in this rapidly changing and dynamic field.

The supplements offered with <u>Fundamentals of Corporate Finance</u> illustrates the authors' commitment to excellence in topic coverage, both in depth and breadth. This <u>Study Guide</u> compliments the goal of the authors and attempts to enhance the learning experience of each student. As with the main text, you will notice that the <u>Study Guide</u> is a student centric tool. Each word is designed to improve on the learning experience. After all, the test of a good "textbook" is not merely the thoroughness with which it covers topics, but how well it conveys the meaning of those topics to you, the student.

The format of the <u>Study Guide</u> is purposely created for ease of use. It tracks the outline of each chapter closely and in many ways can be used as a quick reference source. Many students have found that a quick review of the <u>Study Guide</u> before an actual reading of the chapter may improve comprehension. The thinking behind such a suggestion is that the tired old saying "you can't see the forest for the trees" may actually "hold water." The <u>Study Guide</u> paints a broad picture of the topics being covered, as well as introduces many terms and examples. We view this approach as part of an overall learning experience. The textbook, supplemental materials and your professor all combine to provide a comprehensive presentation of the field of finance.

You will quickly notice that each chapter is formatted in the same manner. A brief description of the topics to be covered in the chapter is presented at the beginning. It is relatively light reading designed to acclimate you to the environment in which the topic resides. This is followed by a "checklist." The checklist helps you organize your thoughts and proceed through the chapter, knowing where emphasis should be placed. Most chapters also provide a list of business information sources. This information is provided in order to help the reader put a face on the material. The biggest concern expressed in academia is "how relevant is this to the real world?" The business information sources will allow you to immediately link the topic you are covering with actual events and situations. The meat of the chapter is the chapter outline. Here you will see the textbook content outlined and summarized for you. Illustrations and formulas are woven throughout the outline in order to make it more comprehensible. A good technique is to periodically return to the chapter outline as you read the book and let it be your guide. After reading the chapter in the textbook you should be able to glance at the outline and fill in relevant content and examples on your own. Hopefully, the outline will seem almost simplistic once a comprehensive review of the chapter is complete. The chapters are concluded with completion questions and problems. The questions focus on concepts, while the problems are primarily numeric. Answers for each are provided at the end of the chapter. These questions and problems supplement the ones in the textbook and provide the user with extra practice.

In the final analysis, users of this Study Guide should find it a wonderful addition to the family of supplements that make up Fundamentals of Corporate Finance by Brealey, Myers, Marcus, Maynes, and Mitra. The family of supplements and textbook, when taken in their totality, provide an excellent learning experience.

Professional courtesy dictates a concluding note. This Study Guide is the one of hopefully, a long series of supplements for the textbook Fundamentals of Corporate Finance by Brealey, Myers, Marcus, Maynes, and Mitra. It represents an update and revision of prior editions. Significant credit must be given to the previous editions prepared by David R. Durst, Thomas E. Stitzel, and Matthew Will. It is our sincere desire that this Canadian revision be viewed as a worthy successor to their work and that the reader benefits from the changes and additions. As with any written endeavour, the ones closest to you bear the burden of your absence. Ironically, the benefit felt by the mass of readers to the written word is created and compiled in the most solitary of settings.

Biography

Dr. Keith C.K. Cheung is the assistant professor of finance at the Odette School of Business, University of Windsor, Ontario. Cheung's research has been published in various economic and business journals including Economics Letters, Euro-Asia Journal of Management and Journal of Business and Public Affairs. His current research interests are in risk management and real options. Cheung has substantial experience teaching introductory and advanced courses in Corporate Finance, Investments Analysis & Portfolio Management, Money, Banking and Financial Institutions to undergraduate and MBA students. His outstanding teaching has already earned him the "Best Professor Award" from the University of Windsor in 2001-2002.

Acknowledgements

I would like to thank my family members for their support. Unfortunately, this study guide cannot make them rich. I also wish to acknowledge the direction and the encouragement provided by the editorial team of Daphne Scriabin, Kelly Dickson and Lynn Fisher. Millions of thanks.

Keith Cheung

CHAPTER 1

THE FIRM AND THE FINANCIAL MANAGER

INTRODUCTION

Like most first chapters of textbooks, the authors provide an introduction to the major areas of study and provide a brief overview of the topics and chapters which follow. Having a good overview of the scope of this course is important. One must have this overview or "big picture" because very soon each chapter will focus us on very detailed subjects. With a good understanding that this overview chapter provides, you will be able to see how the detailed chapter fits into the "big picture" of financial management.

This first chapter provides an orientation to the study of financial management or financial decision making. Given a choice or several alternatives in a business decision, which should I choose? The criteria for choosing, or decision criterion used in this text, is the selection of the alternative which produces the highest value or maximizes value. What creates value in business assets or securities? That is a major topic in this course and several chapters focus on valuation theory, or what we and a lot of other people think affects value. We think that the future cash flow returns associated with a business asset or security affect the value as does the timing and variability or riskiness of those cash flows. So 1) cash flows, 2) timing or when the flow occurs, and 3) variability or riskiness of the cash flows receives considerable time and space in a finance class.

The financial manager or financial decision makers in any business have two major decisions: 1) what assets should we invest in, or the investment decision, and 2) how should we finance the assets, or the financing decision. Both decisions affect the value of the business, so several chapters are devoted to each. The capital budgeting chapters focus on tools for making value-creating investment decisions, while other chapters focus on "financing" issues that are thought to impact value creation.

The choice of business organization has an impact upon the future cash flows, risk of the business, and the ability to raise capital. This choice has an impact upon the future value creating ability of the business, and thus it is important to discuss these concepts early.

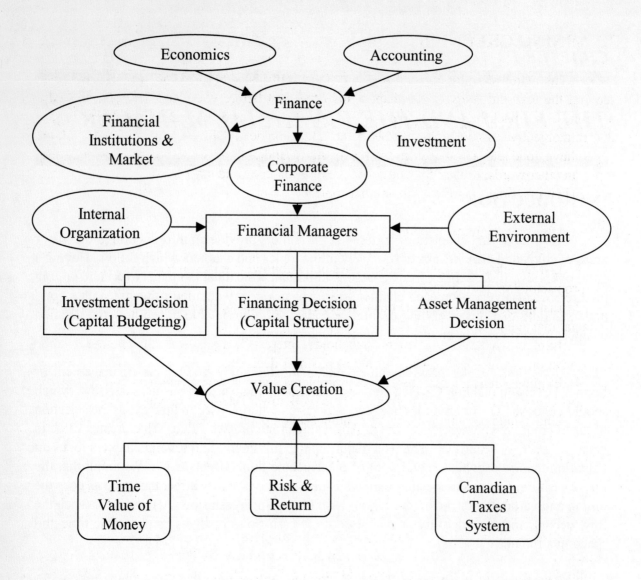

LEARNING CHECKLIST

The major learning objectives of the chapter are listed below. Look at the list *before* reading the text and study guide chapter and *after*, just before you close the book or study session. Come back here and "check off" if you can discuss or write about the item in the learning objective, if you can tell someone else, in some detail, about the topic mentioned, or if you have done reasonably well in the text or study guide sample test questions related to the topic. In other words, if you can "check off" below, you know the material and are ready to test on it. Then it is time to move on to another topic.

After preparing this chapter, you should be able to:

_____1. List the advantages and disadvantages of the following forms of business organization: sole proprietorship, partnership, and corporation.
_____2. List and briefly discuss the business functions and major decisions associated with the financial manager.
_____3. Explain why, even with many stakeholder interests in a business, shareholder wealth maximization is a reasonable basis for major business decisions.
_____4. Explain what is meant by "agency problems," and how shareholders and boards of directors can provide incentives for managers to work toward shareholder value maximization.
_____5. Understand the adverse effect of compensation plans.

SOURCES OF BUSINESS INFORMATION

Your professor has selected an excellent textbook package for you to learn financial management concepts. Finance is a really exciting subject and the concepts and principles discussed in the text are practiced every day by businesses, investors, governments, and financial markets and institutions. To keep up with this every day excitement, we encourage you to follow the current events of business and finance. While the library is a great, and prepaid source of recent business happenings, a subscription to publications such as The Globe and Mail (G&M), The Financial Post, The Wall Street Journal, Canadian Business, Business Week, Fortune, and other business publications is the best way to stay focused on recent business and finance events. In addition, you will learn about conditions in the job market, a hot topic for all business students. If the G&M form is passed around, consider it an opportunity to see the ideas of this class and your other business courses come alive every day. From major business announcements to personal money management, reading these business publications on a regular basis is one good sign that you are developing a professional attitude and are serious about your future.

In chapters to come, this section is devoted to highlighting a few important business and finance publications, many located in your library and the Internet, with which you should be familiar. In the earlier chapters, the important areas of the G&M are featured along with a number of finance and business Web sites that have become popular. Later, important references and periodicals are discussed. Many of you will have assignments beyond this textbook, usually focused on work in the library or the Internet. We hope the materials in this section may be of assistance with those assignments, and for some, help you prepare for a lifelong interest in finance.

CHAPTER OUTLINE, KEY CONCEPTS, AND TERMS

I. **ORGANIZING A BUSINESS**

    A.   The choice of business organization affects the risk and the potential return in the form of after-tax cash flows and thus, the value of the business.

    B.   Compare and contrast the following business organizational forms by:
        1.   The exposure or risks of personal assets from a business venture — limited or unlimited liability.
        2.   The ease and cost of organization and maintenance of the business organization.
        3.   The expected life of the business under each form or business organization.
        4.   The relative tax exposure of the earnings of the business.
        5.   The relative ease of raising capital in financial markets.

	Sole Proprietorship	Partnership	Corporation
Who owns the business	The manager	Partners	Shareholders
Are manager(s) and owner(s) separate	No	No	Usually
What is the owner's liability	Unlimited	Unlimited	Limited
Are the owner and the business taxed separately	No	No	Yes

C.   **Sole Proprietorship**
1.   The sole proprietor business blends the personal and business assets of the individual toward a business venture.
2.   The sole proprietor incurs unlimited liability (exposure of personal assets to business obligations), limited life, business and personal income/assets are viewed by taxing authorities as one, and because of these risks, has considerable difficulty raising funds in financial markets.

D.   **Partnerships**
1.   A partnership is an agreement of sole proprietors to pool their assets and talents in a business.
2.   Like the sole proprietorship, partners are exposed to unlimited liability, limited life of the business, business income is combined with personal income for tax purposes; unlike a sole proprietorship, more than one person is involved, and thus, more capital may be raised in financial markets.

E.   **Corporations**
1.   A corporation is a legal entity separate from its owners called shareholders. The legal entity concept causes the corporation to differ considerably from the sole proprietorship and partnership: corporations are taxable entities, have perpetual lives, and are able to combine the capital of many shareholders, have greater organizational and legal costs, but are more likely to raise capital in financial markets.
2.   Shareholder owners have limited liability, or their personal assets are free from the obligations of the corporations, and shareholders are more inclined to invest in riskier asset ventures to create value.
3.   Shareholders vote for the board of directors, who in turn, appoint senior management, creating a separation of ownership and management of the business.
4.   In a small, closely held business, the owner, board member and manager/worker may be the same person or family, while larger, corporations, with professional boards and management may have a broad base of shareholders or be known as public companies.

F.   **Hybrid Forms of Business Organization**
1.   Businesses can be set up as **limited partnerships**. There are variations on legal concerns. The ultimate purpose is to combine the tax advantage of a partnership with the limited liability advantage of incorporation.
2.   Usually, a limited partner provides funds to a partnership, but plays no active role in the management of the partnership. Also, a limited partner enjoys limited liability losing no more than the amount he or she has invested.

II.   THE ROLE OF THE FINANCIAL MANAGER

A.   The primary functions of the financial manager or financial decision-maker is to raise cash in financial markets (the financing decision), to invest cash (capital budgeting decision), to generate cash from efficient operations, and to allocate cash flows generated for reinvestment or to pay cash dividends.

B.   Funds are raised in financial markets by selling financial assets or securities to investors (stocks and bonds) and investing cash in, in the case of manufacturing firms, in real assets, or physical assets used to produce goods and services.

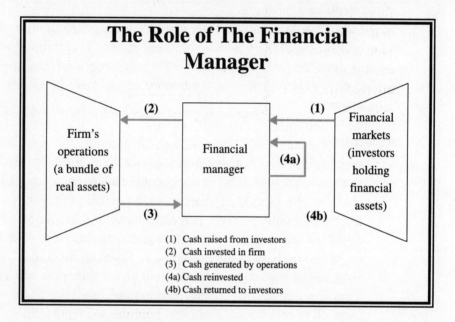

The Role of The Financial Manager

(1) Cash raised from investors
(2) Cash invested in firm
(3) Cash generated by operations
(4a) Cash reinvested
(4b) Cash returned to investors

C.   The Capital Budgeting Decision
1.   The decision as to the amount and which real assets to acquire is a capital budgeting decision.
2.   Where cash if invested affects the amount of future cash flows generated, the timing of those cash flows, and the variability or riskiness of those future cash flows and thus, the value or worth of the capital budgeting decisions.

III. FINANCIAL INSTITUTIONS AND MARKETS

A. **Financial Markets**

1. Financial markets enable businesses to raise funds, enable investors to invest in financial assets, change or trade their portfolio of financial assets, and provide a continuous evaluation or valuation of the firm's securities.

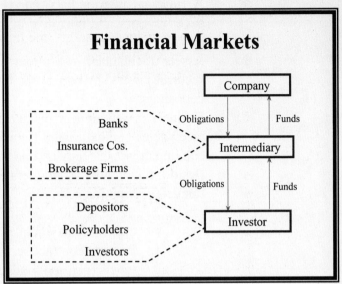

2. The initial sale of securities, where funds are acquired by the business, is called a primary issue or the securities are sold in the primary market.

3. Subsequent trading of the securities in the financial markets is said to trade on the secondary market, such as on stock exchanges or on the over-the-counter (OTC) market, where dealers trade inventories of securities held. Note: no new funds are raised by the firm in the secondary market; however, the firm's securities are evaluated or valued by the secondary market on a continuous basis.

4. Prior to the latest reform, Canada's financial system was organized by four independent sectors: (1) commercial banks (e.g., CIBC), (2) insurance companies (e.g., Freedom 55), (3) trust companies (e.g., Royal Trust), and (4) stock brokerage firms (e.g., Scotia Capital). Nowadays, the regulatory barriers between these four areas no longer exist. Financial institutions are free to go across boundaries offering services.

5. Financial intermediaries can be categorized as (1) depository institutions, (2) contractual savings institutions, and (3) investment intermediaries. Depository institutions make loans and accept deposits from individuals and institutions. Their primary source of income is the "spread". They include banks controlling a large portion of the total domestic assets, trust companies acting as trustees, credit unions and caisses populaires running by members. Contractual savings institutions acquire funds at periodic intervals on a contractual basis. Life insurance companies, property & casualty insurance companies, and pension funds are good examples. Investment intermediaries invest funds on behalf of others. This group includes finance companies and mutual funds.

B. **Financial Institutions**

1. A financial intermediary stands in between (is an intermediary) the saver/investor and borrower of funds, writing a **separate** contract for each.

2. Assets of financial institutions are financial assets such as loans and securities issued by borrowers; liabilities are contracts with investors or depositors.

3. Financial assets appear on two balance sheets as an asset (accounts receivable) and as a liability (accounts payable). Real assets, such as equipment, appear only on one balance sheet.

4. Besides functioning as an intermediary between lenders and borrowers, financial institutions:

    a. Serve as the center of the payments system of cheques and electronic payments.

    b. Provide contract services permitting borrowers (loans) and savers (pension fund reserves) to transfer expenditures across time.

    c. Pool various risks in a portfolio, thus reducing the total variability or risk of the stock portfolio or auto insured customers.

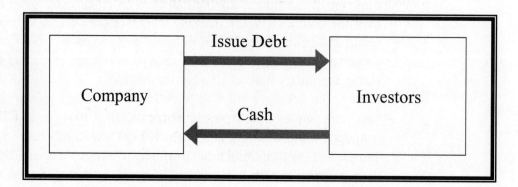

C. **The Financing Decision**

1. The maturity and type of funds raised in financial markets is the financing decision.

2. The selection and mix of long-term debt and equity securities sold in capital markets determine the capital structure of the firm.

D. **Career in Finance**

1. Career opportunities in finance are plenty ranging from entry levels such as bank tellers to senior positions such as chief financial officers.

2. Since each job involves different training, talents, and responsibilities, salaries vary significantly.

IV. WHO IS THE FINANCIAL MANAGER?

A. The financial manager refers to anyone responsible for a significant corporate investment or financing decision. The term is more oriented to the decisions rather than a specific title or job position. This book studies a number of financial manager decision areas, several of which have a significant impact on shareholder value.

B. The classic financial manager titles are the treasurer and the controller, with the former more associated with financing, cash management, and financial market relationships and the latter associated with more traditional accounting functions of financial statements, 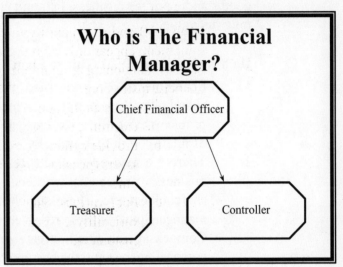 budgeting, and auditing. The chief financial officer, in larger firms, oversees the treasurer and controller and is involved in formulating corporate strategy and financial policy.

C. **Understanding Financial Markets and Institutions**
   1. Knowing the players and procedures of financial markets is an important factor for a financial manager, influencing the cost of funds, terms, and other features of the fund raising activities.
   2. The choice and investment returns of capital budgeting decisions affect the value of the securities issued by the business. Thus, investment and financing decisions are closely related.

V. GOALS OF THE CORPORATION

A. Shareholders want managers to make decisions based upon which alternative will maximize the value of the shareholders' investment.
   1. Making decisions that maximize focuses the financial manager on expected cash flows from investments, the timing of the cash flows, and the variability or riskiness of those cash flows.
   2. Other decision criterion, such as profit or market share maximization do not achieve value maximization. Making decisions based on profit

maximization may focus on accounting income and not consider cash flow, is biased toward short run returns, perhaps ignoring the longer run implications of decisions, and ignores the relative riskiness of the alternatives.

B.   Ethics and Management Objectives — shareholders and the public are concerned that managers operate within the law and maintain the reputation and ethical good standing of the business. Fair and ethical relationships build and maintain long run value.

C.   **Do Managers Really Maximize Firm Value?**

1.   Shareholders are concerned that managers work for maximizing shareholders' wealth and not managers' wealth and lifestyle. Agency problems exist when managers, as agents of shareholders, have a conflict of interest with shareholders.

2.   There are many diverse interests with a "stake" in well being of a business: managers, workers, suppliers, customers, government, shareholders, etc. These stakeholders' interest may conflict at times; managers must work to resolve these diverse interests.

3.   Compensation plans motivate managers to work for their own best personal interest and the best interest of the shareholders, thus resolving some agency problems. However, some plans such as stock options may potentially hurt shareholders.

4.   The board of directors, elected by shareholders, oversees and at times, interferes, if managers do not act in the best interest of shareholders.

5.   Managers whose company does not perform for the best interest of shareholders are candidates for a takeover by a new investor group.

6.   Every public company and its managers are scrutinized and monitored by stock analysts. This specialist monitoring tends to focus managers on value creation.

VI.   **TOPICS COVERED IN THIS BOOK** — Following the definition of the financial manager, this book first studies investment decision making, then financing decisions, then a variety of special issues. Please review the table of contents of your text. Finance in Action: "Finance through the Ages" provides an interesting history for Canadian financial markets.

COMPLETION QUESTIONS

1.   Knowing which assets to buy involves a (*financing/investment*) decision.

2.   Investment decisions are also called (*capital/cash*) budgeting decisions.

3. Knowing how to pay for assets is a (*finance/investment*) decision.

4. A business that is organized without partners or stockholders is called a _____.

5. A business that is owned by stockholders is called a _____.

6. Shareholders (*are/are not*) personally liable for obligations of the firm.

7. _____ assets are used to produce goods and services.

8. Financial assets are called (*tangible assets/securities*).

9. A firm may raise cash in the _____ markets.

10. The firm's mix of long-term financing determines its _____ structure.

11. Long-term financing is available in the _____ markets.

12. A new issue of securities is sold in the (*primary/secondary*) market.

13. The trading of existing securities among investors occurs in the (*capital/secondary*) market.

14. Shareholders want the firm to maximize its (*profits/market*) price.

15. In most large companies where managers are not major owners, a conflict of interest may occur. This is known as an (*agency/broker*) problem.

16. Anyone with a financial interest in the firm is known as a (*shareholder/stakeholder*).

17. The person in a company who is responsible for financing, cash management, and relationships with financial markets and institutions is called the (*controller/treasurer*).

18. The company officer who is responsible for budgeting, accounting, and auditing is called the (*controller/treasurer*).

19. The chief (*executive/financial*) officer oversees the treasurer and controller and sets overall financial strategy.

PROBLEMS

This section presents problems similar to those in the corresponding chapter of the textbook. Those problems serve to illustrate applications of concepts and formulas. In the case of the first chapter, there were no quantitative problems and the relatively few conceptual matters covered have been treated in the Completion section above.

ANSWERS TO COMPLETION QUESTIONS

1. investment
2. capital
3. financing
4. partnership
5. corporation
6. are not
7. Real
8. securities
9. financial
10. capital
11. capital
12. primary
13. secondary
14. market
15. agency
16. shareholder
17. treasurer
18. controller
19. financial

CHAPTER 2

ACCOUNTING AND FINANCE

INTRODUCTION

In this second chapter the authors reinforce a number of basic accounting concepts that you established in your accounting courses. Accounting stresses generally accepted accounting principles (GAAP) as the basis for presenting financial statements. Historical book value was one of the underlying basics of GAAP, but the financial manager and financial markets are focused on estimating market value. Accounting income differs from the financial manager's focus on cash flows, so the authors provide you with a finance perspective of accounting statements and the necessary adjustments needed for a value focus. Value is related to the future cash flows, the timing of the cash flows and the variability or riskiness of future cash flows. Note the futuristic orientation of finance versus the historical perspective of accounting statements.

The last part of the chapter focuses on the Canadian income tax implications for proprietors (personal) and corporations. Taxes paid affect cash flows and cash flows impact value. Therefore, taxes affect value. Learn these few basics, such as marginal tax rate, average tax rate, after-tax concept, etc., for they will be used in future chapters.

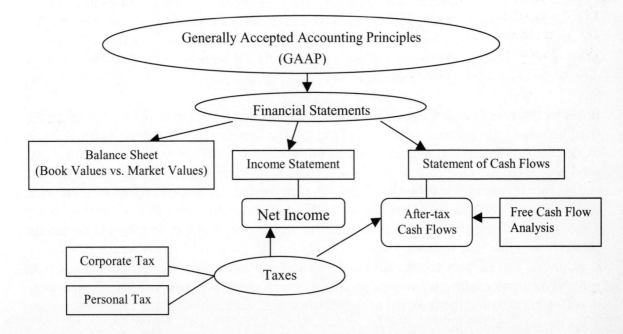

LEARNING CHECKLIST

After preparing this chapter, you should be able to:

_____1. Interpret the accounting information associated with basic financial statement such as the balance sheet, income statement, and the statement of cash flows.

_____2. Distinguish between market and book value.

_____3. Explain why accounting income may differ from cash flow in the period.

_____4. Determine free cash flows.

_____5. Understand the basics of Canadian taxation of personal and corporate income including small business taxes.

SOURCES OF BUSINESS INFORMATION

The Globe and Mail (G&M): It is Canada's national newspaper founded in 1844. We talk about finance in this class. The G&M reports about people and organizations that do it and make money doing it! Like any other presses, G&M has the news headlines on the front page. Besides the usual news coverage in Section A, Report on Business in Section B examines exclusively the financial market activities and issues. There are two other sections: Section R, Globe Review and Section S, Globe Sports.

Current business news is highlighted on the first page of Section B. The "Money & Markets" sub-section provides complete information of all market activities including the Canadian and the overseas markets. Just to name a few. Different indices such as S&P/TSE Composite Index and Dow Jones Industrial Average can be found. The daily performances of various investment instruments such as bonds, stocks, options, futures, and mutual funds are reported under separate headings. Even the corporate earnings are listed. While you can read the full stories from the print, you may want to get the news online. The quick summary "Morning Note" is posted every weekday by 8:45 am Eastern Standard Time before the market opens on their Web site at <www.globeandmail.com>.

Business Internet Search Engines and Directories: You may have received printed materials from financial organizations with some of the information already out-dated. As the finance world changes rapidly, getting the up-to-date information is a challenge. The Internet in many ways is believed to be a great help. Many sites contain the most accurate and latest information that enable you to make sensible decisions. All of the major sites available from your browser such as Netscape or Microsoft Explorer, have a business-related search area. For example, from Yahoo! at <www.yahoo.ca>, located via the Netsearch button in Netscape, there are numerous "search" sites that may help you. You can easily find all kinds of financial numbers such as stock prices, interest rates, etc. In addition, details of financial institutions, news, commentaries, and analyses from the investment community are also available. Most of the information is free. If you want to know the answers to frequently asked questions about a credit card, visit www.mastercard.com/Info/faq.htm.

CHAPTER OUTLINE, KEY CONCEPTS, AND TERMS

I. THE BALANCE SHEET

A. The **balance sheet** presents the accounting value of assets and the source of money used to purchase those assets at a particular time.

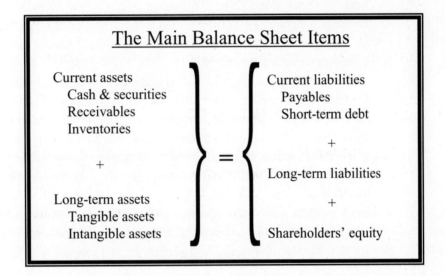

B. Assets are usually listed in descending order of liquidity, or the ability to convert to cash.

 1. Cash and marketable securities, accounts receivables, and inventories are current assets, each of which expect to cycle through cash over the next year.

 2. Longer term fixed assets, both tangible assets like plant and equipment and intangible assets such as patents and trademarks, will not be converted to cash but are expected to generate cash over future accounting cycles.

C. While the assets depict what is owned, liabilities and equity represent what is owed or who provided the funding for the assets.

 1. Current liabilities, such as accounts payable, represent obligations requiring cash payment within the next year.

 2. Current assets minus current liabilities is net working capital, or the extent to which current assets are financed with long-term sources of financing.

 3. Long-term liabilities are debt obligations due beyond one year.

 4. The difference between the accounting value of the assets and the liabilities is the shareholders' equity, representing the original capital contribution plus the earnings retained in the business. See the figure above for a good mental picture of the balance sheet.

D.   **Book Values and Market Values**
1.   Generally accepted accounting principles (GAAP) provide guidelines for preparing financial statements.
2.   According to GAAP, assets and liabilities are usually "booked" at their historical or original cost value.
3.   The *book value* of a business represents the accounting value or the balance sheet value. The book value of net worth or equity is the book value of assets less liabilities, or the historical contributions of owners including original cash contributions (sale of stock) and reinvested earnings (retained earnings.)
4.   While book values are oriented to original cost, market value is oriented to value in use or economic value: the ability to generate future cash flows.
5.   Shareholders and managers are concerned about the market value of their stock, so their focus is on a market value driven balance sheet.
6.   The market value of assets minus the market value of liabilities is the market value of shareholders' equity. See the Jupiter Example 2.1 in the textbook.
7.   Book values are based upon GAAP and market values of assets and liabilities, and thus net worth, are driven by economic value factors studied in later chapters. Seldom are they the same.

II.   THE INCOME STATEMENT

A.   The **income** statement a financial statement listing the revenues, expenses, and net income of the firm in a period of time.

B.   The income statement indicates where operating profit (EBIT) came from (revenues − operating costs − depreciation and amortization) and where operating income was distributed (interest to creditors, taxes to governments, and profits to shareholders). The earnings or losses of discontinued operations are reported separately.

INCOME STATEMENT FOR MOLSON INC., 2001 (Figures in millions of dollars)	
Sales and other revenues	2,483.4
Brewing excise and sale taxes	626.3
Net sales	1,857.1
Cost of sales, selling, and administrative costs	1,505.6
Earnings before interest, taxes, depreciation, and amortization (EBITDA)	351.5
Depreciation and amortization of property, plant, and equipment	49.4
Amortization of intangible assets	38.5
Earnings before interest and taxes (EBIT)	263.6
Net interest expense	68.7
Earnings before taxes	194.9
Taxes	57.7
Earnings (loss) from continuing operations	137.2
Earnings (loss) from discontinued operations	(3.3)
Net earnings	133.9
Allocation of net income	
Cash dividends	40.6
Addition to retained earnings	93.3

C.   **Profits versus Cash Flow**

    1.   Shareholders and managers are concerned about maximizing shareholder value, which is oriented toward estimating and generating cash flows.

    2.   Cash flows and profits from an income statement usually differ because the income statement is interested in measuring profit in a specific time period and certain assumptions vary profit measurement from cash flow measurement.

    3.   Certain noncash expenses, such as depreciation and amortization, are allocated to a specific period to measure accounting profit. These noncash expenses cause profit to be less than what operating cash flow actually is and thus noncash expenses (noncash revenues) must be added back to (subtracted from) profit to estimate cash flow in a period. In addition, capital expenditures, which are capitalized and depreciated or expensed over future periods, incur cash outlays when purchased.

    4.   Another reason why profits and cash flow differ is explained by comparing cash accounting versus accrual accounting. Accrual accounting emphasizes profit measurement in a period: the revenue earned in the period; the expenses incurred in the period. Cash flow is oriented to cash collected versus disbursed in a period. Adjusting entries, accruals, receivables, prepaids, and payables cause accounting profits measured in a period to differ from cash flow in the same period.

    5.   Inventories produced or purchased may incur an outlay of cash, but not be expensed (cost of goods sold) until sold.

III. THE STATEMENT OF CASH FLOWS

A. The **statement of cash flow** is a financial statement that shows the firm's cash receipts and cash payments over a period of time.

B. **The statement of cash flow is divided into three sections.**

1. The cash flow from operating activities for a period is the sum of net income plus (minus) noncash expenses (noncash revenue) plus (minus) the net sources (uses) of cash from changes in various working capital accounts. Decreases (increases) in current asset (current liability) accounts are sources of cash. Increases (decreases) in current asset (current liability) accounts are applications or uses of cash during a period. Note that continuing and discontinued operations affect working capitals.

2. The investment cash flows represent added net (purchase less sale) long-term (capitalized) asset investment in the period.

STATEMENT OF CASH FLOWS FOR MOLSON INC., 2001	
(Figures in millions of dollars)	
Cash provided by operating activities	
Earnings (loss) from continuing operations	137.2
Depreciation and amortization of property, plant, and equipment	49.4
Amortization of intangible assets	38.5
Future income taxes	21.8
Other	(14.9)
Cash provided by operations	232.0
Cash provided from (used for) working capital	44.5
Rationalization costs	(48.3)
Cash provided by operating activities	228.2
Investing Activities	
Business acquisitions (net)	(277.0)
Additions to property, plant, and equipment (net)	(57.0)
Additions to investments and other assets	(8.3)
Proceeds from disposal of investments and other assets	39.0
Cash provided by (used for) investing activities	(303.3)
Financing Activities	
Increase in long-term debt	261.6
Reduction in long-term debt	(166.8)
Securitization of accounts receivable	57.0
Cash dividends	(40.6)
Other	6.8
Cash provided by (used for) financing activities	118.0
Increase (decrease) in cash from continuing operations	42.9
Increase (decrease) in cash from discontinued operations	8.8
Net increase in cash	51.7

3.   The financing cash flows are listed last and include the net change in debt outstanding, cash dividends paid, and the sale or repurchase of common stock.

4.   Since every income statement ledger item and the changes in balance sheet ledger items in the period except the change in the cash/marketable securities account has been listed in the statement of cash flows, the balancing sum of net cash flows must equal the net change in the cash/marketable securities account in the period.

5.   By subtracting capital investments from the amount of business that is generated, the available cash flows for bondholders and shareholders are called free cash flows and the amounts are affected by new security issues.

IV.   ACCOUNTING FOR DIFFERENCES

A.   While accounting is concerned with a presentation of earnings and book values according to GAAP, financial analysts, managers, and shareholders, current and prospective, are concerned with balance sheet and income statement adjustments that estimate market values and cash flows, respectively.

B.   Areas such as valuable intangible assets, not normally listed on the balance sheet, conditional liabilities, such as pension commitments and stock options, are real variables affecting future cash flows and are a part of the value assessment process. There is a decided trend in GAAP toward accounting for market values and measuring cash flows.

C.   Foreign firms must make the accounting accommodations required to be able to penetrate the domestic financial market.

V.   TAXES

A.   Taxes paid to governments affect cash flow available for shareholders. Usually there is a tax implication for every financial decision. The basic tax concepts that follow will assist in making the "tax adjustments" needed for the financial decisions studied in future chapters.

	Firm A	Firm B
Net income	39	65
+ Interest	40	0
Net cash flow	**79**	**65**

B.   Corporate Taxes

Example – *Taxes and Cash Flows can be changed by the use of debt. Firm A pays part of its profits as debt interest. Firm B does not.*

	Firm A	Firm B
EBIT	100	100
Interest	40	0
Pretax income	60	100
Taxes (35%)	21	35
Net income	**39**	**65**

1.   The corporation is taxed on its taxable revenue adjusted for tax deductible business expenses, such as cost of goods sold, salaries, interest paid, and so forth. The tax table in Table 2.4 in the textbook lists the federal and provincial tax rates. To assist small businesses, only the 12% federal rate is applied to the first $200,000 corporate taxable income.

2.   The **marginal tax rate** represents the added taxes per dollar owed for each additional dollar of taxable income. The marginal tax rate is the relevant tax rate for financial decision making analysis. The concept is future oriented, consistent with financial decision making.

3. The **average tax rate** represents the total taxes owed divided by income before taxes. The average tax rate is an historical, after the fact, measure and not a valid decision making tool.

4. Interest expense for the corporation is tax deductible; cash dividends paid to shareholders are not. The after-tax cost of a dollar of interest expense paid, with a 35 percent marginal tax bracket, is $1.00 times (1 – marginal tax rate of .35) or $.65. The cost of a $1.00 of dividends is $1.00. This special tax deduction for interest will have important implications when the financing decision of debt or equity is discussed.

5. Operating losses can be carried back for a maximum of 3 years and forward for up to 7 years.

C. **Personal Tax**

1. Individuals pay income taxes on salaries, on investment income, and on profits of proprietorship and partnership.

2. Income taxes in Canada are progressive, i.e., the higher the income, the higher the tax rates. See Table 2.6 in the textbook. Prior to 2001, provincial income tax was calculated by the tax-on-tax system, now changed to tax-on-income.

3. Dividends are taxed at lower rates to avoid the double taxation of corporate income.

4. When the asset is sold for more than its original cost, a capital gain occurs. Currently, only 50% of capital gains are taxable.

COMPLETION QUESTIONS

1. The financial statement that shows the value of a firm's assets and liabilities at a particular time is called the _____ _____.

2. Payments that are due to the company but have not yet been collected are called accounts (*payable/receivable*).

3. Assets that are unlikely to be used soon or converted into cash in the near future are described as (*current/fixed*) assets.

4. The difference between a company's current assets and its current liabilities is called its net _____ _____.

5. The difference between assets and liabilities represents the amount of shareholders' _____.

6. GAAP stands for _____ _____ _____ _____.

7. The _____ statement shows the revenues, expenses, and net income of a firm over a period of time.

8. EBIT stands for _____ _____ _____ _____
    _____.

9. Net income is either added to _____ _____ or paid out as
    _____.

10. Profits are different from cash flows mainly because of (*appreciation/depreciation*).

11. The practice of matching costs of producing goods with the revenues from selling them
    is known as _____ accounting.

12. The statement of cash flows shows the firm's cash receipts and cash payments (*at a
    particular point in time/over a period of time*).

13. Patents, trademarks, and franchises are examples of (*intangible/tangible*) assets.

14. The treatment of depreciation, reserves, and unfunded pension liabilities are examples
    of (*illegal/legitimate*) differences in accounting practices.

15. Additional taxes owed per dollar of additional income are computed from the
    (*average/marginal*) tax rate.

16. Interest paid by a firm is (*deductible/non-taxable*).

17. The market-value balance sheet is (*backward/forward-looking*).

PROBLEMS

1. Prepare a balance sheet for Nancy's Nursery from the following information. What is
    the shareholders' equity?
    Bank loans (short-term) of $200,000
    Cash of $100,000
    Inventory of $800,000
    Buildings and fixtures $1,500,000
    Accounts receivable of $1,200,000
    Mortgage loan of $1,300,000

2. Nancy's Nursery had sales last year of $750,000. Its cost of goods sold was $500,000
    and general and administrative expenses were $75,000. The other charges were $25,000
    for depreciation and amortization and $30,000 for interest. During the year the company

sold part of the business at a loss of $80,000. Prepare an income statement for NN if it had an average tax rate of 40 percent.

3. A partial balance sheet and income statement for the past two years for North Ocean Bangles is shown below.

BALANCE SHEET, AS OF END OF YEAR
(Figures in $thousands)

Assets	2000	2001	Liabilities and Owners' Equity	2000	2001
Cash	100	200	Payable	200	400
Inventory	400	500	Short-term loans	300	400
Receivables	300	600	Long-term debt	1000	1400
Net plant	2000	2400			

2001 INCOME STATEMENT
(Figures in $thousands)

Sales	1000
Cost of goods sold	700
General and administrative expense	100
Depreciation & amortization	50
Interest	60

a. What is shareholders' equity in 2000 and 2001?
b. What is net working capital in 2000 and 2001?
c. What is the cash flow from operations in 2001?
d. What must have been the new investment in fixed assets in 2001?
e. If NOB has 50,000 shares outstanding what is the earnings per share for 2001?

4. In 2001, the ABC Co. had operating income of $595,000, investment interest income of $50,000 where $30,000 was bond interests and $20,000 was dividends from another Canadian corporation. As the firm had issued securities for financing purposes, it paid $40,000 in interest and $100,000 in dividends to the investors during the year. What is the federal corporate tax? Incorporate the small business tax rate in the calculation.

5. An individual living in British Columbia with wage earnings of $65,000 has invested $25,000 for one year in bonds yielding 6%, what is the after-tax return?

6. Mr. X lives in Ontario. In 2001, he had employment income of $30,000 and dividend income of $1,000. What is his total tax liability?

ANSWERS TO COMPLETION QUESTIONS

1. balance sheet
2. receivable
3. fixed
4. working capital
5. equity
6. Generally Accepted Accounting Principles
7. income
8. earnings before interest and taxes
9. retained earnings, dividends
10. depreciation
11. accrual
12. over a period of time
13. intangible
14. legitimate
15. marginal
16. deductible
17. forward-looking

SOLUTIONS TO PROBLEMS

1. Arrange the accounts by major category and use shareholders' equity as the "plug" or balancing account. Remember that shareholders' equity (also called net worth) = assets – liabilities. These steps produce the following balance sheet:

BALANCE SHEET FOR BONNIE'S BEDDING
(Figures in $thousands)

Assets		Liabilities and shareholders' equity	
Cash	100	Bank loans (short-term)	200
Accounts receivable	200		
Inventory	800	Mortgage loans	1300
Buildings and fixtures	1500	Shareholders' equity	1100
Total assets	2600	Total liabilities and equity	2600

2.   INCOME STATEMENT FOR NANCY'S NURSERY
            (Figures in $thousands)

Sales	750
less Cost of goods sold	500
equals Gross profit margin	250
less Selling and general expenses	75
less Depreciation	25
equals Earnings before interest and taxes	150
less Interest	30
equals Taxable income	120
less Taxes (40%)	48
equals Earnings from continuing operations	72
plus Earnings from discontinued operations	(8)
equals Net income	64

3.

a.   Shareholders' equity equals total assets minus total liabilities. For 2000 this is ($100 + $400 + $300 + $2000) – ($200 + $300 + $1000) or $1300. For 2001 it is $3700 – $2200 or $1500.

b.   Net working capital equals current assets minus current liabilities. For 2000 this is ($100 + $400 + $300) – ($200 + $300) or $300. For 2001 it is $1300 – $800 or $500.

c.   Cash flow from operations equals net income plus increases in current assets plus increases in current liabilities. Note that if current assets declined, the amount would be subtracted from net income. If current liabilities declined the decrease would be subtracted from net income. In this case, cash flow generated from operations equals net income of $80 plus the increase in current assets of $1300 – $800 or $500 minus the increases in current liabilities of $800 – $500 or $300 equals $280 cash flow.

d.   Gross investment in fixed assets equals the increase in net fixed assets plus depreciation in 2001 or ($2400 – $2000) + 50 or $450.

e.   Earnings per share equals net income divided by the number of shares outstanding. For 2001, EPS = $64,000/50,000 = $1.28

4.   First find out the total taxable income.

Income from operating activities	$595,000
Interest income (fully taxable)	30,000
Interest expense (fully deductible)	(40,000)
Dividend income (non taxable)	0
Taxable income	$585,000

Since dividends are paid from after-tax income, they do not affect taxable income here. Applying the small business tax rate of 12%, with a general rate of 27%, the federal tax bill is ($200,000)(0.12) + ($585,000 – 200,000)(0.27) = $127,950.

5. Given the financial situation of this individual, the relevant federal tax rate is 26% and provincial tax rate is 16.7%. Therefore, the combined tax rate becomes 42.7%. Interest income is $(0.06)(\$25,000) = \$1,500$. Tax on interest income is $(0.427)(\$1,500) = \$640.50$. The after-tax interest income is $\$1,500 - \$640.5 = \$859.50$.

6.
Wages		$30,000
Dividends	1,000	
Gross-up (25%)	250	
Taxable dividends		1,250
Taxable income		$31,250

Federal tax:

$30,754(0.16) + ($31,250 – 30,754)(0.22)		$5,029.76
Less: Dividend tax credit ($1,250 × 0.1333)		166.63
Total federal tax		$4,863.13

Provincial tax:

$30,814(0.062) + ($31,250 – 30,814)(0.0924)		$1,950.76
Less: Dividend tax credit ($1,250 × 0.0513)		64.13
Total provincial tax		$1,886.63

Therefore, total taxes are $6,749.76.

CHAPTER 3

THE TIME VALUE OF MONEY

INTRODUCTION

In this first chapter of Part Two entitled "Value," the time dimension of value is presented. The scope of business decisions covers a considerable length of time. The values of cash flows related to those decisions occurring over this wide time period are affected by the time value of money. Most decisions focus on doing something today, e.g., investments, with returns flowing over future time periods. It is important to understand that cash flows in different time periods are not comparable and must be adjusted to a common time period, usually to the present, before comparison and analyses can be performed. This adjustment reflects the opportunity cost of alternative investment and the adjustment focus in most decisions is the current period, the present.

This chapter starts the analytical or arithmetical dimension of business finance that gives this course its reputation. This is the chapter where you make it or break it. If you limp away from this chapter without mastering the concepts and a working knowledge of a financial calculator, the next chapter is even worse.

The chapter starts relatively simple with compound interest and slowly builds. Arithmetic expressions are displayed visually via graphs, and simplified. Unknowns or "what am I solving for" that have plagued half of you since fourth grade are here again. If you have always guessed (what table should I use?), here is a suggestion. Draw a picture. Since these are "time" problems, draw a horizontal line and sketch the problem on the line. The present is on the left, future on the right, with payments (annuity) marked on the time segments of the line. Most of the problems have three variables and ask you to solve for the fourth. Identify the unknown on the time line then associate the interest factor tables with the situation. Better yet, use a financial calculator.

The cash flows discussed in the first part of the chapter are assumed to hold their purchasing power across time periods. Inflation, or the steady decline in purchasing power, is introduced in the last section of the chapter. If the purchasing power of money is declining in the future, then one should "discount" this cheaper value via a higher "I" and a lower present value.

This is the first "valuation" chapter and the authors have carefully included problems and examples in the chapter with valuation concepts, ideas, examples, etc., that will be presented formally in the next few chapters. Review the concepts to come in the next couple of chapters and treat this chapter as a building block to accomplish understanding of the valuation process.

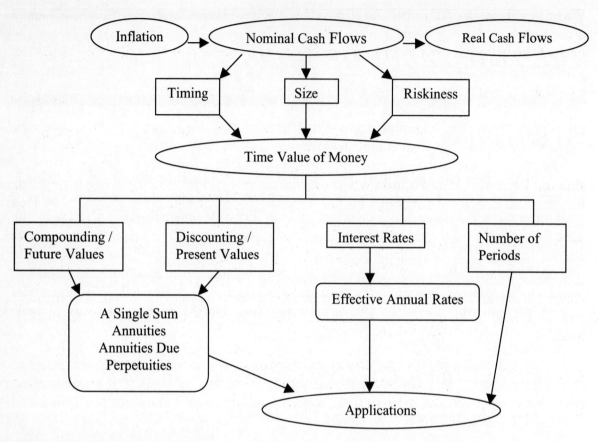

LEARNING CHECKLIST

The real test of this chapter is your ability to work *and understand* the end-of-chapter and study guide problems. After you have worked enough problems, come back here and check off your ability to:

_____1.   Calculate the future value of money invested at a given interest rate.

_____2.   Be able to compare interest rates quoted over time such as calculating the annual effective rate when a monthly interest rate is given.

_____3.   Be able to calculate present value and future values (FV) and know how to distinguish between a present value versus a future value problem.

_____4.   Understand the difference between real and nominal cash flows and between real and nominal interest rates.

_____5.   Have working knowledge of financial calculators.

SOURCES OF BUSINESS INFORMATION

Warnings of Using the Internet for Finance: It is amazing how much information the Internet presents you. However, information has no value unless you know how to analyze it. Hence, the Internet cannot be a substitute for your own judgment. Since the Internet can be overwhelming, you will find yourself hopping from place to place. To avoid such a problem, you need something of a cookbook. That is why we include a section, "Sources of Business Information," to prepare you to be a financial wizard! While you can access a whole world of financial information from your fingertips, there is no guarantee that things you read online are true. Always be cautious of scams on the Internet. Good luck.

Finding Economic Data Online: Where can you find the current mortgage interest rate? The Internet is an extremely useful tool for this. Of course, you can visit the Web sites of various financial institutions for their current rates. For example, go to the Royal Bank of Canada's site at www.royalbank.com/mortgage. The site is updated daily. Cannex at www.cannex.com is another good source providing up-to-date information on mortgage rates from banks and trust companies across Canada. Since the mortgage interest rates are quoted annually, you need to convert the numbers into the correct monthly rates and make your mortgage payments accordingly. Like Cannex, Canoe Web site at www.canoe.ca has also been used by the financial industry.

CHAPTER OUTLINE, KEY CONCEPTS, AND TERMS

I.   FUTURE VALUES AND COMPOUND INTEREST

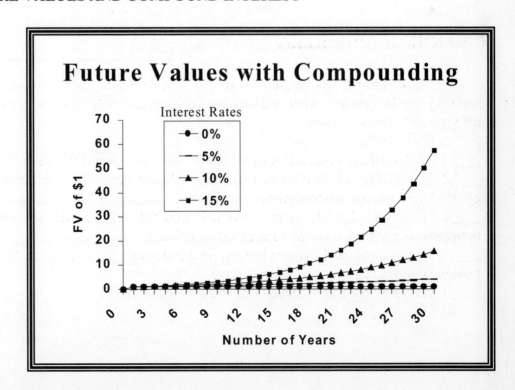

A. Cash flows occurring in different time periods are not comparable unless adjusted for time value.

B. The **future value** is the amount to which an investment will grow after earning interest. Future value = investment $\times (1+r)^t$.

$$\boxed{\begin{array}{l} \text{Future Value of } \$100 = \text{FV} \\[6pt] \text{FV} = \$100 \times (1 + r)^t \end{array}}$$

C. The expression, $(1+r)^t$, refers to **compound interest** or interest earned on interest at the rate, r, for t periods. An investment of $100 for five years at 6 percent interest compounded annually would be $100 \times (1.06)^5 = \$133.82$, with the $33.82 representing the accumulated interest.

D. If the $100 investment above earned 6 percent **simple interest**, or annual interest on the original investment, the sum of the original $100 plus accumulated simple interest would be $100 \times .06 \times 5$ years $= \$30.00$. Note that with compound interest an additional $3.82 is earned in the 5-year period. See Table 3.1 and Figure 3.1 in the textbook for arithmetic and graphic analyses, respectively.

II. **PRESENT VALUE**

A. The value today of a future cash flow is called the **present value**. The present value computation solves for the original investment at a certain rate when one knows the future value. The present value is the reciprocal of the future value calculation. Present value $\times (1+r)^t$ = future value, while the present value = $1/(1+r)^t \times$ future value. See Figure 3.3 for a graphical interpretation of this relationship.

$$\boxed{\begin{array}{l} \text{Present Value} = \text{PV} \\[10pt] \text{PV} = \dfrac{\text{Future Value after t periods}}{(1 + r)^t} \end{array}}$$

B. The interest rate used to compute present values of future cash flows is called the **discount rate**. This will be an important variable when value determination is studied in the next chapter.

C. Present values are directly related to the future cash flows and inversely related to the discount rate, r, and time, t. The higher the future cash flows, the higher the PV; the higher the discount rate and longer the term, the lower the PV.

D. The expression, $1/(1+r)^t$, is called a **discount factor**, which is the PV of a $1 future payment. Discount factors for whole number discount rates and years, are calculated and available for use in Table 3.3 in the textbook.

$$\text{Discount Factor} = \text{DF} = \text{PV of \$1}$$

$$\text{DF} = \frac{1}{(1+r)^t}$$

E. Cash flows occurring at different time periods are not comparable for financial decision making. The cash flows must be time adjusted, at an appropriate discount rate, usually to the "present" for comparison, summation, or other analysis.

F. **Finding the Interest Rate:**
   1. In the expression, $\text{PV} = \text{FV}(1+r)^t$, when the PV, FV, and t are known, $(1 + r)$ may be solved arithmetically.
   2. The discount rate calculated is also called the annual interest rate, growth rate, and internal rate of return, depending on the situation.

$$\text{PV} = \text{FV} \times \frac{1}{(1+r)^t}$$

III. MULTIPLE CASH FLOWS

A. A future stream of cash flows associated with an investment may be compared or summed if adjusted to a common time period, usually the present.

B. The multiple cash flows may be the same amount and be equally spaced over the term (called an **annuity**), may be an annuity with cash flows assumed to be received forever (called a **perpetuity**), or the future cash flow stream may be unequal.

C. The key point is that when discounted to the present, all future cash flows are standardized for comparison, for summing, and other analysis, such as net present value studied later.

$$\text{PV} = \frac{C_1}{(1+r)^1} + \frac{C_2}{(1+r)^2} + \dots$$

IV. PERPETUITIES AND ANNUITIES

A. How To Value Perpetuities

1. The present value of a never ending equal stream of cash flows is called a perpetuity.
2. The PV of a perpetuity is equal to the periodic cash flow divided by the appropriate discount rate or PV (perpetuity) = cash payments/r.

$$PV = \frac{C}{r}$$

B. How To Value Annuities

1. An annuity is an equally spaced level stream of cash flows, such as $50 per year for 10 years.
2. The present value of annuity is the difference between the PV of the cash flows in perpetuity less the PV of the cash flows beyond the relevant annuity period. Arithmetically, the PV of a t year annuity is:

$$PV = C \left[\frac{1}{r} - \frac{1}{r(1+r)^t} \right]$$

where C represents the annuity cash flows per period and r is the appropriate discount rate. The bracketed quantity in the formula above is called an **annuity factor**. Table 3.4 shows annuity factors with varied whole numbers for r and t.

$$PVAF = \left[\frac{1}{r} - \frac{1}{r(1+r)^t} \right]$$

3. A financial calculator refers to annuity cash flows as payments.
4. A loan amortization problem uses the same expression above, solving for C, now the monthly or quarterly payments. The adjustment of annual to more frequent compounding or payments is to multiply the annual t by the number of payments per year and divide the r by the same number.
5. Home mortgage with fixed periodic payments is an excellent example of **amortizing loans** in which part of the payment is used to pay interest and the rest is to reduce principal. As the loan is progressively paid off, the amortization increases with each payment because interest is charged on the outstanding amount only.

C. **Future and Present Value of an Annuity**

1. The future value sum of a series of consecutive, equal payments is called the **future value of an annuity** or:

$$FV = [C \times PVAF] \times 1 + r)^I$$

2. The present value sum of a series of consecutive, equal payments is called the **present value of an annuity**, calculated by multiplying the future value of annuity, above, by $(1 + r)^t$.

3. With an **ordinary** annuity the cash flows (PMT or payments key in a financial calculator) are assumed to flow at the end of the period. An **annuity due** assumes the cash flows occur at the beginning of the period. (See the BGN or DUE key on your financial calculator.)

4. An infinite stream of cash flows growing at a constant rate is called a **growing perpetuity**.

$$PV = \frac{C}{r - g}$$

5. A **growing annuity** is a series (T) of cash flows growing at a constant rate (g).

$$PV = \frac{C}{r - g}\left[1 - \left(\frac{1+g}{1+r}\right)^T\right]$$

6. See details on p. 89 in the textbook about using a financial calculator to solve the annuity problem.

V. **INFLATION AND THE TIME VALUE OF MONEY**

A. **Inflation** is an overall general rise in the price level for goods and services.

B. In the time value of money analysis above, interest rates were assumed to be "real" rates, and the cash flows over the time line were assumed to have the same purchasing power. With inflation the purchasing power of cash flows over a time line declines at the rate of inflation.

C. **Real versus Nominal Cash Flows**

1. One measure of inflation is the Consumer Price Index (CPI). The annualized percentage increases in the CPI are a measure of the rate of inflation.

2. Consumers and investors are concerned about the **real value of $1** or the purchasing power of the dollar or investment return in a period of time.

D. **Inflation and Interest Rates**

1. Actual dollar prices or interest rates are called **nominal** dollars or interest rates. Bonds, loans, and most financial contracts are quoted in nominal interest rates.

2. Nominal rates, adjusted for inflation in a period, are **real interest rates**, or the rate at which the purchasing power of an investment increases.

3. The real rate of interest is calculated as follows:

$$1 + \text{real interest rate} = \frac{1 + \text{nominal interest rate}}{1 + \text{inflation rate}}$$

4. The approximate real rate is the nominal rate minus the inflation rate.

E. **What Fluctuates: Real or Nominal Rates?**

1. Investors and lenders include expected inflation rates in nominal rates to compensate for the loss of purchasing power.

2. Nominal rates include expected real rates of return plus expected inflation rates.

F. **Valuing Real Cash Payments**

1. Since nominal rates include real rates plus expected inflation, discounting nominal future cash flows by nominal rates will give the same answer as discounting real, expected inflation adjusted cash flows by the real interest rate.

2. Current dollar cash flows must be discounted by the nominal interest rate; real cash flows must be discounted by the real interest rate.

G. **Providing For Retirement**

1. Expected inflation is a significant variable in retirement planning, tuition savings plans, choice of vocation, or any long-term financial planning. Even a low rate of inflation can have a major negative effect on people who will receive relatively fixed nominal income or returns.

2. The actual purchasing power rate of return (real rate) on an investment is the nominal expected rate of return, $1 + r$, divided by $1 +$ the expected inflation rate. With high inflation, the realized real rate may be negative.

H. **Real or Nominal?**

1. Most financial analyses in this text will assume nominal rates and will discount nominal cash flows. When one set of cash flows are presented in real term, such as the social security cash flows, then nominal cash flows and rates must be adjusted to compare, contrast, and mix the cash flows. As noted above, do not mix nominal and real or you will have garbage!

VI. ANNUALLY COMPOUNDED INTEREST RATES VERSUS ANNUAL PERCENTAGE RATES

A. The **effective annual interest rate** is the period rate annualized using compound interest. If the one-month rate is 1 percent, the effective annual rate is 12 percent to the twelfth power for there are 12 months in a year. Thus, $(1.01)^{12} - 1 = .1268$ or 12.68 percent. The exponent used is the number of periods in one year.

B. The **annual percentage rate (APR)** is the period rate times the number of periods to complete a year or the interest rate that is annualized using simple interest. In the case above, the one-month rate of 1 percent times the number of months in a year equals 12.00 percent. This is the APR.

C. To convert an annual percentage rate to an effective annual rate, divide the APR by the number of annual interest periods and annualize that period rate. In this example it is $(1 + 0.01)^{12} - 1 = 0.1268$ or 12.68 percent.

COMPLETION QUESTIONS

1. The amount to which an investment will grow after earning interest is a _____ _____.

2. When interest is earned only on the original investment it is called _____ interest.

3. When interest is earned on interest as well as on the original investment it is called _____.

4. The (*higher/lower*) the interest rate the higher will be the future value.

5. The interest rate that is annualized using compound interest is known as the _____ annual interest rate.

6. The interest rate that is annualized using simple interest is the _____ _____ rate.

7. The shorter the compounding period, the (*higher/lower*) will be the effective annual rate.

8. The value today of a future cash flow is called the _____ _____.

9. The _____ _____ is the interest rate used to compute present values of future cash flows.

10. The present value of a $1 future payment is called the _____ factor. It is always (*less/more*) than 1.0 for any positive interest rate.

11. The higher the discount rate, the (*higher/lower*) the present value of $1.

12. A stream of constant, or level, cash payments that never ends is called a _____.

13. The present value of an infinite stream of level payments (*is/is not*) infinite.

14. An annuity is a stream of cash flows that are _____ and spaced _____.

15. The present value of a $1 annuity is called the _____ factor.

16. The perpetuity and the annuity formulas assume that the first payment occurs at the (*beginning/end*) of the initial period.

17. When a loan is repaid by a stream of level payments over its life, the loan is being _____.

18. The amount of principal repayment from a typical home mortgage gradually (*decreases/increases*) over the life of the loan.

19. The expected rate of return that is given up by investing in a project is called the _____ cost of _____.

20. Subtracting the present value of cash flows from the initial investment yields the _____ _____ _____.

21. A risky cash flow in the future is worth (*less/more*) today than the same amount of a more certain cash flow.

PROBLEMS

1. Calculate the present value of $10 for the following combinations of discount rates and time periods:
   a. $r = 5$ percent, $t = 5$ years
   b. $r = 5$ percent, $t = 10$ years
   c. $r = 20$ percent, $t = 5$ years
   d. $r = 20$ percent, $t = 10$ years

2. Compute the future value of $10 cash flow for the same combinations of rates and periods as in problem 1.

3.	Recently, the city of London was looking for a site on which to build a new airport. One location would have involved demolishing the 12th-century Church of St. Michael's. Suppose this edifice had been built for the equivalent of $240 and had increased 5 percent per year in value. What would it be worth today, 1000 years later?

4.	In 10 years, how much would a deposit of $100 grow to in a bank that pays compound interest at a 5 percent rate? How much of the ending balance would be interest earned on the interest paid?

5.	Marlene and Jeff have a target of $100,000 in 20 years for their daughter Ariana's college education fund. How much do they need to deposit in a bank account today if they could earn 5 percent per annum?

6.	Complete the following table by calculating present value, future value, periods, or interest rate for the missing cell on each line:

Present Value	Future Value	Periods	Interest Rate
$500		7 years	4%
$150	$201.59		3%
$320	$349.67	3 years	
	$2430	3 years	5%

7.	What is the equivalent annual rate of interest of 8 percent compounded monthly as compared to semi-annual compounding?

8.	Matthew's father agreed to give him an annual allowance of $1000 until he reaches his 18th birthday, 10 years from today. His older brother, Paul, negotiated payments of $1200 until his 18th birthday which is 7 years from today. If both boys plan to save their money at a bank which pays 6 percent per annum, who has the best deal?

9.	If you deposited $100 six years ago and your passbook savings account shows a balance of $200, what annual percentage rate has the bank been paying?

10.	Using an interest rate of 8 percent, what would be the present value of cash flows of $500 in one year, $600 in two years, and $700 in three years?

11.	Calculate the present value of the following annuities using a 7 percent discount rate:
	a.	Five years of $100 per year with the first payment coming one year from today.
	b.	Five years of $100 payments beginning two years from today.

12.	What would be the monthly payment on a $10,000 auto loan to be repaid over the next 60 months if the monthly interest rate was 1 percent?

13. What would be the opportunity cost of capital for a property that is valued at $100,000 if it offers a return of $10,000 forever?

14. Matt has $100,000 and is expected to live for another 30 years. How much could he have to spend each year, before taxes, if he could earn 7 percent on his money and if he wanted to use it all up by the end of his lifetime?

15. Suppose Matt, as described in problem 14 above, wanted to leave a balance of $10,000 for his favourite charity when he dies. What would be his pre-tax income?

16. How much interest would you pay on a $100,000 home loan over 30 years if you made annual payments and the interest rate was 9 percent?

17. Suppose you want to buy a house and can afford monthly payments of principal and interest of about $1,000. If you finance the loan over 20 years at an APR of 12 percent, what is the maximum price you could pay?

18. What is the effective interest on a 1-year discount interest loan for $5,000 if the interest rate is 5 percent?

19. Olivia's Fashion Centre offers a 2 percent discount on purchases for which cash is payed within 10 days after the purchase. The other choice is to pay the full price in 1 month. What is the effective interest rate of its customers who choose to defer their payments until 1 month?

20. Suppose a firm has bought a new $30,000 machine using a 4-year loan at a 10 percent interest rate. Complete the following table showing the loan repayment.

Time Period	Loan Balance	Year-end Interest Due On Balance	Year-end Payment	Amortization Of Loan
1	$30,000	$3,000	$9,464.12	$6,464.12
2			$9,464.12	
3			$9,464.12	
4			$9,464.12	

ANSWERS TO COMPLETION QUESTIONS

1. future value
2. simple
3. compound
4. higher
5. effective

6. annual percentage
7. higher
8. present value
9. discount rate
10. discount, less
11. lower
12. perpetuity
13. is not
14. equal, evenly
15. annuity
16. end
17. amortized
18. increases
19. opportunity, capital
20. net present value
21. less

SOLUTIONS TO PROBLEMS

1. Present values:
    a. $\$10/(1 +.05)^5 = \$7.84$
    b. $\$10/(1 + .05)^{10} = \$6.14$
    c. $\$10/(1 + .05)^5 = \$4.02$
    d. $\$10/(1 + .20)^{10} = \$1.62$
    Notice the time value of money — at an interest rate of 20 percent, a dollar received 10 years later is only worth 16.2 cents today.

2. Future values:
    a. $\$10 \times (1 + .05)^5 = \$12.76$
    b. $\$10 \times (1 + .05)^{10} = \$16.29$
    c. $\$10 \times (1 + .20)^5 = \$24.88$
    d. $\$10 \times (1 + .20)^{10} = \$61.92$
    Notice the power of compounding — at an interest rate of 20 percent, $1 grows to $6.192 in 10 years!

3. Today's value of St. Michael's would be $\$240 \times (1 +.05)^{900} = \$2820$ trillion. That figure truly shows the power of compounding!!

4. In 10 years the balance would be $\$100 \times (1 + .05)^{10} = \$162.90$. With simple interest, the earnings would be 5 percent of $100 or $5 each year for a total of $50. In that case the balance would be $150 so the interest earned on interest would be $162.90 – $150.00 or $12.90.

5. The deposit today equals the future value discounted back to the present or $100,000/(1 + .05)^{20} = \$37,700$.

6. The future value $= \$55 \times (1 + .04)^7 = \$657.97$.
    To find the number of periods, divide the future value by the present value. $\$201.59/\$150 = 1.344$. Then read from APPENDIX A TABLE A.1 in the row where this value occurs. This is 10 years.
    The interest rate is found by the future value divided by the present value and raising this number to the reciprocal of the time period and then subtracting one to provide the decimal fraction. Thus $(\$349.67/\$320)^{1/3} - 1 = 0.03$ or 3 percent.
    The present value $= \$2430/(1 + .05)^3 = \$720$.

7. The 8 percent rate on a monthly basis is $.08/12$ or 0.0067 percent per month. The annual percentage rate is therefore $(1 + .0067)^{12} - 1 = 0.0843$. With semi-annual compounding, the 6 month rate is $.08/2$ or 0.04 percent. The annual percentage rate then is $(1 + .04)^2 = 1.082$. Notice that the shorter the compounding period, the higher the annual percentage rate.

8. The brothers' deal with their father is computed as the present value of an annuity. It is much easier to use a financial calculator or the present value of an annuity factors found in APPENDIX A TABLE A.3 of the textbook. The latter is a simple multiplication. In Matthew's case this equals $\$1000 \times 7.36$ or $\$7360$. Paul's arrangement has a present value of $\$1200 \times 5.582$ or $\$6698$.

9. When the interest rate is unknown it is probably easiest to use the tables from the textbook. The present value of $100 would be equal to the present value of $200 when that number has been discounted at the appropriate rate. In other words, $\$100 = \$200 \times$ discount factor. The discount factor equals $\$100/\$200$ or 0.5. Looking at the 6-year row of APPENDIX A TABLE A.2, we find the interest is slightly higher than 12 percent.

10. Present values are:
    $$\$500 \times .926 = \quad \$463$$
    $$\$600 \times .857 = \quad \$514$$
    $$\$700 \times .794 = \quad \underline{\$556}$$
    $$\text{Total} \qquad = \$1533$$

11. The present value of the annuities would be:
    a. $\$100 \times 4.1 = \$410.00$
    b. This is a two step calculation. First the present value of a 6-year annuity would be computed and then the present value of a 1-year annuity would be calculated and subtracted from the 6-year amount.
        $\$100 \times 4.767 - \$100 \times .935 = \$383.20$

12. The present value of $10,000 would be equal to the present value of the 60 monthly payments, M, figured at a monthly compounded rate of 1 percent. We need to divide the $10,000 by the present value of an annuity factor found in APPENDIX A TABLE A.3. Note that the table has the far left-hand column labelled "Number of Years." This corresponds with an annual compounding period, the situation found in most problems. In this particular case we have monthly compounding. We then have to mentally replace the "years" with "months" and use the 60 month factor at 1 percent. However, since the table only has entries up to 30 periods, the table factors must be separated into two, 30-month annuities and then combined on a present value basis. For months 1 to 30 the factor is 25.81. For months 31 through 60 the factor is the present value of 25.81, which is $25.81 \times 0.742 = 19.15$. The present value factor for the entire 60 months is thus $25.81 + 19.15 = 44.96$. The monthly payments are: $10,000/44.96 = $222.42.

13. This is a perpetuity. The interest rate on a perpetuity is equal to the annual return divided by the present value of the perpetuity. Here it would be $10,000/$100,000 or 10 percent.

14. The $100,000 is a present value and is equal to the present value of the annual withdrawals figured by including a 7 percent annual earning rate on the balance. Since the annual withdrawals are equal, this is an annuity problem. The $100,000 is divided by the factor that is the present value of an annuity for the 30 periods. This is $100,000/12.41 or $8058. The balance remaining after the 30th withdrawal would be zero. Note that the amount of interest earned during the entire period would be $30 \times $8058 – $100,000 or $141,740!

15. The $10,000 to be left over at the end of 30 years has a present value of $10,000 \times .131$ or $1310. This amount should be subtracted from $100,000 so that the amount that can be allocated to provide the annuity for Matt's annual spending is $98,690. This cuts his yearly amount to $98,690/12.41 or $7953. In other words, by saving $8058 – $7953 or $105 per year for 30 years at 7 percent, Matt can accumulate $10,000.

16. The first step is to compute the annual payments in a manner similar to that done in problem 12. Here the interest rate is 9 percent so the payments are $100,000/10.27 = $9737. This gives total payments of $30 \times $9737 or $292,110. Remember that the annual payments included interest and principal. Since the loan was for $100,000 the interest must be $292,110 – $100,000 or $192,110. Think of this for a moment. The buyer in this situation pays almost double the principal as interest over the life of the loan.

17. This requires calculating the present value of an annuity of $1000 monthly payments, which will be the amount of the loan. The loan will be $90.818 \times $1,000 or $90,818. With the down payment of $20,000 you could afford a house priced at no more than $90,818 + $20,000 or $110,818.

18. The interest is paid at the beginning. It is 5 percent of $5000 or $250. The amount actually received in this loan is $5000 − $250 = $4750. The effective rate is $250/ $5000 = .0526 or 5.26 percent.

19. The "cash" customers will pay 98 percent of their purchase. However, if they delay payment for one month, they would forego the 2 percent discount in return for an additional 20 days. Since there are 365/20 or 18.25 periods in a year, the delay would cost $2/98 \times 18.25 = 37.24$ percent.

20. Note that the annual loan payment can be figured by dividing the loan amount by the present value factor of an annuity as determined from APPENDIX A TABLE A.3. In other words, $30,000/3.1699 = $9,6412.12. For the second year, the loan balance equals the loan balance of the first year minus the amortization of the loan, $30,000 − $6,463.72 = $23,536.28. The year-end interest amount equals the loan balance of the first year times the interest rate, $23,536.28 \times 0.10 = $2,353.63. The principal repayment equals year-end payment minus the interest paid or $9,463.72 − $2,353.63 = $7,110.09. In the same way, the table for the third and fourth years is as follows:

Time Period	Loan Balance	Year-end Interest Due On Balance	Year-end Payment	Amortization Of Loan
1	$30,000.00	$3,000.00	$9,464.12	$6,464.12
2	$23,535.88	$2,355.59	$9,464.12	$7,108.53
3	$16,427.35	$1,642.74	$9,464.12	$7,821.38
4	$ 8,605.97	$ 858.15	$9,464.12	$8,605.97
	0	0	—	—

CHAPTER 4

VALUING BONDS

INTRODUCTION

This chapter continues the cash flow and timing concepts in formal valuation of bonds. The valuation of bonds involves calculation of the present value of expected annuity cash flow payments (interest) followed by the principle (face/par value) at maturity. Bond yields, both promised (yield to maturity) and realized (holding period return) are discussed, as is the inverse relationship between bond prices and interest rates. The discounted cash-flow model, studied in the last chapter, is extended to cover fixed rate bonds. Note that the same concepts are applied in valuing financial assets: cash flows, timing of the cash flows, and the riskiness or variability of cash flows in the form of the discount rate. The authors introduce a number of factors that affect the market rate of return, from expectations of future interest rates, default risk, and expected inflation. The bond market quotations, both Government of Canada and corporate, from <u>The Globe and Mail</u> are presented, providing plenty of examples for learning.

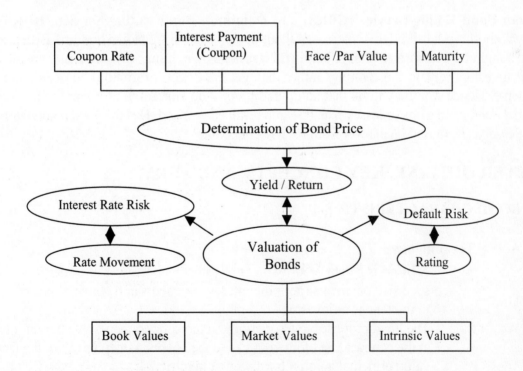

LEARNING CHECKLIST

After studying this chapter, you should be able to:

_____1. Distinguish among the bond's coupon rate, current yield, and yield-to-maturity.
_____2. Understand how bond prices and yields are inversely related.
_____3. Find the impacts of taxes and inflation on the returns of bonds.
_____4. Show how bonds carry interest rate risk.
_____5. Define the default risk and its implication from bond ratings.

SOURCES OF BUSINESS INFORMATION

Investing in Bonds: Many Canadians are not familiar with the investment vehicles except something like GICs or Canada Savings Bonds (CSB). Investing in CSBs is like having your money in a savings account. Buy them at banks earning interest income and cash in when necessary. Information such as current interest rates and terms is available from the Bank of Canada at www.bank-banque-canada.ca. Other types of bonds are more sophisticated. They can be short- or long-term, high- (like junk bonds) or low-risk (like Government of Canada bonds). The Bond Market at <www.bondcan.com> is a good source regarding Canadian bonds. The Web site features a message board and a joke page adds some spice to your bond investments. Another valuable site inclined to the U.S. bond market is www.bondsonline.com.

Canadian Bond Rating Service (CBRS) and Dominion Bond Rating Service (DBRS): These two entities publish relative measures about default risk on Canadian bonds. CBRS was recently bought by Standard & Poor's, but it still issues its own ratings of Canadian firms. It is true that investors rely on those ratings rather than get the direct information to decide their investments. Hence, you may think that an upgrading or a downgrading of a bond will cause substantial bond price gains or losses. The research results are mixed. Has the bond market gone crazy? See if you can find an answer from <www.cbrs.com>.

CHAPTER OUTLINE, KEY CONCEPTS, AND TERM

I.   **BOND CHARACTERISTICS**

A.   **Terminology**
1.   A **bond** is a debt security that obligates the borrower or issuer to make specified payments (periodic interest payments and return of principal) to the lender or investor.
2.   The bond promises to pay periodic interest or coupon to the bondholder at the contract rate of interest, called the coupon rate, plus return the face value principal amount borrowed at maturity.

3. For a fixed coupon rate bond, the coupon rate stays the same throughout the life of the bond. The coupon rate is the market rate, or discount rate, at the time the bond is issued. Thereafter, the market rate may vary; the coupon rate, which determines the periodic interest payment, stays the same.

II. BOND PRICES AND YIELDS

A. **Bond Pricing**

1. The price of a bond is the sum of the present values of the interest payment annuity plus the present value of the single cash flow or face value, usually $1000, at maturity. Using a financial calculator, solve for the present value with the coupon annuity expressed as a payment; the face value at maturity expressed as a single future value (FV).

2. Bond prices are quoted in the financial press as a percentage of their face value. With a face value of $1,000, a price quoted as 103.805 means the bond is worth $1,038.05.

3. When the coupon rate equals the discount rate, the PV price equals the original face value. When market rates of interest are greater (less) than the coupon rate, the PV of the bond is less (greater) than the face value.

4. Bond coupons are usually paid semiannually. To calculate the price of the bond on a semiannual basis, halve the coupon annuity payment and double the maturity of the bond.

$$PV = \frac{cpn}{(1+r)^1} + \frac{cpn}{(1+r)^2} + \ldots + \frac{cpn + par}{(1+r)^t}$$

B. **The Yield to Maturity**

1. The **current yield**, calculated by dividing the annual coupon interest by the price of the bond, is a rough approximation of the expected return on the bond. The current yield assumes that one will hold the bond forever or that the bond is a perpetuity.

2. A better estimate of the expected return on the bond is the **yield to maturity** or YTM. The YTM is the interest rate for which the PV of the bond cash flows (coupons and face value) equals the bond price. The YTM is the approximate market rate of return and assumes that one will hold the bond until maturity.

3. The two separate cash flows of the bond, the coupon and the face value, require that one estimate the YTM as in any equation with more than one unknown (two r values). Most financial calculators calculate the YTM, solving for r or I.

4. Bond coupon rates, for fixed rate bonds, determine the amount of annual coupon and remain the same over the life of the bond. Market interest rates, discount rates, and current borrowing rates change every day. Bond prices vary to give the new bond buyer the market rate of return.

5. Rate of return for a Canada bond is determined by the fixed coupon (i.e., interest) income and the bond price change (i.e., a capital gain or loss). Admittedly, taxes reduce the rate of return on a bond. While interest income is fully taxable, only 50% of capital gains are taxable. After-tax rate of return is found by subtracting the taxes from the relevant cash flows.

6. **Real return bonds (RRBs)** have coupon payments and principal linked to inflation. The real cash flows are fixed, but the nominal cash flows are increased as the consumer price index (CPI) increases. Now, all RRB issues of the Government of Canada have maturities of at least 20 years.

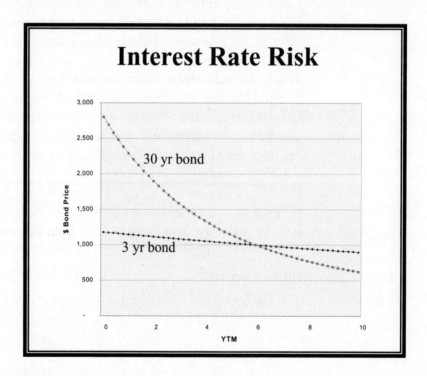

Interest Rate Risk

C. **Interest Rate Risk**

1. Bond prices (PV) vary inversely with changes in market interest rates.
2. The longer (shorter) the maturity of the bond, the greater (less) the change in the bond price for every change in bond discount rates.
3. If the bond is sold before maturity, the seller will receive the market price which, depending on the direction of market rates since the bond was issued, will be higher or lower than face value. This is one dimension of

interest rate risk or the variability of return from the expected YTM caused by selling the bond before maturity.

4.   The actual **rate of return** earned on the bond investment or the holding period return on the bond may be higher or lower than the YTM.

D.   **Reading the Financial Pages**

1.   Bond quotations list prices in terms of percent of face value. Multiply the percentage price quote by the face value, usually $1000, to determine the dollar price.

2.   The prices of government and other dealer traded bonds are quoted on a bid (price the dealer will buy the bond) and ask (price the dealer will sell the bond) basis. See Figure 4.2 in the textbook.

E.   **The Yield Curve**

1.   The **yield curve** is a plot of an issuer's, such as the Canadian Government, bond yields (YTM) by time to maturity.

2.   Expectations of future interest rates has a significant impact upon the shape of the yield curve, while time risks, such as interest rate risk, may also explain the shape of the yield curve.

F.   **Default Risk**

1.   The market yield to maturity on bonds, other than the Canadian government bonds, include a **credit risk premuim**, or added yield to cover the market's expected default loss on risk bonds.

2.   The credit risk premium is the difference between the yield on a risky bond and a Canadian bond of similar maturity.

3.   The higher the expected loss in yield from the risky bond, the higher the credit risk premium.

4.   Bond rating firms, like Moody's and Standard and Poor's, rate the default risk of risky bonds.

5.   High investment grades are in the range from AAA to BBB; speculative or **junk bonds** are rated below BBB.

6.   The vertical yield difference between securities of varying default risk is the default risk premium.

COMPLETION QUESTIONS

1. A _____ is simply a long-term debt.

2. The amount of interest received each year by the bondholder is called the _____.

3. The amount of principal that is repaid when the bond matures is also known as the (*book/face*) value, or (*par/real*) value, or (*market/maturity*) value.

4. The coupon payment on a bond is a(n) (*annuity/premium*).

5. The coupon payment on a bond can be found as the sum of the (*future/present*) value of the coupon payments plus the present value of the final payment, which is usually the (*face/market*) value.

6. Most bonds in Canada pay interest (*annually/semiannually*).

7. When the dollar amount of the coupon is divided by the market price of the bond the result is called the (*coupon/current*) yield.

8. The (*current yield/yield to maturity*) is the discount rate that makes the present value of the bond payments equal to its market price.

9. As interest rates rise the market prices of bonds (*fall/rise*).

10. For a similar change in interest rates, the prices of longer-term bonds will change (*less/more*) than the prices of shorter-term bonds.

11. The earnings on a bond over a year divided by the dollar amount invested is known as the (*rate of return/yield to maturity*).

12. The fractions of bond prices are generally quoted in _____ of a dollar.

13. The bid price quote is the price at which a bond dealer will (*buy/sell*).

14. Entries in the financial pages showing government bond price quotes have a column headed "Yield." This number is the same as the (*current yield/yield to maturity*).

15. The relationship between time to maturity and yield to maturity is known as the _____ _____ _____ _____ _____. The graph of this relationship is called the _____ _____.

16. Normally long-term rates are (*higher/lower*) than short-term rates. This means the yield curve is usually (*downward/upward*) sloping.

17. Two reasons why investors more often receive a higher return on long-term bonds compared to short-term bonds are because the former have (*less/more*) price fluctuations and because the proceeds from maturing bonds can be invested (*later/sooner*).

18. The additional yield that is promised on a corporate bond over a treasury bond having a similar coupon and maturity is called the _____ premium.

19. Bonds rated below investment grade are called _____ bonds.

20. The higher the bond rating or grade, the (*higher/lower*) the expected yield.

21. To measure returns in purchasing power terms, an adjustment to (*constant/nominal*) dollars is made to account for _____.

22. The rate at which the purchasing power of an investment increases is called the _____ interest rate.

23. Inflation will cause the purchasing power from an annuity to (*decrease/increase*) as time passes.

24. Two ways for a company to raise new money involve _____ and _____.[1]

25. It is (*true/false*) that a default-free bond has an AAA rating.

PROBLEMS

1. A 10-year old Bailey's bond pays $100 interest each year. Its last market price was $1064. What is its coupon rate, current yield, and yield to maturity?

2. What would be the coupon that Bailey would likely set on a new 10-year issue offered while the same market conditions as those specified in problem 1 above.

3. Bonnie is considering buying a bond having 15 years until maturity and a coupon of 9 percent. She wants a 10 percent yield to maturity. What is the maximum price she should pay for this bond?

4. Suppose there is a 9 percent coupon bond outstanding that matures in 5 years and offers a yield to maturity of 9 percent. What will be its price?

---

[1] Other correct terms are borrowing and equity.

49

5. Jim purchased the bond described in the preceding problem for $950 a year ago. What is the rate of return that he would have received on this bond over the past year?

6. If inflation this past year had been 4 percent, what would have been the real rate of return on the bond described in problem 5 above?

7. Small Industries' bonds sell for $885, will mature in 8 years, and offer a yield to maturity of 8 percent. What is the coupon rate?

8. Calculate the price of the bond that Bonnie was considering in problem 3 if interest rates rose dramatically causing the yield to maturity on that bond to suddenly increase by 1 percentage point to 11 percent?

9. Compare the situation faced by Debi who was looking at a 2-year bond that was identical to the one Bonnie was considering in all other respects. In other words, what would be the change in price for the short-term bond if interest rates rose by the same 1 percent from 10 to 11 percent?

10. Cathy started as an accountant 40 years ago at an annual salary of $4000. Her son-in-law expects to begin his accounting career earning $32,000. If the cost of living increased 7 times over the past 40 years, who entered the workforce with higher purchasing power?

11. If you expect to receive a 7 percent interest rate from a certificate of deposit, what real interest rate will you earn if inflation is 4 percent per year?

12. Suppose you plan to have savings totalling $1,000,000 when you retire in 30 years. What would be the purchasing power in terms of today's dollars of that amount if inflation averages 4 percent each year?

13. If you think you will live 25 years beyond retirement and the real interest rate during that period is 3 percent, what would be your annual annuity in today's dollars from the savings plan described in the preceding problem?

14. Neverend Life Insurance Co. has issued a perpetual bond with a coupon of 6 percent. What price would the bond sell for today if the required rate of return is 12 percent?

ANSWERS TO COMPLETION QUESTIONS

1. bond
2. coupon
3. face, par, maturity
4. annuity

5.   present, face
6.   semiannually
7.   current
8.   yield to maturity
9.   fall
10. more
11. rate of return
12. decimal
13. buy
14. yield to maturity
15. term structure of interest rates, yield curve
16. higher, upward
17. less, sooner
18. default
19. junk
20. lower
21. nominal, inflation
22. real
23. decrease
24. debt, stock
25. false

SOLUTIONS TO PROBLEMS

1.   The coupon amount or rate on a bond is fixed for its life at the time it is issued. In this problem the dollar amount is specified as being $100 per year.

The *coupon rate* is calculated by dividing the annual interest by the face value (also called par value): $100/$1000 = 0.10 or 10 percent.

The *current yield* is the coupon amount divided by the current bond price: $100/$1064 = 0.94 or 9.4 percent.

Yield to maturity (YTM) is a much more difficult calculation. YTM is the special interest rate that will make the present value of the bond's payments (the coupon and the principal) equal to the current price. Unfortunately there is no direct way to solve for YTM using an equation. A trial-and-error process is involved. However, financial calculators are programmed to do this very quickly. Otherwise tables can be used but they require more time and computations. For example:

$$\begin{aligned} \text{current price} &= \text{present value} \\ &= \text{pv of coupon amount} + \text{pv of principal} \\ &= \text{coupon} \times \text{annuity factor} \\ &\quad + \text{principal} \times \text{present value factor} \\ &= \$100 \times \text{factor} + \$1000 \times \text{factor} \end{aligned}$$

Since we know that the current price is above par value, the interest rate for this particular bond is currently below the coupon rate so the first guess is 8 percent.

$$\text{Present value} = \$100 \times 6.710 + \$1000 \times 0.463$$

= $1134 which is not equal to the current price of $1,064.50. Try 9 percent:

$$\$1064 = \$100 \times 6.418 + \$1000 \times .422$$
$$= \$1063.80 \text{ which is very close to the price of } \$1064$$

so the YTM is 9 percent.

2. Issuers of bonds must offer yields that are competitive. The convention is to set the coupon on new bonds at the yield to maturity offered by outstanding bonds of similar maturity, risk, and other factors. Since Bailey's has a bond outstanding with 10 years of life remaining and that yields 9 percent, it would choose a 9 percent coupon. This would allow it to sell at par value of $1000.

3. Bonnie would pay an amount that would be below the par value so that the 9 percent coupon plus the gain from her purchase price to the par value (redemption value) would offer her a required return of 10 percent (the yield to maturity). This price would be:

$$\text{pv of coupon amount} + \text{pv of principal} = \$90 \times 7.606 + \$1000 \times .239$$
$$= \$923.54$$

4. The price will be equal to the present value of all future returns as illustrated in each of the preceding problems. Thus

$$\text{price} = \$90 \times 3.890 + \$1000 \times .650 = \$1000^*.$$

*Note this is within round-off error of $1000 which is par value. This reinforces the earlier statement that whenever the coupon and yield to maturity are the same, any bond will sell at par value.

5.
$$\text{Rate of return} = \frac{\text{interest} + \text{capital gain}}{\text{original price}}$$
$$= \frac{\$90 + (\$1000 - \$950)}{\$950}$$
$$= .1474 \text{ or } 14.74\%$$

6.
$$\text{Real return} = \frac{1 + \text{nominal return}}{1 + \text{inflation}} - 1$$
$$= \frac{1 + .1474}{1 + .04} - 1$$

7. Remember that

$$\text{Price} = \text{coupon} \times \text{annuity factor} + \text{principal} \times \text{pv factor}$$
$$\$885 = \text{coupon} \times 5.747 + \$1000 \times .540.$$

$$\text{The coupon} = \frac{\$885 - \$540}{5.747} = \$60$$

This means the coupon must be 6%.

8. The price at the higher yield to maturity of 11 percent will be:

$$\$90 \times 7.191 + \$1000 \times .209 = \$856.19$$

This compares with $923.54 in problem 3. It means that a 1 percent increase in YTM results in a decrease of $67.35 or 7.3%

9. Here we compare the value of the 2-year bond at a 10 percent yield with what happens if rates go to 11 percent. The original bond value would be:

$$\$90 \times 1.736 + \$1000 \times .826 = \$982.24$$

At 11 percent this bond would fall to:

$$\$90 \times 1.713 + \$1000 \times .812 = \$966.17$$

This is a drop of $16.07 or 1.6 percent which is considerably less than the decline of 7.3 percent figured for the longer-term bond. The conclusion is that longer-term bonds are much more volatile than short-term bonds for a given change in interest rates.

10. Cathy's son-in-law's equivalent purchasing power in comparison to hers would be $32,000/7 or $4571 which is substantially greater. It means that the starting salary of accountants, given these numbers, has outpaced the cost of living increases.

11. As in problem 6,

$$\text{Real return} = \frac{1 + \text{nominal rate}}{1 + \text{inflation rate}} - 1$$

$$= \frac{1 + .07}{1 + .04} - 1 = 1.029 \text{ or } 2.9\%$$

12. The cost of living would have risen by the 4 percent compounded annual rate for 30 years which would be $(1.04)^{30}$ or 3.243 times. This means the purchasing power would be $1,000,000/3.243 or $308,356.46.

13. The lump sum of $308,356.46 computed in the preceding problem would be equivalent to an annuity of $308,356.46/17.41 or $17,711.46 per year for 25 years if the real interest rate was 3 percent.

14. The bond pays a coupon of 6 percent or $60 per year. If the required return was 12 percent the bond would sell for $60/0.12 or $500.

CHAPTER 5

VALUING STOCKS

INTRODUCTION

This chapter extends the valuation concepts explored in valuing bonds and applies them to equity securities. The same basic principles apply. Basic determination of cash flows and discount rates are at the core of valuing stocks. While bonds have default risk, stocks also have risk associated with the unknown nature of future cash flows.

These valuation techniques involve non-contractual and varied future cash flows, which are characteristic of all common stock. Covering an increasingly complex variety of cash-flow patterns from constant dollar (no-growth), constant growth (Gordon Model), and growth over a specific time period, the authors provide valuation techniques for a variety of common stock and business cash-flow patterns. The following chapters apply these concepts to specific value-creating, cash-flow generating projects.

As in prior chapters, the required/expected rate of return concept is reinforced. These rate-of-return discussions provide an important building block for the later study of capital budgeting and risk analysis.

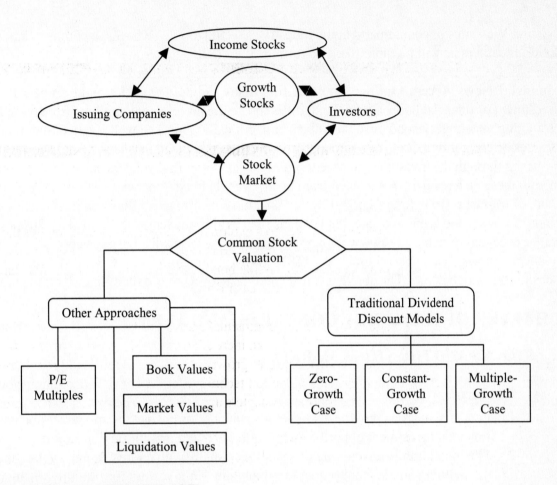

LEARNING CHECKLIST

After studying this chapter, you should be able to:

_____1. Understand the stock trading reports in the financial pages of newspapers.
_____2. Calculate the present value of a stock given forecasts of future dividends and future stock price.
_____3. Use stock valuation formulas to infer the expected rate of return on a common stock.
_____4. Interpret price-earnings ratios.

SOURCES OF BUSINESS INFORMATION

Keep it or Dump it after Bad News? Frankly, there is no well-established rule for trading. In addition to examining a company's financial and operating history, you must understand its markets, competitive challenges, and outlooks. Updating yourself on its recent activities, you can weigh the chances for success and income against the risks of failure and loss. Remember that you cannot rely solely on the official information although many companies have their annual reports, press releases, etc. available. Some examples can be found online with RBC www.royalbank.com and AT&T Canada www.att.com. To broaden your research, check out the existing Web sites of counterparts in the industry as well. Despite setbacks, a company having solid fundamentals will be more likely to turn itself around.

Financial News Access Online: You can find many online newsletters and articles from investment or financial publications. First, differentiate the professional opinions from the sale-promoting materials. Second, read the information critically. Third, be well aware of the frauds. Besides offering information, newsgroups are sometimes organized for discussions. Spend time browsing through the investment newsletters and magazines to find your favourites. Only check in with these on a regular basis to keep from being overwhelmed. Financial institutions, e.g., the Bank of Montreal www.fcfunds.bomil.ca, not only have their investor news online, but also all kinds of market and economic data. Publications such as "MoneySense" or "Canadian Business" can be accessed from the sites www.moneysense.ca and www.canadianbusiness.com. The world financial news can be found at CNN www.cnnfn.com or CBS MarketWatch <cbs.marketwatch.com>. The above is a just small taste of what is called finance on the tube.

CHAPTER OUTLINE, KEY CONCEPTS, AND TERM

I. STOCKS AND THE STOCK MARKET

   A. Introduction
1. Financial markets provide a source of financing for businesses and governments; a financial investment opportunity for individual and institutional investors.
2. The initial, funds-raising sale of securities, usually with an investment banker, is in the **primary** market; subsequent trading between investors for liquidity, financial investing, and portfolio rebalancing is in the **secondary** market.

   B. **Reading the Stock Market Listings**
1. Figure 5.2 in the textbook lists a number of stock quotations. Note price changes in eighths, an "annualized" quarterly dividend, and the dividend yield as the annualized dividend divided by the closing price.
2. Why do the dividend yields vary? Expected price appreciation and risk.
3. The price/earnings (P/E) ratio is the closing price divided by the earnings per share. Commonly used in valuation assessment, the ratio indicates the number of years of current earnings the market is willing to pay to own the stock.

II. BOOK VALUES, LIQUIDATION VALUES, AND MARKET VALUES

   A. **Terminology**
1. **Book value** of common shareholders represents the accounting value of assets less the accounting value of liabilities.
2. Book value is biased toward historical or original costs.
3. **Liquidation value** of common shareholders represents the quick sale of individual assets less liabilities owed.

4.   **Going concern value** represents the difference between a minimum liquidation value and actual or "true" value (market), the worth of an on-going business by investors considering, 1) future earning power of existing tangible and intangible assets, 2) the value of future investment opportunities of the firm, and 3) intangible assets.

5.   **Market value** represents the value assigned to a firm by investors in a reasonable market driven by the expected level and variability of cash flows. When the market/book ratio exceeds one, the economic value of the assets exceeds the accounting value or the expected rate of returns to shareholders exceeds their minimally acceptable rate of return.

III. VALUING COMMON STOCKS

A.   **Today's Price and Tomorrow's Price**

1.   The expected and actual, realized rate of return to common stockholders comes from 1) cash dividends, DIV_1, and 2) capital gains or losses, $P_1 - P_0$.

2.   Investors compare expected returns, based on expected dividends and price changes, with minimum required returns, comparable returns on similar securities (opportunity costs).

3.   If expected returns exceed comparable returns elsewhere, investors will want to purchase the stock, bidding the price up and the expected return down to the minimum acceptable return.

4.   At any market price, expected returns equal that required by investors.

5.   All securities of the same risk are priced to offer the same expected rate of return.

6.   Actual returns may substantially differ from the expected returns due to the taxes.

$$\text{Expected Return} = r = \frac{Div_1 + P_1 - P_0}{P_0}$$

B.   **The Dividend Discount Model**

1.   The **dividend discount model**, or discounted cash flow model, states that share value equals the present value of all expected future dividends.

2.   With a specific investment time period or horizon, H, the intrinsic share value (value determined by the evidence) is:

$$P_0 = \frac{Div_1}{(1+r)^1} + \frac{Div_2}{(1+r)^2} + ... + \frac{Div_H + P_H}{(1+r)^H}$$

3.   The stock price at the horizon date, P_H, is the present value of cash dividends received beyond the horizon date.

4.   As the horizon date changes, the present value of the stock will remain the same as dividends are expected to grow at the rate of "r" (Example 5.2, Table 5.4, and Figure 5.3 in the textbook).

5.   At extreme horizon dates the present value of P_H becomes insignificant; thus the dividend discount model--share value equals the present value of future, expected dividends.

IV.   SIMPLIFYING THE DIVIDEND DISCOUNT MODEL

A.   **The Dividend Discount Model With No Growth**

1.   When all earnings are paid as cash dividends, no growth is possible (reinvestment = depreciation to maintain the current stock of capital).

2.   The stock value of a no-growth firm is the expected dividend capitalized (perpetuity) at the required rate of return or:

$$Perpetuity = P_0 = \frac{Div_1}{r} \; or \; \frac{EPS_1}{r}$$

Assumes all earnings are paid to shareholders.

B.   **The Constant-Growth Dividend Discount Model**

1.   The **Constant-Growth Discount Model** is an arithmetic expression calculating the present value of a perpetual stream of cash flows, DIV, growing at a constant rate of growth, g, and discounted at a required rate of return, r:

$$P_0 = \frac{Div_1}{r - g}$$

2.   With a sustained positive growth rate in the economy and business activity, the Gordon Model and its assumptions are reasonable.

3. DIV_1 represents the dividend received at the end of period one.

4.   The constant-growth formula is valid only when "g" is less than "r."

5. P_0 is directly related to DIV_1 and g; inversely related to r.

C. **Estimating Expected Rates of Return**

1. In constant-growth business situations, if g is capitalized in the market in higher stock prices, r may be a proxy for the market expected rate of return on similar risk situations.

2. The expected rate of return is a combination of the dividend yield, DIV_1/P_0, and capital appreciation rate, g.

3. The required rate of return, r, is a market-determined rate related to the risk-free rate adjusted upward for risk, given expectations of DIV_1 and g. The stock price, P_0, adjusts to equate the market-expected rate with the required rate of return.

D. **What If Short-Term Growth Rates Don't Fit The Market?**

1. The no-growth and constant-growth dividend discount models above assume two patterns of cash flows while reality presents the analyst with many variations. The dividend discount model is easily adapted.

2. Changing future dividend patterns from non-growth to constant-growth to variable-growth rates over a given horizon requires that the analyst estimate the stock price by forecasting the cash-flow patterns and discounting the cash flows at the market-required rate of return.

3. The terminal value, P_H, represents the present value of the cash flows beyond the horizon.

V. **GROWTH STOCKS AND INCOME STOCKS**

A. **Income vs. Growth Stocks**

1. **Income stock** returns are derived from the dividend yield, DIV/price, and are associated with businesses with a high **payout ratio**, the fraction of earnings paid out as dividends.

2. **Growth stock** returns are derived from a combination of no or relatively small dividend yields (low payout ratio) and a high **plowback ratio** (the proportion of current period earnings or free cash flow retained in firm), and earning high asset returns, in excess of that required by the market, on reinvested earnings.

3. The **sustainable** growth rate, g, discussed in the constant-growth rate discussion above, relates to the expected asset returns on reinvested capital adjusted for the proportion of earnings plowed back into the firm. Dividends (payout ratio) limit the level of reinvested capital and the growth potential of future earnings and dividends.

$$g = \text{return on equity} \times \text{plowback ratio},$$

where the return on equity is the expected return on equity capital plowed back into earning assets.

4. Similar stock prices ($41.67) will result from a 100 percent payout ratio and any less payout where the plowed back earnings earn just the required rate of return.

5. When rates of return on reinvested capital exceed the required rate of return, added value, often called "value added" or the **present value of growth opportunities** or **(PVGO)**, is capitalized in the market price of the stock.

B. **The Price-Earnings Ratio**

1. Higher price-earnings ratios are associated with higher expected growth opportunities and lower earnings-price ratios, reflecting that some portion of the required rate of return is expected to be derived from growth opportunities. An unreasonably high P/E ratio can result from the understated earnings.

2. Expected future earnings are expected cash flows less any reinvestment associated with the economic depreciation of earning assets or earnings (cash flow) above that needed to maintain the earning power of the firm.

COMPLETION QUESTIONS

1. Owners of the corporation are (*debtholders/shareholders*) who expect a risk premium in the form of (*higher/lower*) returns compared to lenders.

2. Sales of new securities occur in the (*primary/secondary*) market.

3. Already-issued securities are bought and sold in the (*primary/secondary*) market.

4. Canadian stock exchanges operate as an (*electronic/auction*) market.

5. (*Toronto Stock Exchange/Canadian Venture Exchange*) lists shares of new, smaller companies.

6. Given the Bid/Ask prices of $46.50 and $47.25, your buying price for a share is (*$46.50/$47.25*).

7. The term NASDAQ stands for _____ _____ _____ _____ _____ _____.

8. Periodic cash distributions from the firm to its shareholders are called (*dividends/interest*).

9. Unlike bonds that normally pay a fixed amount of interest, common shareholders hope profits will grow enabling the firm to pay (*higher/lower*) dividends.

10. The ratio of stock price to earnings per share for a company is called the _____ _____ multiple.

11. The term "odd lot" refers to (*the human race/trades for less than 100 shares*).

12. According to the balance sheet (*book/market*) value is equal to assets minus liabilities. This is also called the net _____ of the firm.

13. Because the value of a firm's assets as reported on their balance sheet is equal to their original cost minus the depreciation, their (*book/market*) value will often be very different.

14. Net proceeds that would be realized by selling the firm's assets and paying off its creditors is called the _____ value of the firm.

15. The actual value of a successful company is called its _____ _____ value.

16. A firm may be worth more "alive than dead" due to its extra _____ _____, its _____ assets, and the value of its (*current/future*) investments.

17. A financial statement that uses the actual or true value of all the firm's assets and liabilities is known as a _____ _____ balance sheet.

18. The cash payoff to owners of common stocks comes from _____ and _____ gains or losses.

19. All securities of the same risk (*are/are not*) priced to offer the same expected rate of return.

20. The _____ _____ model computes the share value as the present value of all future dividends.

21. The present value of a stock (*equals/is greater than*) the present value of future dividends out to the investment horizon plus the present value of the forecasted stock price at the horizon. This relationship holds for (*any/only one*) horizon date.

22. When no growth of dividends is expected, the value of the stock will be equal to the dividend divided by the (*discount rate/yield to maturity*).

23. In the constant growth dividend model the share value is equal to next year's (*dividend/interest*) divided by the difference between the expected rate of return and the growth rate.

24. The (*payout/plowback*) ratio is the fraction of earnings that are paid out as dividends.

25. Growth stocks usually have relatively (*high/low*) payout ratios.

26. A company's growth rate is equal to the product of its return on (*assets/equity*) and its (*payout/plowback*) ratio.

27. If the present value of growth opportunities is positive, the required rate of return will be (*greater/less*) than the earnings-price ratio.

PROBLEMS

1. Peter's Pickle Chips (PPC) paid $2 in dividends this past year. Analysts expect this payment will grow at 6 percent annually for the indefinite future.
   a. What stock price is forecast with this model if a discount rate of 10 percent is appropriate (use the constant growth model)?
   b. What are the expected dividends for the next 2 years (i.e., DIV_1 and DIV_2)? What is the present value of these 2 dividends?
   c. What will be the estimated value of PPC 2 years from now? What is the present value of this price discounted to the present time (time zero)?
   d. Add the discounted price of PPC stock 2 years from now to the present value of the dividends in the first 2 years (i.e., add the results of parts b and c). Compare the summation to the answer in part a, they should be equal (there may be small rounding error of a few pennies).

2. Suppose the Allman Brothers Grocery Stores Inc. currently has a $1.50 dividend per share. This dividend is expected to grow at 4 percent into the future and the appropriate discount rate for a stock with Allman's risk profile is 8.5 percent.
   a. What is the forecasted stock price for Allmans using the constant growth model?
   b. What happens to Allman's price if the discount rate rises to 10 percent?
   c. What happens to Allman's price if the expected growth in dividends rises to 5 percent? Use the original discount rate of 8.5 percent.

3. Fillmore West pays a $3 dividend right now and its stock sells for $43. The best estimate of Fillmore's required return is 13 percent. Given this information and using the constant growth stock price model, what is the constant growth rate for Fillmore?

4. Bankcity's perpetual preferred stock pays a $2 dividend and is priced to yield 13 percent. What is price of this issue according to the constant growth model?

5. Silver Creek Gold Company (SCG) has an average return on equity of 12 percent over the past 5 years. Analysts believe this rate is sustainable for the foreseeable future.
    a. If SCG's plowback ratio is 45 percent what is its expected growth rate?
    b. If SCG's dividend is expected to be $1.75 next year ($DIV_1$) and the required return is 12 percent, what is the constant growth estimate for SCG stock price?
    c. What will happen to SCG's growth rate and stock price if they invest in projects that yield less than 12 percent?

6. Hacker's Cigarettes Company expects sales, earnings, and dividends to decline 5 percent in the foreseeable future due to rising taxes and falling demand. If their dividend is currently $3.50 and the required return is 15 percent, what would the constant growth model predict for Hacker's stock price?

7. Hardball Software stock sells for $46 with an estimated discount rate of 16 percent. Analysts estimate next year's dividend at $2.10 and Hardball plans to reinvest 75 percent of its earnings back into the business. What is Hardball's rate of return on its reinvested earnings (ROE)?

8. In the Wall Street Journal, you notice a cellular telephone stock that sells for $28.50 and earned $1.80 per share during the current year.
    a. What is the price/earnings (P/E) ratio for this firm?
    b. What return will you theoretically earn on this stock next year if you buy it at the above price and earnings do not change? (Recall that earnings belong to the shareholders.) Does this seem like an adequate compensation for the risk of investing in stocks?
    c. In general, what do investors expect to happen to the earnings of firms that have high P/E ratios?

9. You live in Ontario and your marginal federal tax rate is 16% and your marginal provincial tax rate is 6.2%. The dividend gross-up factor is 125%, the federal dividend tax credit is 13.33% of gross-up dividends, and the provincial dividend tax credit is 6.6% of gross-up dividends. You want to compare your after-tax income if $1,000 is received as dividends and capital gains.

ANSWERS TO COMPLETION QUESTIONS

1. shareholders, higher
2. primary
3. secondary
4. electronic
5. Canadian Venture Exchange
6. $47.25
7. National Association (of) Securities Dealers Automated Quotation
8. dividends
9. higher
10. price earnings
11. trades for less than 100 shares
12. book, worth
13. market
14. liquidation
15. going concern
16. earning power, intangible, future
17. market value
18. dividends, capital
19. are
20. dividend discount
21. equals, any
22. discount rate
23. dividend
24. payout
25. low
26. equity, plowback
27. greater

SOLUTIONS TO PROBLEMS

1. This problem illustrates forecast and valuation based on the constant-growth dividend discount model.

   a. $P_0 = \dfrac{DIV_1}{r - g} = \dfrac{\$2.12}{(.10 - .06)} = \$53$

   b. Dividends increase by 6 percent per year:

   $DIV_1 = \dfrac{\$2.12}{(1 + .10)^1} = \$1.93$

Present values of the second year's dividend:

$$DIV_2 = \frac{\$2.25}{(1+.10)^2} = \$1.86$$

c. $$P_2 = \frac{DIV_3}{r-g} = \frac{\$2.25(1.06)}{(.10-.06)} = \frac{\$2.38}{.04} = \$59.55$$

Present value of the above stock price (note: it is received at the end of year two, the same time the second dividend is received):

$$P_0 = \frac{\$59.55}{(1+.10)^2} = \$49.21$$

d. The summation of $49.21 + $1.93 + $1.86 = $53.00. You should see that the constant-growth dividend discount model used in answer a is simply a shorthand way of calculating the present value of all the future dividends in the special case of a constant growth in dividends.

2. It is evident after we do the math, but it should be intuitively obvious that rising discount rates reduce stock price and rising growth in dividends increases stock price. Keep your thinking cap on when you do these problems and it is easier to avoid silly mistakes (like fat fingers that punch the wrong button on the calculator).

a. $$P_0 = \frac{DIV_1}{r-g} = \frac{\$1.50(1.04)}{(.085-.04)} = \$34.67$$

b. $$P_0 = \frac{DIV_1}{r-g} = \frac{\$1.50(1.04)}{(.10-.04)} = \$26$$

c. $$P_0 = \frac{DIV_1}{r-g} = \frac{\$1.50(1.06)}{(.085-.04)} = \$35.33$$

3. Since $P_0 = DIV_1/r-g$ we can substitute in the known variables and solve for the growth rate. Thus:

$$P_0 = \frac{DIV_1}{r-g} = \frac{DIV_0(1+g)}{r+g} = \$43 = \frac{\$3(1+g)}{(.13-g)} \text{ or } 5.6\%$$

4. Since the payout on this preferred stock issue does not grow (there are preferred stock issues that pay floating rate dividends) the g in our formula is zero. Thus:

$$P_0 = \frac{DIV_1}{r - g} \text{ and } P_0 = \frac{\$2}{.13} = \$15.38$$

5. A rough estimate of SCG's sustainable growth is that it will be able to earn the same return on its equity investments in the future that it has earned in the recent past. The earnings "plowed back" into the firm are called retained earnings (i.e., equity), the rest of the earnings are paid out as dividends and do not help the firm grow.

   a. For SCG:
      g = return on equity × plowback rate
      $$= 12\% \times .45 = 5.4\%$$

   b. $P_0 = \frac{DIV_1}{r - g}$ and $P_0 = \frac{\$1.75}{.12 - .054} = \$26.52$

   c. Investing in projects that return less than expected by shareholder (i.e., required return) reduces the firm's growth rate and the stock price.

6. The constant growth model has trouble handling high rates of growth (it is not reasonable to expect a firm to grow at high rates for indefinite periods of time, competition always catches up), but the model has no trouble with negative growth rates, as Hacker's demonstrates:

$$P = \frac{DIV_1}{r - g} \text{ and } P_0 = \frac{\$3.50(1 - .05)}{[.15 - (-.05)]} = \$16.63$$

7. First solve for Hardball's growth rate:

$$P_0 = \frac{DIV_1}{r - g} \text{ so } g = r - \frac{DIV_1}{P_0} = 0.16 - \frac{\$3.10}{\$46} = \$.0926$$

Assuming it's reasonable to expect that Hardball's growth rate will be:

$$g = \text{ROE} \times \text{plowback ratio}$$
$$.0926 = \text{ROE} \times .75$$
$$\text{ROE} = .0926/.75 = 12.35\%$$

8.   a.   P/E = $28.50/$1.80 = 15.83

      b. $1.80/$28.50 = 6.3 percent. This return looks low for a firm invested in a business as competitive as the cellular telephone market.

      c.   Investors that pay high P/Es expect earnings will increase in the future. If the earnings do not increase then investors will have paid too much for the stock.

9.

		Dividends	Capital Gains
Income		$1,000	$1,000
Dividend gross-up		$250	0
Less Non-taxable gains		0	($500)
Taxable income		$1,250	$500
Income tax	@16%	$200	$80
	@6.2%	$77.5	$31
Less DTC	@13.33%	$166.63	0
	@6.6%	$82.5	0
Taxes payable		$28.37	$111
Income after-tax		$971.63	$889

CHAPTER 6

NPV AND OTHER INVESTMENT CRITERIA

INTRODUCTION

This chapter continues the valuation theme, but shifts to an internal, managerial focus oriented to the discussion and evaluation of several investment decision criteria. How should managers select long-term investments? In your economics class, profit maximization (PM) was used as the decision criterion. Profit maximization worked well under the simplistic assumptions of no risk and immediate returns from investment. PM is *not* an effective decision criterion in the real world of long-term and variable (risky) investment returns. A better decision criterion is needed. The net present value decision criterion fits the manager's needs to be concerned with long-term, multiple periods, variable or risky returns, and a focus on cash-flow returns. The net present value and internal rate of return decision criteria are consistent with shareholder wealth maximization, for they focus on expected cash flows, when the flow occurs, and the riskiness of the cash flow.

You must now make a transition from the former section and chapters related to valuation in a macroeconomic or general setting to this microeconomic setting related to making decisions within the business. Managers must assess the expected value added contributions of new investment projects. The net present value measures each project's expected contribution to shareholder wealth. This chapter is a continuation of the valuation theme from the last chapter.

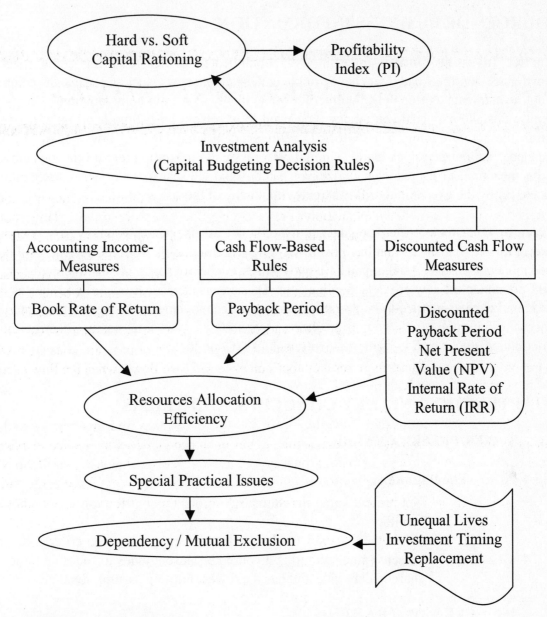

LEARNING CHECKLIST

This chapter is a skills-specific chapter that focuses on training you to:

_____1. Calculate the net present value of an investment and learn the NPV decision rule.
_____2. Calculate the internal rate of return of a project and learn the IRR decision rule.
_____3. Compare and contrast the NPV and IRR with the payback and discounted payback decision rule and book value rate of return decision rule, which do not always increase shareholder wealth.
_____4. Use the profitability index decision rule when capital rationing occurs.

SOURCES OF BUSINESS INFORMATION

Practice Investing Online: Investing is a complicated matter requiring some specific knowledge. Don't feel bad if you have trouble understanding newspaper and magazine columns about investments. Fortunately, the Internet offers plenty of sites to help you along. Worrying about a mistake may cost you money; you want to have some real-time hand-on experience before the actual trading. The "Green Line Investment Challenge" at www.ichallenge.net/phcanada is a fantastic stock market simulation for a small registration fee. While you compete in this most realistic game to win a prize, you can buy and sell shares of stocks at current market prices. Enjoy the excitement of Bay Street without any of the risk.

Screening Out Stocks: After knowing enough of how markets operate, you may have your own criteria for picking stocks that have potential. The screening tools from the Internet will do a good job. For Canadian markets, you have two choices: Globeinvestor at www.globeinvestor.com and Carlson Online at www.carlsononline.com. The screens have all search criteria such as P/E ratio, market cap and price-to-book-value ratio, and price movements during any time interval. Since the Internet offers powerful filtering capabilities, you can easily identify those undervalued stocks or fast-rising momentum stocks. Good luck.

CHAPTER OUTLINE, KEY CONCEPTS, AND TERMS

I.   **NET PRESENT VALUE**

    A.   **The Rationale**

        1.   Net present value measures each project's contribution to shareholder wealth.

        2.   While there are several long-term investment decision criteria, the net present value method is favoured because it tends to focus on building shareholder value and has the fewest limiting assumptions.

    B.   **A Review of the Basics**

        1.   **Capital budgeting decisions**, the process of choosing investment projects, are important because they usually involve large cash outlays with cash flow return over a long period of time. The *four* steps in the capital budgeting decision process are:

            a.   Forecast the future project cash flows, noting when the flow occurs.

            b.   Estimate the opportunity cost of capital. The **opportunity cost of capital** is the expected rate of return given up by investing in the project under review.

            c.   Calculate the present value of the future cash flows discounted at the opportunity cost of capital rate. The present value of the cash flows represents the maximum amount that investors would pay for the investment.

d.   NPV Decision Rule: The present value sum of the future cash flows *minus* the investment outlay is the **net present value**. If the net present value is positive (greater than zero), make the investment. If the net present value is negative, forgo the investment. If the present value is the maximum amount one would pay for the investment relative to the cost, the NPV represents the added value of the investment. NPV = PV of future cash flows minus required investment.

e.   The expected net present value of a project is the added shareholders' wealth provided by the project.

$$NPV = C_0 + \frac{C_t}{(1+r)^t}$$

C.   Valuing Long-Lived Projects

1.   Added net present values generated by investments are represented in higher stock prices.

2.   The net present value method is a proxy for financial market investor analysis of business investments.

3.   Projects that are expected to generate negative net present values will reduce shareholders' wealth by the expected negative NPV.

$$NPV = C_0 + \frac{C_1}{(1+r)^1} + \frac{C_2}{(1+r)^2} + ... + \frac{C_t}{(1+r)^t}$$

Note: C_0 is negative presenting a cash outflow.

II.   OTHER INVESTMENT CRITERIA

A.   **Internal Rate Of Return**

1.   An alternative to the NPV method is the **internal rate of return**, which is the discount rate that, having discounted the expected cash flows, will produce a present value equal to the cost of the project. In this case, a discount rate that will generate an NPV of zero.

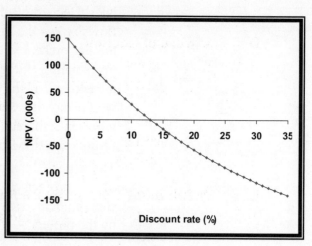

2.   The rate of return decision rule — invest in any project offering a rate of return higher than the opportunity cost of capital. See Figure 6.3 in the textbook for an illustration.

B.   **A Closer Look at the Rate of Return Rule**

1.   The rate of return, or the **internal rate of return, or IRR**, or the discounted cash flow (DCF) rate of return, is the discount rate at which NPV equals zero.

$$\text{Rate of Re turn} = \frac{C_1 - \text{investment}}{\text{investment}}$$

2.   If the rate of return is greater than the opportunity cost of capital, the NPV of the project is greater than zero.

3.   If the NPV of a project is less than zero (negative) the rate of return is less than the opportunity cost of capital.

4.   The rate of return rule and the NPV rule are equivalent.

C.   **Calculating the Rate of Return for Long-Lived Projects**

1.   The IRR of a single future cash flow (PV) or an annuity flow (PV of annuity) may be determined easily and arithmetically as the discount rate that equates the cost of the project with the present value of the future cash flows.

2.   The IRR of a multiple, uneven cash flow stream involves more than one unknown and is not easily solved arithmetically. One must iterate, often several times, selecting an expected IRR and discounting the cash flows until the NPV of the project is zero.

3. The rate of return rule will give the same decision as the NPV rule as long as the NPV of a project declines smoothly as the discount rate increases. See Figure 6.2 in the textbook.

D. **A Word of Caution**

1. Do not confuse the IRR with the opportunity cost of capital. The IRR is the rate of return on the cash flows of the investment.

2. The opportunity cost of capital is the minimum IRR acceptable to the firm. The opportunity rate of return is an estimate of the minimum acceptable rate of return demanded by investors in financial markets on similar risk investments.

E. **Pitfalls of the Rate of Return Rule**

1. While the IRR is easier to understand than the NPV, the NPV should be used as a final decision criterion for an investment.

2. The IRR method has a number of theoretical pitfalls that encourages the use of the NPV method:

    a. Pitfall 1: mutually exclusive projects. Where **mutually exclusive projects** are facing the financial manager, one must be selected and the other deferred or passed by. In cases where competing projects serve the same purpose, select the project with the highest expected NPV. The IRR may give a conflicting choice relative to the NPV, which focuses more accurately on shareholder value. Analysis of the IRR on an *incremental basis* will give decisions consistent with the NPV.

    b. Pitfall 1a: mutually exclusive projects involving different outlays, same lives. Small projects may be erroneously selected over larger projects using the IRR. When NPV is higher as the discount rate increases, a project is acceptable only if its internal rate of return is less than the opportunity cost of capital.

    c. Pitfall 2: lending or borrowing. The IRR does not distinguish between a lending (investing) or a borrowing (borrow and invest) situation, whereas the NPV clearly points out the negative aspects of the borrowing strategy.

    d. Pitfall 3: multiple rates of return. Any change in sign $(+, -)$ in period cash flows produces as many IRRs as there are changes in the cash flow directions of the investment. Many investments, such as oil or gas wells, entail added outlays after several periods of positive cash flows, producing the arithmetical possibility of multiple IRRs. Use the NPV, offsetting the discounted negative cash flows against the positive cash flows.

F.   **Payback**

1.   A popular and relatively simple cash flow investment decision criteria is the payback defined as the time until cash flows recover the initial investment of the project.

2.   The payback rule states that the investment should proceed if the payback period is less than a specified cut off period.

3.   While cash flows are considered, the timing of the cash flows and the cash flows beyond the payback period are not considered. The payback method ignores the risk of the project cash flows and the opportunity rate of return of investors.

4.   The payback method is a popular, simple evaluation method for short-lived projects.

G.   **Discounted Payback**

1.   Use discounted cash flows to determine the payback period.

2.   This rule considers the timing of cash flows.

H.   **Book Rate of Return**

1.   Another decision criterion, **book rate of return (accounting rate of return)** or the average accounting income per period divided by the book value of the investment.

$$\text{Book rate of return} = \frac{\text{book income}}{\text{book assets}}$$

2.   The book rate of return does not consider cash flows, the timing of the cash flows, nor the investors' opportunity rate of return.

III.   PROJECT INTERACTIONS

A.   **Special Situations**

1.   The capital budgeting decision analyses, to this point in the chapter, have considered mutually exclusive alternatives. In either Project A *or* Project B, the proper decision rule was to select the project with the higher NPV.

2.   There are other mutually exclusive decision analysis considerations that occur frequently that complicate our simple NPV rule. *Three* situations are discussed below.

B.   **Investment Timing**

1.   *When* to make an investment is a difficult decision in a dynamic world, where new cost-saving technology is always improving and NPVs are greater if delayed until later.

2.   The right time to purchase an ever-increasing NPV investment is indicated by the highest present value of future NPVs, found by discounting the estimated NPVs of projects made in future periods by the opportunity cost of capital.

C. **Long-Lived versus Short-Lived Equipment**

1. When comparing mutually exclusive projects that have unequal project lives, one must analyze the costs of the projects, the outlays and the annual costs of the projects.

2. Calculate the equivalent **annual cost** of both machines. *Decision Rule:* Accept the project with the lowest equivalent annual cost.

$$\text{Equivalent annual cost} = \frac{\text{present value of costs}}{\text{annuity factor}}$$

3. The equivalent annual cost is the annual (annuity or payment) project cost that equates the present value cost of the project (outlay and annual costs) at the opportunity rate of return. The equivalent annual cost is the level annual charge or cost necessary to recover the present value of investment outlays and operating costs.

D. **Replacing an Old Machine**

1. Most equipment is replaced before the end of its useful economic life or its depreciable life. Replacement decisions most often involve replacing old with new with different useful cash-flow lives.

2. Calculate the equivalent cost, annuity payment which equates the PV cost at the opportunity rate of return, of the new project's costs compared to the period cost of the old project.

3. If the equivalent period cost of the new project is less than the period cost of the old project, accept the new; if greater, delay the replacement and review later.

IV. **CAPITAL RATIONING**

A. **Capital Rationing Decision Criterion**

1. A business maximizes shareholders' wealth by accepting *every* project with a positive NPV.

2. The above statement assumes that only negative NPVs establish a limit on the capital budget of a business and that any financing needed can be raised in financial markets.

3. **Capital rationing** exists if there is a limit on the amount of funds available for investment. There are two forms of capital rationing: soft rationing and hard rationing.

B.   **Soft Rationing**

1.   Soft rationing exists if businesses themselves, or their senior managers, place limits on the size of the capital budget.

2.   Soft rationing limits can be relaxed if added NPV investments are available; financing is provided easily by financial markets.

C.   **Hard Rationing**

1.   Hard rationing or limits on the capital budget are set by financial markets (investors).

2.   With funding constraints, positive NPV projects are forgone.

3.   With hard rationing, the firm must choose projects, to the limit of its financing ability, from among a list of projects with positive NPVs.

4.   Within a hard rationing constraint, choose the projects with the highest **profitability index** to the limit of the financing budget. The profitability index is the ratio of the sum of present values of the project divided by the initial cost of the investment. It is a relative measure of the value (present value) of a project compared to its cost. The higher profitability index projects have higher PVs relative to the scarce capital invested.

D.   **Pitfalls of the Profitability Index**

1.   Using the profitability index decision rule in situations without capital rationing may give erroneous choices, similar to the IRR.

2.   Using the profitability index without capital rationing wrongly favours small, short-lived projects over large, long-lived projects with higher NPVs.

COMPLETION QUESTIONS

1.   The capital budgeting decision involves choices of (*investment projects/who to hire for staffing needs*).

2.   The opportunity cost of capital is the expected rate of return (*earned/given up*) by investing in a project.

3.   If the present value of a project's payoffs is (*greater/less*) than the investment outlay, the decision should be to go ahead with the project.

4.   Managers increase shareholders' wealth by accepting all projects with a (*negative/ positive*) net present value.

5.   For most projects, the higher the discount rate, the (*higher/lower*) will be the net present value.

6. The common practice is to discount a project's cash flows at (*different/identical*) rates.

7. The internal rate of return (IRR) is the discount rate at which the project's NPV equals _____.

8. If the opportunity cost of capital is less than a project's internal rate of return, the NPV will be (*negative/positive*).

9. For the IRR rule to work, the project's NPV must (*fall/rise*) as the discount rate increases.

10. When there are multiple changes in the cash flows over a project's life, the (*IRR/NPV*) rule does not work.

11. Two or more projects that cannot be pursued simultaneously are called _____ _____ projects.

12. The (*IRR/NPV*) rule can only be used successfully in selecting among mutually exclusive projects if incremental cash flows are used.

13. The term capital (*budgeting/rationing*) refers to a limit on the amount of funds available for investment.

14. The ratio of the present value of a project's cash inflows to the investment amount is called the _____ _____.

15. The time it takes for cash inflows from a project to recover the initial investment is known as the _____ _____.

16. The payback calculation fails to account for (*cash flows/profits*) after the payback period as well as the time value of money.

17. The book rate of return is equal to the average (*cash flow/net profit*) divided by the average book value over a project's life.

PROBLEMS

Use the project information below to answer problems 1–9:

Year	Project C		Project D	Project E
0	–$10,000		–$14,000	$12,000
1	3,500		4,800	3,700
2	3,500		4,800	3,700
3	3,500		4,800	3,700
4	3,500		4,800	3,700

1. Assuming an opportunity rate of return of 10 percent, calculate the net present value of the projects above. List the steps involved in calculating and interpreting the NPVs.

2. Using the NPV rule, which project(s) above would you accept and why would you accept the project(s) if:
   a. Projects C, D, and E were mutually exclusive?
   b. Projects C, D, and E were not mutually exclusive?

3. Calculate the internal rate of return for each project above. State the IRR decision rule. Which of the projects are acceptable using a 10 percent opportunity rate of return?

4. If the opportunity rate of return were to increase, how high would it have to be to reject all three projects above?

5. Calculate the profitability index for each project above.

6. If only $15,000 were available for the projects above, which, if any, of the projects above would you accept? Why? (Hint: we are assuming a capital rationing situation.)

7. If the projects above were mutually exclusive, and without capital rationing, which would be selected for investment?

8. Using the IRR and NPV calculations above, and with shareholder maximization as your decision criterion, which of the projects above would you select? Why?

9. Calculate the payback period for each of the projects above. With shareholder maximization as your decision criterion, which of the projects above would you select? Why?

10. Michelle could purchase a building for $400,000 and expect to sell it three years from now for $650,000. If alternative rates of return are expected to earn 14 percent in the

period, should she buy this building? Use both the NPV and IRR methods and decision rules.

11. If you were to pay $1000 for an art appreciation course that is expected to give you at least $200 per year in enjoyable benefits for life, what is your opportunity rate of return today if you refuse to take such a course?

12. In the above problem 11, if your opportunity rate of return were 10 percent, what is the NPV of the art appreciation class?

13. A $100,000 machine with a useful life of three years is expected to produce cash profit before depreciation of $50,000 per year for three years. Assuming straight-line depreciation, calculate the average rate of return on average book value.

14. Two machines costing $100,000 and $112,000 are each expected to generate $35,000 in cash flows per year for 5 years. With an opportunity rate of return of 15 percent,
   a. Which machine would you take if the machines were not mutually exclusive?
   b. If only one of the machine investments will be made, which, if any, would you take?
   c. What is the internal rate of return on each machine? What does the IRR decision rule indicate? With this information, which machine should you take if shareholder maximization were your basis for your decision?

15. A $100,000 land investment made by Katie may be sold for $110,000 one year later. What is the rate of return on this one-year investment? If her opportunity rate of return is 15 percent, should she accept the project?

16. A 10 percent coupon bond, $1000 face value, is purchased for $800 and will be held to maturity 3 years from today. Assuming interest paid annually 1 year from today, what is the internal rate of return on the investment?

17. In the bond problem above, if your opportunity rate of return is 12 percent, would you buy the bond today? Why?

18. The standard acceptable payback period is 4 years. Consider the following cash flows of a project.

Year	0	1	2	3	4	5
CFs ($)	– 100	50	30	10	20	50

With a cost of capital of 10%, should this project be undertaken according to the discounted payback period rule?

ANSWERS TO COMPLETION QUESTIONS

1. investment projects
2. given up
3. greater
4. positive
5. lower
6. identical
7. zero
8. positive
9. fall
10. IRR
11. mutually exclusive
12. IRR
13. rationing
14. profitability index
15. payback period
16. cash flows
17. net profit

SOLUTIONS TO PROBLEMS

1. Calculate NPVs at 10 percent opportunity rate of return. (4n, 10i, PV Annuity) = 3.170.

   NPV Evaluation:

   a. List the expected cash flows and when they are expected — see project information.

   b. Find the present value of the future cash flows, discounting at the opportunity rate of return of 10 percent:

      Project C: PV = $3,500 (3.170) = $11,095

      Project D: PV = $4,800 (3.170) = $15,216

      Project E: PV = $3,700 (3.170) = $11,729

c. Calculate the NPV by subtracting the cost of the project from the PV of the discounted cash flows above.

	Project C	Project D	Project E
PV	$11,095	$15,216	$11,729
– outlay	10,000	14,000	12,000
NPV	$ 1,095	$ 1,216	$ – 271

The NPV of Projects C and D are greater than zero and acceptable, while the NPV of Project E is less than zero.

2. With reference to the NPVs of Projects C, D, and E above.

    a. If only one project may be accepted (they are mutually exclusive), Project D with the highest NPV of $1,215 should be selected.

    b. If the projects above were not mutually exclusive or competing, accept all projects with positive NPVs. Projects C and D will be accepted for the amount that we would have to pay. Project E has a negative NPV and should be rejected because the PV of $11,729 is less than the $12,000 that we must pay for the project.

3. Let X = Unknown Interest Factor, PV Annuity, 4 years

Project C IRR: $10,000 = $3,500 X so X = $10,000/$3,500
X = 2.8571 IRR is approximately 15%. (Look on 4 year
PV Annuity line in APPENDIX A, TABLE A.3)

Project D IRR: $14,000 = $4,800 X = $14,000/$4800
X = 2.9167 IRR is approximately 14%

Project E IRR: $12,000 = $3,700 X = $12,000/$3,700
X = 3.2432 IRR is approximately 9%

Financial calculator:

Project C	Project D	Project E
$10,000 PV	$14,000 PV	$12,000 PV
$ 3,500 PMT	$ 4,500 PMT	$ 3,700 PMT
4 n	4 n	4 n
Calc. I = 14.96%	Calc. I = 13.95%	Calc I = 8.95%

Under the IRR decision rule, accept all projects with IRRs greater than opportunity rate of return:

Project C = IRR of 15% which is > 10% opportunity rate; accept

Project D = IRR of 14% > 10% opportunity rate; accept

Project E = IRR of 8.95% < 10% opportunity rate; reject

4.   Under the IRR decision rule, as long as the IRR equals the opportunity rate of return, shareholders will be earning their minimally acceptable rate of return, their opportunity rate. When the opportunity cost of capital exceeds the highest IRR of Project C or 15%, returns to shareholders will be below their minimally acceptable rate of return or be below what other, alternative investments would offer.

5.   The profitability index for the projects are calculated below. The profitability index (PI) is calculated by dividing the PV sum of discounted cash flows by the cost (outlay) for the project. The PI decision rule is to accept projects with PIs greater than one; reject projects with PIs less than one. For competing projects under a strict capital rationing constraint, select the project with the highest PI.

Project C PI = $11,095/$10,000 = 1.11 > 1; Accept

Project D PI = $15,216/$14,000 = 1.09 > 1; Accept

Project E PI = $11,729/$12,000 = .98 < 1; Reject

6.   Under this hard capital rationing situation, select the highest PI project from the acceptable projects. Project C has the highest present value per outlay.

7.   Without capital rationing and assuming Projects C, D, and E are not mutually exclusive, select Projects C and D with positive NPVs and IRRs greater than the 10 percent cost of capital.

8.   The NPV rule is consistent with shareholder wealth maximization. Projects C and D are acceptable with positive NPVs.

9.   The payback period is the length of time it takes the annual cash flows to cover or *pay back* the original investment.

Project C Payback Period = $10,000/$3,500 = 2.86 years

Project D Payback Period = $14,000/$4,800 = 2.92 years

Project E Payback Period = $12,000/$3,700 = 3.24 years

Under the payback period decision rule if one project is to be chosen, Project C, with the shortest payback period would be selected. All projects that pay back within policy limits will be acceptable under the payback decision rule. In this question, shareholder value is the decision criterion, so the highest positive NPV is favoured. This means Project D first, then Project C will be accepted. The payback evaluation is not consistent with shareholder wealth maximization.

10. NPV = – $400,000 + $650,000 (14i, 3n, PV$)
     NPV = – $400,000 + $650,000 (.675)
     NPV = $38,750
     IRR: $650,000/$400,000 = 1.625 IRR is 17.6%
     Financial calculator: $400,000 PV
                                     $650,000 FV
                                     3N
               Calculate I = 17.57%
          Decision Rules:
          NPV > 0; accept
          IRR = 17.6% > 14%; accept

11. For a $1000 investment with a $200 annual return for life (perpetuity), the expected rate of return is:

     $200/$1000 = . 20 or 20%

12. NPV = – $1000 + 200 (10i, 30n, PV Annuity)
     NPV = – $1000 + $200 (9.427)
     NPV = $885.4 (30n)
     NPV = $993.4 (60n)

In problem 11, the expected return of 20 percent exceeds the opportunity rate of return of 10 percent and is consistent with a positive NPV, calculated in problem 12.

13. Average book rate of return = average annual income/average annual book assets

Year	0	1	2	3
Gross book value	$100,000	$100,000	$100,000	$100,000
Cumulative depreciation	0	$ 33,333	$ 66,666	$100,000
Net book value	$100,000	$ 66,667	$ 33,334	0

So the average annual book value is $50,000.

Year	1	2	3
Cash profit before Depr.	$50,000	$50,000	$50,000
minus Depr.	$33,333	$33,333	$33,333
Net income	$16,667	$16,667	$16,667

Average book rate of return = $16,667/$50,000 or 33%

14. a. With the same cash flows and lower investment, the lower cost $100,000 investment seems better, but we must calculate the NPV of each project to see if the investments contribute to shareholder value or earn the shareholder opportunity rate of return.

NPV = – $100,000 + $35,000 (15i, 5n, PV Annuity)
NPV = – $100,000 + $35,000 (3.352)
NPV = $17,320

NPV = – $112,000 + $35,000 (15i, 5n, PV Annuity)
NPV = – $112,000 + $35,000 (3.352)
NPV = $5320
Accept both if not mutually exclusive.

b. If mutually exclusive, take the investment with the higher NPV, the $100,000 investment.

c. The IRR evaluation should give the same decision.

$100,000 = $35,000 (5n, PV Annuity, IRR?)
IRR: $100,000/$35,000 = 2.857 from APPPENDIX A TABLE A.3 the IRR is 22 percent

84

Financial calculator: $100,000 PV

$35,000 PMT

5 n

Calculate I = 22.1%

$112,000 = $35,000 (5n, PV Annuity, IRR?)
IRR: $112,000/$35,000 = 3.200 from APPENDIX A TABLE A.3 the IRR is 17 percent

Financial calculator: $112,000 PV

$35,000 PMT

5 n

Calculate I = 16.99%

The IRR for both investments is greater than the 15 percent opportunity rate of return and are acceptable. If mutually exclusive, take the $100,000 machine earning the highest NPV to maximize shareholder value.

15. $$\text{Rate of Return} = \frac{\text{Profit}}{\text{investment}} = \frac{C_1 - C_0}{C_0}$$

$$= \frac{\$110,000 - \$100,000}{\$100,000} = .10 \text{ or } 10\%$$

With alternative investments of 15%, the investor would reject this investment opportunity.

16.

Year	Cash Flows	Interest Factors
0	– $ 800	1
1	$ 100	PV, single cash flow
2	$ 100	PV, single cash flow
3	$1100	PV, single cash flow

Estimate the interest factors that, times the cash flows and summed, equals the outlay of $800 or NPV = 0. Or,

NPV=0 = $-800 + 100 (3n, PV Ann., IRR?) + 1000 (3n, PV Ann., IRR?)

With two unknowns in the equation, one must estimate the IRR that generates a NPV = 0.

Financial calculator: $-$ $800 PV

$100 PMT

$1000 FV

3 n

Calculate I = 19.4%

17.   The IRR of 19.4% exceeds the 12% minimum acceptable rate of return. Make the investment. Or,

NPV = $-$ $800 + $100 (12i, 3n, PV Ann.) + 1000 (12i, 3n, PV $)

NPV = $-$ $800 + $100 (2.402) + $1000 (.712)

NPV = $152.20 > 0, buy the bond at $800. The investor would have been willing to pay $800 + $152.20 or $952.20 for the bond, accepting a 12 percent IRR or expected yield to maturity on the bond.

18.   To find the discounted payback period, we need to calculate the present value of each cash flow from the project using the cost of capital as the discount rate.

Year	0	1	2	3	4	5
CFs ($)	$-$ 100	50	30	10	20	50
PV@10%	$-$ 100	45.45	24.79	7.51	13.66	31.05
Cumulative PV	$-$ 100	$-$ 54.55	$-$ 29.76	$-$ 22.25	$-$ 8.59	22.46

Since the discounted payback period = 4 + (8.58/31.05) = 4.276 years which exceeds 4 years, the project is rejected.

CHAPTER 7

USING DISCOUNTED CASH-FLOW ANALYSIS

INTRODUCTION

This chapter builds upon the last chapter and focuses on estimating the expected cash flows of an investment project. There are a number of general concepts and rather detailed procedures that you must master. One of the more important concepts is that of determining the "incremental" cash-flow impact of a new project. The standard question for you to ask is, "What changes, given the decision to make the investment?" The Blooper Industries example is a good discussion example that enables one to cover most of the concepts and rules developed in the chapter. Use the Blooper Industries example as a review to test your skills. When working the cash-flows examples, complete the analysis with an assessment of the NPV and IRR and their corresponding decision rules to accept or reject. This enables you to tie the last chapter and this one into a continuous process.

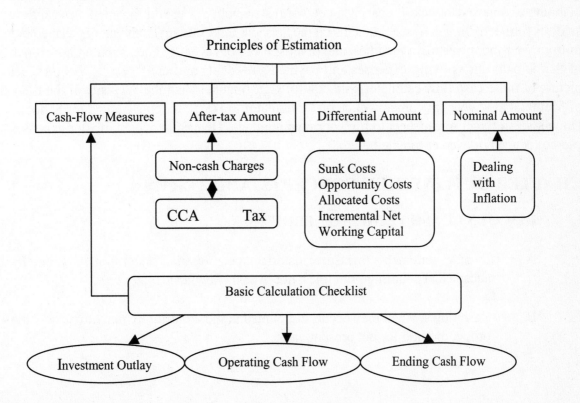

LEARNING CHECKLIST

In this skill-specific chapter you should be able to accomplish the following after reading the chapter and working the end-of-chapter problems:

_____1. Differentiate cash flow from profits. Remember discount expected cash flows, not expected profits.

_____2. Estimate the incremental cash flows of an investment project, including the incidental effects of an investment on other company cash flows.

_____3. Be able to point out and deal with sunk costs and opportunity costs associated with an investment project.

_____4. Remember to include estimated changes in net working capital for an investment (beginning and end) and to exclude the interest costs (financing costs) associated with financing a project. The opportunity cost of capital includes the cost of financing.

_____5. Business taxes in Canada and the capital budgeting decision.

SOURCES OF BUSINESS INFORMATION

Analyze the Financial Situation: To a great extent, successful investing is attributed to planning as opposed to luck. Preparing a net worth statement is a useful first step. A cash flow analysis further helps you to see problems on the horizon. First, add up all the money that comes in from your job, investment incomes, and other sources of revenue. Then subtract how much of that is paid out as living expenses and payments on debts and credit cards. With a clear picture of those cash flow estimates, you control your finance. Visit the Web site of the Bank of Montreal at www.bom.com and click on "Calculator to Help Students Budget for School." Download an Excel spreadsheet to run your own numbers. Determine which of your expenses can be reduced or even eliminated.

CHAPTER OUTLINE, KEY CONCEPTS, AND TERMS

I.   DISCOUNT CASH FLOW, NOT PROFITS

A.   Income statements measure historical performance according to generally accepted accounting principles, not in cash-flow terms.

B.   Cash flows, when they occur, discounted at the opportunity rate of return is the proper method for net present value.

II. DISCOUNT *INCREMENTAL* CASH FLOWS

A. **Include All Indirect Effects**
   1. Project cash-flow analysis should consider the differential cash flows that occur given the acceptance of the project.
   2. Incremental cash flows represent the cash-flow changes that the new project creates, or the cash flow *with* the project *less* the cash flow *without* the project.

   $$\text{Incremental Cash Flow} = \text{cash flow with project} - \text{cash flow without project}$$

   3. All differential cash-flow implications of the project must be considered, including the impact of the new project on *any* other aspect of the business cash flows.

B. **Forget Sunk Costs**
   1. Cash flows not related to the project are irrelevant in the project cash-flow analysis.
   2. Cash flows that occur regardless of whether the project investment is made are sunk costs and are not relevant to the current project.

C. **Include Opportunity Costs**
   1. Include opportunity cost cash flows, such as the value of land which you could otherwise sell, as a relevant cost of an investment project.
   2. The **opportunity cost**, or the best alternative value option of the land owned prior to the investment consideration, is a part of the investment outlay.

D. **Recognizing The Investment In Working Capital**
   1. The incremental **net working capital**, added current assets less added current liabilities, represents relevant cash-flow costs of initiating a project and should be part of the NPV analysis. Working capital recovered at the end of the project is a relevant cash flow.
   2. Ignoring working capital, or the fact that varying levels of incremental net working capital may occur throughout the life of the project, or ignoring the recovery of working capital are *three* common errors in project cash-flow analysis.

E. **Beware of Allocated Overhead Costs**
1. Overhead costs, such as heat and light, incurred whether the project investment is made or not, are irrelevant to the project cash-flow analysis.
2. Include only the additional or incremental cash-flow costs, only when they occur, in the project analysis.

III. DISCOUNT NOMINAL CASH FLOWS BY THE NOMINAL COST OF CAPITAL

A. If the discount rate or the opportunity rate of return used in project analysis is in nominal terms, versus inflation adjusted or in real terms, relevant project cash flows should be in nominal terms as well. One may use real, inflation adjusted discount rates and cash flows, but consistency in this matter is what is important.

$$1 + \text{real interest rate} = \frac{1+\text{nominal interest rate}}{1+\text{inflation rate}}$$

B. Expected cash flows, if inflation is expected during the life of the project, must be adjusted upward to nominal values. The adjustment should reflect the added price changes in the prices of the products, labour costs, etc., rather than a general inflation rate, such as the Consumer Price Index.

IV. SEPARATE INVESTMENT AND FINANCING DECISIONS

A. When the cash flows of an investment are analyzed, *how* the investment is financed, or the financing cost of the project, is ignored.

B. How the project is financed, and the financing costs, are variables affecting the opportunity rate of return, and are used to discount the cash flows. Financing the project and its impact is considered when calculating the opportunity rate of return, (studied later in the book).

C. The value of the investment is considered by itself, independent of financing choice.

V. CALCULATING CASH FLOW

A. A project total cash flow is the sum of three components: capital investment, investment in working capital, and cash flow from operations.

B.   Capital Investment — The money spent to begin any new project can be significant. Such large expenditures to start projects may produce tremendous value to the firm, however, the immediate impact may very well be a reduction in current cash flow. When determining the firm's total cash flow, the expenditures on new investments must be subtracted.

C.   Investment in Working Capital — All new projects entail the conversion of cash assets into other types of assets. Items such as inventory, raw materials, and finished products drain cash from the firm. Coinciding with these asset conversions may be changes in accounts receivable and accounts payable balances.

D.   Cash from Operations — The most recognizable source of cash is the firm's operations. Do not be deceived into thinking that this number can be pulled directly form the income statement. There are slight modifications, most notably depreciation, which must be made in order to arrive at a true cash flow. All of these adjustments are simple math, yet sometimes require investigative powers to locate all corporate transactions that impact the cash flow of a firm.

VI.   Business Taxes and Capital Budgeting Decision

A.   **Depreciation and Capital Cost Allowance (CCA)**

1.   The amount of write-off on depreciable assets is known as **capital cost allowance (CCA).**

2.   CCA is one of the important deductions for tax purposes, but it is not a cash outflow and hence is viewed as a "non-cash" expense.

B.   **Asset Class System**

1.   In Canada, all depreciable assets are grouped under different classes and most of these classes use the declining balance depreciation method.

2.   Each class is assigned a CCA rate (d) for calculating depreciation expense in each year. The CCA rates vary from 4% to 100%. See Table 7.1 in the textbook.

3.   The half-year rule applies when the asset is put into use, allowing firms to claim only half of the total CCA eligible in the year.

4.   The balance remaining in an asset class that has not yet been depreciated in the year is called **undepreciated capital cost (UCC)**. That is, UCC is the book-value of each asset class at a given point of time and its value is affected by the purchase/sale of assets and the termination of the pool.

C. **Sale of Assets**

1. When an asset is sold, the UCC is reduced by the amount so-called "adjusted cost of disposal" which is the lesser of the asset's sale price or its initial cost.

2. In case of a simultaneous purchase and sale of assets, the net acquisition matters. Need to find the total cost of all additions and subtract the adjusted cost of capital of all assets in that class.

3. If net acquisition is positive, the first year one-half rules applies, but the half-year rule does not apply if net acquisition is negative.

D. **Termination of Asset Pool**

1. On the disposition of one or more assets, if there is nothing left in the pool, then one of the two situations arises.

2. **Terminal loss** occurs when no asset remains in the pool, but the UCC is still positive. Terminal loss is fully tax-deductible. With terminal loss, the pool is closed and ceases to generate CCA tax savings.

3. A **recaptured depreciation** occurs if the sale renders UCC of the pool negative. A recapture is that negative UCC balance of the asset class after deducting the adjusted cost of disposal and is added back to taxable income.

4. If sale price exceeds the original cost of the disposed asset then, along with a recapture, there also will be a **capital gain**.

5. After netting out any capital losses, only 50% of the capital gains are taxed.

E. **Present Values of CCA Tax Shields**

1. As long as the asset pool is not completely terminated, firms can have tax savings from the CAA deduction over an infinite period.

2. Present value of CCA tax shield is influenced by several factors. Here is a general computational formula.

$$\left[\frac{CdT_C}{r+d} \right] \left[\frac{1+0.5r}{1+r} \right] - \left[\frac{SdT_C}{d+r} \right] \left[\frac{1}{(1+r)^2} \right]$$

VII. EXAMPLE: BLOOPER INDUSTRIES

A. Work carefully through the Blooper Industries example, reinforcing concepts mentioned earlier.

	Year:	0	1	2	3	4	5	6
1.	Capital investment	10,000						
2.	Working capital	1,500	4,075	4,279	4,493	4,717	3,039	0
3.	Change in working capital	1,500	2,575	204	214	225	−1,678	−3,039
4.	Revenues		15,000	15,750	16,538	17,364	18,233	
5.	Expenses		10,000	10,500	11,025	11,576	12,155	
6.	CCA of mining equipment (asset class 38, $d = 30\%$)		1,500[1]	2,550	1,785	1,250	875	612 ...
7.	Pretax profit		3,500	2,700	3,728	4,538	5,203	
8.	Tax (35%)		1,225	945	1,305	1,588	1,821	
9.	Profit after tax		2,275	1,755	2,423	2,950	3,382	

[1]In the first year, CCA is computed using the half-year rule.
Note: Some entries are subject to rounding error.

B. **Calculating Blooper's Project Cash Flows**

1. All of the outlay, $10 million, is assumed to be made now or in the zero period, with no salvage value expected at the end of the project life.

2. Note the changes in net working capital, or net added current assets needed, early in the project. Later, as the project winds down, net current assets are no longer needed and contribute to the positive cash flow.

3. Revenues are estimated through the periods in which revenues are thought to be generated. Do not arbitrarily cut-off the periods of cash-flow generation.

4. Lines four and five are assumed to be cash flow revenue and expenses, with depreciation to be the only noncash revenue/expense in the analysis.

5. Project cash flows are the sum of *three* components: investment outlay of the project, investment in project net working capital, and project cash flow from operations.

6. Cash flows from operations may be determined from the data *two* ways: calculate the sum of cash inflows and outflows, or add back depreciation (noncash expense) to net after-tax profit.

Year:	0	1	2	3	4	5	6
Revenues		15,000	15,750	16,538	17,364	18,233	
−Expenses		10,000	10,500	11,025	11,576	12,155	
=Profit before tax		5,000	5,250	5,513	5,788	6,078	
−Tax at 35%		1,750	1,838	1,930	2,026	2,127	
=Operating cash flows (excluding CCA tax shield)		3,250	3,412	3,583	3,762	3,951	

C. Calculating the NPV of Blooper's Project — Cash flows are conservatively assumed to occur at the end of the year.

D. **Further Notes and Wrinkles Arising from Blooper's Project**

1. Nominal amounts of CCA are fixed, given inflation, yielding lower real tax shield cash flow.

2. All depreciable assets are placed into different classes and each class has its own CCA rate determined by Canada Customs and Revenue Agency (CCRA).

3. The half-year convention assumes that the asset was purchased at mid-point of the first year with one-half of the capital cost added to the pool and one-half in the following year. The reason is to discourage firms from acquiring depreciable assets at year-end.

4. The CCA provides a faster depreciation rate (double-declining balance) and tax shield recovery compared to the **straight-line depreciation** rate, which provides for equal depreciation amounts over the useful life of the project.

5. The CCA depreciation tax shield affects cash flow and is relevant for capital budgeting analysis.

6. Salvage value cash flows involve the net cash received from the disposal *less* any taxes (sold for more than book value) on the sale or *plus* any tax shield (sold for less than book value) loss (book loss times the marginal tax rate).

	Year:	0	1	2	3	4	5	6
1.	Capital investment	−10,000						
2.	Change in working capital	−1,500	−2,575	−204	−214	−225	1,678	3,039
3.	Cash flows from operations (excluding CCA tax shield)		3,250	3,412	3,583	3,762	3,951	
4.	Total cash flows (excluding CCA tax shield)	−11,500	675	3,208	3,369	3,537	5,629	3,039

COMPLETION QUESTIONS

1. Wise investment decision making relies, in part, on identifying (*cash flows/net profits*).

2. Capital expenditures (*are/are not*) deducted from revenues when calculating profits.

3. When sales are made on credit they are recognized in the calculation of (*cash flows/net profits*).

4. Cash flows for project evaluation (*are/are not*) determined by subtracting cash flows occurring without the project from those that would happen if the project were accepted.

5. Incremental cash flows (*do/do not*) include sunk costs.

6. Incremental cash flows (*do/do not*) include opportunity costs.

7. Changes in net working capital associated with the project (*should/should not*) be included in cash flow calculations.

8. If no additional overhead costs will be created, (*no/a proportion of*) overhead costs should be allocated to the project's cash flow.

9. To account for the effects of inflation, (*nominal/real*) cash flows should be discounted by the (*nominal/real*) interest rate.

10. Project financing costs (*should/should not*) be included in the cash flow calculations.

11. Revenues minus the total of expenses and (*depreciation/taxes*) equals cash flow from operations.

12. Cash flow from operations can be found by adding (*depreciation/ salvage value*) to net profits.

13. The reduction in taxes attributable to the depreciation allowance is called the depreciation _____ _____.

14. The depreciation tax shield (*decreases/increases*) cash flows.

15. The declining balance CCA method enables a firm to realize (*depreciation sooner/more total depreciation deductions*).

16. In comparison with straight line depreciation, CCA (*decreases/increases*) the value of the depreciation tax shield for most asset classes.

17. The salvage value of an asset that has been fully depreciated is treated as a (*gain/loss*) for tax purposes.

18. When only one project will be selected from two or more choices, the projects are said to be (*interdependent/mutually exclusive*).

19. When a project decision concerns when to make an investment, the choice should be the year that offers the (*highest/lowest*) NPV of benefits.

20. The _____ annual cost calculation is used to evaluate projects that do the same thing but which have unequal lives.

PROBLEMS

1. Mel's Music, Inc. expects to sell $500,000 of instruments and supplies this coming year. Depreciation on his furnishings and rental instruments will be $50,000. He will pay $300,000 for labour and the items he sells. The rent on his store is $60,000 and he figures taxes will be 40 percent of taxable income. Compute his expected net profit.

2. Use the three methods outlined in the textbook to compute the operating cash flow for Mel's.

3. MaryAnn's Medical Supplies had sales last month of $100,000 and operating expenses of $90,000. During that month she reduced her accounts receivable by $12,000 and increased her bank loan by $8,000. What was the net cash flow for her business?

4. Jason's Jump Rope Company (JJRC) decided to purchase a new delivery vehicle at $100,000 for 4 years. If this truck belongs to Class 38 with a CCA rate of 30 percent, what would be the undepreciated capital cost (UCC) of the truck at the end of the second year? Incorporate the half-year rule.

5. Suppose JJRC sold the vehicle described in problem 4 for $40,000 at the end of year 4. After the sale, there was nothing left in the asset class. Assuming the combined tax rate is 40 percent, what would be the net cash realized from the sale?

6. Jackie's Jelly Beans, Inc. (JJBI) is considering buying a new mixing machine for $50,000. It would replace an existing machine having a trade-in value of $10,000 that is also equal to its book value. Production cost savings with the new machine are estimated to be $20,000 per year. The life of the new mixer is 10 years and it would have a zero market value at that time. The cost of capital is 12 percent, the tax rate is 40 percent, and straight line depreciation is used. What are the project cash flows?

7. For JJBI in the above problem:
   a. Calculate the net present value (NPV).
   b. Calculate the internal rate of return (IRR).

8. Tell how the NPV and IRR would change if the accelerated cost recovery schedule (ACRS) were used instead of straight line depreciation for the data presented in problem 6. You don't need to actually make the calculations, just describe the effect of using ACRS.

9. What would be the equivalent annual cost of the machine described in problem 6?

10. Geree is considering buying a personal computer system for her home use for $5,000. She estimates the PC will have a 3-year useful life and that it will have no significant value at the end of 3 years.. She can also lease the system for the same period for $1,000 annually. Which is the lowest cost alternative if her opportunity cost is 14 percent?

11. Suppose Geree's husband, Shell, thinks he can negotiate a better lease arrangement for the computer. What would be the maximum payment for each of the three years that would be necessary to make the two options have an equal cost?

ANSWERS TO COMPLETION QUESTIONS

1. cash flows
2. are not
3. cash flows
4. are
5. do not
6. do
7. should
8. no
9. nominal, nominal
10. should not
11. depreciation
12. depreciation
13. tax shield
14. increases
15. depreciation sooner
16. increases
17. gain
18. mutually exclusive
19. highest
20. equivalent

SOLUTIONS TO PROBLEMS

1. From data given in the problem, the following statement can be prepared:

    INCOME STATEMENT FOR MEL'S MUSIC, $

Revenue	500,000
Variable expenses	300,000
Fixed expenses	60,000
Depreciation	50,000
DEBIT	90,000
Taxes (40%)	36,000
Net income	54,000

2. Net income plus depreciation approach:
    $54,000 + $50,000 = $104, 000$

    Cash inflow – cash outflow analysis: (this method simply subtracts all of the cash outflows from the cash inflows)
    $$\$500,000 - (\$300,000 + \$60,000 + \$36,000) = \$104,000$$

    Depreciation tax shield approach: (this case adds the after-tax cost of the net cash flows to the tax savings of the non-cash charges)
    $$(\$500,000 - \$300,000 - \$60,000) \times 0.60 + \$50,000 \times 0.40 = \$104,000$$
    Note that all three methods result in the same value.

3. MaryAnn's sales efforts generated $100,000 – $90,000 or $10,000. She also generated cash by reducing her accounts receivable by $12,000 and $8,000 by increasing her bank loan. These actions provided $20,000 so her total new cash was $10,000 + $20,000 or $30,000.

4.

Year	Beginning UCC	Applicable UCC	CCA Charges @30%	Ending UCC
1	$100,000	$50,000	$15,000	$85,000
2	$85,000	$85,000	$25,500	$59,500
3	$59,500	$59,500	$17,850	$41,650
4	$41,650	$41,650	$12,495	**$29,155**

    At the end of the fourth year, JJRC shows a UCC of $29,155.

5. The firm has $40,000 from selling the vehicle. The adjusted cost of disposal is the minimum of ($40,000, $100,000) = $40,000. With an ending UCC of $29,155, deduct $40,000 from the pool leaving a negative balance of $10,845. A CCA recapture occurs and it is fully taxable. Net proceeds = $40,000 – (0.4)($10,845) = $35,662. If the sale proceeds exceed the initial cost of the disposed asset, then there also will be a capital gain, along with a recaptured depreciation. However, it does not happen in this question.

6.

Cost of new mixer	$50,000
less trade-in allowance	10,000
Net outlay	$40,000
Annual savings	$20,000
less depreciation ($50,000/5)	10,000
Taxable income	$10,000
Tax	4,000
Net profit	$ 6,000
add depreciation	10,000
Cash flow	$16,000

The $40,000 outlay is followed by net cash flows in years 1 to 5 of $16,000. Note that the cash flow would be reduced by any additions to working capital. This is illustrated in problem 11 of the textbook.

7. a. The NPV = (PV factor) × $16,000 – $40,000
   = 3.605 × $16,000 – $40,000 = $17,680

   b. IRR: Remember that:
   PV of inflows – PV of outflows = 0
   PV factor × $16,000 = $40,000
   PV factor = $40,000/$16,000 = 2.5
   the IRR is almost 29 percent.

8. Think what happens when declining balance depreciation is used in place of straight-line depreciation—the higher charges occur earlier. This means greater deductions leading to lower taxable income and lower taxes and lower net profit in the earlier years.

However, the cash flow is higher! This is because the only change to cash flows is a reduction in the outflow for taxes in the earlier years. Note that the total amount of depreciation is unchanged. CCA thus makes it possible to shift cash flows from later years to earlier years. Since money has a time value, we would rather have it sooner. The result is to increase the project's NPV and the IRR as well. Accordingly, the present value of tax savings derived from the CCA calculation is larger than the one associated with straight-line depreciation.

9. The equivalent annual cost is the cost per period with the same present value as the cost of buying and operating the new mixer. In this case the 5-year annuity that is equivalent to the investment outlay is:

$$= \$50,000/\text{PV of annuity}$$
$$= \$50,000/3.605 = \$13,860.$$

10. The cost of buying:

$$= \$5,000 - \$1,000 \times \text{PV factor}$$
$$= \$5,000 - \$1,000 \times 2.914$$
$$= \$2,086$$

The cost of leasing:

$$= \$1,000 \times \text{PV factor}$$
$$= \$1,000 \times 2.914$$
$$= \$2,914$$

So it is cheaper to buy the computer.

11. The maximum lease payments would be the annual amounts whose present value is equal to the net present value of the purchase option. Thus:

$$\$2,086 = \text{lease payment} \times \text{PV factor}$$
$$\text{lease payment} = \$2,086/2.914 = \$716$$

CHAPTER 8

PROJECT ANALYSIS

INTRODUCTION

Past chapters focused on the general concepts and specific techniques of the capital budgeting evaluation. This chapter extends those ideas to a more realistic setting within a business. In every business, large and small, the capital budget is assembled, negotiated, reassembled, and finally is presented to senior management and the board of directors. A small proprietor may assess the value of new equipment by herself over morning coffee. As the business grows, the people, dimensions, and breadth of competing opportunities grows exponentially! All this is planning, estimating, and setting a course in an uncertain future. A plan should not be a single point in a very uncertain future, but provide a basis for considering alternative results to varying future conditions. "What if" analysis, scenario analysis, break-even analysis (accounting and NPV), etc., are techniques searching for a "feel" for the future. A capital plan should consider several alternative economic situations; a review of new investments should consider the most critical variables that will "make or break" the success of the project. In addition to the useful planning techniques, the chapter offers a good planning perspective for you as a future manager: We do not know what the future holds, but we have a good feel for the results, and are ready, when specific things happen. Read and study the chapter within a planning format and overview, rather than looking at a series of specific planning techniques.

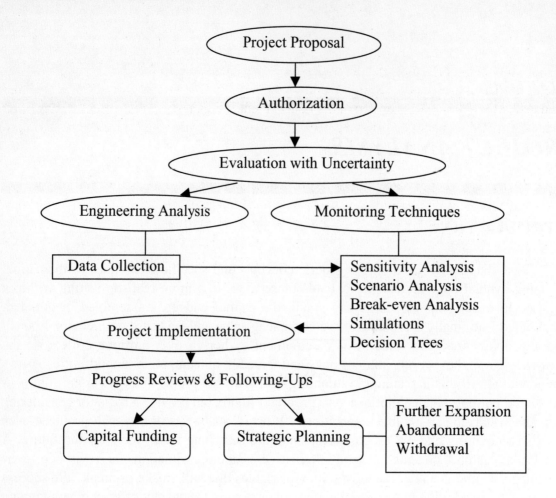

LEARNING CHECKLIST

After preparing this chapter you should be able to:

____1. Appreciate the practical problems of capital budgeting in large corporations.
____2. Be able to define and differentiate sensitivity analysis, scenario analysis, and break-even analysis.
____3. Recognize the importance of managerial flexibility in the capital budgeting process.
____4. Common practices of capital budgeting for Canadian firms.

SOURCES OF BUSINESS INFORMATION

Economic Information: Checking out the broad picture is always a sensible move before you invest. Find out how the economy is doing, both nationally and regionally. For example, if the economy weakens, how will this change affect your investment selections? Statistics Canada's CANSIM (Canadian Socio-economic Information Management System) database and information retrieval service provide detailed and timely statistical information for both the private and public sectors in English and French. This system contains data about national accounts, labour, manufacturing, construction, trade, agriculture, and finance. Selected demographic and social data such as population estimates are also available. The CANSIM Time Series Database is administered by the Dissemination Division at Statistics Canada and is updated daily. If you are interested in the issues of education, justice, health, and culture, look into the CANSIM II multidimensional database. However, the complete CANSIM database can be found at www.statcan.ca.

A Sad Reality for the Canadian Companies: If firms have a face to show public, it's their Web sites. When you first Web-link to an organization, you get its homepage. These homepages are essentially a billboard designed to attract new clients. Unfortunately, they are taken lightly as a simple public relations exercise. Either you may not find anything too elaborate, or you only find online sales pitches. Of course, you will be frustrated. Since more people are joining the Internet and doing things online, they create strong demand for electronic relationships. It is happy to see many Canadian companies particularly in the financial industry wake up. For example, visit the CIBC at www.cibc.com/tip to sign up for online banking.

CHAPTER OUTLINE, KEY CONCEPTS, AND TERMS

I.   **HOW FIRMS ORGANIZE THE INVESTMENT PROCESS**

      A.   **The Process**
          1.   There are two important steps in the investment process: the capital budget and project authorization.
          2.   They include the planning and proposals of investment, followed by evaluation and approval.

      B.   **Stage 1: The Capital Budget**
          1.   The **capital budget** is a list of planned investment projects.
          2.   The list may be compiled from the bottom up (divisions and departments) or from the top down (strategic planning).
          3.   Project plans from the bottom up bear the specific knowledge of people close to the customer and other business dimensions; senior management has the perspective of corporate strategy and the big picture of the firm's operations.

      C.   **Stage 2: Project Authorization**
          1.   *Four* different project areas are common in a business:
              a.   Outlays required by law, such as safety equipment, or projects required under company policy are evaluated to find the lowest cost.
              b.   Maintenance or cost reduction projects, such as replacement decisions.

   c. Projects related to expanding the capacity of existing business activity.

   d. Investment projects in new products or services.

  2. The required outlays, number one above, are mandated and the lowest cost for compliance is the decision rule. The other three types of projects should use the NPV method as a decision criterion.

D. **Problems and Some Solutions**

  1. Making sure that assumptions are consistent among competing proposals is important. A top-down set of assumptions, such as an economic forecast, focuses assumptions in a narrow, consistent range.

  2. Keeping the manager reward system consistent with shareholder returns encourages a long-run focus in investment evaluation, and helps eliminate conflicts of interest.

  3. Competition for scarce funds may lead to an inflation of estimated project cash-flows or benefits, and an overstatement of the estimated project NPV.

  4. Capital rationing techniques, which force divisional managers to send only the best projects forward, and intense scrutiny of projects are project-screening techniques that assure only the best projects are accepted for investment.

II. **SOME "WHAT-IF" QUESTIONS**

A. **Different Possibilities** — Project cash flows and NPVs may be estimated under different assumptions to improve the decision process.

B. **Sensitivity Analysis**

  1. Changing a single, specific variable within a range from most likely to optimistic to pessimistic and evaluating the NPVs is called **sensitivity analysis**.

  2. Sensitivity analysis reveals the significant variables, which, if varied or mis-estimated, would significantly change the NPV and acceptability of the project.

  3. Sensitivity analysis assumes that the individual variables are independent of each other. This is usually not the case. Sales cannot be varied without significantly affecting certain costs. This interrelationship between variables limits the extent that one variable can be changed without altering another, and thus, narrows the range of the sensitivity analysis.

Sensitivity Analysis (Finefodder's example)

Sensitivity Analysis

	Year 0	Years 1 - 12
Investment	– 5,400	
Sales		16,000
Variable costs		13,000
Fixed costs		2,000
Depreciation		450
Pretax profit		550
Taxes @ 40%		220
Profit after tax		330
Operating cash flow		780
Net Cash Flow	– 5,400	780
		NPV = $478

Possible Outcomes

	Range		
Variable	Pessimistic	Expected	Optimistic
Investment (000s)	6,200	5,400	5,000
Sales (000s)	14,000	16,000	18,000
Var Cost (% of sales)	83%	81.25%	80%
Fixed Costs (000s)	2,100	2,000	1,900

C. **Scenario Analysis**

1. Like sensitivity analysis, scenario analysis involves the same change of variables to see the impact on NPV, but scenario analysis differs from sensitivity analysis in that a particular combination of variables under specific assumptions is compared with another scenario of assumptions.

Sensitivity Analysis (Finefodder's example — continued)

NPV Calculations for Pessimistic Investment Scenario

	Year 0	Years 1 - 12
Investment	− 6,200	
Sales		16,000
Variable costs		13,000
Fixed costs		2,000
Depreciation		450
Pretax profit		550
Taxes @ 40%		220
Profit after tax		330
Operating cash flow		780
Net Cash Flow	− 6,200	780
		NPV = ($121)

NPV Possibilities

	NPV (000s)		
Variable	Pessimistic	Expected	Optimistic
Investment (000s)	− 121	478	778
Sales (000s)	− 1,218	478	2,174
Var Cost (% of sales)	− 788	478	1,382
Fixed Costs (000s)	26	478	930

---

2. Simulation analysis, an extension of scenario analysis, generates many scenarios and, with an estimate of their probability, generates NPV estimates for a wide range of scenarios.

III.   BREAK EVEN ANALYSIS

A.   Break-Even Analysis

1.   In any business venture forecast, **break-even analysis**, or an estimate of the sales point where total revenue equals total expenses is an important focus point for managerial analysis.

2.   Estimating the accounting break-even point level of sales of a project requires identifying the level of fixed costs involved in the project and the variable cost/sales ratio related to the project.

Break-Even Analysis (Trinova Airliner example)

Break Even Analysis

	Year 0	Years 1 – 6
Investment	$900	
Sales		$15.5 \times$ Planes Sold
Var. cost		$8.5 \times$ Planes Sold
Fixed costs		175
Depreciation		$900/6 = 150$
Pretax profit		$(7 \times$ Planes Sold$) - 325$
Taxes (50%)		$(3.5 \times$ Planes Sold$) - 162.5$
Net profit		$(3.5 \times$ Planes Sold$) - 162.5$
Net Cash Flow	– 900	$(3.5 \times$ Planes Sold$) - 12.5$

B.   **Accounting Break-Even Analysis**

1.   The sales break-even point is estimated to be the fixed costs including depreciation divided by the percentage of sales contribution margin, or the fixed costs including depreciation divided by 1 minus the variable cost to sales ratio:

$$\text{BEP Sales} = \frac{\text{Fixed costs inc. depr.}}{\text{Added profit for each unit sold}}$$

$$= \frac{\text{Fixed costs inc. depr.}}{\text{Price} - \text{variable cost / unit (contr. margin)}}$$

$$= \frac{\text{Fixed costs inc. depr.}}{1 - \text{variable costs / sales or \% contribution}}$$

2.   A project that *just* breaks even in accounting income terms will have a negative NPV.

> **Answer**
>
>   The break even point, is the # of Planes Sold that generates a NPV = $0.
>
>   The present value annuity factor of a 6 year cash flow at 10% is 4.355
>
>   Thus,
>
> NPV = – 900 + 4.355 (3.5 × Planes Sold – 12.5)

C.   **NPV Break-Even Analysis**

1.   NPV break-even analysis calculates the level of sales that generates an NPV of zero or an internal rate of return that equals the opportunity rate of return of investors.

2.   With the cost of the project = the present value of cash flows = NPV of zero, the level of sales that generates the periodic cash flows needed to generate the given present value is the unknown.

3.   The PV of cash flows = annuity factor (periods/opportunity rate) × (depreciation per period) + [(1 – tax rate)(sales × contribution margin – fixed cost and depreciation)]. The bracketed quantity represents net income plus depreciation or the after-tax cash flows. Sales higher than the zero NPV sales will produce positive NPV.

4. The sales level that produces an NPV of zero is always *higher* than the sales level for the accounting break-even point.

Break-Even Analysis (Trinova Airliner example — continued)

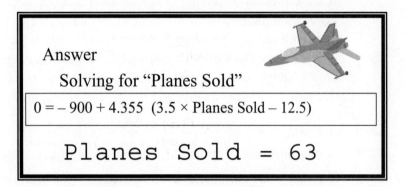

Answer
   Solving for "Planes Sold"

$$0 = -900 + 4.355 \ (3.5 \times \text{Planes Sold} - 12.5)$$

```
Planes Sold = 63
```

D. **Operating Leverage**

1. The accounting break-even point depends upon the level of **fixed costs**, or the costs incurred regardless of the level of output, associated with the project and the variable cost/sales ratio or the profit on each extra sale. **Variable costs** are costs that vary directly with sales.

2. Projects with a high proportion of fixed costs generate higher NPVs when sales are high than projects with low proportions of fixed costs (high proportions of variable costs). The contribution to fixed cost, sales less variable costs, contributes to fixed cost until the break-even point and thereafter contributes to profit/cash flows. The high fixed cost project will have a high contribution to profit for each higher level of sales.

3. A project with fixed costs is said to have **operating leverage**. The extent of operating leverage or the extent of fixed costs versus variable costs/sales is called the **degree of operating leverage** (DOL).

$$\text{DOL} = \frac{\% \ \text{change in profits}}{\% \ \text{change in sales}}$$

4. The degree of operating leverage is the percentage change in profits given a 1 percent change in sales, or:

$$\text{DOL} = 1 + \frac{\text{fixed costs}}{\text{profits}}$$

5. Arithmetically, the DOL is one plus the fixed costs/profit ratio, measured at a specific level of sales, or:

6. The risk of a project, or the variability of the realizable NPV, is directly related to the degree of operating leverage of the project. The higher the fixed costs, the greater the variation in cash flows given a change from estimated sales.

IV. FLEXIBILITY IN CAPITAL BUDGETING

A. **The Rationale**
  1. In addition to reviewing all variations of possible cash flows associated with a project, selecting projects with a high degree of flexibility provides managers with the opportunity to adjust to future, unknown, competitive and economic factors associated with the project.
  2. Decision trees assist in measuring the value of management options to vary a future course of action associated with a project with sequential decisions.

B. **Decision Trees**
  1. A **decision tree** diagrams alternative sequential decisions and possible outcomes.
  2. Expected cash flow outcomes and the probability of the outcome provide the opportunity to calculate a conditional probability expected NPV of all future cash flow possibilities.
  3. The NPV becomes the discounted, at the opportunity rate of return, expected value payoff of alternative outcomes.

C. **The Option to Expand**
  1. Projects that develop in stages, or are developed with future flexibility in mind, provide managers with options to expand at each stage or to change the nature of the project in the future in response to market forces.
  2. The cost of the option is the opportunity costs of not doing the entire project now.

D. **Abandonment Options** — Managers must recognize and evaluate the option to abandon a project at every point after they make the initial investment.

E. **Flexible Production Facilities**
  1. Building in an option to change its production or raw material mix provides future flexibility for the manager.
  2. The cost of the option is the flexibility changes built into the project compared to a single purpose design of the project.

F. **Investment Timing Options**
  1. Any project proposal provides the manager the option to invest or accept the project.
  2. The option to invest can be exercised now or later.

3. One must weigh the value of cash flows lost by delaying the project versus the possibility of adding new information about the future cash flows or possible success of the project if it is postponed for a time.

V.   CAPITAL BUDGETING PRACTICES FOR CANADIAN FIRMS

A.   Discounted Cash Flow (DCF) method
1. Over 75 percent of the surveyed firms favour this approach.
2. The more complicated the project, the more likely the DCF.
3. IRR is more frequently used than NPV.

COMPLETION QUESTIONS

1. The list of planned investment projects for a firm is called the (*capital/cash*) budget.

2. Estimating the effect of changes in the forecasts of key variables such as sales and costs is called (*scenario/sensitivity*) analysis.

3. (*Scenario/Sensitivity*) analysis employs a set of assumptions for interrelated variables.

4. When a computer is used to calculate outcomes from hundreds or thousands of possible combinations of variables, it is called (*financial/simulation*) analysis.

5. Break-even analysis determines the level of (*profits/sales*) needed to achieve zero profits.

6. When the cash flows from operations equal the initial investment, the NPV will be (*negative/zero*).

7. The determination of revenues needed to make the present value of inflows equal to the present value of outflows is done in a (*NPV/future*) value break-even analysis.

8. Fixed costs (*do/do not*) vary with different levels of sales.

9. Variable costs (*are constant/rise*) as output increases.

10. Labour and material costs are (*fixed/variable*).

11. The higher the proportion of fixed costs the (*higher/lower*) the break-even point.

12. The lower the level of fixed costs the (*higher/lower*) will be the operating leverage.

111

13. The degree of operating leverage is equal to the percentage change in (*costs/profits*) divided by the percentage change in (*costs/sales*).

14. A diagram of alternative sequential decisions and possible outcomes from those decisions is called a _____ _____.

15. Estimation of the probabilities of different possible outcomes from an investment project is called _____ analysis.

16. The closing down of a nuclear generating station is an example of (*negative/positive*) abandonment value.

17. Flexibility in production facilities and multiple sources of raw materials is appropriate because the future is (*certain/uncertain*).

18. A survey reports that most firms use (IRR/NPV) to evaluate various capital investments.

PROBLEMS

1. Last year the AA Division of Long Life, Inc. produced 10 million batteries at a total cost of $0.60 per unit. The chief financial officer estimates they could double production this year without having to add additional fixed costs. The total costs would grow to $10 million. What are the variable costs per unit?

2. How much are the fixed costs in problem 1?

3. Louisville Loopers expects to make baseball bats with labour and material costs of $7 per unit. They will wholesale them for $14 each. Investment in depreciable plant and equipment will be $15 million, which is to be allocated over the useful life of 15 years. Annual fixed charges for all other costs are $600,000. What is the accounting break-even point?

4. What is the net present value break-even point in problem 3 if the tax rate is 40 percent and the cost of capital is 10 percent?

5. What is the lowest degree of operating leverage for a profitable company with no fixed costs?

6. A manufacturer of memory chips estimates $200 million of sales with a 10 percent profit margin for the coming year. The degree of operating leverage is 8. What will be its profits if it only achieves 90 percent of its sales forecast?

7.   Suppose the manufacturer in problem 6 has a banner year with sales reaching 110 percent of projections. What will be the profits?

8.   A group of investors is contemplating backing a new Broadway musical that will cost $10 million to produce. There is a 50 percent chance that the show will be successful and return a present value of $15 million. However, there is an equal probability that the show will be a financial failure and result in a present value of inflows of $5 million. They believe if they pay an extra $4 million to hire superstars "Marvelous Marilyn" and "Rugged Ron" that they will assure a successful outcome. Should they hire MM and RR?

9.   Given a project with a fixed cost of $10,000, depreciation of $6,000 per year, a selling price for the product of $3 per unit, and an 8,000 unit break-even point, what is the variable cost per unit?

10. The XYZ Co. is considering launching a new product with a 2-stage project. Stage I requires an initial investment of $10 million now and is expected to have cash flows after-tax of $12 million or $5 million with 50%-50% chances in Year 1. Depending on this market test, the company decides whether or not entering Stage II. Only if the Year 1 cash flow turns out to be $12 million, another $50 million then will be invested. If invested, the sequential cash flows after-tax expected are $20 million per year for 4 years (in Years 2 to 5).

     The required return for Stage I is 15% due to a greater uncertainty. The normal required return is 10%. Use the decision tree analysis to evaluate this project.

ANSWERS TO COMPLETION QUESTIONS

1.   capital
2.   sensitivity
3.   Scenario
4.   simulation
5.   sales
6.   negative
7.   NPV
8.   do not
9.   rise
10. variable
11. higher
12. lower
13. profits, sales

14. decision tree
15. simulation
16. negative
17. uncertain
18. IRR

SOLUTIONS TO PROBLEMS

1. Last year the total costs for the 10 million batteries at a cost of $0.60 per unit were 10 × $0.60 or $6 million. This year the added production was 10 million units for an incremental cost of $10 – $6 or $4 million. On a cost per unit basis this would be $4/10 or $0.40 for each battery.

2. Remember that total costs equal variable costs plus fixed costs. In problem 1 the variable costs last year were 10 million units × the variable cost per unit of $0.40 or $4 million. Subtracting this from the total cost of $6 million yields a fixed cost of $2 million. As a check we can compute the fixed costs in the latest year as the difference between the total costs of $10 million and the variable costs of 20 million units × the variable cost per unit of $0.40. This equals $2 million which is the same fixed cost as for the prior year. This should be the case because the problem states that production could be increased without having to incur any additional fixed costs.

3. The break-even point is where revenues minus costs equals zero. (It is important to note that taxes do not enter into the calculation because they are based on having a profit to tax — no profit, no tax.) Depreciation = $15 million/ 15 = $1 million per year. So fixed costs = $400,000 + $1,000,000 = $1,400,000. This must be covered by the contribution margin on the sales. In other words, each unit sold contributes to the coverage of fixed costs. In this case each bat contributes $14 – $7 or $7 so the break-even point will be $1,400,000/$7 or 200,000 bats per year.

4. To compute the present value break-even point, cash flows are needed. Here we are seeking the sales volume that generates cash inflows that are sufficient to offset the cash outflows using present values. The cash inflows are profits after taxes plus the depreciation tax shield. The present value of these cash flows will equal the investment outlay at the break-even volume. Remember the annual depreciation is $1,000,000 so the tax shield will be $.4 \times \$1,000,000$ or $400,000 per year. The present value factor for a 15-year annuity at 10 percent is 7.606. Using the tax rate of 40 percent and letting Q equal the break-even volume, the equation becomes:
$$\$15,000,000 = [\{\$14Q - (\$7Q + \$1,400,000)\} \times (1 - .4) + \$400,000] \times 7.606$$
$$Q = 574,316 \text{ bats per year}$$

5.   Recall that the degree of operating leverage is 1 plus the ratio of the fixed costs to profits. In the case of a profitable firm with no fixed costs, the degree of operating leverage is 1. This is the lowest degree of operating leverage.

6.   The percentage change in profits equals the percentage change in sales × the degree of operating leverage. In this case a sales decline of 10 percent would result in a drop in profits of $10 × 8$ or 80 percent. Profits at the projected level would have been 10 percent of sales of $200 million or $20 million. If sales were only 90 percent of the forecast, profits would decline by 80 percent or by $16 million. In other words, a 10 percent shortfall in sales causes profits to fall to $4 million.

7.   Profits would increase by the increase in sales × the degree of operating leverage. This would be $10 × 8$ or 80 percent. Expressed on an absolute basis profits would rise from the original forecast level of $20 million to $36 million. (The increase is 80 percent or $20 million of $16 million.)

8.   In the worst-case scenario, the expected net present value is – $10 million + $5 million or a loss of $5 million. They should hire the players for $4 million to avoid the 50 percent chance of the $5 million loss.

9.   The profit margin is ($10,000 + $6,000)/8,000 or $2 per unit. The variable cost is the difference between the selling price and the profit margin or $3 – $2 = $1 per unit.

10.   Consider the following decision tree diagram.

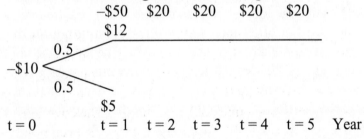

In Year 1, Stage II NPV = $20 × PVAF(10%, 4) – $50 = 20(3.17) –50 = $13.4 million
Stage II expected NPV (in Year 1) = 0.5 ($13.4) = $6.7 million
Stage II expected NPV (in Year 0) = $6.7 × PVIF(15%, 1) = $5.83 million
Stage I expected CFAT = 0.5($12) + 0.5($5) = $8.5 million
Stage I NPV (in Year 0) = $8.5 × PVIF(15%, 1) – $10 = 8.5(0.87) –10 = –$2.61 million
So, NPV = $5.83 – $2.61 = $3.22 million and the project should be accepted.

CHAPTER 9

INTRODUCTION TO RISK, RETURN, AND THE OPPORTUNITY COST OF CAPITAL

INTRODUCTION

While this is the beginning of a new section related to the discussion of risk and return, it is really a "bridging" section between the asset investment materials of the last section and the financing section that follows this one. The past and prospective investment projects of a business establish a risk profile that determines the opportunity rate of return. There is no cost of capital, required rate of return, nor opportunity rate of return *independent* of where the funds are invested. This connection or bridge of financing and financial markets to the capital budgeting process is an important concept to understand when taking your finance course, because it ties the chapters and course together. This chapter introduces risk concepts, historical rates of return, and the opportunity rate concept. In the next chapter these concepts are inserted in the capital budgeting process. Risk, an important factor in the valuation theme, is focused on financial risk, related to the variability of returns. Your prior experience with risk is with pure risk, the risk of real assets, where the "tail" is single-sided. It is the risk of a loss to something you now have. What is the risk of someone looting your apartment when you are in class? Few students will return to their "digs" to find it cleaned and refurnished, a proxy for the upside return occurrence or second "tail" of possible occurrences or positive benefit. One tail on pure risk and two tails for investment returns! Students often define investment risk as the risk of loss, bringing in their pure risk focus. Investment risk has two tails (as in a normal curve) with an expected average in the middle, and lower and higher to the left and right of the average (mean).

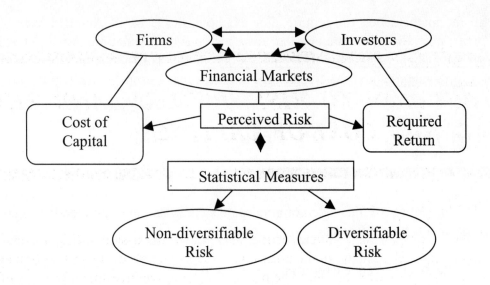

LEARNING CHECKLIST

After preparing this chapter, you should be able to:

_____1. Estimate the opportunity cost of capital for an "average risk" project.
_____2. Calculate the standard deviation of returns for individual common stocks or a stock portfolio.
_____3. Understand how and why diversification reduces total risk.
_____4. Distinguish between unique risk, which can be diversified away, and market risk, which cannot.

SOURCES OF BUSINESS INFORMATION

Check Out the Risk Profile: To properly set investment policy, you should specify your risk tolerance. It is important to know the maximum amount of additional risk that you will accept for a given increase in expected return. You are willing to assume a higher level of risk in order to obtain a higher rate of growth, or you just want to minimize the risk of any loss of your money to ensure a solid income. One means of establishing your risk tolerance is to identify your most desirable choice from a set of questions. Judging from the answers, you know what type of investor you are, aggressive or passive. You can find many online documents with advice on how to analyze your risk tolerance. An excellent site can be found from Merrill Lynch at www.merill-lynch.ml.com/investor/risktol.

Online Calculators: You may have the confidence to select your investment candidates. To avoid any chaos, you want to keep a good balance in your portfolio. Don't put all your eggs in one basket. So you know the benefit of diversification. But you still have a hard time to decide the weight for your favourites. Luckily, the Internet provides many online financial calculators that can do all the mathematics you require. For example, the Bank of America Web site suggests an investment allocation strategy that matches your own situation. Answer the 12 questions at www.bankamerica.com/tools/sri_assetall.html. Or read "Focus on Your Needs" from www.networth.galt.com/invesco/Needs.html to determine your investment strategies.

CHAPTER OUTLINE, KEY CONCEPTS, AND TERMS

I.   RATES OF RETURN: A REVIEW

    A.   Security return, either stock or bonds, are a combination of dividend or interest payments plus any capital gain or loss.

    B.   The annual percentage return on investment is:

$$\text{Percentage Return} = \frac{\text{Capital Gain} + \text{Dividend}}{\text{Initial Share Price}}$$

    C.   The above return is a nominal return, reflecting how much more money one has at the end of the year.

$$\text{Dividend Yield} = \frac{\text{Dividend}}{\text{Initial Share Price}}$$

    D.   The same percentage return or total return is the sum of the dividend yield (annual dividends/initial share price) plus the capital gain yield (annual capital gain/initial share price).

$$\text{Capital Gain Yield} = \frac{\text{Capital Gain}}{\text{Initial Share Price}}$$

    E.   The real rate of return is the nominal rate adjusted for the inflation rate in the period or the additional purchasing power one has with the investment return:

$$1 + \text{real ror} = \frac{1 + \text{nominal ror}}{1 + \text{inflation rate}}$$

II.   SEVENTY-FIVE YEARS OF CAPITAL MARKET HISTORY

A.   Principles

1.   Managers must estimate current and future opportunity rates of return for investment evaluation. Estimating the opportunity rate begins with a study of historical rates of return on varying risk investments.

2.   The level of risk and required rate of return are directly related. Investors require higher rates of return for increased risk.

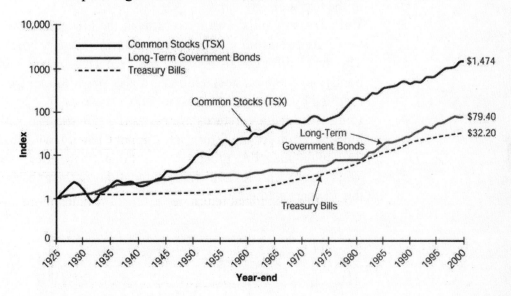

B.   Market Indexes

1.   Several **market indexes** measure the investment performance of the overall market.

2.   The TSE 300 Composite Index, based on a portfolio of the 300 largest TSE stock, is a value-weighted index covering a relatively broad and active trading in the Canadian market. The Index excludes control blocks composed of more than 20 percent of outstanding shares. While the Index itself does not include the paid-out dividends, the TSE 300 Total Return does. To reflect the fact that no stock weighted more than 10 percent in the portfolio, the TSE 300 Capped Index is created using the prices of the TSE 300 stocks. However, the Index recently has been replaced by the S&P/TSX Composite Index, which is not required to list exactly 300 stocks.

3.   The **Dow Jones Industrial Average** is an equal share index of 30 industrial stocks. It is an index of a few important firms, independently of how many shares each company has outstanding.

4.   The **Standard and Poor's Composite Index** is a share-weighted index of 500 firms, covering about 70 percent of the value of stocks traded.

Compared to the Dow, the S&P 500 is a broader index and is adjusted for the relative number of shares available to investors.

5. The Nikkei Index (Tokyo) and the Financial Times Index (London) are just a few other market performance indices.

C. **The Historical Record**

1. The historical returns of Treasury bills, long-term Treasury bonds, corporate bonds, and common stock are compared in Figures 9.1 and 9.2 in the textbook.

2. With Treasury bills' average returns at the low end of the risk scale, a **maturity premium** is added for long-term Treasury bond returns.

3. The return differentials between risk-free Treasury bills and corporate bonds and common stock returns is a **risk premium**, or the added return required by investors to invest in risky securities.

4. Long-term average returns are a starting point in estimating required rates of return for the future, and the opportunity rate of return used in the capital budgeting process.

5. The riskier securities had wider fluctuations in their yearly returns over the 75 years studied.

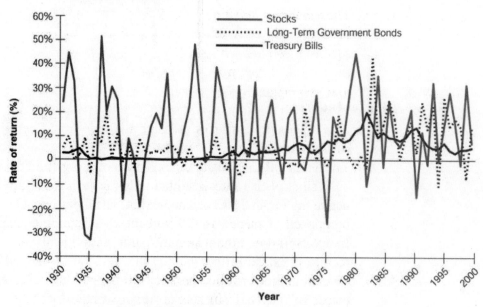

D. **Using Historical Evidence to Estimate Today's Cost of Capital**

1. The opportunity rate of return given up to invest in the projects of a business are equivalent to the returns on a market portfolio of common stocks.

2. Estimated stock returns fluctuate yearly (7 percent average risk premium) around the Treasury bill rate. This assumes that there is a normal, stable risk premium on the market portfolio and that past returns are reliable predictors of future returns.

3. Historical returns provide a benchmark for estimating current and future required rates of return. The market portfolio returns, assumed to be stable and similar to historical returns, may serve as proxy for average-risk project opportunity rates of return.

III. MEASURING RISK

A. **Historical variation**

1. Variation around a central tendency or mean may be presented visually by constructing a histogram (Figure 9.3) in the textbook and studying the dispersion or spread of possible outcomes.

2. Another method is calculating a measure of variation used as a proxy for measuring risk, such as the variance or standard deviation. Risk relates to the variability of future returns.

B. **Variance and Standard Deviation**

1. The **variance** statistic is the average value of squared deviations from the mean. The **standard deviation** is the square root of the variance.

Coin Toss Game-calculating variance and standard deviation

(1) Percent Rate of Return	(2) Deviation from Mean	(3) Squared Deviation
+ 40	+ 30	900
+ 10	0	0
+ 10	0	0
- 20	- 30	900

Variance = average of squared deviations = 1800 / 4 = 450

Standard deviation = square of root variance = $\sqrt{450}$ = 21.2%

2. The *greater* the variance or standard deviation, the *greater* the dispersion, volatility, or variability of returns, and the *greater* the risk. See the above figure for the calculation of the variance and standard deviation.

3. In general, variance is the probability-weighted average of squared deviations around the expected return. Standard deviation is the square root of variance.

4. The population variance, with known probabilities of each possible outcome, is different from sample variance that has unknown probabilities. The sample variance is an estimate based on a set of observations. To get the number, we divide the sum of squared deviations by the number of observation minus 1.

C.   **Measuring the Variation in Stock Returns**

1.   Calculating historical average investment returns and the variability of those returns, the comparison of average returns and volatility indicates that historical risk and return are directly related.

2.   Higher risk is associated with higher average returns.

3.   One might assume that historical returns and variability (long period) would extend into the future for estimating investor-required or opportunity rates of return.

4.   Investors will expect a higher rate of return, risk premium over the Treasury bill rate, with higher standard deviation of returns.

Year	Rate of Return	Deviation from Average Return	Squared Deviation
1995	14.5	−1.4	1.9
1996	28.3	12.4	154.9
1997	15.0	−0.9	0.8
1998	−1.6	−17.5	305.6
1999	31.7	15.8	250.1
2000	7.4	−8.5	72.1
Total	95.45		785.5

IV.   **RISK AND DIVERSIFICATION**

A.   **Portfolios**

1.   Our measures of variation apply to groupings of securities or portfolios as well as single securities.

2.   The variability or risk of a portfolio, or a market portfolio such as the TSE 300 Composite, is *not* the simple average of the individual stock variability. The portfolio risk is *less* than the average risk of the individual securities.

B.   **Diversification**

1.   The reduced risk of the portfolio is caused by **diversification** effects of spreading the portfolio across many investments.

2.   Portfolio diversification works because prices of different stocks do not move exactly together or are not perfectly correlated (+1). Diversification works best, or the risk-reducing effects of diversification works best, when the stock returns are negatively correlated. Diversification reduces the variability of returns on the portfolio compared to the average variability of the individual stocks.

C.   **Asset versus Portfolio Risk**

1.   While historical returns on individual securities are good proxies for estimating future returns on individual securities, historical standard deviations of returns are *not* good risk proxies for stocks held in a portfolio.

2.   Since stocks and other securities are usually held in portfolios, because of the diversification effect, the relevant risk of a stock to be added to the portfolio is the impact of the added stock on the portfolio variability or risk. The incremental risk of a stock added to a portfolio depends on how the stock varies compared to the portfolio variation. If the historical correlation between the stock and portfolio are high positive (+1), there is no diversification effect of the added stock. If the relationship is negative, zero or low positive, the addition of the stock lowers the portfolio variance or standard deviation or risk.

3.   Incremental risk does not depend upon the added stock's variability; it depends upon how the stock affects the portfolio's variability when it is added to the portfolio.

4.   Correlation coefficient, a number between –1 and 1, measures the degree to which two stocks move together.

D.   **Market Risk versus Unique Risk**

1.   The diversification effect or the reduction in portfolio risk takes place with the addition of added securities until about 20 or 30 are included in the portfolio. Beyond that, the diversification effect of added securities is minimal.

2.   While diversification eliminates the **unique risk** of individual securities, one cannot eliminate the **market risk** or systematic risk, the risks that affect the entire stock market.

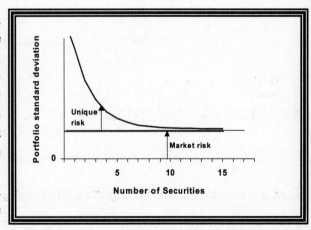

3.   For a diversified portfolio, only the market risk matters. When one discusses securities investment or investors, it is assumed that the security is held in a diversified portfolio and the relevant risk is market risk.

V. THINKING ABOUT RISK

A. *Three* added risk concepts are presented below.

Message 1: Some Risks Look Big and Dangerous But Really Are Diversifiable

1. Individual project risk may not be as high when the project is part of a portfolio of business investments. As in the discussion above, the relevant risk is the incremental risk effect on the investment portfolio or the impact on the total business effort.

Message 2: Market Risks Are Macro Risks

2. Investors holding diversified portfolios are concerned with macroeconomic risks, or the impact of business cycle, exchange rates, etc., on investor decisions related to investment and disinvestment in financial markets. Specific or unique risk is not relevant.

3. Managers must deal with unique risk exposure in addition to market risk, but only market risk affects the opportunity rate of return of the firm.

Message 3: Risk Can Be Measured

4. The risk, measured by the variance or standard deviation, of individual stocks can be easily measured, but when diversification is assumed for investors, only the incremental risk effects of adding a security to a portfolio is relevant.

5. In the next chapter this relevant risk, or the individual stock's relationship with fluctuations in the market portfolio, is discussed and measured.

COMPLETION QUESTIONS

1. Return s from stocks come from (*dividends/interest*) and _____ gains or losses.

2. (*Nominal/Real*) returns indicate buying power.

3. A measure of the investment performance of the overall market is a (*industry/market*) index.

4. The Dow Jones Industrial Average includes (*less/more*) stocks than the Standard and Poor's Composite Index.

5.   Short-term Treasury bills are (*less/more*) risky than long-term Treasury bonds.

6.   Corporate bonds are (*less/more*) risky than common stocks.

7.   The extra average return from investing in long-term versus short-term Treasury securities is known as the _____ premium.

8.   On an historic basis, the higher the risk the (*higher/lower*) the return.

9.   The expected market return is equal to the interest rate on Treasury bills plus the (*normal/real*) risk premium.

10.   The opportunity cost of capital for (*safe/risky*) projects is the rate of return offered by Treasury bills.

11.   Measures of dispersion are used to measure (*return/risk*).

12.   A measure of volatility that is the average value of squared deviation from the mean is called _____.

13.   Another measure of risk is the square root of variance which is also called the _____ _____.

14.   The (*expected/historical*) return is equal to the probability-weighted average of possible outcomes.

15.   Common stocks as a group have a (*higher/lower*) standard deviation compared to corporate bonds.

16.   Diversification (*increases/reduces*) variability because prices of different stocks (*do/do not*) move exactly together.

17.   Counter cyclical stocks do well when others do (*poorly/well*).

18.   _____ risk refers to risk factors affecting only a particular firm. It is also called (diversifiable/non-diversifiable) risk.

19.   Another name for systematic risk is _____ risk.

20.   Systematic risk (*can/cannot*) be eliminated.

21.   Drilling for oil and fire insurance are examples of (*diversifiable/market*) risk.

22.   Grocery chains have (*less/more*) market risk compared to automobile manufacturers.

PROBLEMS

1. Tim purchased a stock for $25 per share and sold it one year later for $30 after having received dividends of $1 per share. What was his rate of return?

2. If the inflation rate during the year Tim had the stock described in the preceding problem was 8 percent, what was his real rate of return?

3. Using the DJIA method and starting at 100, construct a measure of price changes in the stock market from a sample of the 3 stocks as shown in the figure below:

STOCK PRICE IN $ PER SHARE			
PERIOD	A	B	C
1	15	25	80
2	20	23	86
3	17	28	69

4. If the average annual compound rate of return for all large Canadian common stocks between 1926 and 2000 was 12.8 percent and the risk-free return averaged 6.5 percent, what was the average risk premium (excess rate of return)?

5. In one year when inflation was 12 percent, the real return on long-term bonds was –3 percent. What was the nominal return that year? Why did investors accept the negative real return? What could they have done about it?

6. Suppose a stock is projected to sell for $30 per share in a year from now. What price would you pay today for that stock if it was expected to pay a dividend this coming year of $4 per share and if you required a return of 12 percent?

7. What would be the value of the stock described in problem 6 if instead you required a return of 18 percent?

8. Suppose you own stock in a company that is widely expected to be acquired by another firm but antitrust consideration might block the merger. If the deal fails to go through the price will fall from the present $50 per share to $40. If the combination is approved your shares will increase to $60. The probability of a positive outcome within the next year is 0.7 with a 0.3 chance that the acquisition will not occur. What is your expected return?

9. You are considering investing in a particular stock with an expected return of 8 percent at least. This stock will deliver 20 percent returns in the good state, but –10 percent returns in the bad state. What is the lowest probability of the good state in order to justify the investment?

ANSWERS TO COMPLETION QUESTIONS

1. dividends, capital
2. Real
3. market
4. less
5. less
6. less
7. maturity
8. higher
9. normal
10. safe
11. risk
12. variance
13. standard deviation
14. expected
15. higher
16. reduces, do not
17. poorly
18. Unique, diversifiable
19. market
20. cannot
21. diversifiable
22. less

SOLUTIONS TO PROBLEMS

1. The only returns from common stock are in the form of dividends and capital gains or losses based on the difference between the price paid and the price at which the shares are sold.

$$\text{Rate of return} = \frac{\text{dividends} + \text{capital gains}}{\text{initial price}}$$

$$= \frac{\$1 + (30 - 25)}{\$25}$$

$$= .24 \text{ or } 24\%$$

2.

$$\text{Real return} = \frac{1 + \text{nominal rate}}{1 + \text{inflation rate}} - 1$$

$$= .148 \text{ or } 14.8\%$$

3.

PERIOD	AVE. PRICE, $	% CHANGE	CALCULATED AVE.
1	40	—	100.0
2	43	7.5	107.5
3	38	−11.6	95.0

4. The actual return minus the risk-free rate equals the risk premium:
$$11.8\% - 4.8\% = 7\%$$

5. Recall that the approximate real return equals the nominal rate minus the rate of inflation. This means the nominal rate is about equal to the real rate plus the inflation rate. In this case the nominal rate $= -3 + 12 = 9$ percent.

   Investors did not expect inflation would be so high or they never would have accepted a 9 percent return. They were hurt by having inflation exceed their fixed return but there was nothing they could do about it. They did make up for the loss of purchasing power by requiring higher nominal rates later.

6. The return on a share of stock over one year is equal to the dividend plus the capital gain or loss divided by the initial price. Expressed in symbols this is:

$$k = \frac{D + (P_1 - P_0)}{P_0}$$

solving this equation for P_0

$$P_0 = \frac{D + P_1}{k + 1}$$

$$= \$30.36$$

7.   This is a case of becoming less optimistic about the future that translates into higher risk. The higher risk means a higher required return. If nothing else changed, the maximum price you would pay would be:

$$P_0 = \frac{\$4 + \$30}{1 + .18}$$

$$= \$28.81$$

This is one explanation why stock prices fall when investors become more conservative in their view of the future. The way they can achieve the higher required returns is to decrease their valuation of stocks which means they will not pay as much for shares. The weakened demand will result in a drop in share prices.

8.   The expected stock price is the sum of the products of the possible prices multiplied by the likelihood of their occurrence. The price would be:

$$60 \times 0.7 + 40 \times 0.3 = \$54$$

$$\frac{\$60 - \$54}{\$50}$$

The expected return would be:

$$= .12 \text{ or } 12\%$$

9.   Let W be the required probability. Since 8% = W(20%) + (1 – W)(–10%), we are solving for W = 0.6.

CHAPTER 10

RISK, RETURN, AND CAPITAL BUDGETING

CHAPTER IN PERSPECTIVE

This chapter continues to build the bridge between asset investment, capital budgeting, and financial markets. This chapter continues our study of risk measurement, starting with calculation of beta, the variability of an investment's return relative to fluctuations of the market portfolio. Beta is a relative risk measure; the risk of a company's stock relative a broad-based market portfolio of stocks. Students with their new financial/statistical calculator should be able to crank out a regression line. Try the text example.

The concepts of risk and return have been building slowly in the text and now are concluded in this chapter. Later in the chapter, risk and capital budgeting concepts are combined in a short but important discussion of the project cost of capital. The last section in the chapter is the connecting link of CAPM to the asset side of the balance sheet.

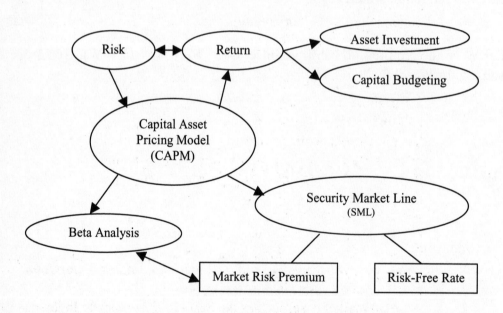

LEARNING CHECKLIST

After preparing this chapter you should be able to:

____1. Measure and interpret the market risk, or beta, of a stock. What does beta measure?
____2. Relate the market risk of a security to the rate of return that investors demand.
____3. Calculate the opportunity cost of capital for a specific project.

SOURCES OF BUSINESS INFORMATION

An Explosive Industry: Admittedly, one way to reduce the risk with stock market investing is to diversify. However, it may be easier said than done. You usually need about 15 to 20 stocks to achieve the benefit of diversification. The reality is that you may not have enough resources to play the game. Instead, you could turn to mutual funds as an alternative to cope with the risk involved. Mutual funds are great investments, but they need careful studies. Like other investments, there are all kinds of mutual funds in the market. While you choose the types of mutual funds that best match your risk preference, you can diversify your portfolio with a reasonable cost. A number of organizations offer online information or interactive tools to help. The "Six Steps to Selecting a Mutual Fund Investment" from Scotia Capital at www.scotiacapital.com is worth mentioning.

Company Profiles: If you are thinking about investing in a company, you want to know more about that company. A thorough research of the company must be undertaken. The company's profile including address, phone numbers, executive names, recent sales figures, and company statutes, etc. is available online. Try www.finance.yahoo.com for the U.S. companies. You may be surprised that stock betas and other risk measures of Canadian companies are sometimes impossible to find on their Web sites.

CHAPTER OUTLINE, KEY CONCEPTS, AND TERMS

I.   **MEASURING MARKET RISK**

    A.   **Concepts**
1. Only "macro" events affect the value of the **market portfolio**, or a portfolio of all assets in the economy.
2. A broad market base, such as the S&P/TSX Composite Index, is often used as a proxy for the market portfolio.
3. Firm specific or unique risk are averaged out or diversified away when considering the market portfolio.
4. A measure of a stock's risk relative to the risk of the market portfolio is called the stock's **beta**, and is expressed as the Greek letter β.

B. **Measuring Beta**

1. Investors with diversified portfolios are not concerned about the specific or unique risk of a stock, only the impact of the stock on the risk of the entire portfolio.

2. The relative risk of the stock compared to the portfolio risk or beta is the relevant risk to consider when a new stock is added to the portfolio.

3. Defensive stocks historically tend to vary less than the market portfolio; aggressive stocks have a history of more variation relative to the market portfolio.

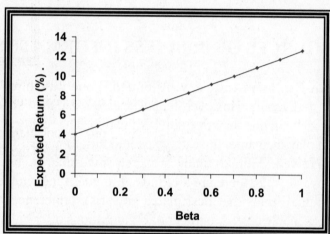

4. Beta is the slope of the regression line of the individual stock returns relative to the market portfolio returns. If the slope indicates a change in historical stock returns *similar* to the market (-1 to +1), the beta has a value of 1. If the variations in the stock return, given a 1 percent variation in the market returns, is less than the market variation, the beta is *less than* 1 and the stock is noted as a "defensive" stock. If the slope of the line through the points found by plotting the stock's returns relative to a 1 percent change in the market portfolio is *greater than* 1, the beta has a value greater than 1.

5. Any stock's return is comprised of two parts. The first is explained by the macro events in the market or the market rate of return. The second part of the return is related to the specific or unique risk of the stock relative to the market rate of return, or the stock beta.

6.   The beta is calculated by 1) observing monthly rates of return for the stock and the market; 2) plotting the observations as in Figure 10.1 in the textbook; and, 3) fitting a regression line showing the average returns to the stock (dependent variable) at

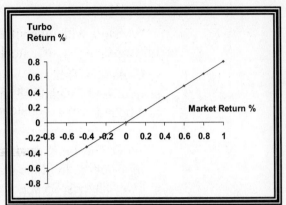

different market returns (independent variable). The slope of the line, beta, relates the change in stock returns, given a change in market return.

7.   Alternatively, use the correlation coefficient or the covariance to find the beta of stock j. The beta is the sensitivity of a stock's return to the return of the market portfolio.

$$\beta_j = \frac{\text{cov}(r_j, r_m)}{\sigma_m^2} \quad \text{or} \quad \beta_j = \frac{\rho_{j,m}\sigma_j}{\sigma_m} \quad \text{where} \quad \rho_{j,m} = \frac{\text{cov}(r_j, r_m)}{\sigma_j\sigma_m}$$

C.   **Betas for Inco and Westcoast Energy**

1.   Betas for Inco and Westcoast Energy are calculated in Figure 10.2 in the textbook. Sixty months' return of the stocks and market are plotted and a regression line is calculated and drawn.

2.   The beta is the "b" in the (a + bx) function of the straight line drawn or the slope of the line. It indicates the change in the stock return, given a change in the market rate of return.

3.   Inco had a beta of 1.33, or a stock variation 30 percent higher than the market variability over the period. Westcoast Energy tended to vary less than the market in the same period (beta of 0.48).

4.   Table 10.1 in the textbook lists selected common stocks and their betas for a specific period.

D.   **Portfolio Betas**

1.   Diversification decreases the variability from unique risk but not from market risk.

2.   The beta of a portfolio is an average of the stock betas weighted by the investment in each security. One may construct a higher risk than the market average portfolio (portfolio beta greater than 1), or a portfolio with an average risk less than the market (portfolio beta less than 1).

3.   A large portfolio of diversified stocks would approximate the market index and have a portfolio beta around 1. An index mutual fund is a "market portfolio" of stocks with a beta close to the value of 1.

I. RISK AND RETURN

A. Calculations

1. Canadian Treasury bills have very low risk and a beta of zero, or no relationship with the variations of the market stock portfolio which has a beta of 1.0.

2. The difference between the return on the market and the T-bill rate is called the **market risk premium**, or the risk premium demanded by investors to hold the market portfolio rather than T-bills.

3. Over the past 75 years, the market risk premium has averaged over 7.0 percent per year.

4. The expected rate of return on any portfolio combining T-bills and the market portfolio lies on a straight line between *all* T-bills (4 percent) and *all* stocks of the market portfolio (11 percent).

5. The risk premium is proportional to the portfolio beta. A portfolio with one-half T-bills and one-half the market portfolio of stocks would have a beta of .5, and a risk premium of one-half the market portfolio risk premium.

6. The market risk premium is the market return *less* the return on T-bills.

7. Beta measures risk of the stock relative to the market. The expected risk premium on an individual stock is the stock return less the risk-free rate or beta *times* the market risk premium.

8. The total expected return on a stock is the risk-free rate plus the risk premium of the stock.

    Expected Return on stock = risk-free rate + risk premium.

$$\text{Market risk premium} = r_m - r_f$$
$$\text{Risk premium on any asset} = r - r_f$$
$$\text{Expected Return} = r_f + B(r_m - r_f)$$

9. The above formula showing the expected return as the sum of the risk-free rate plus the risk premium is called the **capital asset pricing model (CAPM)**. The rate of return on an individual stock is dependent upon the risk-free rate and the risk premium which is related to the market risk premium and the risk of the stock relative to the market risk premium, its beta.

B.   **Why the CAPM Works**

1.   The CAPM assumes well-diversified investors; market risk is the only relevant risk.

2.   The expected return on a portfolio is equal to the risk-free interest rate plus the expected portfolio risk premium.

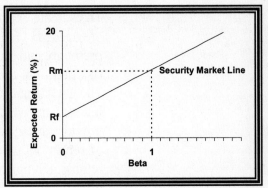

C.   **The Security Market Line**

1.   A plot of expected rates of return of varied risk (beta) portfolios is called the **security market line**. This is illustrated in the figure above.

2.   According to the CAPM, expected rates of return for all securities and all portfolios lie on this line.

3.   The required risk premium for any investment is given by the security market line.

4.   A stock with a given beta that is expected to earn a return higher than that on the security market line will be purchased by investors, bidding up the stock price and lowering the expected rate of return to the security market line. Investors keep expected returns on the security market line.

5.   The security market line is the risk-return trade-off of investors.

6.   The CAPM states that the expected risk premium on an investment should be proportional to its beta.

7.   The CAPM explains the risk-return trade-off well in the period 1931 to 1991, though the SML tends to understate low risk returns and overstate high beta portfolios. In the period 1966–1991, however, there is little relationship between portfolio betas and the return on the portfolio. Other variables such as growth of GDP, yield spread, and firm size outside the simplified CAPM are involved in establishing returns besides beta. Arbitrage pricing theory (APT) is one example.

8.   The CAPM, though not the only model of the risk-return trade-off, is a good practical rule of thumb. It presents a simplified approach noting that extra required returns are required by investors to take added risk, and investors are primarily concerned with market risk that cannot be diversified away.

D. **Using the CAPM to Estimate Expected Returns**

1. To estimate expected investor returns for a selected stock, *three* numbers are needed: 1) the risk-free rate of interest, 2) the expected market risk premium, and 3) the beta of the stock, or the historical variation in stock risk premium relative to the market risk premium.

2. The CAPM may also be used to estimate the discount rate for new capital investments when calculating net present value. The security market line provides a standard for investment project acceptance. If the internal rate of return on a project exceeds the opportunity rate of return (investor returns in a portfolio of equal risk securities), the firm should make the investment.

3. For any risk level or beta, project returns below the security market line are unacceptable and have negative NPVs.

II. **CAPITAL BUDGETING AND PROJECT RISK**

A. **Concept** — Before the CAPM, financial manager's intuition indicated that riskier projects are less desirable than safe projects and that riskier investments must have higher expected rates of return relative to safe projects.

B. **Company versus Project Risk**

1. The estimated required rate of return of investors on a firm's securities is called the **company cost of capital**. The cost of capital is the discount rate used in calculating the NPV of investment projects and is the minimum acceptable rate of return when compared to the internal rate of return (IRR).

2. The cost of capital is determined by average risk of a company's assets and operations. The cost of capital is applicable as a discount rate only on projects with the average risk of the business.

3. The **project cost of capital** is a risk-adjusted minimum acceptable rate of return used as a discount rate on a specific project. The project cost of capital depends on project risk, not the company cost of capital, representing an average risk project.

C. **Determinants of Project Risk**

1. Project risk is usually assumed to be associated with the variability of cash flow of the project itself, but what matters is the relationship between the project's cash flows and the total firm (portfolio) variability or the project's beta.

2. Projects that tend to have high operating leverage (high fixed costs) tend to have high project betas.

3.   Follow the pure play approach, using the cost of capital of another company involved exclusively in the same type of project, to estimate project cost of capital.

D.   **Don't Add Fudge Factors to Discount Rates**
1.   Concern over the downside features of risk encourages managers to add risk premiums to discount rates in project analyses, thus forsaking many value-creating projects.
2.   Special risk factors should be incorporated into the cash flow estimation, not the discount rate. Special risks are often unique risks that are diversified away with other projects.

COMPLETION QUESTIONS

1.   Macro risk (*can/cannot*) be eliminated by diversification.

2.   _____ risk is measured by the sensitivity of an investment's returns as related to fluctuations in the market.

3.   The Canadian market portfolio is represented by the (*Dow Jones Industrial Average/ S&P/TSX Composite Index*).

4.   The sensitivity of a particular stock's return to the return from the market portfolio is measured by _____.

5.   Defensive stocks have (*high/low*) betas.

6.   The returns from aggressive stocks will vary (*less/more*) than the market return.

7.   Aggressive stocks will have betas that are (*less/more*) than 1.0.

8.   If the returns from the market were expected to increase by 10 percent, a stock with a beta of 0.9 would be expected to return an extra _____ percent.

9.   An attraction of (*over-the-counter stocks/mutual funds*) is that they offer small investors diversification at low cost.

10. An (*index/mutual*) fund is expected to track the market as a whole. Such a fund has (*considerable/extremely small*) unique risk.

11. The difference between the return on the market and the return on risk-free Treasury bills is termed the _____ _____ _____ .

12. The beta for Treasury bills is (0/1.0).

13. The _____ _____ _____ _____ states that the expected return on any security is equal to the risk-free return plus the security's beta multiplied by the market risk premium.

14. When the Treasury bill return is 5 percent and the market risk premium is 10 percent, a portfolio with a beta of 1.2 will be expected to return (*12/17*) percent according to CAPM.

15. The _____ _____ _____ shows the relationship between expected return and beta.

16. Investors expect a (*penalty/reward*) for both waiting and worrying. (THIS IS A FUNDAMENTAL PRINCIPLE OF FINANCE — think carefully about its meaning.)

17. CAPM can be used to estimate the (*discount rate/internal rate of return*) for capital budgeting projects.

18. For capital budgeting projects with high risks beta should be (*decreased/increased*).

19. The expected rate of return by investors in a company is determined by the average (*return/risk*) from the company's assets and operations.

20. The discount rate that is the minimum acceptable expected return on a project given its risk is known as the project _____ _____ _____ .

21. Projects involving revenues that are strongly dependent on the state of the economy tend to have (*high/low*) betas and a (*high/low*) cost of capital.

22. Projects that have (*high/low*) fixed costs will tend to have (*high/low*) betas.

23. Discount rates for high risk projects (*should/should not*) reflect the market risk of the project and (*should/should not*) be adjusted to offset errors in the cash flow forecast.

PROBLEMS

1. What is the capital asset pricing model (CAPM)? Explain the concept and express the model as an equation.

2. What will be the beta for a Myranda's portfolio that is invested 40 percent in Treasury bills and 60 percent in a group of stocks that track returns from the S&P/TSX Composite Index?

3. Suppose that in a year of strong economic growth, an airline stock is expected to provide a return of 30 percent and the market return is expected to be 20 percent. On the other hand when the economy is stagnant, the expectations are for returns of 4 percent for the airline and 8 percent for the market. Estimate the beta for the airline stock.

4. What will be the expected return from the portfolio specified in problem 2 if the risk-free rate is 6 percent and the expected market return is 14 percent?

5. Compare the return expected for the airline stock in problem 3 when the market return is expected to be 12 percent and 18 percent. The Treasury bill rate in both cases can be assumed to be 7 percent.

6. What conclusions can be drawn from the returns estimated for the airline stock in problem 5?

7. What is the standard deviation of a well-diversified portfolio with a beta of 0.9 when the standard deviation of the market returns is 30 percent?

8. When the market return increases by 2 percent, stock M averages increases of returns of 4 percent. What is stock M's beta?

9. For a project having a beta of 0.8, what is the appropriate discount rate for evaluating its potential investments if the market risk premium is 10 percent and the Treasury bill rate is 7 percent?

10. Suppose the internal rate of return on the potential project described in problem 9 is 20 percent. Should the firm make the investment proposed?

11. For a company having a beta of 1.1, a current stock price of $40 per share, and an expected dividend this coming year of $2.80 per share, what is the projected stock price one year from today? (Assume the market risk premium is 12 percent and the risk-free rate is 6 percent.)

12. A company is considering an investment that offers a net cash flow of $100,000 per year for the indefinite future. The risk of this project is felt to be the same as the average for all stocks. If the Treasury bill rate is 8 percent and the market return is expected to be 14 percent, what is the maximum investment outlay that should be made?

13. The covariance between the returns of two stocks X and Y is 0.002. If the standard deviation of returns for X and Y are 10 percent and 20 percent, respectively, what is the correlation coefficient?

ANSWERS TO COMPLETION QUESTIONS

1. cannot
2. Market
3. S&P/TSX Composite Index
4. beta
5. low
6. more
7. more
8. 9
9. mutual funds
10. index, extremely small
11. market risk premium
12. 0
13. capital asset pricing model
14. 17
15. security market line
16. reward
17. discount rate
18. increased
19. risk
20. cost of capital
21. high, high
22. high, high
23. should, should not

SOLUTIONS TO PROBLEMS

1. CAPM is a model that helps explain the trade-off between risk and return for a security. Risk is measured for a particular security relative to the variation of returns for the overall market. The expected return (r) is based on the expected return for the overall market (r_m) and the current risk-free rate (r_f). CAPM states that the expected return for a particular security is equal to the risk-free rate plus a premium. This premium is the product of the premium return for the overall market and the riskiness of the individual security (β). In symbols the CAPM is expressed as:

$$r = r_f + \beta(r_m - r_f)$$

2. The portfolio beta will be the weighted average of the securities comprising the portfolio. Remember that the beta for Treasury bills, which are risk-free, is zero and, by definition, the beta for the market is 1.0. The portfolio beta is thus:
$$0 \times 0.4 + 1.0 \times 0.6 = 0.6$$

3. The beta can be estimated by dividing the change in the return for a particular stock by

$$\frac{30-4}{20-8} = 2.17$$

the change in the return for the overall market. In this case beta for the airline is: 2.17.

4. According to the CAPM:
$$r = r_f + \beta(r_m - r_f)$$

$$r = 6 + 0.6 \times (14 - 6) = 10.8\%$$

5. When the market return is 12 percent, CAPM predicts the airline stock return will be:
$$= 7 + 1.6 \times (12 - 7)$$
$$= 15\%$$
When the market return is 18 percent, the airline stock return is expected to be:
$$= 7 + 1.6 \times (18 - 7)$$
$$= 24.7\%$$

6. The high degree of sensitivity of returns for the airline stock compared to the market is caused by the high beta. The conclusion is that if one expects the market to increase it is advisable to be invested in stocks with betas above 1. In other words, if a bull market is forecast, high beta stocks should be chosen. Of course if the market is weak, the high beta stocks will experience an even poorer performance. Also the sensitivity of a stock to the market is a general relationship that does not always hold true.

7. The standard deviation for a well-diversified portfolio is related to the market which, by definition, is fully diversified through beta as:
$$\text{beta}_{\text{portfolio}} = 0.9 \times 30 = 27\%$$

8. Beta is a measure of sensitivity of the returns from a particular security, or portfolio of securities, to changes in returns from the overall market. In this case when the market return increases by 2 percent, stock M increases by twice as much. Therefore its beta is 2.0.

9. The appropriate discount rate is the required return calculated from CAPM as:
$$r = 7 + 0.8 \times 10 = 15\%$$

10. The IRR of 20 percent means the NPV is zero at that discount rate. At lower discount rates the NPV will be positive. Since the appropriate discount rate for this project is 15 percent, the calculation will result in a positive NPV so the project should be <u>accepted</u>.

11. First we need to calculate the required rate of return:
$$r = r_f + \beta(r_m - r_f)$$
$$r = 6 + (1.1 \times 12)$$
$$r = 19.2\%$$
The next step is to recognize that the required rate of return is also equal to the

$$r = \frac{\$2.80}{\$40} + \frac{P_1 - \$40}{\$40}$$

dividend yield plus the capital gain or:
$$P_1 = (.192 - .07 + 1) \times \$40 = \$44.88$$

12. According to the CAPM, the required rate of return is:
$$= 8 + 1.0 \times (14 - 6)$$
$$= 16\%$$
For a perpetuity, the value is:
$$= \$100,000/.16 = \$625,000$$
This is the maximum price that should be paid to provide a 16 percent return. If the outlay is less, the return will be higher.

13. $$P_{xy} = \frac{0.002}{(0.1)(0.2)} = 0.1$$

CHAPTER 11

THE COST OF CAPITAL

INTRODUCTION

This chapter, like the entire section, continues to bridge the relationship between investor concerns and minimum required returns and the internal decision-making processes of a business. The cost of capital or required rate of return concepts are covered in this chapter. While the opportunity rate of return concept was introduced generally several chapters ago, the specific theory and processes involved in estimating the cost of capital are covered in this chapter.

The opportunity cost of capital is used in the NPV and IRR evaluation of investment opportunities. This shareholder involvement or perspective in the investment process says that if the cost of capital return is generated as the return on investment, shareholders will receive their minimally acceptable rate of return. If they receive less, they are likely to sell the stock and move to investments that provide competitive rates of return relative to risk assumed. What if returns higher than the opportunity cost of capital are earned on investments? More investors will be attracted to the stock, the current stock owners will be pleased and will want to buy more stock, and the stock price is likely to increase.

What determines this opportunity rate of return? The market determines the cost of capital; management only estimates what it will be, based on a current evaluation. This market determined rate of return required on one business is the rate forgone on similar investments of similar risk (opportunity cost). Like the NPVs and IRRs in the capital budgeting chapters, reasonable accuracy of the estimate is a function of the quality of inputs. Like the cash flow estimates in capital budgeting, estimating the required rate of return today and over the life of the investment requires considerable insight in addition to technique. Remember, there is no cost of capital independent of where funds are invested. Note the relationship between capital budgeting and financial markets. Finally, do not get mired in the details and fail to keep a broad perspective. This is a chapter where the "trees" can keep you from seeing the "forest."

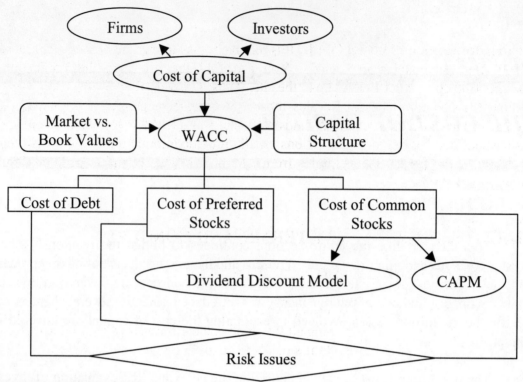

LEARNING CHECKLIST

After studying this chapter you should be able to:

____1. Select the balance accounts representing a company's capital structure.

____2. Estimate the current, required rates of return on the securities issued by the firm in the past.

____3. Calculate the weighted average cost of capital.

____4. Understand when the weighted average cost of capital is or is not the appropriate discount rate for a new project. Note how this "financing" chapter ties loosely with "investing."

SOURCES OF BUSINESS INFORMATION

Mutual Funds On the Web: There is no shortage of information online to help you learn about mutual funds. You can find a good overview at www.ific.ca from the Investment Funds Institute of Canada that is a self-governing organization representing the Canadian mutual funds industry. On the Web site, you can also access their glossary of mutual fund terms. Mutual funds have advantages and disadvantages. You need to take the time to understand what you are getting into. Since mutual funds are likely to be a part of your retirement nest egg, you should start this "pooled-investments" in your RRSP account soon. Clearly there must be some merits to mutual funds; otherwise, the industry would not experience such a solid growth. While the professional talent is one benefit to mutual funds, management fees is the big concern.

Further Research on Mutual Funds: It is relatively easy to find the Web sites of most major mutual fund companies in Canada. You can find the list from the Fund Library at www.fundlib.com. After linking up to the site, you see very detailed information of each type of fund the company carries. Besides those investment companies, most banks and trust companies have also offered mutual funds particularly as a RRSP investment. To enhance your basic background research, organizations usually provide information of the investment team in charge of the funds. See examples from Altamira at www.altamira.com and Trimark at www.trimark.com.

CHAPTER OUTLINE, KEY TERMS, AND CONCEPTS

I. THE COST OF CAPITAL

A.   The cost of capital for an all-equity financed firm is the required return on the firm's assets. Owning all the stock is the same as owning all the assets and the expected return on the stock is the expected return on the assets.

B.   Note the following identities:
1.   Value of business = value of stock
2.   Risk of business = risk of stock
3.   Rate of return on business = rate of return on stock
4.   Investor's required return = investor's required return from business from stock

C.   The **capital structure**, or the market value mix of debt and equity securities, features the sources of financing as a portfolio of financing funding a portfolio of assets.

D.   The cost of capital is the weighted average of returns (weighted by market value) on debt and equity, which is equal to the expected rate of return on the portfolio of assets.

E.   The cost of capital is the discount rate for evaluating new, similar risk asset investments.

Cost of Capital Example (Geothermal)

> *Geothermal Inc. has the following structure. Given that geothermal pays 8% for debt and 14% for equity, what is the Company Cost of Capital?*

Market Value Debt	$194	30%
Market Value Equity	$453	70%
Total Firm Value	$647	100%

$$\text{WACC} = (.3 \times 5.2\%) + (.7 \times 14\%) = 11.4\%$$

II. CALCULATING THE WEIGHTED AVERAGE COST OF CAPITAL

A. General Principles

1. The cost of capital is the opportunity cost of capital for the firm's existing assets. The cost of capital is used to assess or value new assets with risks similar to existing assets.
2. In the following sections, cost of capital concepts are discussed as is the weighted average cost of capital (WACC), a method for estimating the company cost of capital when debt capital is present, and an after-tax cost of debt capital must be calculated.

B. Calculating Company Cost of Capital as a Weighted Average

1. When only equity is financing a business, the CAPM may be used to calculate the company cost of capital.
2. When debt securities finance a portion of assets, the cost of capital is a weighted average of the returns demanded on the debt and equity securities. It is the expected return on the portfolio of all the firm's securities, which in turn is driven by the expected return on the business assets, or $V = D + E$.
3. The cost of capital is the expected return on assets, r_{assets}/V, which is equal to the expected income returns to the debt portion of total assets, $(DV \times r_{debt})$, plus the expected income returns to equity portion of total assets, $(EV \times r_{equity})$.

$$r_{assets} = \frac{\text{total income}}{\text{value of investments}}$$

$$r_{assets} = \frac{\left(D \times r_{debt} \right) + \left(E \times r_{equity} \right)}{V}$$

$$r_{assets} = \left(\frac{D}{V} \times r_{debt} \right) + \left(\frac{E}{V} \times r_{equity} \right)$$

C. **Three Steps in Calculating Cost of Capital**

1. Calculate the market value of each security as a proportion of the firm's total value.
2. Determine the current required rate of return on each security.
3. Calculate a weighted average of the required returns.

D. **Market versus Book Weights**

1. The cost of capital is the expected rate of return that investors require on the business assets, based on the market value of the securities of the firm.
2. The market value of securities versus book values should be used as weights when calculating the weighted average cost of capital.

E. **Taxes and the Weighted-Average Cost of Capital**

1. Taxes are important considerations in the cost of capital calculation because interest payments on debt are deductible. At a 35% tax rate, the after-tax cost of $1 of interest paid is $1 \times (1-.35)$ or $.65. This interest tax shield of $1 \times 35\%$ or $.35 on $1 reduces the pre-tax cost of debt by $(1- \text{tax rate})$. The after-tax cost of debt with a required pre-tax return of 8% is $8\% \times (1-.35) = 5.2\%$.
2. The after-tax version of the company cost of capital is called the **weighted average cost of capital**, which is the expected rate of return on a portfolio of all the securities of the firm and the discount rate for the NPV evaluation of new investments of similar risk.

F. **Wrapping Up Geothermal**

1. The use of lower cost, tax-deductible debt lowers Geothermal's cost of capital below that of an all-equity firm.

2. The WACC is the minimum acceptable rate of return on Geothermal's investment. The expected internal rate of return (IRR) exceeds the WACC and the NPV analysis indicates that the new project will add $9.5 million to the net wealth of Geothermal's owners.

$$ WACC = \left[\frac{D}{V} \times (1 - Tc)r_{debt} \right] + \left[\frac{E}{V} \times r_{equity} \right] $$

G. **Checking Our Logic**

1. If Geothermal earns the cost of capital on assets, 11.4 percent, the debt security holders will earn their required rate of return, 8 percent, and shareholders will earn their required rate of return of 14 percent.
2. If Geothermal earns an IRR greater than (less than) the cost of capital, shareholders will earn a return higher (lower) than their required rate of return of 14 percent. Creditors will earn only their fixed rate, required rate of return of 8 percent in all periods.
3. Projects with actual NPVs greater than zero will earn shareholders a return greater than the required rate of return on equity. Projects earning IRRs less than the cost of capital will produce actual NPVs less than zero and returns to equity below the required rate of return.

III. **MEASURING CAPITAL STRUCTURE**

A. Some of the practical problems involved in measuring the cost of capital include 1) identifying market values, and 2) determining the current market value of securities.

B. Market value weights are preferred over book value weights. Publicly traded share prices may be listed in newspapers. Market value estimates may be calculated by finding the present value of future cash flows discounted at the current interest rates.

C. The market value of equity may be estimated by multiplying the share price by the number of shares outstanding.

IV. **CALCULATING REQUIRED RATES OF RETURN**

A. Estimate the current, required rate of return on each security the firm has outstanding. For bonds, the current yield to maturity is a good proxy; for stocks, estimates using the CAPM or dividend discount model are reasonable numbers.

B. **The Expected Return on Bonds** — The yield to maturity, or the yield calculated to equate future cash flows with the price of the bond, is a good proxy for expected bond returns for healthy firms.

C. **The Expected Return on Common Stock**
1. The cost of equity capital may be estimated using the CAPM, where the expected return on equity is equal to the sum of the risk-free, T-bill rate plus the firm's beta times the market risk premium.
2. The dividend discount model may be used to estimate the required rate of return on equity, $P_o = DIV_1/(r_{equity} - g)$, where P_o is the current price, DIV_1 is the expected first year's dividend, and g is the expected growth rate. Solving for r_{equity}, the equation is transformed into the sum of the dividend yield plus the dividend growth rate or:

$$r_e = \frac{Div_1}{P_0} + g$$

D. **The Expected Return on Preferred Stock**
1. The estimated market value of preferred stock is found by dividing the constant dividend by the current required rate of return on similar risk preferred stock in the market. The price is equal to expected annual dividend divided by r_{pfd}.
2. Solving for the required rate of return on the preferred, use the following estimates:

$$r_{preferred} = \frac{Div_1}{P_0}$$

V. BIG OIL'S THE WEIGHTED AVERAGE COST OF CAPITAL

A. The weighted average cost of capital is the weighted sum of the after-tax cost of debt plus the cost of equity.

B. This section provides you with a simple example of the math involved in such calculations.

VI. INTERPRETING THE WEIGHTED AVERAGE COST OF CAPITAL

A. **When You Can and Can't Use WACC**
1. The WACC is the rate of return that the business must expect to earn on its average-risk investments in order to provide the opportunity rate of return to all its investors, debt and equity.
2. Investment projects under consideration with higher or lower risk than average business risk should be discounted with rates above or below the WACC.

149

B. **Some Mistakes People Make Using the WACC**

1. Because debt is tax deductible and its after-tax cost is far less than the cost of equity, one may reason that funding the project with increased proportions of debt will lower the WACC.

2. As the debt ratio increases, the incremental cost of debt, both explicit interest rates and implicitly through increases in the cost of equity capital, raises the WACC.

C. **How Changing Capital Structure Affects Expected Returns**

1. If there are no corporate taxes, a change in the capital structure does not affect the WACC, though it does affect the incremental cost of each component of the capital structure.

2. The shareholder's required rate of return adjusts to the changing capital structure and its component parts in order to keep the WACC the same.

D. **Revisiting the Project Cost of Capital**

1. When there are no corporate taxes, the cost of capital of a project is unaffected by how it is financed. With taxes, the best financing mix must be selected. The project's weighted-average cost of capital **(WACC)** must reflect the overall risk and the optimal securities mix of funding.

VII. **Flotation Costs And The Cost Of Capital**

A. Flotation Costs Represent The Costs Of Issuing Or "Floating" New Securities.

1. Flotation costs increase the cost outlay of investment projects and lower NPVs.

2. Recognizing flotation costs as an upward adjustment in the cost of capital is not as practical or as logical as including flotation costs as a negative cash flow outlay.

B. The Cost of Capital Depends Only On The Risk Of The Project

1. Flotation costs should be treated as a negative, incremental cash flow.

2. Flotation costs do not increase the required rate of return.

COMPLETION QUESTIONS

1. When a firm has no debt, all its assets are financed with _____.

2. When a firm has (*considerable/no*) debt its value is equal to the value of its stock.

3. The (*capital/financial*) structure is the mix of debt and equity.

4. The company _____ of _____ is the weighted average of the returns required by debt and equity investors.

5. The weighting factors for debt and equity are based on (*book/market*) values.

6. The inclusion of income taxes will lower the cost of (*debt/equity*) capital.

7. The cost of equity is (*raised/unaffected*) by the existence of income taxes.

8. A project with a zero NPV will generate (*excess/sufficient*) funds for investor requirements.

9. The stock price for a firm having a market value of $200 million and 5 million shares outstanding must be _____ per share.

10. According to the CAPM, the cost of equity capital is (*higher/lower*) for high beta stocks.

11. According to the CAPM, when the market risk premium decreases, the cost of equity capital for all firms will (*decrease/increase*).

12. According to the dividend discount model, the cost of equity is higher for (*faster/slower*) growing firms.

13. The cost of preferred stock is (*higher/lower*) for higher dividends.

14. If income tax rates were increased, the cost of debt would (*decrease/increase*).

15. The weighted average cost of capital is adjusted (*downward/upward*) when evaluating above average risk projects.

16. As more financing for assets comes from debt, the cost of equity will (*decrease/increase*).

17. The market risk of a firm's projects is known as the (*asset/liability*) beta.

18. The cost of debt is (*greater/less*) than the cost of equity.

ANSWERS TO COMPLETION QUESTIONS

1. equity
2. no
3. capital

4. cost, capital
5. market
6. debt
7. unaffected
8. sufficient
9. $40
10. higher
11. decrease
12. faster
13. higher
14. decrease
15. upward
16. increase
17. asset
18. less

PROBLEMS

1. Allequity Corporation is a manufacturing firm with an equity beta of 1.1. Currently Treasury Bill rates are 5 percent and the market-risk premium is estimated at 8 percent. What is the required rate of return by the shareholders of Allequity Corporation? What is Allequity's cost of capital? What is the minimum acceptable rate of return on new investments?

2. Bryon Corp. issued 20 year bonds two years ago when rates were 7 percent. The $1000 face value bonds are now selling at $940. What is the current required rate of return on Bryon Corp. bonds assuming annual interest payment?

3. With marginal tax rates of 40 percent, what is the current after-tax cost of capital for Bryon Corp. bonds? See problem 2.

4. Bryon Corp. estimates the market value of its equity to be $20 million and its debt, $10 million. The total assets listed on the balance sheet are $30 million. If equity investors now require an 18 percent rate of return on equity, what is the estimated weighted average cost of capital (WACC) for Bryon Corp? See problems 2 and 3 above. If Bryon Corp. recently evaluated an investment project with a positive NPV, what is the approximate rate of return on the investment?

5. Akron Tire issued preferred stock several years ago with a face value of $100, paying a dividend of 9 percent. Recently the preferred was trading at $105. What is the approximate required rate of return on preferred if Akron Tire decided to sell an issue of preferred stock?

6. Buchtel Industries has the following capital structure. If the corporate tax rate is 40 percent, what is the WACC for Buchtel Industries?

Security	Market Value	Required rate of return
Debt	$5 million	10%
Preferred stock	$3 million	12%
Common stock	$8 million	18%

7. Buchtel Industries above is evaluating a project which is expected to generate a $50,000 cash flow for 5 years with a salvage value in the 5th year of $25,000. What is the maximum amount that Buchtel Industries should pay for the project? If they pay this amount, what is the expected NPV of the project?

8. What is the expected rate of return on a project with a NPV of zero, financed with equal amount of debt costing 12 percent and equity with an opportunity rate of return of 20 percent? What is the WACC, assuming no taxes paid. If the firm is considering financing with 52 percent debt, how would the IRR on the project and the company's WACC change?

9. Monitor Software has a WACC of 14 percent. Its stock sells for $8, currently pays a dividend of $.50, and has a growth rate of 8 percent. If the debt outstanding is priced to yield to 10 percent, what are the proportions of debt and equity? Assume no taxes.

10. A business with 40 percent debt, yielding 10 percent before a tax rate of 40 percent, and the rest equity with an opportunity cost of capital of 20 percent, is contemplating an investment with an NPV of zero. Calculate the WACC, listing the steps involved in calculating the WACC.

11. In problem 10 , should the business make the investment?

12. If the stock of Geothermal, pp. 333–334 in the chapter, is selling at $24 and the equity required rate of return is 20 percent, what is the WACC of Geothermal?

13. In problem 12 , would you recommend that Geothermal make the expansion?

14. In problem 12, what annual amount must Geothermal earn on the investment to provide bondholders and stockholders their required rate of return?

SOLUTIONS TO PROBLEMS

1. The required rate of return (RRR) is the risk-free rate plus the beta times the market-risk premium (required return on the market portfolio minus the risk-free rate) or:

    RRR = .05 + 1.1(.08) = 13.8%

    Since Allequity has no debt, the required return on the stock is the cost of capital and the <u>minimum</u> acceptable return on any new investments.

2. The recent yield to maturity is a proxy of the pre-tax required rate of return on bonds of Bryon Corp. At a price of 94 percent of face value or $940 with annual coupon payments of 7 percent of $1000 or $70 for 18 years with a final cash flow of $1000 at maturity,

    Financial calculator: $940 PV, $1000 FV, $70 PMT, 18 N
    I = 7.62% yield to maturity

    The approximate market rate of return on Bryon Corp.'s long-term debt is 7.62 percent.

3. The after-tax cost of debt is the pre-tax rate of 7.62 percent times 1 minus the marginal tax rate of 40 percent or:

    After-tax cost of debt = 7.62%(1 − .4) = 4.57%

4. The WACC for Bryon Corp., using the market value of debt and equity as weights is:

    WACC = (10/30).0457 + (20/30).18 = 13.52%

    If a recent investment proposal had a positive NPV after discounting the expected cash flows at the cost of capital, 13.5 percent, the rate of return of the project is greater than 13.5 percent.

5. The required rate of return (RRR) on the preferred stock of Akron Tire is the yield now demanded by the market or,

    RRR = $9 dividend/$105 price = 8.57%

6. Buchtel Industries has a total market value of $16 million and an after-tax cost of debt of 10%(1 − .4) = 6%.

    WACC = 5/16 × .06 + 3/16 × .12 + 8/16 × .18 = 13%

7. Using the WACC calculated in problem 6 above, discount the 5th year, $50,000 annuity and single cash flow (5th year) value of $25,000 at 13 percent:

PV = $50,000(3.517) + $25,000(.543) = $189,425

The present value or maximum investment of $189,425 would generate an internal rate of return of 13 percent, yielding the sources of funding, including equity, their required rate of return.

8. WACC = .5(.12) + .5(.20) = 16%

If the project cash flows discounted at the WACC of 16 percent yields a NPV = 0, the expected IRR on the project equals the WACC of 16 percent. Any variation in the funding mix should not affect the expected return on the project, but just divide the cash flow earnings among the sources of funding.

9. This problem works back from the WACC of 14 percent to determine the debt/total value and equity/total value ratios. Using the constant growth estimate of price as the expected dividend in period one, $.50(1.08) = $.54, divided by the difference between the required rate of return on equity and the growth rate or:

$$r = \frac{Div_1}{P} + g$$

r = $.54/$8 + .08

r = .1475%

Let x = Debt/total value ratio
$1 - x$ = Equity/total value ratio

WACC = .10x + .1475(1 − x) = .14

x = 15.8% debt proportion
$1 - x$ = 84.2% equity proportion

10. The after-tax cost of debt is 10%(1 − .4) = 6%

WACC = .06 (.4) + .20 (.6) = .144 or 14.4%

1. Calculate the proportional weights of each source of capital, using market values.
2. Determine the required rate of return today of each security.
3. Calculate the WACC.

11. If the project has an NPV of zero calculated by discounting expected cash flows at the 14.4 percent WACC, the IRR on the project equals 14.4 percent and will provide the required rate of return to each source of capital. Assume a $100,000 investment invested at 14.4 percent, the WACC, generating $14,400 each year and available for interest on the debt and returns to equity. Forty percent or $40,000 of the $100,000 investment is financed by debt; 60 percent or $60,000 is financed by equity.

    $ 14,400 14.4% return on $100,000
    – 2,400 $40,000 debt @ 10% cost of debt(1–.4)
    $ 12,000 Available for $60,000 equity contribution or

$12,000/$60,000 = 20% return on equity

Both debt and equity will receive their required rate of return if the investment is invested at the WACC or if the NPV on an investment equals zero.

If the project earns an IRR greater than the WACC, or if the NPV is greater than zero, the shareholders will receive a return greater than their RRR. For example, if the investment earns a 20% return, the returns to equity on the $60,000 of contributed equity is:

    $20,000 ($100,000 × 20%)
     –2,400 after-tax cost of debt (does not change)
    $17,600 earnings available for common

$17,600/$60,000 equity or a 29.3 percent rate of return on equity. The expected rates of return (IRR) on equity on positive NPV projects exceed the WACC.

12. If Geothermal's stock were priced at $24, the market value capital structure would be:

    Debt $194.0 million (26.3%)
    Equity 543.6 million (73.7%)
        $737.6 million 100.0%

    WACC = .263(.08) + .737(.2) = .168 or 16.8%

The market value of the assets is the same as the value of the securities, $737.6 million. The increased proportion of equity and recent higher required rates of return (now 18 percent) increased the WACC to 16.8 percent.

13. The expected IRR on the project of 15 percent is less than the WACC of 16.8 percent. Jo Ann would recommend that the project be rejected because the IRR is less than the WACC.

14. The investment must earn the WACC or 16.8 percent to earn the required rate of return for shareholders.

$5,040,000 (16.8% return on $30 million)
− 631,000 (.263 × $30 million × .08 cost of debt)
$4,409,000 (Available for common investment of .737 × $30 million or
            $22,110,000)

$4,409,000/$22,110,000 = .20 or 20%

The project is expected to only earn 15 percent per year or .15 × $30 million = $4.5 million, less than the $5.04 million (above) needed to compensate investors at their RRR. The proof is:

$4,500,000 (15% return on $30 million)
− 631,000 (cost of debt)
$3,869,000 return on $22,110,000 equity.

The ROE is $3,869,000/$22,110,000 = .175 or 17.5 percent. The 15 percent project return would earn shareholders 17.5 percent which is less than the 20 percent needed to retain investors in the stock at $24. If the investment is made, selling pressure on the stock is likely to drop the price to provide the RRR of 20 percent.

CHAPTER 12

CORPORATE FINANCING AND THE LESSONS OF MARKET EFFICIENCY

INTRODUCTION

This is the first of three chapters related to financing in financial markets. An earlier section reviewed asset investment, followed by the last section covering concepts bridging asset investment and financial markets (financing). To understand the variables and the process of making financing decisions, one must first consider a few assumptions related to the financial markets and investors. These are covered in this chapter.

The first section of the chapter covers the efficient market hypothesis in a very readable, practical presentation. Varying degrees of efficiency are covered as are classic issues such as timing and other issues related to less than efficient markets. Your former experiences with efficient markets was in your microeconomics course. Comparing the pure competitive model of economics with the efficient markets discussion with multiple period decision periods and variability of results of decisions (risk) will help you make the transition from prior knowledge to this chapter.

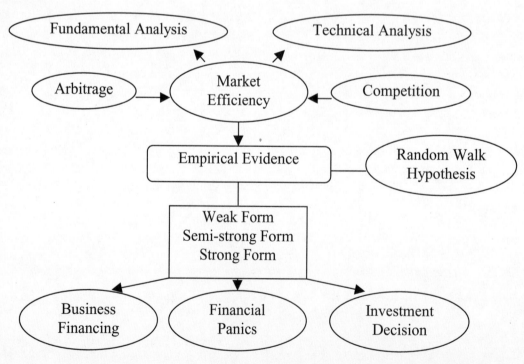

LEARNING CHECKLIST

This is a challenging concepts chapter. Read and study to grasp the concepts and be able to:

____1. Show how competition among investors leads to efficient markets.
____2. Cite evidence that supports the hypothesis that security markets are efficient, or evidence that financial markets are less than efficient.
____3. Understand the implications and impact of market efficiency on business financing decisions.

SOURCES OF BUSINESS INFORMATION

Economy Watch: People talk about interest rates going up and down as if all rates move together. However, a loan of 1 month is fundamentally different from a loan for 5 years. Short-term and long-term rates behave quite differently. Take a look at the business section of a newspaper such as www.nationalpost.com/financialpost, and you will see various interest rates across a wide range of possible future loan maturity dates. What matters is the overall movement of interest rates. Since those rates are used every day by real people making real financial, legal, and economic commitments. Virtually, they say about the future of the economy. For example, with a large mortgage, if you believe that the interest rate will soon rise, then you may want to convert to a longer-term mortgage at the relatively low interest rates currently available. The concern is whether it is cheaper to raise money today or tomorrow.

Everything Must be Paid: You probably have heard about the dollar-cost averaging investment. With this method, you buy securities in regular allotments instead of all at once. The idea is to avoid committing all your money and losing sleep. In principle, buying in stages allows you to purchase more units when prices are down while keeping a structured investment plan when values are higher. In practice, dollar-cost averaging can be quite expensive since commissions would apply for each transaction. Believe or not, there are reports suggesting you get higher returns by investing in one lump-sum as opposed to in-stages through dollar-cost averaging. Visit a few Web sites such as www.smartmoney.com and www.yahoo.com, to check out what the stock investing experts say in this matter. Anyway, dollar-cost averaging should be best viewed as forced savings. What do you think about gradual investing versus not investing at all?

CHAPTER OUTLINE, KEY CONCEPTS, AND TERMS

I. **DIFFERENCES BETWEEN INVESTMENT AND FINANCING DECISIONS**

    A.   Financing decisions are more complicated than investment decisions for the variety of securities to sell is large and continually expanding, the number of financial institutions providing financing is extensive, and the market is very competitive.

    B.   In some ways financing decisions are easier than investment decisions. Financial decisions may be reversed more easily than investment decisions. The level of competition in financial markets is extensive so it is hard to make an incorrect financial decision. All prices, rates, and terms are fair, or are true values, and unlike investment decisions that usually provide positive net present values, financing decisions usually provide fairly priced, zero NPVs.

    C.   Funds are raised, or securities are sold in efficient capital markets, or markets where security prices rapidly reflect all relevant information, currently available, about asset values.

    D.   In efficient markets all securities are fairly priced, so financing is always a zero NPV transaction.

    E.   The rest of the chapter discusses the efficient market hypothesis, providing a background of the idea, its logic, and several tests of market efficiency.

II. **WHAT IS AN EFFICIENT MARKET?**

    A.   **A Startling Discovery: Price Changes Are Random**

        1.   Research by Maurice Kendall indicated that security market price changes were unrelated to prior price changes with no predictable trends or patterns or that the prices tended to be a **random walk** over time. See Figure 12.1 in the textbook.

        2.   Support of the efficient market theory is indicated in the scatter diagram of daily price changes of the stock of Weyerhaeuser during a 30-year period. The dots are evenly distributed in the four quadrants, indicating no recurring pattern of price changes, or that price changes are random.

3. Another test of the efficient market theory is to review the level of correlation between daily price changes. Much research has indicated little correlation or low correlation coefficients (close to zero). New information is random; prices react accordingly.

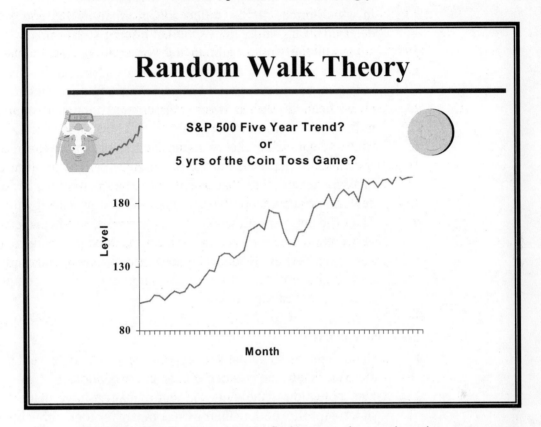

4. **Technical analysts** attempt to find patterns in security price movements and trade accordingly. Their trading tends to quickly offset any price trend and keep the markets efficient.

B. **Three Forms of the Efficient-Market Theory**

1. The first form of market efficiency is **weak-form efficiency** which is a situation in which market prices rapidly reflect all information contained in the history of past prices. Past price movements are random; the past cannot predict future price changes.

2. **Fundamental analysts** attempt to find under- or over-valued securities by analyzing "fundamental" information, such as earnings, asset values, etc., to uncover yet undiscovered information about the future of a business. They look ahead trying to forecast future information; technical analysts are studying past prices, looking for predictable patterns. New information is quickly reflected in the price of the stock, and investors were not able to earn superior returns by buying or selling after the announcement date.

3.   A second form of market efficiency, **semi-strong form efficiency**, is a market situation in which market prices reflect all publicly available information.

4.   A third form of market efficiency, **strong-form efficiency**, is a situation in which prices rapidly reflect *all* information that could be used to determine true value. In this market pricing situation, all prices would always be fairly priced and no investor would be able to make superior, accurate forecasts of future price changes. Even professional portfolio managers do not consistently outperform the market, thus supporting the creation of "index" portfolios, assembled to match popular market indices.

5.   The efficient market theory implies that security market prices represent fair value. Some argue this cannot be since prices go up and down, and that fair value should change very little. Fair market value changes with new information about the future cash flows associated with a security.

6.   The efficient-market theory implies that portfolio managers work in a very competitive market with little or no added advantage over the next portfolio manager. They make few extraordinary returns, not because they are incompetent, but because the markets are so competitive and there are few easy profits.

C.   **No Theory is Perfect**

1.   Though the efficient markets hypothesis is well supported by research, there are a few unexplained events and exceptions.

2.   One exception is the evidence that managers have made consistently superior profits trading their own company's stock, probably with good insider information, but testing the strong-form efficiency theory. The

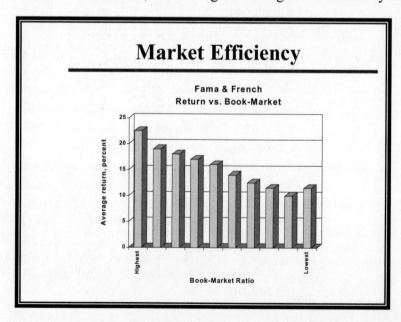

managers know more about the company's opportunities than other market participants.

3. Small firm stocks have consistently outperformed large firm stocks, especially in January, questioning even the weak-form efficiency hypothesis. The fact that other yet-explained variables are involved is the likely answer.

D. **The Crash of 1987**

1. The 11 percent drop in the TSE 300 Composite Index and the 20 percent decline in the S&P 500 on Monday, October 19, 1987, led many to question the efficient-market theory. Critics assumed the market had no new information, that prices were irrationally high before the crash, or irrationally low after the crash.

2. A slight drop in market growth prospects could have produced the decline.

3. The challenge related to studying common stock valuation has *two* implications:

    a. Investors value stocks related to yesterday's price, which is assumed to be correct. When the prior price is deemed to be incorrect, an adjustment is made to find the fair value of the market.

    b. The assumption that yesterday's price was the true fair value is difficult to verify. Price adjustments of significant magnitude may be plausible if adjustments are explained on a relative basis.

III. **LESSONS OF MARKET EFFICIENCY**

A. **Markets Have No Memory**

1. Even though the efficient-markets theory assumes that past prices contain no information about future prices, or that prices are a random walk, financial managers often act as if they did not accept such a hypothesis:

    a. Managers are reluctant to issue stock after a decline, waiting for a rebound.

    b. Managers favour the issuance of equity over debt after an increase in equity values. They are attempting to sell when the stock is high, reducing the dilution of EPS.

    c. Managers are reluctant to sell equity if favourable announcements are to be made in the future, but inside information has nothing to do with past prices, only the future of the firm.

B.	**There Are No Financial Illusions**
1.	Investors are not concerned with accounting income and its measurement or timing, only cash flows.
2.	Creative accounting is an invisible curtain to analysts, but managers feel others benefit with their "smoke and mirrors" accounting methods.
3.	Research indicates that such creative announcements produce no long-term value, and that only information related to future cash flows are "value relevant" information to the market.

C.	**There Are No Free Lunches on Wall Street or Bay Street**
1.	Trust market prices in an efficient market. There is no better deal tomorrow.
2.	Term structure differences in interest rates offer no deal for today or tomorrow. The markets' expectations of future interest rates determine the rate differences over time. Choosing short or long-term rates for financing or investment will likely yield or cost the same over the long term.

COMPLETION QUESTIONS

1.	Competition in financial markets is (*less/more*) thorough than in most product markets.

2.	Financial markets in which security prices rapidly reflect all relevant information about asset values are called _____ capital markets.

3.	Prices that are equally likely to rise or fall on any particular day, regardless of price movements on previous days, are said to follow a _____ _____ .

4.	With remarkable unanimity statistical researchers have concluded that there is (*little/much*) useful information in the sequence of stock prices.

5.	_____ analysts are persons who attempt to find patterns in security price movements.

6.	According to (*strong/weak*) -form efficiency, market prices rapidly reflect all information contained in the history of past prices.

7.	_____ analysts are persons who attempt to value securities by examining information about the firms's earnings, assets, and business prospects.

8.	In semi-strong-form efficiency investors (*can/cannot*) make superior profits by using information that is publicly available.

9. The strong-form efficiency means that people having private information (*can/cannot*) consistently outperform the market after taking account of differences in risk.

10. Investors who agree with strong-form efficiency would be more likely to buy (*index funds/individual stocks*).

11. Stock prices (*do/do not*) represent fair values because they do rise and fall.

12. According to (*strong/weak*) -form efficiency, approximately half of a group of professional portfolio managers will outperform the market in any particular year.

13. If stock prices were consistently more volatile in one month compared to all other months, this would be (*consistent/inconsistent*) with weak-form efficiency.

14. Small company stocks have significantly (*higher/lower*) returns in January, compared to larger firms.

15. The "January Effect" (*is/is not*) consistent with weak-form market efficiency.

16. Sudden downturns in the stock market, like the crash of 1987, can be explained by a sudden (*decrease/increase*) in investor expectations about the future growth rate in dividends.

17. The belief that markets have (*considerable/no*) memory and that prices follow a random walk is another way of stating the (*strong/weak*)-form efficient market theory.

18. Researchers have shown that investors (*are/are not*) mislead by accounting changes designed to (*deflate/inflate*) earnings.

19. If a company splits its stock two-for-one and has no changes to report in its future prospects, its stock price will (*fall by one-half/stay the same*).

20. If interest rates are lower on 2-year bonds in comparison with those on 1-year bonds, the market is forecasting a (*decrease/increase*) in short-term interest rates.

PROBLEMS

1. Bill Begee, head of Korrison-Minudsen, has instructed his chief accounting officer to employ the most aggressive accounting practices that are legal so as to report the highest possible earnings for the company. What likely effect will this action have on K-M's stock price?

2. If security markets are truly efficient, explain why all stocks don't provide the same return to investors?

3. "According to the strong-form of the efficient markets hypothesis (EMH), there are no surprises in security markets." Explain why this is not a true statement.

4. Professional investors should be able to outperform the market. Explain why this statement is true or false according to the EMH.

5. Chief financial officers of companies are well-advised to time their security offerings. Explain whether or not this is the case according to the EMH.

6. What does a downward sloping yield curve indicate that investors are expecting to happen to long-term interest rates?

ANSWERS TO COMPLETION QUESTIONS

1. more
2. efficient
3. random walk
4. little
5. Technical
6. weak
7. Fundamental
8. cannot
9. cannot
10. index funds
11. do
12. strong
13. consistent
14. higher
15. is not
16. decrease
17. no, weak
18. are not, inflate
19. fall by one-half
20. decrease

SOLUTIONS TO PROBLEMS

1. The effect will be nothing substantial either in the short- or long-run. This is because investors are very savvy and are typically not fooled by manipulation of financial statements. Creative accounting does not succeed in distorting underlying values that are reflected in stock prices.

2. All stocks don't provide the same returns to investors because different stocks have different risks. The expected returns reflect these perceived risks. Investors will only purchase higher risk stocks <u>if</u> they expect to be rewarded accordingly. On the other hand, investors will accept lower returns if they believe the risk of realizing those returns is lower.

3. The quoted statement in this problem is simply not an accurate interpretation of the efficient markets hypothesis (EMH). The EMH does not hold that investors know the future. Investors are not perfect forecasters. Rather the EMH states that security prices reflect information that is currently available. No one knows exactly what will happen tomorrow. Investors act on what is known today and their actions result in prices that are based on this information. Surprises certainly do occur but investors expect future returns that match their risk assessments.

4. There is a level of anticipated risk in the market. Investors expect to receive rewards corresponding to that level. But these returns have occurred on average for many cases over long periods of time. A similar generalization can be made for professional investors who are seeking undervalued stocks relative to the value determined by perceived riskiness. Thus over the long-run and for numerous instances, the returns will indeed have higher average amounts. Professional investors tend to do this. They are in the market for long periods of time and are making hundreds and hundreds of investments. If they undertake higher than average risks, they will tend to have higher than average returns and thus "beat the market." But many of these professionals will fail to meet the averages from time to time, especially those who are consistently taking the higher risks. Some analysts tend to make more insightful use of available information, which also helps them to realize superior returns from time to time.

5. No one without special knowledge that will have a predictable effect on values will be able to consistently earn higher returns than expected, given the level of perceived risk. Financial managers may be able to make more informed judgments about the future potential performance of their firm. However, the marketplace is the ultimate determiner of value. Even the insider doesn't know what will happen to other firms, to the economy, or to the stock market. Furthermore, company executives may be overly optimistic or super-aggressive as was hinted in problem 1. The most obvious example of the folly of believing that financial managers should be able to wisely time

the security market actions is in the case of interest rates. Statistical analyses of historical interest rate patterns cast overwhelming doubt on those who claim to be able to know what will happen to interest rates.

6.   When the yield curve is downward sloping, short-term rates are higher than long-term rates. This situation is an indication that investors expect a decline in long-term rates. When this is the case, investors try to lock-in the current long-term rates by buying long-term bonds. This tends to drive their price up resulting in lower yields. Also investors will be shifting out of short-term debt that tends to force the short-term debt prices down resulting in higher short-term yields. These actions cause the downward slope in the yield curve.

CHAPTER 13

AN OVERVIEW OF CORPORATE FINANCING

INTRODUCTION

This is the second chapter on business financing. It covers the many varieties of financing alternatives available in financial markets. There is an in-depth discussion of common stock, preferred stock, and debt securities. Much of the discussion focuses on the standard terms of common stock, etc., that most of you learned in accounting. Here, try to focus on the risk/return considerations of each of the characteristics, features, or covenants discussed. Each feature affects the future cash flows, their timing, and variability. Keep this valuation theme in your mind as you study the details. At the end of the chapter is a section related to historical patterns of corporate financing. This section provides a good historical perspective for understanding today and, important to you, the future. The bond refunding decision is discussed in the appendix.

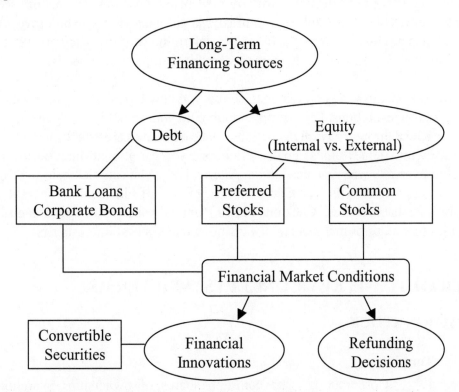

LEARNING CHECKLIST

After studying this chapter, you should be able to:

_____1. Compare and contrast the three major securities discussed, common stock, preferred stock, and bonds as to maturity, claims on income, claims on assets in case of liquidation, and voice in management of the firm.

_____2. Name and discuss variations of the above securities and special terms or covenants that increase or decrease the risk/return potential for investors and the issuing business.

_____3. Summarize recent trends in the use made by firms of different sources of financing.

_____4. Explain the bond refunding decision.

SOURCES OF BUSINESS INFORMATION

Bonds or Stocks, not Tea or Coffee? How should you include debt or equity instruments in your portfolio? It is not an easy question. Generally speaking, bonds offer stable interest income and relative safety of principal. Stocks may be poor in providing steady income, but are good at price appreciation. Furthermore, stocks have greater tax advantages. Having noticed all these, you get really excited about stocks. However, your financial situation and investment objective are the guiding keys for the selection. Are you a security-conscious, an income-seeking or growth-oriented investor? The Bank of Montreal MatchMaker at www.bmoinvesting.com/ec/matchmaker.asp provides a simple "self-test" to determine your investing profile. Based on the information, you choose what is the best mix to suit your particular needs.

Make a Plan: As you know, a good roadmap shows you how to reach your destination. Look at those New Year's resolutions. For example, double up your monthly mortgage payments or maximize your RRSP through payroll deductions. Once objectives are established, you are very much on your own to achieve these goals. Of course, you can mount them on the wall and remind yourself everyday what you need to do. Alternatively, you can seek help from qualified financial planning professionals. The Canadian Association of Financial Planners (CAFP) at www.cafp.org is a reliable source. Click on "Find a Planner" search icon. This organization has a code of ethics that requires members to always put a client's best interests first.

CHAPTER OUTLINE, KEY CONCEPTS, AND TERMS

I.   **COMMON STOCK**

    A.   **Terminology**

        1.   Corporations issue common shares of ownership. Shareholders or stockholders own the shares and may trade the shares.

2. Common stock has several classifications or "sets" of shares. The total possible number of shares that the company may issue are the shares **authorized** by a vote of the common stock. Of the authorized, usually a large proportion are **issued**, and the rest are authorized, not issued. Of the issued, most are **outstanding**, except the **treasury** shares which have been repurchased by the company in the U.S. In Canada, however, treasury stock is not allowed. Consequently, the number of shares issued always equals the number of shares outstanding.

3. The number of outstanding shares are used to calculate dividends and earnings per share.

4. When a share is issued or sold it is recorded or "booked" usually at a nominal, low **par value**. If sold above par, the remainder is recorded in the **paid-in capital** or capital surplus account of the general ledger. Today, common shares mostly do not have a par value due to the changes in the Canadian Business Corporations Act.

5. Cumulative earnings, not paid out in dividends, but reinvested in the firm, are accounted for in the **retained earnings** account.

6. Net common stockholders equity is the sum of the common stock account recorded at par value, the paid-in surplus, and the retained earnings, less the amount of repurchased or treasury stock. The amount represents the historical value of money raised from the sale of stock plus earnings retained over the past, less the amount of shares repurchased.

B. **Book Value versus Market Value**

1. Net common stockholders equity is recorded at original, historical book value.

2. The market value of common equity is the product of the number of shares *outstanding* times the current market value per share.

3. The market value is determined in the market based on the prospects of future cash flows, their timing, and the riskiness of the cash flow.

4. Market value is usually greater than book value if the managers have been investing in positive, added value creating, net present value investments. If actual NPVs are negative for the business over time, the economic or market value will be less than the accounting or book value.

Book Value vs. Market Value Example (Canadian Pacific, Ltd.)

Common Stock

Example — Canadian Pacific Ltd (CP) Book Value vs. Market Value (12/2002)
Total Shares Outstanding = 314 million

Common Shares	1,695,000,000
Additional Paid-in Capital	227,500,000
Retained Earnings	7,274,400,000
Foreign Currency Translation Adjustments	138,600,000
Net Common Equity (Book Value)	$9,335,500,000

December 2002 Market Price = $42.75
# of Shares   × 314 million

Market Value $13.4 billion

C. **Dividends**

1. The board of directors declare dividends. They are not contractual like interest payments to creditors.

2. Unlike interest expense, dividends are deemed a return of capital by Canada Customs and Revenue Agency (CCRA), and are not a *deductible* expense.

D. **Stockholders' Rights**

1. Stockholders, as owners of the corporation, have ultimate responsibility for the actions of the company.

2. Shareholders delegate most decisions to the board of directors they elect, and the management that is appointed by the board. Some decisions related to the number of authorized shares, mergers, etc., are retained by shareholders.

172

3.　　The board, comprised of insiders, (corporate officers), and non-executive directors appoints top managers and provides an overview of managerial activities and performance for the shareholders.

E.　**Voting Procedures**

1.　　Shareholders vote for members of the board of directors, using one of two voting methods.

2.　　When each vacant board seat is voted upon *one at a time*, with one vote per share, a majority vote is needed for election. Under this **majority** voting method, a dominant shareholder group, electing one board member at a time, can usually elect their candidates to all positions.

3.　　Under the **cumulative** voting procedure all directors are elected in one vote. Minority group shareholders may cumulate their votes (number of shares times directors elected) and cast a block of votes. The largest block of votes appoints the first director and so on.

4.　　Shareholders may delegate or proxy their vote to others, usually management-oriented shareholders or dissident shareholder groups. A **proxy contest** occurs when shareholder groups compete with existing management for control of the board and the corporation.

5.　　The Ontario Securities Commission (OSC) recently introduced regulations intended to give the votes of the minority shareholders the same acknowledgement for important corporate decisions such as mergers as those of majority shareholders.

F.　**Classes of Stock**

1.　　While a single class of common stock is prevalent, some corporations have various types of restricted shares, such as restricting the voting rights or dividend rights of one of the classes.

2.　　A **coattail provision** ensures the rights to participate in takeover bids are granted for subordinate voting shares.

G.　**Corporate Governance in Canada and Elsewhere**

1.　　The separation between ownership (principals) and management (agents) may create a potential conflict of interest between owners and managers. The study of this conflict and resolutions is called agency theory.

2.　　The Japanese structure of holding companies and interlocking directorships and share ownership is called a *kiretsu*. The combination of industrial and financial firms provides for less "public" borrowing or financing and a better focus on long-term versus short-term performance.

3.　　Similar arrangements, *chaebols*, can be found in South Korea and central Europe.

II.   PREFERRED STOCK

A.   The terms of **preferred stock**, especially the priority of claims on the declared dividend pool and the claim on assets in case of liquidation, are ahead of those of common stock.

B.   In exchange for the above preferred treatment, preferred stockholders usually waive their full voting rights and accept a fixed dividend return.

C.   The **net worth** of a corporation is the sum of the common and preferred stockholders' equity accounts. When no preferred is outstanding, net worth and common stockholders' equity are the same.

D.   Preferred dividends, like common dividends, are not tax deductible. Preferred dividend income, if received by a Canadian corporation through its investment in preferred stock, is not taxed. As a result, preferred share financing is popular here.

E.   If declared, preferred dividends are paid before common dividends are paid, and usually are cumulative. Cumulative preferred is very common and requires that if dividends are passed in one period (common would have been passed also), the averages will be paid in the future before any common dividends are paid.

F.   Even without a final repayment date, preferred stocks can be redeemable at the call price by the firm, or retractable by the investors at a specific date.

G.   Some preferred stocks are **floating-rate preferred** with their dividend varying or floating with the change in a specific index or interest rate level.

H.   Some preferred shares are convertible into common shares at a preset price before an expiration date.

III.   CORPORATE DEBT

A.   **Concepts**

1.   Common and preferred stock represent ownership and voting control in a corporation; corporate borrowings are non-ownership contractual obligations to receive amounts of capital for corporate investment projects, pay a usually fixed cost interest rate on the debt, and repay the principal at maturity or in payments (sinking fund).

2. Interest expense on debt is tax deductible, unlike common and preferred dividends. A company with a 34 percent tax rate would effectively pay (1 − .34) or 66 cents on any dollar of interest expense.

B. **Debt Comes in Many Forms**

1. There are many variations of interest rates, terms, repayment provisions, seniority of claims in case of liquidation, collateral, and risk.

2. The interest rate paid, or coupon rate, is the going market rate at the time the money is borrowed. Some bonds are zero coupon, discount bonds; others have rates that are adjustable. The bank **prime rate** or *LIBOR* varies with market interest rates.

3. **Funded debt** is debt payable after one year; unfunded debt is short-term bank loans, a current liability. Funded debt such as bonds often have long maturities.

4. Debt comes due! Repayment may be at maturity, but more commonly is paid-off in instalments or payments. A **sinking fund** is an arrangement for periodic payments to a fund, or to reduce the amount outstanding (buy back bonds).

5. **Callable bonds** are able to be paid-off early, the price stipulated in the contract, at the discretion of the borrower. Firms are more likely to call bonds when interest rates have fallen or when their investments have generated high levels of cash flows. Sometimes a bond is call-protected for a certain time period during which firms cannot issue a call.

6. Some unsecured, general creditors may, for a higher interest rate, be positioned as **subordinated debt**, which means if the firm defaults the senior general creditors are paid-off from the dissolution of assets before the subordinated creditors.

7. If collateral, such as plant and equipment, railroad cars, or land is pledged backing the debt obligation, the bonds are **secured bonds**.

8. Funded debt may, at the corporation's option, be *rated* by rating services such as Dominion Bond Rating Service, Moody's, or Standard and Poor's. If the securities have minimum default risk, they will be awarded an **investment grade**. Below investment grade, securities have the infamous title of **junk bonds**.

9. Bonds issued in specific currency denominations such as Swiss franc and sold in the corresponding countries are called foreign bonds. Euro dollars are dollar denominated short-term deposits held in foreign banks outside Canada. Don't mix up with the euro which is the new European common currency. A bond denominated in Canadian dollars that is sold internationally is called a euro bond.

10. Securities may be sold to the broad general public class of investors called a **public offering**, or "placed" with a small group of investors, usually financial institutions, called a **private placement**. The publicly

175

offered, and later publicly traded, securities are more likely to have a ready market in case investors wish to sell the securities.

11.   Lenders impose a number of conditions on borrowing companies, called **protective covenants**.

12.   Variations of debt, such as a **lease**, are common. Instead of borrowing and buying a productive asset, such as machinery, the business may lease, not own, paying lease payments instead of debt instalments.

C.   **An Example: The Terms of Heniz's Bond Issue** — See Table 13.3 in the textbook for a description of Alcan's bond issue. Note the above mentioned terminology and characteristics of the bonds. Look up its market price in The Globe and Mail.

D.   **Innovation in the Debt market**

1.   As conditions and needs of investors and corporations change, new types of funding contracts arise.

2.   The Canadian government has issued so-called **indexed bonds** whose payments are tied with the inflation rate. Other bond's return may be indexed to the price or value of a commodity or interest rate.

3.   **Reverse floaters** are variable rate bonds that pay a higher rate when other interest rates fall, and vice versa.

4.   Many types of loans and assets are being repackaged (i.e., securitized) and resold as **asset-backed bonds**. Securitization can be done through multi-sellers or a single-seller.

IV.   **CONVERTIBLE SECURITIES** — Some bonds may be issued with options that grant the investor the right to *buy* shares of common stock (warrants) or the option to *trade* the bond for a stated number of shares of common stock (convertible).

V.   **PATTERNS OF CORPORATE FINANCING**

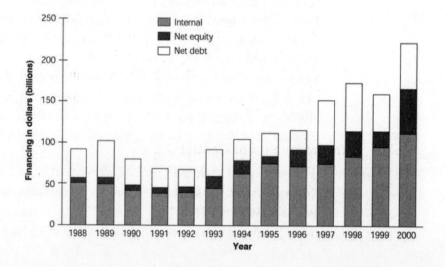

A. **Choices**

1. Funds for investment may be raised from external (debt or equity security issues) or internal sources, such as cash flows from operations.
2. **Internally generated funds**, derived mostly from net income retained in the period plus non-cash depreciation expenses (cash flow from operations) are a major source of funds for both Canadian corporations and businesses of other countries.

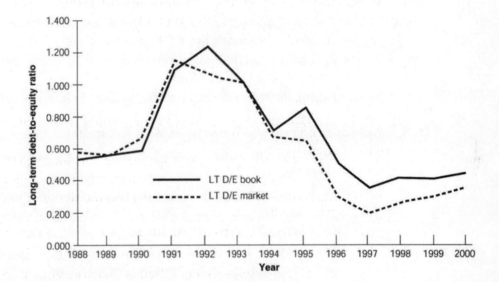

B. **Do Firms Rely Too Heavily on Internal Funds?**

1. Research by Gordon Donaldson indicates that a business' growth or investment growth rate is determined by the growth rate of internally generated funds, rather than the quantity of positive NPV investments.
2. Managers that do not wish to be critically assessed or monitored by the financial markets and financial institutions when financing externally might follow this strategy.
3. The costs of financing externally is avoided when internally generated funds are used as in the possible downward movement in stock prices when a new equity issue is announced. Investors feel managers "signal" lower expected profits when new equity is issued, rather than a debt issue announcement where expectations are for higher profits in the future.

C. **External Sources of Capital**

1. The financing trends of early 1990s reveals that debt issues were popular. During late 1990s, net equity issues were negative suggesting stock buybacks were also popular.

2.   However, following the downturn in stock market prices, share repurchase programs have been declining. Stable (book value) debt-to-equity ratios are observed lately.

3.   Compared with firms in the G-7 countries, Canadian corporations have increased their use of debt financing recently.

VI.   Bond Refunding Decision

A.   Basic Issues

1.   The call feature of a bond allows the issuing firm to redeem the bond earlier than its maturity.

2.   Refunding a bond issue involves buying back existing bond and replacing it with a new one.

3.   Falling interest rates are the driving force behind the refunding decision.

B.   Net Investment Costs Associated with Refunding

1.   When the firm calls the bond, it pays a fixed call price that is usually above the par.

2.   Such a non-tax-deductible **call premium**, the difference between the call price and the par value, is part of the incremental cost.

3.   Other cost involved is the **flotation cost** on a new issue that can be amortized over its life or 5 years, whichever is less.

4.   Since the firm issues a new bond before retiring the old one, there is a overlapping period from 1 to 3 months during which both issues are outstanding. Although the firm has to suffer **additional interest** on the old issue, this interest is tax deductible.

C.   Net Savings Associated with Refunding

1.   The difference between the yearly after-tax interest costs on the 2 issues determines the annual savings.

2.   As these savings will continue to be generated every year over the life of the new bond, their present values matter.

D.   Net Present Value Associated with Refunding

1.   Refunding a bond is similar to a capital budgeting decision relying on the NPV analysis. Only refunding projects with positive values should be undertaken. See the spreadsheet on p. 407.

COMPLETION QUESTIONS

1. Sources of finance are classified as _____ or _____.

2. Equity has a (*priority/residual*) claim on the firm.

3. Shares that are held by the company that have been issued but are not outstanding are called _____ stock, which are not allowed in Canada.

4. (*Book/Par*) value is the value of stock shown on the certificate.

5. Another name for additional paid-in-capital is capital _____.

6. Earnings not paid out as (*dividends/interest*) are retained earnings.

7. Book value is a (*backward/forward*) looking measure.

8. _____ value is usually greater than book value because of inflation and capital investments in projects with present values that exceed initial costs.

9. On most matters shareholder control is exercised through voting on (*board of directors/ company officers*).

10. The voting system in which all the votes of a shareholder can be cast for one board candidate is known as _____ voting.

11. The process in which outsiders compete with existing management for shareholders' votes is called a _____ contest.

12. A firm may have two or more classes of common stock which differ in their right to _____ and/or to receive _____.

13. Preferred stock has priority over (*bondholder/common stockholders*).

14. Net worth or _____ value (*does/does not*) include preferred stock.

15. If a firm goes out of business, preferred stockholders claims are (*behind/ahead of*) those of bondholders.

16. Preferred dividends (*are/are not*) deductible from taxable income.

17. (*0/50*) percent of dividends received by one Canadian corporation from another Canadian corporation are treated as taxable income.

18. Preferred stock paying dividends that vary with short-term interest rates are called _____-_____ preferred.

19. The deductibility of interest means, in effect, that the government (*discourages/subsidizes*) the use of debt.

20. _____-rate loans are tied to variations in the prime rate or the London _____ _____ _____ _____ (LIBOR).

21. Debt that is repayable more than one-year from the date of issue is called _____ debt.

22. A (*floating/sinking*) fund is established to retire debt before maturity.

23. A (*callable/secured*) bond may be repurchased by the firm before maturity at a specified price.

24. The call and sinking fund provisions (*do/do not*) effectively place a limit on capital gains for the investor.

25. A bond that is subordinated has claims that are junior to some other (*creditors/share-holders*).

26. Secured debtholders have claims on specified collateral that are (*junior/senior*).

27. _____ bonds have unusually high risks and high expected returns.

28. Eurodollars are dollar deposits held (*by foreigners/in banks outside Canada*).

29. Bonds that are sold throughout the world are called _____.

30. Private individuals (*do/do not*) usually buy private placements.

31. A protective covenant is a restriction placed on (*borrowers/lenders*).

32. A lease is similar to (*debt/preferred stock*).

33. Bonds having payments that are tied to some measure of prices are called_____ bonds.

34. Asset-back bonds have value derived from (*a pool of assets/claims on assets of a firm*).

35. The right to buy shares from a firm at a specified price before a set date is called a _____.

36. A convertible bond has a provision that allows the (*investor/issuer*) to exchange the bond for a predetermined number of shares.

37. Internally generated funds equals profits not paid out as dividends plus _____.

38. The cost of internally generated funds is (*less/more*) than the cost of money raised from a new stock issue.

39. Debt ratios in Canada are (*higher/lower*) than those found in most developing nations.

40. Refunding is likely if the cost of borrowing has (*risen/fallen*) since the old securities were issued.

41. Time remaining to maturity (*is/is not*) a factor for refunding an issue.

42. Refunding can be more beneficial to the (*bondholder/issuing firm*).

PROBLEMS

1. Bonnie's Boleros, Inc. (BBI) has authorized 1 million shares of common stock. How many shares are outstanding if the shareholders' equity portion of the balance sheet is:

ACCOUNT	$THOUSANDS
Common stock ($1 par)	200
Paid in surplus	400
Retained earnings	2000
Common equity	2600
Treasury stock	100
Net common equity	2500

2. If the treasury shares in problem were purchased on the open market for $5 per share, how many share of BBI are currently outstanding?

3. If BBI sold 50,000 shares of authorized but unissued stock for $10 per share, how would the shareholders' equity accounts change?

4. Suppose BBI issued 50,000 shares of preferred stock at $10 per share. How would this affect the shareholders' equity accounts shown in problem 1?

5.	Suppose a company has 8 directors being nominated for re-election by the owners of 1 million outstanding shares. How many shares would need to be controlled in order to elect at least 1 director if the cumulative voting process was in place?

6.	How many votes does the owner of 100 shares have to cast in the election described in the preceding problem?

7.	How many shares would be needed to elect at least one director in the situation outlined in problem 5 if majority voting procedures were in effect instead of cumulative voting?

8.	What would be the likely explanation for a case where Kali Company bonds are selling at a price that offers a yield to maturity of 9 percent when its preferred stock is yielding 8 percent? (Assume a 40 percent tax rate applies).

9.	The ABC Co. is considering whether or not to call an outstanding perpetual bond issue of $20 million today and re-issue them with a lower interest rate. The existing bonds pay 6 percent of par that was acceptable when the bonds were initially issued. Recently, the interest rate has gradually fallen down to 3 percent. The company thinks that bonds paying 3 percent of par can be issued as replacements. The call premium is $150 per bond and the total administrative costs are $1.5 million. Should the company refund the old issues? Assume the bond has a par value of $1000.

10.	Which of the following will tend to increase the cost of debt for a firm?
	a.	Subordination clause
	b.	Convertibility feature
	c.	Debenture classification

ANSWERS TO COMPLETION QUESTIONS

1.	debt, equity
2.	residual
3.	treasury
4.	Par
5.	surplus
6.	dividends
7.	backward
8.	Market
9.	board of directors
10.	cumulative
11.	proxy
12.	vote, dividends
13.	common stockholders

14. book, does
15. behind
16. are not
17. 0
18. floating, rate
19. subsidizes
20. Floating, Inter-bank Offered Rate
21. funded
22. sinking
23. callable
24. do
25. creditors
26. senior
27. Junk
28. in banks outside Canada
29. Eurobonds
30. do not
31. borrowers
32. debt
33. indexed
34. a pool of assets
35. warrant
36. investor
37. depreciation
38. less
39. lower
40. fallen
41. is
42. issuing firm

SOLUTIONS TO PROBLEMS

1. The par value per share multiplied by the shares issued equals the dollars of common stock entered on the balance sheet. So the shares issued must be:
   $$\$200,000/\$1 = 200,000$$

2. Since $5 per share was paid with a total outlay of $100,000, the number of treasury shares must be:
   $$\$100,000/\$5 = 20,000$$
   The number of shares outstanding equals the shares issued minus any treasury shares or:
   $$200,000 - 20,000 = 180,000$$

3. BBI would receive $10 for each of the 50,000 shares sold or a total of $500,000. This would be accounted for by adding the product of the 50,000 shares and the $1 per share par value to the par value account and 50,000 times the remaining $9 per share or $450,000 to the paid in surplus account.

4. There will be no effect on any of the shareholders' equity accounts because each of those shown in problem 1 pertained only to the common equity. While preferred stock is an equity security, it is limited as to claim and does not impact on the common stockholder for balance sheet entries.

5. There will be 8 votes for each share held. This means a total of 8 × 1 million or 8 million votes eligible to be cast in this election with the positions going to the top 8 vote-getters. Therefore, the minimum number of votes needed to elect 1 director is 1 million. This is equivalent to 1 million/8 or 125,000 shares.

6. Shareholders receive 8 votes for each share held so the owner of 100 shares would have 800 votes. These could be spread evenly or allocated to one or more of the nominees.

7. Under majority voting, the majority rules. This means that one share more that one half of the outstanding number of shares is needed to elect the directors. In this case it would be 500,001 shares. In most elections the number of shares actually voted is less than the number that are outstanding so as a practical matter it takes somewhat less than half of the outstanding shares to control the election. The important point is that one more than half the votes cast will elect all of the directors. No directors can be elected by the under 50 percent minority.

8. Taxes are the likely explanation. Companies (but not individuals) that receive dividends from another company only pay taxes on 30 percent of the dividends received. Companies (and individuals) must pay taxes on all interest received from corporate bonds they hold. For example, firms that pay taxes at the rate of 40 percent would have after-tax yields of $(1 - .4) \times 9$ or 5.4 percent on the bonds. The after-tax yield on the preferred stock is:
    $\{1 - (.3 \times .4)\} \times 8 = 7.04$ percent. The after-tax figures are in line with the risk and return relationship that says preferred stock is always riskier than the bonds issued by the same company.

9. $$\text{NPV} = \left[\frac{(0.06 - 0.03)}{0.03}\right]($20,000,000) - $150\left[\frac{$20,000,000}{$1,000}\right] - $1,500,000$$
    $= 20,000,000 - 3,000,000 - 1,500,000 = $15,500,000 > 0.$
    The refunding is worthwhile.

10. a. The subordination clause will increase the yield that firms must offer to investors because some other debt will be senior to the subordinated issue. This adds to the riskiness of that issue so investors will require a higher rate of return.

 b. The convertibility feature is a significant addition to the desirability of a bond. Investors therefore will not require as high a coupon as they would if the bond was not convertible.

 c. A debenture bond is not backed by any pledge of specific assets. This means in the case of trouble, they will have no preference over other creditors. The higher risk translates into higher expected returns.

CHAPTER 14

HOW CORPORATIONS ISSUE SECURITIES

INTRODUCTION

For most students this section is one of the most interesting and exciting, and this chapter in particular. Why? The initial public offering (IPO) is where all the sweat-equity of a business cumulates in riches. Mr. Bell, of Taco Bell, sold his taco stands to the public and eventually to Pepsico with a combination secondary and IPO and took home millions. In this chapter the process of going public, the role of investment banking, and a discussion of venture capitalists are presented. There are always a number of interesting current events from The Wall Street Journal and other sources to enrich this well-written chapter. Look for the large "tombstone" ads in the third section of the WSJ, or stop in at a local brokerage office in town and ask for copies of offering prospectus, which are given to investors thinking of buying newly issued securities.

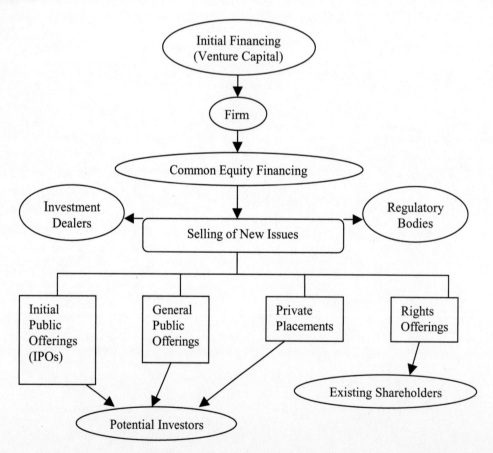

LEARNING CHECKLIST

After studying this chapter you should be able to:

____1. Understand how venture capital firms design successful deals and how they obtain their return on their investment.

____2. Understand the process of making an initial public offering (IPO) and the costs of an IPO. Who receives the "costs" of going public?

____3. Know the process and terms associated with a new security offering by an established firm (not an IPO), both a public cash offering and a private placement. Who are the parties involved?

____4. Explain the role and services of the underwriter in an issue of securities.

____5. Know how the new and small firms get their financing.

SOURCES OF BUSINESS INFORMATION

Initial Public Offerings Online: When you are drowning in tears by the disappointing stock market performance, investing in an IPO is also an excellent way to lose your shirt! Since an IPO is the first time that a company offers shares to the public, buying shares by then surely provides a head start of a new investment opportunity. While nothing is ever too good to be true, an IPO has its drawbacks. The IPO Center associated with the Microsoft Network at http://moneycentral.msn.com/investor/market/ipomain.asp offers information on upcoming IPOs. Under "New Filings," is a complete list of companies that have filed, but not yet started trading. To see companies that are trading now, visit "IPO Performance." To learn about IPO, check out the "IPO Basics."

Going Public: In order to make Canadian public securities filings accessible to all, the Canadian Securities Administrators (CSA) and the Canadian Depository for Securities (CDS) have developed a Web site at www.sedar.com. As an investor, you can find and retrieve company or mutual fund profiles, new filings and the latest news at the System Electronic Document Analysis and Retrieval (SEDAR). As an agent, you can speed up the filing process required by the Canadian securities regulatory bodies. If you are curious about the rules for electronic filing, information can be found online as well.

CHAPTER OUTLINE, KEY CONCEPTS, AND TERMS

I. VENTURE CAPITAL

A. Equity capital provided to a promising new business is called **venture capital**. Venture capital is provided by wealthy individuals (angels), investment companies, and some pension funds.

Venture Capital

First Stage Market Value Balance Sheet ($mil)

Assets		Liabilities and Equity	
Cash from new equity	0.5	New equity from venture capital	0.5
Other assets	0.5	Your original equity	0.5
Value	1.0	Value	1.0

B. The success of the new business is directly related to the entrepreneur who originated the business.

C. The growing business generates the entrepreneur's capital along with capital contributed by venture capitalists.

D. The big payoff for the entrepreneur and venture capitalist is when the firm goes public.

Venture Capital

Second Stage Market Value Balance Sheet ($mil)

Assets		Liabilities and Equity	
Cash from new equity	1.0	New equity from 2nd stage	1.0
Other assets	2.0	Equity from 1st stage	1.0
		Your original equity	1.0
Value	3.0	Value	3.0

II. THE INITIAL PUBLIC OFFERING

A. Definition

1. If the developing business is going well, it is time for the original investors to cash in by selling stock to the investing public for the first time, called an **initial public offering (IPO)**.

2. When newly issued shares are sold to the investor public, it is called a primary issue (money raised by the firm). When original shareholders sell a number of their shares in an IPO, it is called a secondary offering (money raised goes to the selling stockholders).

B. Arranging a Public Issue

1. Before the IPO, an **underwriter** is selected to assist in arranging the procedural requirements, to buy the issue from the firm, and finally, to sell the issue to the investor public.

2. Under a firm commitment, the underwriter pays a fixed price to the firm for the stock then sells the stock to the public for, hopefully, a higher amount. The difference is called the **spread**. If it is too risky to offer a firm commitment, the underwriter may sell the stock for the firm at the best price, called a best efforts underwriting.

3. Before a public offering is made, the firm must comply securities acts and regulations enforced by different provinces. A registration statement detailing the facts of the company and issue is filed with the appropriate provincial commission where the securities are sold. A summary of the registration statement called a **prospectus**, both a preliminary, "red herring" (from red writing on the side) or final copy after all terms are finalized, is given to all investors considering the investment. While securities laws are similar among provinces, the Ontario Securities Commission (OSC) is a leader in the field given the overall importance of the Toronto Stock Exchanges (TSE) in Canada.

4. In order to accelerate the sales, an underwriter is willing to practice **under-pricing** or to sell the securities below their true values. A simple average of 10 percent in the TSE market suggests that under-pricing is a significant cost of a stock underwriting. Other costs of the underwriting include administrative (legal, accounting) costs and the spread taken by the underwriter. Overall, the underwriter gets the spread, the public investors get the under-pricing, the professionals get their take, and the firm gets the remaining cash.

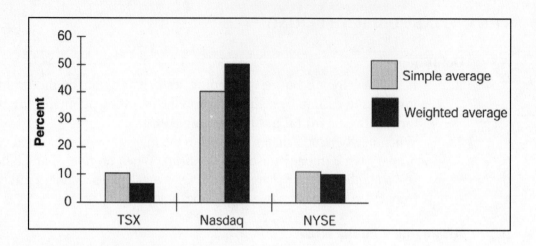

III. THE UNDERWRITERS

A. Role

1. The underwriter has *three* functions: providing advice (pricing and timing), buying the issue from the company (risk taking), and selling the issue to the public.

2. A group of underwriters, or a syndicate, is usually formed to share the risk of buying the issue. A larger selling group of underwriters and broker/dealers is formed to sell the issue quickly. The spread is split among the lead underwriter, syndicate, and selling group.

B. Who Are the Underwriters?

1. Underwriters comprise the large Canadian investment dealers listed in Table 14.1 in the textbook and thousands of other investment banks, brokers, dealers located domestically, and increasingly, internationally.

2. Most underwriting involves a negotiated price with the firm and in a few utility holding companies and governmental bodies, competitive bidding determines which investment dealer and what price/yield will be paid.

3. For large issues, a group of underwriters called a **syndicate** or banking group will be formed to better handle the sale. Syndication also helps to spread the risks.

Underwriter	No. as Lead	Value of Issues ($)	No. as Non-Lead	Value of Issues ($)	Total No. of Deals	Value of Issues ($)
RBC Dominion Securities	126	8,409	201	6,571	327	14,980
TD Securities	112	8,274	216	6,312	328	14,586
CIBC World Markets	110	6,627	212	6,750	322	13,376
BMO Nesbitt Burns	59	5,078	214	6,324	273	11,402
Scotia Capital	81	4,896	198	6,348	279	11,244
Merrill Lynch	45	4,552	144	4,633	189	9,184
National Bank Financial	58	2,689	172	3,433	230	6,122
Goldman Sachs	8	860	24	1,349	32	2,209
Credit Suisse First Boston	8	1,530	11	652	19	2,182
Saloman Smith Barney	13	1,502	6	281	19	1,783

IV.   LISTING ON THE STOCK MARKET

A.   Having "gone public," a firm has the option of listing its shares for trading on a security exchange, such as the TSE (Toronto Stock Exchange) or CDNX (Canadian Venture Exchange).

B.   Only the securities of a "listed" company are eligible for trading on an exchange. To be listed, a company must meet certain qualifications and pay the requisite fee. See Table 14.5 in the textbook for the TSE listing requirements.

C.   The decision to list shares has the pros and cons. While publicity creates a beneficial effect on the listing company, disclosure requirements may expose the embarrassments of a firm.

V.   RIGHTS ISSUES AND GENERAL CASH OFFERS BY PUBLIC COMPANIES

A.   **Rights Offering**
   1.   After the IPO, additional common stock issues may be sold by a business seeking financing. This is called a **seasoned offering**. The stock may be offered to existing shareholders, called a **rights issue**, or sold to the general public.
   2.   In a rights issue, shareholders would be able to purchase additional shares at a price below current market price, called **subscription price**. A 25 percent increase in shares would entitle a shareholder to buy 1 share at the lower price for every 4 that they own. This practice is to ensure the interests of the current shareholders are protected.

3. **Standby underwriting agreement**, and **over-subscription privilege** are used to avoid a situation where share price falls below the subscription price.

4. Rights issues are less common in Canada than in other countries.

B. **General Cash Offers**

1. If a rights issue is not elected, additional stock may be sold to the general investing public, called a **general cash offer**.

2. In Canada, large and well-known companies often use **bought deals** for their seasoned equity issues.

3. Under the **Prompt Offering Prospectus (POP) System**, qualified firms are allowed to use a short-form filing process instead of a full prospectus to gain a fast approval.

4. In the US, firms have different practices filing one registration statement for several issues of the same security over a period of time. This process, called a **shelf-registration**, provides quicker access to capital markets.

C. **Costs of the General Cash Offer**

1. The costs of an underwriting include the under-pricing of the issue, the spread to the underwriters, and the administrative costs.

2. From Figure 14.3 in the textbook, the cost of underwriting different types of security issues expressed as a percent of the proceeds confirms the economies of scale in an issuance.

3. Due to the smaller risk involved, issue costs are lower for debt securities than for equity.

D. **Market Reaction to Stock Issues**

1. Does adding more shares depress stock prices below true value and decrease the motivation to sell stock? The answer is no. If a stock price were to drop just because of added supply, the yield on the stock would be higher than alternative risk investment, and investors would bid the stock price back up the investor required rate of return.

2. Research indicates that prices do drop slightly (3 percent) after the announcement of a stock offering, and that is a considerable amount of funds each year for business. If it cannot be added to supply alone which causes the market to depreciate the stock, what is it? Investors are signaled by the announcement of stock issue that management feels the stock is overpriced by the market and are rushing in to sell stock. If managers thought the stock were undervalued, they would probably sell debt or forgo the investment, rather than drop the stock price to investors by an announcement of a stock offer.

VI.   THE PRIVATE PLACEMENT

A.   Instead of a public offering of securities, a firm may negotiate a **private placement** of the securities with a small number of knowledgeable investors, such as an insurance company.

B.   Since the general public is not involved, relevant provincial commissions do not require registration, prospectus, etc. The issue may be placed quickly and at a lower cost of financing.

C.   Since the investor has purchased a security with little or no marketability, the yield demanded by the investor will likely be higher.

D.   The usually small and medium firms and investors can custom tailor the issue so that both are satisfied. A good direct relationship established through private placement is also critical for large firms.

APPENDIX: FINANCING OF NEW AND SMALL ENTERPRISES

A.   Compared with the U.S., Canadian venture capital industry is still in the infant stage although it has grown significantly over the last 10 years.

B.   Funds from private, non-bank-related firms and labour-sponsored funds, each counts for 40 percent of the new venture capital funds. The rest belongs to corporate, government, and hybrid funds.

C.   Table 14.A1 in the textbook lists important attributes of classic venture capital investing.

D.   The type of venture capital funding available to a firm will be influenced by the stage the business is at during its life cycle.

E.   In Canada, there are a wealth of federal, provincial, and local resources such as the Business Development Bank of Canada (BDC), Atlantic Canada Opportunities Agency (ACOA), and municipal government economic offices.

COMPLETION QUESTIONS

1.   The money invested to finance a new firm is called (*bank loans/venture capital*).

2.   In an initial public offering a firm sells its (*bonds/stock*) to raise funds.

3. In an underwriting a firm (*guarantees/makes its best effort*) to provide a company with new money.

4. The difference between the offering price of a security and the price received by the issuer is called the _____.

5. The document that provides information to potential investors in a security offering is called a _____.

6. Underwriters typically (*over/under*) price initial public offerings.

7. The larger the offering the (*higher/lower*) the costs, expressed as a percentage of funds raised, of going public.

8. The role of (*brokers/underwriters*) in a new issue includes advising on the terms, buying the new issue, and reselling it to the public.

9. With large issues, underwriters may form a (*corporation/syndicate*) to handle the sale.

10. Underwriters may sell the new issue at (*above/below*) its stated offering price.

11. Utility holding companies are required to choose their investment dealers by _____ bids.

12. In a few cases, companies offer new shares only to their existing shareholders through a _____ issue.

13. In the vast majority of instances, already-public companies needing additional funds do so through a (*general/tender*) offer.

14. _____ allows well-established companies to make a short-form filing to regulators that permits issues to be quickly offered.

15. Costs to the issuer are (*higher/lower*) for bonds compared to common stocks.

16. A new issue of common stock in already-public firms will typically cause a slight (*decline/increase*) in the price of the stock after the announcement.

17. When a public corporation sells more stock the price of existing shares (*will/will not*) fall if the firm does not earn an adequate return on the money raised.

18. The new stock issues signal that the market has (*overpriced/underpriced*) the securities.

19. Shares bought in a private placement (*can/cannot*) be re-sold to individual investors.

20. Firms that sell bonds in a private placement will usually pay a slightly (*higher/lower*) rate.

PROBLEMS

1. Explain how a rights issue can be used to enhance a stock offering.

2. Chelsea's Classics Inc., a publicly-held firm, recently announced plans to raise new equity funds for expansion. They will have a rights offering at a subscription price of $20 per share with 10 rights necessary to buy each new share. The 1 million shares currently outstanding are trading for $25 per share. How much new money will be raised through this offering?

3. What will be the expected stock price after the rights issue described in problem 2?

4. If flotation costs are expressed as a percentage of the dollar amount of a new offering, rank the following from the highest to the lowest.
   a. $50 million bond
   b. $100 million bond
   c. $50 million stock
   d. $100 million stock

5. Which offering will return the most money to the issuing company:
   a. a $50 million 9 percent, 20-year bond that is sold to the public with an underwriting fee of 1 percent and other expenses of $100,000 or
   b. a $50 million 20-year, 9.2 percent coupon bond privately placed for total fees of $100,000?

6. Which bond described in problem 5 is actually cheaper for the issuer?

7. What other factors might influence the decision to choose a method for the proposed offering as described in problem 5?

8. Tressa Corporation plans to sell 80,000 shares of stock at the current market price of $50 per share. The firm has 200,000 shares already outstanding with a book value of $60 per share. What will be the new book value immediately after the new stock is issued?

9. What will be the likely market price immediately after the stock issue as described in problem 8?

10. Should individuals buy into several venture capital funds to diversify their portfolios? Explain.

ANSWERS TO COMPLETION QUESTIONS

1. venture capital
2. stock
3. guarantees
4. spread
5. prospectus
6. under
7. lower
8. underwriters
9. syndicate
10. below
11. competitive
12. rights
13. general
14. Prompt offering prospectus (POP) system
15. lower
16. decline
17. will
18. overpriced
19. can not
20. higher

SOLUTIONS TO PROBLEMS

1. Rights are used as sweeteners to make a stock offering more attractive to existing shareholders. Most uses of this vehicle occur because the firm's by-laws require it whenever new stock is sold to the public. The concept is to allow existing shareholders to buy new shares at a discount from the currently quoted market price. In actuality, the total value of each shareholder's stake will be unchanged after the offering is completed. The market price per share will decline after the offering so that the total value of the outstanding shares equals the pre-offering value plus the amount of new money that is invested in the new shares. Market value is not created by a rights offering — only other changes in the market cause total shareholder value to change. See problem 2 for an illustration of the rights offering process.

2. Since 10 rights are needed for each new share and there are 1 million shares outstanding, the number of new shares is 1,000,000/10 or 100,000. Each new share will provide $20 to the company so the total funds raised will be 100,000 × $20 or $2 million.

3.   The market value of the firm before the issue is 1 million shares times the market price of $25 per share or $25 million. This will increase by the amount of new money added ($2 million as shown in problem 2) so the total shareholder wealth is $27 million. This can be understood by reasoning that the shareholders had cash before the offering and they allocated a total of $2 million of it to the investment in College Classics. The $27 million is wealth that will not be changed during the process of the rights offering. The share price of the 1 million original shares plus the 100,000 new shares will be $27 million/1.1 million or $24.55.

4.   The $50 million stock offering is the highest because stock issues cost more than bond issues and smaller offerings are relatively more expensive compared to larger offerings. This means the ranking for the other issues will be the $100 million stock, then the $50 million bond, and the $100 million bond offering will be the lowest.

5.   a. The costs of the public offering will be the $300,000 expense plus the underwriting fee of 1 percent of the $50 million or $500,000 for a total of $800,000. The net proceeds will be $50,000,000 – $800,000 = $49,200,000.
        b. The private placement will yield net proceeds of $50,000,000 – $100,000 = $49,900,000.

6.   This problem requires the use of present value calculations to determine if it is worth paying more for the fund raising in order to save interest costs during the life of the bond. From the solution to problem 5 we know that it costs $800,000 – $100,000 or $700,000 more to make a public offering. The annual interest costs would be $50,000,000 × .09 = $4,500,000. The annual interest costs for the privately placed issue would be $50,000,000 × .092 = $4,600,000. The savings with the public offering would be $4.6 – $4.5 or $100,000 for each of the 20 years that the bonds will be outstanding. The appropriate discount rate is 9 percent since the comparison base is the public offering. The present value of the interest savings is $100,000 × 9.129 = $912,900. This is greater than the initial added cost of $700,000 so the public offering should be chosen.

7.   Even though the present value analysis in problem 6 favoured the public offering, a private placement could be selected because it provides the potential for greater flexibility. When the negotiations are being conducted at the outset, it is possible that the privately placed issue will have fewer restrictions placed on the company. Later, during the life of the bond, there is a higher likelihood that the original terms can be modified because it is much easier to negotiate with the small number of investors involved in a private placement. The more flexible nature of the situation with a private placement can offset the higher costs.

8.   The company is selling 80,000 shares at $50 per share for a total of $4,000,000. This will be added to the existing book value of 200,000 shares at $60 per share or

$12,000,000. This amount plus the new funds of $4,000,000 will provide a total book value of $16,000,000. (The typical accounts affected are the par value of the common stock and the paid in surplus.) The book value of each of the 280,000 shares outstanding after the new issue will be $16,000,000/280,000 or $57.14.

9.   The market price after the offering will likely be unchanged at $50 per share. Only if investors feel the new money will be invested for a positive present value will the share price increase.

10. From the investor's point of view, venture capital investments will have a low correlation with the other assets in the individual portfolio. However, venture capital funds themselves are highly correlated with marker factors. Having said that, individual venture investments offer diversification potential, but venture capital funds or pools do not. In summary: buying one venture may give investors diversification potential, but buying several funds in the hopes of additional diversification may not make any financial sense.

CHAPTER 15

THE CAPITAL STRUCTURE DECISION

INTRODUCTION

Does capital structure and dividend policy affect the value of the business? Such has been the discussion in finance for years. What are the conditions in which debt and dividend policy does not impact the value of the business? Modigliani and Miller were presented the Nobel Prize for their work in this area. The authors feel that the MM argument provides a good start for this section on capital structure.

Just as the pure competitive model provides us a look at market conditions where price is minimized and quantity maximized, an early review of the MM thesis is an important start before looking at an economy *with* taxes, agency costs, bankruptcy, etc. As the simplistic assumptions are relaxed, we find that capital structure mix and dividend policy *does affect* investor cash flows, required rates of return, and value. While some finance texts are reluctant to mention the MM thesis, these authors introduce and explain the MM ideas with ease. Discussing the MM ideas here provides a connection to early chapters (value is in assets), provides conditions necessary where capital structure is irrelevant or does not impact value, and finally links the contributing factors that may affect value: investment, debt, and maybe dividend decisions.

Some of the most important ideas of this course are presented in this chapter. Your understanding of these concepts should tie the course together to this point and provide you the concepts necessary to proceed to the coming chapters.

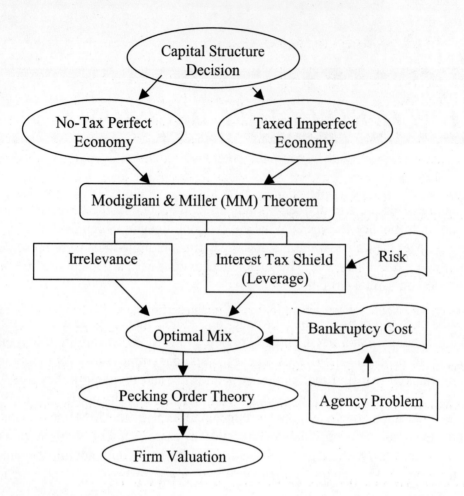

LEARNING CHECKLIST

This is an important concepts chapter and after preparing the chapter you should be able to:

_____1. Analyze the effect of debt finance on the risk and required return of equity holders.
_____2. Understand the advantages and disadvantages of debt and how increasing debt affects the value of the business.
_____3. Discuss the various costs of financial distress that is associated with increased debt levels.
_____4. Explain why the debt-equity mix varies across firms and across industries.

SOURCES OF BUSINESS INFORMATION

A Catalyst for Success: Beyond dispute, the venture capital industry aids the overall economy by providing the financing to create new businesses. Those start-ups also help existing businesses by generating new growth opportunities. Venture capital should be taken as a long-term commitment. While you get swept up in the excitement of trading stocks, you must realize that venture capital investing is a different ball game. First, your money is highly illiquid and probably will be locked-in for quite a few years. Second, since firms seeking venture capital are usually new and more risky, your investment is aiming to earn at least 40 percent to 60 percent annual return. Third, you need to prepare for involvement in the project more than just to provide funds. If you think about this alternative investment, visit and become a member with the trade association of venture capitalists at the US website www.nvca.org. Hopefully, you can build not only your personal wealth, but also the companies'.

Business News on the Web: There are a number of business/financial news services available on the Web. The Canadian site <www.baystreet.ca> is an excellent mix of investing resources covering business headlines, North American and global market updates, audio news reports from CBC, and daily commentary from the financial experts. The CBC's business page at www.cbc.ca/business has a similar setup. The "Personal Finance" section offers a characteristic feature. Some material is presented in audio and video format. Another all-purpose personal finance/investing site is www.quicken.ca.

CHAPTER OUTLINE, KEY CONCEPTS, AND TERMS

I.   **HOW BORROWING AFFECTS COMPANY VALUES IN A TAX-FREE ECONOMY**

    A.   **Capital Structure and Value**

        1.   The value of business assets, assuming there is no tax deductibility of interest, is not affected by the capital structure mix of debt and equity.

        2.   The present value of the cash flows from assets, the value of assets, is equal to the value of securities issued by the business. Changing the mix of securities does not affect the value of the assets.

        3.   The right-hand side of the balance sheet, assets, determines the *size* of the pizza; the mix of securities on the left-hand side of the balance sheet determines *how* the pizza is sliced. The only way to increase the amount of pizza is to increase the value of assets (pizza), not slicing (financing) in a new combination of slices.

        4.   This theory or idea won Franco Modigliani and Merton Miller (MM) a Nobel Prize.

II.   MM's ARGUMENT

A.   The value of business asset is not affected by the capital structure mix. This is known as MM's proposition I (debt irrelevance proposition). Debt policy should not matter to shareholders. It is the assets that count for value.

B.   Why should leveraging, or substituting debt for equity in the capital structure, affect the value of assets? Investors do not need businesses to add leverage to their investment portfolio. Financial institutions will lend investors money if they want, so adding debt to the business capital structure is no big thing, or certainly nothing of value to investors.

River Cruises — All Equity Financed

Data

Number of shares	100,000
Price per share	$10
Market value of shares	$1 million

Outcome	State of the Economy		
	Slump	Expected	Boom
Operating income	$75,000	125,000	175,000
Earnings per share	$.75	1.25	1.75
Return on shares	7.5%	12.5%	17.5%

C.   **How Borrowing Affects Earnings Per Share**

1.   The existence of debt can impact the earnings of a company in two important ways. The first is by reducing earnings available to shareholders. The second is by reducing the need for equity capital.

2.   Tables 15.3 and 15.4 in the textbook show how the inclusion of debt into a firm's capital structure can alter the earnings per share. For now, we will assume the change is cosmetic in nature and represents mathematical gymnastics. The impact on risk is coming right up!

D.   **How Borrowing Affects Risk and Return**

1.   Increasing the amount of debt versus equity, called **restructuring**, *does* increase shareholder's expected return. If leverage is favourable with the return on assets exceeding the cost of debt, earnings and returns to shareholders will increase.

2.	These higher expected returns are not without a cost. The cost is increased risk to the shareholders, for now with debt, there is a prior claim (creditors) on their income stream and assets, in case of failure.

3.	Shareholders, with debt above them, have prospects for higher returns, but added risk. The net effect in the valuation process is that the expected future cash flows have gone up, with the use of debt, but so has the shareholder required rate of return. The increased cash flows in the valuation function have increased, but are offset by the increased discount rate. There is no change in the value of the assets or the stock of the shareholders.

4.	The **operating risk** or **business risk**, or the risk or variability of the operating income or earnings before interest and taxes (earnings before distributions are made to sources of funds) is not affected by the capital structure mix.

5.	While the operating risk is not affected by increased proportions of debt or use of **financial leverage**, the **financial risk**, or risk (variability or returns) to shareholders has increased with increased use of debt. With increased financial leverage and increased financial risk, shareholder required rates of return increase. The higher expected value from the use of debt are cancelled out by the higher discount rate applied to the higher cash flows. The value of the assets are left unchanged or are not affected by changing the mix of debt and equity.

E.	**Debt and the Cost of Capital**

1.	The weighted average cost of capital (WACC) is the expected return on the assets, and correspondingly, the securities of a business and is the required rate of return on any new average risk investment project.

2.	In an all equity business the WACC = r_{assets} = r_{equity}, or the expected return on assets equals the expected rate of return on equity.

3.	When debt is added or the capital structure mix changed, the cost of debt, and equity, must be weighted by their relative market value proportions so that:

$$WACC = r_{assets} = r_{debt}[D/(D+E)] + r_{equity}[E/(D+E)]$$

4.	The WACC or the r_{assets} does not change as debt is added to the capital structure. This concept is **MM's proposition II** which states that the expected return on the common stock increases as the debt/equity ratio increases. Why doesn't the WACC change? As more low cost debt is added to the capital structure, the required rate of return on equity increases to offset the advantage of low cost debt. The WACC does not change; the market value of the firm does not change. Debt does not matter in this situation where the deductibility of interest is not a factor.

5.   Debt has an explicit cost in the form of an interest rate, and an incidental, implicit cost impact on the required rate of return on equity as debt is added to the capital structure. Debt is no "cheaper" than equity and the use of debt does not affect the WACC, nor the value of the firm.

6.   Figure 15.3 shows the offsetting effects of lower cost debt, even if risk-free, added to the capital structure relative to the increasing required rate of return of equity of greater financial leverage. One offsets the other and the expected return on assets, r_{assets}, is not affected by changing the capital structure mix.

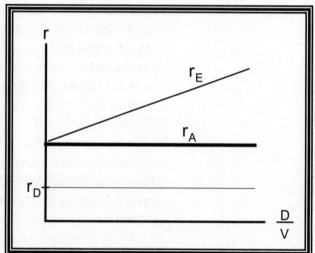

7.   Adding a bit of reality does not change the conclusion. In Figure 15.4 in the textbook risky debt is considered, where with increases in the debt/equity ratio, the cost of debt increases as creditors get edgy about sharing the income stream, and the rate of increase in the shareholder's required rate of return begins to slow as bondholders begin to bear a greater share of the risk. The conclusion is the same: the WACC or expected return on assets or the cost of the package of debt and equity (WACC) does not change. Debt does not affect the value of the assets!

III.   CAPITAL STRUCTURE AND CORPORATE TAXES

A.   Impacts

1.   Reality says that financial managers are concerned about finding that "right" mix of capital structure that produces the lowest or optimal cost of capital. This indicates that there are other factors working beyond MM's assumptions.

2.   The presence of taxes, bankruptcy costs, potential conflicts of interests between creditors and shareholders, and ways that financial decisions could affect investment decisions *do* affect the value of assets.

3.   If this is true, what is the value of the MM propositions? How did they win a Nobel Prize with a theory with such limiting assumptions? Their propositions provided the foundation upon which we study reality or the

real-world situation as it exists. Just as the pure competitive model studied in microeconomics was used as a basis for evaluating existing market structure, MM's basic theories provide a basis for explaining how these other variables affect asset or business values.

B. **Debt and Taxes at River Cruises**
1. Interest expense is deductible against taxable income, which means that the combined income of debt and equity holders is increased with the use of debt. See Table 15.5 in the textbook.
2. The added value is the **interest tax shield**, or the tax savings resulting from the deductibility of interest payments.
3. The annual interest tax shield is the product of the interest paid, (r_{debt} × D), times the tax rate, T_c. Since the creditors or bond holders receive their same interest payment and no more, the added annual value of the tax shield accrues to shareholders.
4. Assuming a constant level of debt, the value over time of the tax shield is the annual tax shield capitalized or divided by the current cost of debt capital, or, another way, is the product of the amount of debt, D, times the corporate tax rate, T_c:

$$\text{PV of Tax Shield (assume perpetuity)} = \frac{D \times r_D \times T_C}{r_D} = D \times T_C$$

C. **How Interest Tax Shields Contribute to the Value of Stockholder's Equity**
1. There are three claims on the operating income of business: creditors, shareholders, and government.
2. The deductibility of interest is a tax shield that diverts government taxes to the shareholders. Thus the tax shield increases the value of an all-equity business by the amount equal to the value of the tax shield, T_cD, or:

Value of levered firm = value if all-equity financed + T_cD
     See Figure 15.5 in the textbook.

D. **Corporate Taxes and the Weighted-Average Cost of Capital**
1. The value of the corporate tax shield is represented in the lower after-tax cost of debt. Lower after-tax costs of debt lowers the WACC and increases the present value of stream of asset cash flows.
2. The value of the tax shield is represented in the value of the assets.

E.   **The Implications of Corporate Taxes For Capital Structure**

    1.   If the value of the tax shield increases as the debt/equity ratio increases, as in Figure 15.6 in the textbook, why doesn't all business borrow as much as they can?

    2.   There are other factors, such as the increased costs of possible financial distress that offsets the value of the tax shield at high debt/equity ratios.

IV.   COSTS OF FINANCIAL DISTRESS

A.   **General**

    1.   As the debt/equity increases, the **costs of financial distress**, or the costs of possible bankruptcy, increases.

    2.   The market value of the business is equal to the value of an all-equity business *plus* the present value of the tax shield *less* the present value of financial distress.

    3.   The added costs of financial distress overtakes the added value of the tax shield at some point and may lower the value of the firm at some high debt/equity ratio. See Figure 15.7 in the textbook.

    4.   The theoretical optimum capital structure is the debt/equity level in which the PV of the tax shield is just offset by the PV costs of financial distress. This debt/equity level will not only maximize market value of the business, but also minimize WACC for the firm. See Figure 15.8 in the textbook.

B.   **Bankruptcy Costs**

    1.   Bankruptcy occurs as the value of a business declines. Bankruptcy does not cause the value of a business to decrease. It is a court-directed legal process that occurs when the value or the financial conditions of a business deteriorate to the point where the bills are not paid or the value of the equity is zero.

    2.   If bankruptcy occurs the costs are deducted from the remaining value of the business and shareholders are the last in line for any proceeds. Shareholders are likely to lose their investment in this situation.

C.   **Evidence on Bankruptcy Costs** — Research indicates that the costs of bankruptcy for large firms is a relatively small proportion of the value of the securities.

D.   **Direct Versus Indirect Costs of Bankruptcy** — While direct bankruptcy costs are relatively small, the indirect costs associated with bankruptcy related to managerial limitations and efforts to correct the economic problems may be significant.

E.   **Financial Distress Without Bankruptcy**

    1.   As long as bills are paid, a firm in financial distress may avoid bankruptcy, reduce costs, and begin a turnaround.

    2.   Often a valueless firm may take added risk to bet on a turnaround, or linger for a significantly long time before an interest payment is missed or some bankruptcy act occurs.

    3.   All stakeholders want the troubled firm to recover although their interests may be in conflict.

F.   **What the Games Cost**

    1.   Until bankruptcy occurs, owners still control investment and operating strategy. With little remaining to lose, managers/owners may bet the creditor's money in a risk turnaround venture, thus increasing the costs of financial distress.

    2.   Added equity invested in a financial distressed situation for a reasonable project may reward creditors, not reward owners, and the project may be ignored.

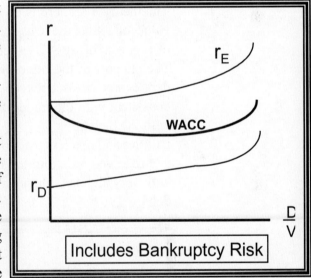

    3.   Positive NPV projects that tend to be in the creditors' interest and not shareholders may be avoided, especially if close to bankruptcy. Shareholders may be interested in getting their money out, not putting more into the business that may go to creditors.

    4.   It is in stockholders' interest to avoid high-debt situations where "betting games" may occur because stockholders generally lose. Borrowing contracts are generally in favour of creditors if problems should occur. Thus owners' required rates of return for investment in high-debt firms may keep debt/equity ratios in the moderate range. Protective covenants reduce the flexibility of firms to make decisions and loss of flexibility reduces the value of firms.

G.   **Costs of Distress Vary With Type of Asset**

1.   Real asset firms tend to lose less value in bankruptcy than firms with significant intangible assets, such as research and development firms who depend upon human capital.

2.   From the arguments above, companies with safe, tangible assets such as real estate and high taxable income should have high debt-to-equity ratios, while people-oriented firms with little or no taxable income should have low debt-to-equity ratios.

3.   Although debt capacity is a practical consideration for individual firms, most company ratios are consistent with their respective industry averages.

V.   EXPLAINING FINANCING CHOICES

A.   **The Trade-off Theory**

1.   The theory that there is an optimum debt/ratio that maximizes market value, offsetting the benefits of the tax shield against the increasing costs of financial distress is called the **trade-off theory**.

2.   The support of the trade-off theory is evidenced by a wide variety of debt/equity ratios between industries and companies, but with some consistent with the trade-off theory and some operating inconsistently with the theory.

3.   Utilities and retailers tend to borrow heavily and their assets are tangible and relatively safe, but the most successful companies, such as Merck, with very high taxable profits, tend to forgo the tax shield advantage of debt.

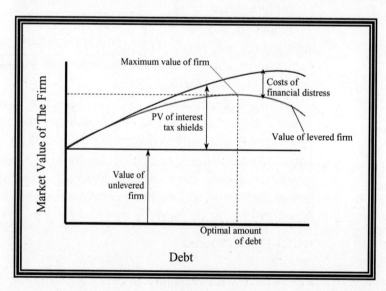

B. **A Pecking Order Theory**

1. Research has shown that stock sales announcements tend to drive stock prices down, indicating that investors think managers feel the stock price is overvalued if they attempt to sell equity.
2. Likewise, the announcement of a debt issue has little or no effect upon equity prices.
3. The above observations indicate a pecking order theory of capital structure alternative ways to fund investment.
4. Businesses prefer to issue debt rather than equity if internally generated cash flow is insufficient. Use of internally generated funds does not have the signalling effect, positively or negatively, that external funding does.
5. If external funds must be raised, equity will be used reluctantly, reserved as the residual in the financing pecking order.
6. Under the pecking order theory there is no target debt/equity ratio because there are two kinds of equity: internally generated earnings retained and external stock sales. Internal equity is the first choice for financing ahead of debt, and finally, external equity funding.
7. Profitable firms have sufficient internally generated capital to fund their high NPV investments. Hence, they have all equity or low debt ratios.
8. Less profitable firms tend to issue more debt as they run out of internally generated funds quickly and turn to debt as the next source of funding in the pecking order.

COMPLETION QUESTIONS

1. Firms try to use the particular combination of debt and (*assets/equity*) that will maximize their overall market value.

2. The mix of a firm's financing sources is known as its _____ _____.

3. According to reasoning of Modigliani and Miller's (MM) proposition I, financial managers (*can/cannot*) increase value by changing the mix of securities used to finance a company.

4. Restructuring is the process of changing a firm's capital structure (*by/without*) changing its assets.

5. If the return on assets is greater than the cost of debt, the return to shareholders will be (*decreased/increased*) by borrowing.

6. Business risk is associated with variations in operating (*costs/income*).

7. Risk to shareholders resulting from the use of debt is known as _____ risk.

8. Financial leverage (*decreases/increases*) the variability of shareholders returns.

9. The weighted average cost of capital is equal to the expected return on (*assets/debt*).

10. MM's proposition II states that the required rate of return on equity increases as the firm's debt-to-equity ratio (*decreases/increases*).

11. The (*explicit/implicit*) cost of debt is interest and the (*explicit/implicit*) cost is the higher return demanded by shareholders.

12. Another way of expressing MM's proposition II is to say that the expected return on (*assets/equity*) does not change no matter what the level of borrowing is.

13. The existence of income taxes results in a cost advantage for (*debt/equity*) because (*dividends/interest*) is deductible for companies.

14. The interest tax shield is equal to the corporate tax rate (*divided/multiplied*) by the dollar amount of interest paid.

15. The modified MM proposition I states that the value of the leveraged firm is equal to the firm's value with all equity financing (*minus/plus*) the present value of the tax shield.

16. A tax-related disadvantage to borrowing recognizes that some returns to (*debtholders /stockholders*) come as capital gains that may be deferred and eventually taxed at a lower rate.

17. (*Benefits/Costs*) of financial distress arise from bankruptcy or near bankruptcy.

18. In the case of bankruptcy, the _____ become the new owners.

19. The (*direct/indirect*) costs of bankruptcy are measured by legal and administrative fees.

20. For companies in financial distress but not yet in bankruptcy there is a strong temptation to bet the future on (*creditors'/shareholders'*) money.

21. Firms facing bankruptcy often (*do/do not*) have difficulty attracting new equity capital because returns on the new investment (*will/will not*) have to be shared with creditors.

22. A theory of capital structure states that there is a _____ between the interest tax shield and the distress costs of debt.

23. A relatively (*low/high*) debt-to-equity ratio is observed in the pharmaceutical industry.

24. According to the pecking order theory of capital structure, firms prefer to issue (*debt/equity*) if internally generated funds are insufficient.

25. Ready access to cash or debt financing is referred to as financial (*slack/distress*).

PROBLEMS

1. Refer to Table 15.2 of the textbook and suppose that River Cruises offers a $300,000 bond issue with a 10 percent coupon. Assume it uses the entire proceeds to repurchase stock on the open market at its current price of $10 per share. If you ignore any impact of the restructuring on stock price and use an income tax rate of 40 percent, what would be the expected earnings per share given a normal state of the economy?

2. Recompute earnings per share for the situation prescribed in problem 1 if no debt was issued and the tax rate was 40 percent.

3. What conclusion can be drawn from the calculations in problems 1 and 2?

4. If the beta of River Cruises as described in the problem was 1.2, what must be the beta on River Cruises' assets?

5. Leverage, Inc. has $100,000 of capital including $30,000 of debt at an interest rate of 9 percent. If shareholders expect a return of 20 percent, what is the expected return on total assets? (Ignore taxes.)

6. Suppose Leverage, Inc. decided to restructure its balance sheet by issuing enough debt to repurchase stock to bring the debt/equity ratio to 1.0. Assuming its debt is default-free, what would be:
   a. The expected return on assets?
   b. The expected return on equity?

7. No Growth, Inc. (NGI) has EBIT of $100,000. If it has no debt financing, what will be the value of the firm if it indeed does not expect to grow, it pays taxes of 40 percent, and a discount rate of 12 percent is appropriate?

8. What is meant by the term "interest tax shield"?

9. What is the present value of the interest tax shield for a firm with $1 million of a 7 percent perpetual debt issue, if the tax rate is 40 percent and the discount rate is 10 percent?

10. What would the present value of the interest tax shield change in problem 9 if:
   a. The debt issue had a 10-year maturity? and
   b. The WACC was 15 percent?

ANSWERS TO COMPLETION QUESTIONS

1. equity
2. capital structure
3. cannot
4. without
5. increased
6. income
7. financial
8. increases
9. assets
10. increases
11. explicit, implicit
12. assets
13. debt, interest
14. multiplied
15. plus
16. stockholders
17. Costs
18. creditors
19. direct
20. creditors'
21. do, will
22. trade-off
23. low
24. debt
25. slack

SOLUTIONS TO PROBLEMS

1. The debt issue will provide funds to repurchase $300,000/$10 per share or 30,000 shares. After this occurs, the number of outstanding shares will be reduced from 50,000 to 20,000. The interest on the new debt will be 10 percent of $300,000 or $30,000 per year. This lowers taxable income from $125,000 to $95,000. The after-tax income will be $(1 - 0.4) \times \$95,000$ or $57,000. The earnings per share will be $57,000/20,000 or $2.85.

2. The taxable income was $125,000. The after-tax income would be $(1 - 0.4) \times \$125,000$ or $75,000. The earnings per share in this case would have been $75,000/50,000 or $1.50.

3. The use of leverage is profitable for the shareholders. Earnings per share increased from $1.25 to $2.85 by borrowing and using the proceeds to repurchase some of the shares outstanding. This is made possible because the after-tax interest cost incurred is more than offset by the reduction in the number of shares outstanding. The positive or negative aspect of leverage depends on the level of pre-tax profits. If the company encountered a downturn in profitability, the use of debt financing would exacerbate the problem just as it helped make the firm even more profitable in the situation where the restructuring occurred.

4. Since the beta for debt is zero, the beta for the total assets must be 70 percent of the equity or $0.7 \times 1.2 = 0.84$.

5. The firm must earn $0.09 \times \$30,000$ or $2,700 for the debt. For the equity it must earn $0.20 \times \$70,000$ or $14,000. The total earnings must then be $16,700. The return on assets will be $16,700/$100,000 or 16.7 percent.

6. a. The return on assets, given the default-free assumption, will be unchanged by the restructuring so it will remain at 16.7 percent. There will be a higher return expected on the equity to offset the higher cost of interest payments as shown in part b below.

   b. A debt/equity ratio of 1 means the proportions of debt and equity are equal. The total return on assets for the new financing structure will be:

   $$0.5 \times r_{equity} + 0.5 \times .09 = .167$$
   $$r_{equity} = .244 \text{ or } 24.4 \text{ percent}$$

7. The value of the firm will be equal to the present value of all future earnings. The after-tax earnings are $(1 - 0.4) \times \$100,000$ or $60,000 per year. Recall that a stream of a constant amount has a value of that amount divided by the expected rate of return. (This is the procedure for valuing preferred stock and perpetual bonds.) The value of NGI will be $60,000/.12 or $500,000.

8. The interest tax shield refers to the tax savings resulting from the deductibility of interest payments. It recognizes the "partnership" of government with business by allowing taxes to be lowered by reducing taxable income by payments to debtholders. Remember that dividend payments are not deductible when figuring taxes so there is encouragement for borrowing as a source of funds. The encouragement is the interest tax shield.

9. The amount of the interest tax shield depends on the amount of interest payments, the tax rate, and the discount rate. In this case the firm will pay 0.07 × $1,000,000 or $70,000 per year. This will reduce taxes by 0.40 × $70,000 or $28,000 annually. In present value terms this is $28,000/.10 or $280,000.

10. a. The tax savings are unchanged at $28,000 per year but the present value is of an annuity for 10 years at 10 percent. For each $1 this is 6.145 so the tax shield value is 6.145 × $28,000 or $172,060.

   b. Just as the value of the tax shield was reduced by shortening the life of the bond, the value will also be reduced by increasing the discount rate. With a 15 percent discount rate for 10 years, the present value will be 5.019 × $28,000 or $140,532.

CHAPTER 16

DIVIDEND POLICY

INTRODUCTION

In finance, we are fairly convinced that investment decisions are the key to value creation. In the last chapter, we saw that the government tax shield adds to this value by the use of debt, but to some limit. In this second of "do capital structure decisions matter?" chapters, you are provided excellent coverage of an area that half your professors do not think is relevant: dividend policy. As in the last chapter, starting with the conditions under which dividends are irrelevant, then adding more realistic assumptions is a proven method for learning the concepts. The valuation theme, and the factors affecting value, connects this chapter with the theme of the text, and adds another piece of the puzzle.

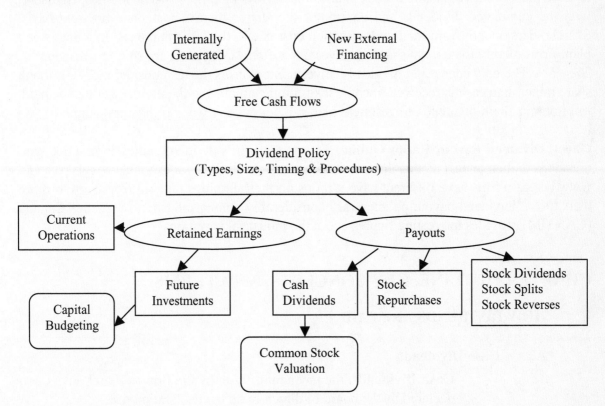

LEARNING CHECKLIST

After studying this chapter you should be able to:

____1. Describe the process by which dividends are paid by a corporation.

____2. Explain why, under special conditions and assumptions as set forth by M&M, dividend policy should not affect the value of a business.

____3. Explain why dividends may be used by managers to signal the prospects of their business.

____4. Show how tax rate differences on cash dividends versus capital gains might affect dividend policy based on clientele effect.

SOURCES OF BUSINESS INFORMATION

Dividend Reinvestment Plans (DRIP): Companies such as Alcan, Bank of Montreal, and BCE have offered dividend reinvestment plans whereby shareholders can simply reinvest their cash dividends in additional shares of the corporation. Depending on the needs of equity capital, two types of plans are used. In an old stock plan, a trustee buys the firm's shares on the open market with the cumulated dividends and distributes the shares to investors on a pro rata basis. Shareholders benefit from the low transaction cost due to the large purchase. In a new stock plan, firms merely issue extra shares to investors. Often, such shares are sold at a discount of 3% – 5%. The only concern of dividend reinvestment plans is the tax consideration. Although share rather than cash is received, income taxes on the amount of the dividends must be paid. Information about dividend reinvestment plan can be found at www.dripcentral.com.

Check Dividend Payout Ratios Online: To know a firm's dividend policy in practice, you must look at their annual reports that can found on their Web sites, for example, www.cp.ca and www.bce.ca. Firms have different payout ratios on their earnings ranging from zero to more than 100%. Dividend payout policies vary considerably among industries. Statistics Canada (CANSIM) provides interesting figures about the industrial variations.

CHAPTER OUTLINE, KEY CONCEPTS, AND TERMS

I.   **HOW DIVIDENDS ARE PAID**

    A.   **Cash Dividends**

        1.   **Cash Dividends**, the payment of cash by the firm to shareholders, are declared by the board of directors on the declaration date.

        2.   A regular dividend is a level the board hopes to maintain in the future; a dividend payment called a special or extra dividend is viewed as a one-time payment.

3. The dividend is paid on the payment date to all shareholders of record on the record date which is announced on the declaration date.

4. To be a shareholder of record, and thus receive a dividend, one must have purchased the stock before the **ex-dividend date**, which is four business days before the record date.

5. The stock price should drop by the amount of the dividend on the ex-dividend date.

6. Instead of cash dividends, many companies have automatic reinvestment plans in which additional shares of stock are purchased. The business keeps the cash and shares are given to shareholders.

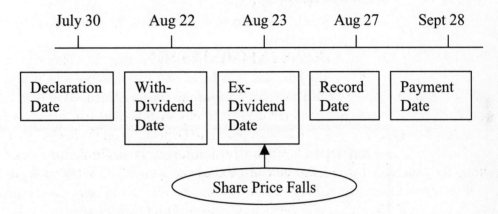

B. **Some Legal Limitations on Dividends**

1. Creditors may limit or prevent the payment of dividends until the debt is paid.

2. The Canadian Business Corporations Act and provincial acts may also limit dividend payment (reduce cash, reduce retained earnings) if the payments would lower capital below the amount of retained earnings, thus impairing invested capital. Also, dividend payment is prohibited if it results in the firm being unable to pay its liabilities when they are due or if such liabilities exceed the firm's assets.

C. **Stock Dividends, Stock Splits, and Reverse Splits**

1. A **stock dividend** is distribution of additional shares to shareholders. The cash is kept in the firm for investment; shareholders receive added shares. A 10 percent stock dividend would issue 1 share per 10 owned by stockholders.

2. A **stock split** is an issuance of added shares to shareholders. No cash is exchanged, only a change in the number of shares issued and the par value.

217

3. A stock dividend is a mini-stock split. No cash is involved and the book value of shareholder's equity does not change. They are accounting entries; a recapitalization. With more shares outstanding, the market value *per share* drops because more shares are outstanding, but the *total market value of the firm does not change.*

4. A reverse split is the opposite of a stock split. A 1-for-2 reverse split means shareholders give up two existing shares for one new share. With fewer shares outstanding, share price increases to an optimal trading range.

D. **Stock Repurchase**

1. A **stock repurchase** occurs when the company buys back stock from shareholders.

2. A stock repurchase has the same impact of a dividend: The cash account in the business is reduced and the shareholders as a group have more cash. The book value of the equity is reduced in both cases.

Example – Cash dividend versus share repurchase

Assets		*Liabilities & Equity*	
A. Original balance sheet			
Cash	$150,000	Debt	0
Other assets	850,000	Equity	1,000,000
Value of firm	1,000,000	Value of firm	1,000,000
Shares outstanding = 100,000			
Price per share = $1,000,000 / 100,000 = $10			

Example – Cash Dividend versus Share Repurchase

Assets   *Liabilities & Equity*

   B.   After cash dividends @$1/share

Cash	$50,000	Debt	$0
Other assets	850,000	Equity	900,000
Firm value	$900,000	Firm value	$900,000

Shares outstanding = 100,000
Price per share = $900,000 / 100,000 = $9

Example – Cash Dividend versus Share Repurchase

Assets   *Liabilities & Equity*

   C.   After stock repurchase @$10/share of 10,000 shares

Cash	$50,000	Debt	$0
Other assets	850,000	Equity	900,000
Firm value	$900,000	Firm value	$900,000

Shares outstanding = 90,000
Price per share = $900,000 / 90,000 = $10

II.   HOW DO COMPANIES DECIDE ON DIVIDEND PAYMENTS?

A.   Survey research of business indicates that dividend payments may be determined a variety of ways:

      1.   The business may have a predetermined long-run **dividend payout ratio**, which establishes the percentage of earnings to be paid in dividends.

      2.   Managers tend to focus on dividend *changes* rather than absolute levels.

      3.   Dividend changes follow shifts in long-run, sustainable levels of earnings, rather than short-run fluctuations in earnings.

      4.   Managers are reluctant to make changes in dividend payments that are likely to be reversed in the future.

B.   A constant payout ratio means that dividends will vary as earnings vary. Companies tend to change dividends steadily in response to a sustainable increase in earnings. Cash dividends per year were more stable than earnings. See Figure 16.2 in the textbook.

C.   Future earnings prospects by managers are built into dividend policy. Higher earnings tend to follow higher dividends and lower earnings follow low dividends.

III.   WHY DIVIDEND POLICY SHOULD NOT MATTER

A.   **Efficiency and Value Arguments**

1.   *If markets are efficient*, dividend policy should not affect shareholder value. Assuming that a business' capital budgeting decision (accept all positive NPVs) and borrowing decisions have been made, it then becomes a choice as to *how* to raise equity capital: internally from earnings paying cash common dividends or financing externally from the sale of stock?

2.   Dividend policy, with the capital budgeting and debt policy *established*, is then the choice between internal equity or paying dividends and using external equity.

3.   This area of dividend policy has a variety of opinions as to how or if dividend policy affects the value of the business. Some are of the opinion that value is affected by dividend policy, some such as the MM proposition in the next paragraph think dividend policy has no effect on value, and finally, some think that dividends cost the shareholders added taxes to the point where dividends may have a negative impact upon value.

B.   **Dividend Policy Is Irrelevant in Competitive Markets**

1.   If efficient, competitive markets exist, then the **MM dividend-irrelevance** theory is reasonable. Given an investment program and debt policy, the equity portion of the financing may come internally, from retained income, or raised externally and at low cost in equity markets.

2.   If earnings exceed the necessary equity funding for the capital budget, the *residual* can be paid in dividends. If the equity capital needed for investment exceeds the internally generated earnings, external equity can be raised inexpensively in financial markets.

3.   The existing shareholders' value will remain the same if external debt is sold for they now have their dividends plus the now diluted market value of their shares.

4.   If dividends are not paid, how can existing shareholders generate cash if needed? MM's answer for those who need cash is to sell a few shares of stock in efficient markets. The added value created by positive NPVs and financed with retained earnings, will be represented in higher stock prices. After selling a few shares each period, the investor's total net worth has not changed.

5.   With efficient markets, it does not matter if earnings are retained and, with expected positive NPVs, shareholder value is built up via capital gains, or if dividends are paid out as dividends and the equity needed is raised in financial markets. The investor's net worth (value) is only affected by the prospects of expected NPVs from the new investments. Value comes from assets, not financing, with efficient markets.

Example - Assume ABC Co. has no extra cash, but declares a $1,000 dividend. They also require $1,000 for current investment needs. Using M&M Theory, and given the following balance sheet information, show how the value of the firm is not altered when new shares are issued to pay for the dividend.

Record Date		Pmt Date	**Post Pmt**
Cash	1,000	0	**1,000** (40sh @ $25)
Asset Value	5,000	5,000	**5,000**
Total Value	6,000	5,000	**6,000**
# of Shares	200	200	**240**
price/share	$30	$25	**$25**

NEW SHARES ARE ISSUED

C.   **Dividend Irrelevance — An Illustration**

1.   The shareholders of Rational Demi-conductor are the same regardless of which dividend policy is followed (pay or not pay dividends).

2.   The investor's value remains the same because, in the case of no dividends, the efficient financial markets are able to provide, via capital gains, shareholders with the added value of expected positive NPV investment funded by retained earnings.

```
┌─────────────────────────────────────────────────────┐
│                                                       │
│   Example - continued - Shareholder Value             │
│                                                       │
│                      Record      Pmt       Post       │
│      Stock           6,000       5,000     6,000      │
│      Cash                0       1,000         0      │
│                                                       │
│                                                       │
│      Total Value     6,000       6,000     6,000      │
│                                                       │
│   Stock = 240sh @ $25 = 6,000                         │
│                                                       │
│      Assume shareholders purchase the new issue with  │
│      the cash dividend proceeds.                      │
│                                                       │
└─────────────────────────────────────────────────────┘
```

D.   **Calculating Share Price**

1.   When dividends, which serve as a residual to fund the equity portion of the capital budget, are low or not paid in a period, investors with current cash needs can easily sell appreciated (investments were made in positive NPV investments) shares at a fair price to provide them cash.

2.   When dividends are paid, the firm must fund the equity-contributed cash from the sale of new equity providing the funds needed to finance all positive NPV projects. The total value of the firm does not change because of the dividend policy.

IV.   **THE ASSUMPTION BEHIND DIVIDEND IRRELEVANCE**

A.   **General Arguments**

1.   Given efficient capital markets, MM argues that dividends do not affect the value of the business. In this section, other arguments counter the MM ideas.

2.   One argument is that dividends now have added value over capital gain maybe later. Managers can stabilize dividends, but not the market price of the firm's stock. *But*, as long as investment debt policy is held constant, the overall cash flows of the business are the same regardless of the dividend policy. The risks that shareholders bear are related to the investment and debt policies, not the dividend policy. Investors, by themselves with efficient markets, can adjust any riskiness associated with the dividends now, appreciation later argument by altering their investment portfolio between risky common stock and cash assets.

3.   An efficient market provides, at fair prices, for transfers in ownership created by shifts in dividend policy all the while the total value of the business is unaffected by dividend policy, only investment and debt policy through the tax shield.

B.   **Why Dividends May Increase Firm Value**
1.   When markets are less than efficient, dividend policy may affect firm value. The impact of dividend policy upon firm value then depends on the extent of market inefficiency.
2.   Given high proportional transaction costs on the sale of stock, investors may be better off if the company constantly pays the dividend.

C.   **Dividends as Signals**
1.   Firm value is not increased by increased dividends; firm value increases if management's increase in dividends signals the presence of high NPV opportunities.
2.   In markets where there is little information, increased dividends portend increased future cash flows or dividend policy is a form of communications to the market about future prospects.
3.   Just as dividend increases add expectations of favourable future prospects, dividend cuts are assumed by the market as a signal of bad news to come.

V.   **TAXES AND DIVIDEND POLICY**

A.   **Supporting Logic**
1.   There is an argument that, just as corporate deductibility of interest affects value, differential taxation of cash dividends and capital gains may provide a value edge of one dividend policy (dividends) over another (no dividends, capital gains).
2.   If cash dividends are taxed at a rate higher than capital gains, shareholder's after-tax return is higher if no dividend is paid, earnings are retained and invested, and the return is taken as a capital gain.

B.   **Why Pay Any Dividends at All?**
1.   If dividends are taxed at a high rate, and they have been in the past, why pay dividends at all?
2.   Firms do not pay any tax on dividend income received from another Canadian firm.
3.   With the higher tax rate on dividends, firms should attempt to retain earnings and minimize the extent to which they issue stock, as long as all positive NPV investments are being pursued.

4. Clientele effect exists. While some shareholders prefer current income demanding a firm to pay out a high percentage of its earnings, others like the firm to retain most of its earnings for reinvestment. Thus, a firm attracts a specific clientele who is drawn by its dividend policy.

C. **Taxation of Dividends and Capital Gains with Recent Tax Law Changes**
    1. Before 1972, there were no taxes on capital gains making cash dividends unattractive.
    2. Tax reforms in 1980s have increased taxes on capital gains. The elimination of the $100,000 lifetime capital gain exemption is an example.
    3. In 2000, the federal government reduced the taxable portion of capital gains from 75% to 50%.
    4. The tax laws effectively narrow the difference between the tax rates on dividends and capital gains for individuals.
    5. Tax on dividends must be paid immediately, while capital gain taxes are paid when the gain is "realized." Such a delay favours the after-tax, time adjusted capital gain return alternative.

	Firm A	Firm B
Next year's price	$112.50	$102.50
Dividend	$ 0	$ 10.00
Total *pretax* payoff	$112.50	$112.50
Today's stock price	$100	$ 98.90
Capital gain	$ 12.50	$ 3.60
Before-tax rate of return (%)	$\frac{12.5}{100} = .125 = 12.5\%$	$\frac{13.60}{98.90} = 0.138 = 13.8\%$
Tax on dividend at 30%	$0	.30 × $10 = $3.00
Tax on capital gain at 20%	.20 × $12.50 = $2.50	.20 × $3.60 = $.72
Total after-tax income (dividends plus capital gains less taxes)	(0 + 12.50) − 2.50 = $10.00	(10 + 3.60) − (3.00 + .72) = $9.88
After-tax rate of return (%)	$\frac{10}{100} = .10 = 10\%$	$\frac{9.88}{98.90} = .10 = 10\%$

COMPLETION QUESTIONS

1. Directors who expect to maintain the same payment in the future declare (*extra/regular*) cash dividends.

2. The record date always occurs (*after/before*) the payment date.

3. On the ex-dividend date owners of the stock (*will/will not*) receive dividends that were declared earlier.

4. (*No/Some*) restrictions apply on the payment of dividends as long as the company has sufficient cash.

5. Distributions of additional shares to a firm's stockholders is known as a stock _____ or a stock _____.

6. A stock repurchase had the same effect as a (*cash/stock*) dividend.

7. Dividends divided by (*cash flow/earnings*) equals the dividend payout ratio.

8. Dividends tend to follow (*long/short*) -run shifts in earnings.

9. Changes in dividends (*are/are not*) viewed as forecasts of future earnings.

10. Dividends fluctuate (*less/more*) than earnings.

11. A firm that is planning for a large expansion would likely pay (*high/low)* dividends.

12. _____ policy is the trade-off between retaining earnings and paying out cash and issuing new shares.

13. One view of dividend policy is that high dividends bring about high taxes that (*decreases/increases*) the value of the firm.

14. According to Modigliani and Miller (MM), the value of the firm (*is/is not*) affected whether the firm pays any dividends or not.

15. MM's argument for the irrelevance of dividend policy (*does/does not*) assume a world of certainty; it (*does/does not*) assume efficiency in capital markets.

16. People who believe dividends are "good," because they add value, base their argument on the fact that dividends are a (*risky/safe*) stream of cash instead of the (*certain/uncertain*) future of capital gains and/or some investors prefer spendable income from dividends because they are legally restricted from using capital gains or because dividends are a cheap and convenient way for them to receive cash from a company.

17. Another argument favoring high dividends is based on a firm's ability to convert dividends into (*capital gains/cash flows*) that are taxed at lower rates.

18. The argument for low dividends is based on a firm's ability to convert dividends into (*capital gains/cash flows*) which are taxed at lower rates.

19. Canada Customs and Revenue Agency (CCRA) has the authority to prevent companies from disguising (*dividends/interest*) as a stock (*issue/repurchase*).

20. The higher the tax rate paid on dividends received the (*stronger/weaker*) the incentive to pay dividends.

21. In Canada, any company receiving a dividend from another Canadian company pays income tax on only (*0/50*) percent of the dividends received.

22. A reduction in the capital gains tax rate (*decreases/increases*) the incentive to pay dividends.

PROBLEMS

1. Arrange the following dates in chronological order as they occur during the dividend payout procedure:

   Payment date
   Record date
   With-dividend date
   Declaration date
   Ex-dividend date

2. What is the dividend yield for a firm that recently announced a quarterly dividend of 50 cents per share when its stock is trading at $25 per share?

3. If nothing else happened to affect stock prices when would the dividend payment cause an impact on stock price?

4. What is the payout ratio for a company that is expected to earn $3.20 per share for the current year if its latest quarterly dividend was $0.32 per share?

5. Give an example showing how a stock dividend will affect the price of that stock?

6. Ryan's Rafts Company has 100,000 shares outstanding and declares a 20 percent stock dividend. If the total market value of the shares is $1 million before the stock dividend is paid, what will be the price per share after the dividend is paid, assuming nothing else happens to influence the stock price?

7. Suppose a firm with 50,000 shares outstanding has a market capitalization value of $1 million. If it has declared a dividend of $1 per share and the average tax rate on dividends is 30 percent, what will be the expected price per share on the ex-dividend date?

8. Bonto Ltd., reported earnings of $20 million and dividends of $12 million in its most recent year. The company has 5 million shares outstanding but has just announced plans for a 2-for-1 stock split. Assuming a current (pre-split) stock price of $80 per share, what are the dividends per share:
   a. Before the split?
   b. After the split what will the expected annual dividend rate be?

9. What will be the expected stock price of Bonto after the split?

10. What is the market value of Bonto
    a. Before the split?
    b. After the split?

11. Living in Ontario, you have $52,500 of taxable income from your employment in 2001. Meanwhile, you also own 4,000 shares of the ABC Co. that pays a total dividend of $2 per share during the year. Ignoring surtaxes charged, what is your after-tax dividend income?

ANSWERS TO COMPLETION QUESTIONS

1. regular
2. before
3. will not
4. Some
5. dividend, split
6. cash
7. earnings
8. long
9. are
10. less
11. low
12. Dividend
13. decreases
14. is not
15. does not, does
16. safe, certain
17. capital gains

18. capital gains
19. dividends, repurchase
20. stronger
21. 0
22. decreases

SOLUTIONS TO PROBLEMS

1. The process of paying dividends involves a set of standardized procedures. First the board of directors meets and **declares** a dividend. They establish a **record** date. By standard agreement this sets the **ex-dividend** date as 4 business days *before* the record date. People who buy the stock on that day or any day thereafter will not be entitled to receive the dividend that was previously declared. The **with-dividend** date is then understood to be the last day before the stock is traded without the right to receive the previously declared dividend. The dividend will actually be **paid** several weeks after the record date. Thus, in chronological order, the dates are: declaration, with-dividend, ex-dividend, record, and finally the payment date.

2. Dividend yields are computed as the total expected annual amount of dividends divided by the current market price for the stock. The $0.50 quarterly payout translates to $2 per share for the year. The dividend yield would be $2/$50 or 4 percent.

3. From the time after the declaration date through the with-dividend date, the price will only move due to other factors affecting the company or the market in general. On the ex-dividend date purchasers of the stock will not be entitled to receive the previously declared dividend. This is the date that the stock will fall by the amount of the dividend.

4. The payout ratio is the amount of dividends expected to be paid for the year expressed as a percentage of the earnings for that year. The annual dividend for this situation is expected to be $4 \times \$0.32 = \$1.28$ per share. The dividend payout ratio is: $\$1.28/\$3.20 = 0.4$ or 40 percent.

5. Assuming there is no news affecting the stock or the stock market, the individual stock price will fall by the percentage of the stock dividend. Thus for a stock trading at $60 per share which has a 15 percent stock dividend, the new stock price will be $60/1.15 or $52.17 per share.

6. The firm will be sending new shares to its shareholders. But that is all that happens. The company has not received any money, nor has its earning power increased as a result of the transaction. The value of the firm remains unchanged, as does the value of each shareholder's total share holding. After the 20 percent stock dividend there will

be 100,000 × 1.2 or 120,000 shares outstanding. The share price before the dividend was $1,000,000/100,000 shares or $10 per share. The new price will be $1,000,000/120,000 or $8.33 per share. The increase in the number of shares exactly offsets this decline in stock price. For example, the owner of 100 shares before the dividend had a market value of $10 × 100 or $1,000. After the dividend that person has 120 shares × $8.33 or $1,000 of market value.

7.   This problem incorporates the effect of income taxes. The share price before the dividend was $1,000,000/50,000 shares of $20. If we ignore taxes the ex-dividend price will be $20 − $1 or $19 per share. Because the investor pays 30 percent of the dividend in taxes, the net benefit of the $1 dividend is only $1 × (1 − 0.3) or $0.70 per share. So the new stock price will be $20 − $0.70 or $19.30.

8.   a. The $12 million of dividends are paid on the 5 million shares so the amount for each share is $12 million/5 million or $2.40.
     b. There will be twice as many shares outstanding after the split or 10 million. Because the company has not indicated that they are increasing the dividend rate, the total amount of dividends will remain the same. This means the expected dividends per share after the split will be $12 million/10 million or $1.20.

9.   Because of the 2-for-1 split the stock price will fall by one half to $40 per share. The value of each individual shareholder's stock will be unchanged. For example, someone who owned 100 shares before the split had a value of 100 × $80 per share or $8,000. After the split that person had 200 shares at $40 per share for a value of $8,000.

10. a. The market value of the 5 million shares of Bonto before the split was 5 million shares × $80 per share or $400 million.
     b. After the split the market value is 10 million shares × $40 per share or $400 million. Market value is not affected by this type of transaction. Only when investors expect a change in basic forces surrounding the company and the market itself will there be a change in the valuation.

11. 2001 individual tax rates and brackets

Federal:	16%	22%	26%	29%
	$0	$30,755	$61,561	$100,001+
Ontario:	6.20%	9.24%	13.39%	
	$0	$30,815	$61,631+	

	Federal @22%	Ontario @9.24%

Dividend received
   (4,000 × $2) = $8,000
Add: gross up @25% = 2,000

Taxable dividends $10,000

Income tax (Tax rate × $10,000)	$2,200	$924
Less: dividend tax credit		
DTC = 0.1333 × $10,000	1,333	
DTC = 0.0513 × $10,000		513
Taxes payable	$ 867	$411

Total taxes payable $1,278

Dividends after-taxes ($8,000 − $1,278) = $6,722.

CHAPTER 17

FINANCIAL STATEMENT ANALYSIS

INTRODUCTION

This is the first chapter of a three-chapter series covering working capital management topics. Financial analysis is first covered followed by financial planning, and finally, working capital management and short-term financing. Working capital greases the skids for the efficient utilization of capital assets that produce value. Too little working capital (current assets) and production and sales are hindered; too much working capital and the rate of return on capital diminishes. Working capital is justified as long as the incremental rate of return of an added dollar invested in working capital exceeds the opportunity rate of return of capital.

This chapter categorizes the scope of financial ratio analysis into *five* areas: 1) leverage, 2) liquidity, 3) efficiency or turnover, 4) profitability, and 5) market value. Several ratios are covered for each area, including an explanation of why the ratio is a good proxy for the concept. You studied ratio analysis in your second accounting course. Focus your thoughts on how each of the five areas, and their ratio measures, affects the value of a business. This "value" orientation is the main focus of finance, so be sure to carry the theme into this chapter. Table 17.9 in the textbook presents a variety of ratios for several industries.

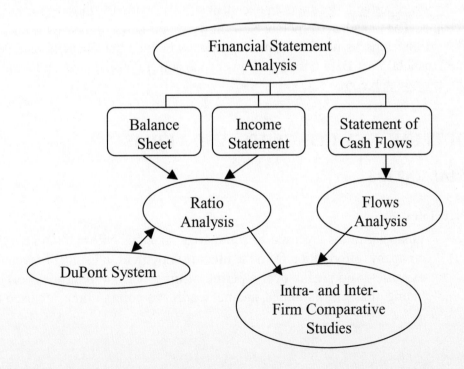

LEARNING CHECKLIST

After studying this chapter you should be able to:

____1. Calculate and interpret ratio measures of leverage, liquidity, profitability, asset management, and market valuation for a business.
____2. Use the Du Pont formula to understand the components of profitability measures such as return on assets and return on equity.
____3. Examine the statement of cash flows
____4. Evaluate the potential pitfalls of ratios based on accounting data.
____5. Understand market value added and economic value added.

SOURCES OF BUSINESS INFORMATION

Financial Post Information: In this chapter, you have seen a variety of financial ratios for a few industries. These averages are published by various organizations. In Canada, the Financial Post at www.financialpost.com is one of the most popular sources. The FP Data Group uses the Global Industry Classification Standard (GICS) putting the TSE 300 firms into 23 broad classes. The FP Investor Suite provides corporate and financial information. Both operating data and financial ratio averages can be found there.

Financial Data Finder: Statistics Canada's Web site at www.statcan.ca publishes detailed corporate financial statistics on balance sheet and income statement data that are broken down by industry classification and business size. While you want to check out the information for your own research, you may need some basic tutorials and tools. The Online Library of Financial Report at www.reportgallery.com is an excellent site for reviewing most of the ratios discussed in this chapter. The Canadian Corporate News at www.cdn-news.com is an interesting start. Other sources of benchmarks for Canadian corporations include the financial database available from the Financial Post Data Group at www.canoe.com/FP/home.html and Dun & Bradstreet Canada at www.dnb.com.

CHAPTER OUTLINE, KEY CONCEPTS, AND TERMS

I.   FINANCIAL RATIOS

    A.   **Principles**

        1.   Financial ratios are used to summarize financial information about a company. Information from the **income statement**, a listing of revenue, expenses, and profits over a period of time, and the **balance sheet**, a listing of assets, liabilities, and net worth at a point in time, are used to

calculate financial ratios related to the performance and risk level of a business.
2.   A balance sheet and income statement is often calculated as a **common-size** statement by dividing the balance sheet ledger items by total assets, and income statement items by total revenue.
3.   Five types of risk/return areas are studied in this chapter, using financial ratios as proxies to measure each risk.

B.   **Leverage Ratios**

1.   The use of fixed cost financing, either debt or preferred stock, is called financial leverage. Financial leverage presents a risk/return opportunity. Shareholders may magnify their earnings/returns by the use of fixed cost financing but, on the other hand, debt is a fixed cost, contractual commitment to pay regardless of the asset earning rate.

2.   Creditors, owners, and suppliers are interested in the extent to which a firm has sought the tax shielded benefits from financial leverage producing debt.

3.   Leverage ratios are of two types: balance sheet ratios comparing leverage capital to total capitalization (long-term debt and equity) or total assets, and coverage ratios that measure the earnings or cash-flow times coverage of fixed cost obligations.

4.   The long-term debt ratio measures the proportion of the capital structure that is made up of debt and lease obligations:

$$\text{Long-term debt ratio} = \text{long-term debt} + \text{value of leases} \div (\text{long-term debt} + \text{value of leases} + \text{equity})$$

The higher the ratio the greater the use of financial leverage, posing an increased risk/return situation for investors.

5.   The debt to equity ratio measures the amount of long-term debt plus value of leases to equity or the amount of leverage capital in relation to the equity cushion under the debt obligation:

$$\text{Debt-equity ratio} = [\text{long-term debt} + \text{value of leases}] \div \text{equity}$$

6.   The total debt ratio measures total liabilities, current and long-term, relative to total assets or the proportion of assets financed by debt:

$$\text{Total debt ratio} = \text{total liabilities} \div \text{total assets}$$

Whether or not to include operating leases, total liabilities differ.

7.   A coverage ratio, such as the times interest earned ratio, measures an amount available relative to amount owed. How many times is the obligation covered?

$$\text{Times interest earned} = \text{EBIT} \div \text{interest payments}$$

One may include principal payments necessary per period in the denominator to review the ability of operating earnings to cover the total debt obligation of principal and interest.

8.   The cash coverage ratio broadens the numerator to cash flow from operations relative to the interest payments:

$$\text{Cash coverage ratio} = (\text{EBIT} + \text{depreciation and amortization}) \div \text{interest payments}$$

9.   The fixed charge coverage ratio recognizes that lease and current debt repayments must be paid in time to avoid possible bankruptcy. Convert these fixed payments to a before-tax basis by dividing by $(1 - \text{tax rate})$.

Fixed charge coverage ratio = (EBIT + depreciation and amortization) ÷ (interest payments + grossed-up current debt repayment + grossed-up current lease obligations)

C.   **Liquidity Ratios**

1.   Liquidity ratios attempt to measure the ability to pay obligations such as current liabilities and the pool of assets available to cover the obligations. **Liquidity** is the ability of an asset to be converted to cash quickly at low cost. Converting an asset to cash occurs in one of two ways. Sell the asset, hoping it has reasonable liquidity, or in the case of a financial asset, like accounts receivable or Treasury bill, maturity brings cash. Working capital circulates from inventory to accounts receivable to cash, etc. Accounting value estimates of liquid assets are reasonable estimates of their value.

2.   Current assets (the pool of circulating cash assets available to be allocated to pay bills) *minus* current liabilities(the pool of obligations the business must pay in the near future) is an analytical amount called net working capital (NWC). NWC is a rough measure of the current assets left over if the current liabilities were paid. The NWC to total assets ratio estimates the proportion of assets in net current assets, another name for NWC:

$$\text{NWC/total asset ratio} = \text{net working capital} \div \text{total assets}$$

3.	The current ratio is the classic liquidity ratio, but is merely a variation of the idea above — what pool of circulating assets is available relative to the pool of current obligations:

Current ratio = current assets ÷ current liabilities

4.	Continuing the theme of assets available to pay obligations, the quick or acid-test ratio eliminates inventories, the least liquid current asset, from current assets:

Quick ratio = (cash + marketable securities + receivables) ÷ current liabilities

5.	The cash ratio eliminates inventories and receivables from current assets to review the cash assets relative to the current liabilities:

Cash ratio = (cash + marketable securities) ÷ current liabilities

6.	The interval measure of liquidity measures the firm's pool of liquid, quick assets (above) to the daily expenditures from operations and gives an estimate of the number of days' obligations that are circulating in the quick assets. The more days, the greater the ability to meet obligations:

Interval measure = (cash + marketable securities + receivables) ÷ average daily expenditures from operations

The denominator represents annual cash (not depreciation) expenses divided by 365.

D.	**Efficiency Ratios**

1.	Another area of financial analysis, efficiency ratios, measures how effectively the business is using its assets. "Using" relates to liquidity or profitability or performance. The numerators used in efficiency ratios are activity-based items, such as sales, cost of sales, etc., while the denominators are generally some average balance sheet amount. Turnover ratios are often converted to a time-line focus by dividing turnovers ratios into 365 days.

2.	The asset turnover ratio measures the sales activity derived from total assets, or the revenue generated per dollar of total assets. The asset turnover is also an important component of asset profitability studied later, measuring the revenue per dollar invested:

Asset turnover ratio = sales ÷ average total assets

235

Sales, a measure of activity, may be compared to a variety of balance sheet accounts (e.g., fixed assets, net working capital, stockholders equity, etc.) to measure the revenue generating efficiency of the account.

3. The inventory turnover ratio, using the cost of goods sold representing the cumulative amount of inventory sold in a period as the numerator and average inventory (beginning plus ending divided by two) as the denominator, measures the number of times the value of inventory turns over in a period:

$$\text{Inventory turnover} = \text{cost of goods sold} \div \text{average inventory}$$

The inventory turnover may be converted to a time line concept, the number of days' sales in inventories, by finding the reciprocal ($1/\times$) of the inventory turnover times 365 or:

$$\text{Days' sales in inventories} = \text{average inventory} \div (\text{cost of sales}/365)$$
$$\text{or} = [1 \div (\text{inventory turnover})] \times 365$$

4. The average collection period applies the same concept above to accounts receivables. The average collection period is the estimated number of days it takes to collect receivables:

$$\text{Average collection period} = \text{average receivables} \div \text{average daily sales}$$

The more days' sales outstanding, the greater amount of capital is tied up in accounts receivables relative to sales.

E. **Profitability Ratios**

1. Profitability refers to some measure of profit relative to revenue or an amount invested. The net profit margin measures the proportion of sales revenue that is profit available for sources of funds (net income + interest). Net profits after taxes is commonly used in this ratio, but net profits is biased by the relative amount of leveraging or debt financing in the business:

$$\text{Net profit margin} = (\text{net income}) \div \text{sales}$$

2. The gross profit margin reflects the mark-up over the cost of products sold representing cost control.

$$\text{Gross profit margin} = (\text{sales} - \text{cost of goods sold}) \div \text{sales}$$

3. The operating profit margin is an overall measure of a firm's operating performance. It is also known as the basic earning power.

$$\text{Operating profit margin} = (\text{EBIT} - \text{taxes}) \div \text{sales}$$

4. A good performance ratio is the return on total assets including current and fixed (ROA), which is part of the Du Pont analysis.

$$\text{Return on assets} = (\text{net income} + \text{interest}) \div \text{average total assets}$$

Since the financial leverage affects the ROA, operating performance alone is measured by the adjusted return on assets.

$$\text{Adjusted ROA} = (\text{net income} + \text{interest} - \text{interest tax shields}) \div \text{average total assets}$$

5. Based on total capital, the high return on invested capital somehow indicates the monopoly power a firm owns.

$$\text{Return on invested capital} = (\text{net income} + \text{interest} - \text{interest tax shields}) \div (\text{average total debt} + \text{preferred and common equity})$$

6. The return on equity (ROE) measures the profitability of the common stockholders' equity or return per dollar of invested equity capital.

$$\text{Return on equity} = \text{net income} \div \text{average equity}$$

7. The proportion of earnings that is paid out as dividends is called the payout ratio.

$$\text{Payout ratio} = \text{dividends} \div \text{earnings}$$

8. The complement of the payout ratio is the plowback ratio, or the proportion of earnings retained in the period.

$$\text{Plowback ratio} = (\text{earnings} - \text{dividends}) \div \text{earnings} = \text{earnings retained in period} \div \text{earnings}$$

9. The plowback ratio times the return on equity (ROE) is an estimate of the growth rate in common equity from internally generated earnings, or the sustainable growth rate in assets that the business can support from internal earnings without changing the total debt/equity asset ratio.

$$\text{Growth in equity from plowback} = (\text{earnings} - \text{dividends}) \div \text{equity} = [(\text{earnings} - \text{dividends}) \div \text{earnings}] \times (\text{earnings} \div \text{equity}) = \text{plowback} \times \text{ROE}$$

II.   THE DU PONT SYSTEM

A.   The **Du Pont System** is a process of analyzing component ratios (also called decomposition) of the ROA and ROE to explain their level or changes.

B.   The ROA is comprised of the product of the profit margin, what the firm earns on every dollar of sales, times the asset turnover or the extent to which a business utilizes its assets:

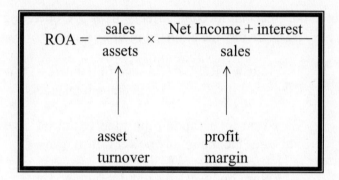

$$\text{ROA} = \frac{\text{sales}}{\text{assets}} \times \frac{\text{Net Income} + \text{interest}}{\text{sales}}$$

asset turnover   profit margin

Both the profit margin and asset turnover can be broken down in sub-components (decomposed) to assess the cause of the level or changes in the ROA. The ability to earn on assets is comprised of expense control per sales (profit margin) and the effective use of assets to generate revenue (asset turnover). A level of ROA can be generated or changed by affecting the margin or turnover.

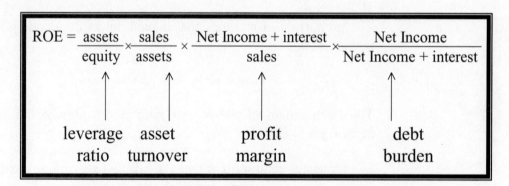

$$\text{ROE} = \frac{\text{assets}}{\text{equity}} \times \frac{\text{sales}}{\text{assets}} \times \frac{\text{Net Income} + \text{interest}}{\text{sales}} \times \frac{\text{Net Income}}{\text{Net Income} + \text{interest}}$$

leverage ratio   asset turnover   profit margin   debt burden

C.   The ROE is comprised of the ROA *times* the leverage ratio *times* the debt-burden ratio, or the ROE is related to the effective, profitable use of assets, the extent of financial leverage, and the level of interest rates paid on debt

III. ANALYSIS OF THE STATEMENT OF CASH FLOWS

A. As cash is the king in finance, using the **free cash flow (FCF)** is a new approach to value the return of an investment.

B. Although there is no standard definition of FCF, the FCF is widely defined as the cash flow from operating activities (i.e., net income plus depreciation and amortization) minus the cash flow for investing (i.e., capital expenditures plus changes in working capital).

C. While such an approach better measures how much actual cash the business generates, cash-flow-based ratios will provide reliable assessments.

IV. USING FINANCIAL RATIOS

FINANCIAL RATIOS FOR SELECTED INDUSTRY GROUPS, SECOND QUARTER, 2000								
	Wholesale and Retail	Biotechnology and Pharmaceuticals	Technology	Food and Beverage	Communications and Media	Auto, Parts and Transportation	Oil and Gas	Steel
Long-term debt ratio[a]	0.26	0.14	0.15	0.51	0.69	0.19	0.34	0.47
Cash flow from operations/total debt	0.5	−0.46	−0.69	0.3	0.32	1.59	0.99	0.113
Current ratio	1.68	11.07	3.54	2.46	1.18	1.98	1.74	2.02
Quick ratio	0.66	7.21	2.96	0.83	0.86	1.17	1.5	0.79
Times interest earned	5.73	−10.26	−33.09	7.72	5.54	34.29	19.64	2.7
Total asset turnover	2.2	0.26	0.86	1.33	0.55	1.26	0.56	1.1
Operating profit margin	3.62	−33.56	−22.21	14.61	15.98	10.11	37.62	6.18
Return on total assets (%)	4.57	−14.55	−11.97	7.54	2.7	6.73	11.72	5.2
Return on equity (%)	7.89	−16.3	−18.8	16.36	−36.96	11.23	27.92	5.03

[a] Long-term debt/(Long-term debt + equity)

A. Cautions

1. Generally acceptable accounting principles have considerable leeway in accounting for asset/liability values and income, so that it is often difficult to make an absolute comparison of company ratio with other companies or the industry ratios.

2. Goodwill is difficult to assess. Some commitments to pay, such as pensions, lease obligations, and guarantees, are not always shown as a liability.

B. Choosing a Benchmark

1. Knowing reasonable ranges for the above ratios calculated requires practice, comparison of the trends over time, and compared to averages, a successful business or similar benchmark for comparison.

2.   Industry ratios are available from a number of sources. Differences from averages or earlier trends is not wrong, but provides a beginning for understanding why the differences or changes occurred.

V.   MEASURING COMPANY PERFORMANCE

A.   Efficient markets have come to realize that an accounting statement has limited use when determining the value of the firm. All the ratio analysis skills in the world can not tell you the market value of a firm. Nor can they tell you why market value of some firms continues to rise above expectations.

B.   **Stern Stewart & Co.** employ two measurements to track just such information. **Market Value Added (MVA)** tells us the difference between the market value of common stock and its book value. Their other measurement, Economic Value Added (traditionally referred to as residual income), tells us the net dollar return after deducting the cost of capital.

$$EVA = Residual\ Income$$
$$= Income\ Earned - income\ required$$
$$= Income\ Earned - [Cost\ of\ Capital \times Investment]$$

C.   **THE ROLE OF FINANCIAL RATIOS**
1.   Never forget that financial ratios can provide "invaluable" information about a firm, its health and its risks. At the same time, it does not necessarily lead us to "valuable" information either. Specifically, when it relates to market values and economic values.
2.   The accountant tends to over emphasize ratios and the financial manager tends to under estimate them. Be mindful that the truth lies somewhere in the middle.

COMPLETION QUESTIONS

1.   The purpose of financial statement analysis (*is/is not*) to analyze a firm's overall performance and to assess its current financial standing.

2.   The five types of financial ratios are: _____, _____, _____, _____, and _____.

3. (*Leverage/Liquidity*) ratios show how easily the firm can get cash.

4. The (*balance sheet/income statement*) presents a snapshot of a firm at a given point in time.

5. An example of an asset not shown on the balance sheet is (*employees/trademarks*).

6. Shareholders' equity (*excludes/includes*) preferred stock.

7. The common size balance sheet presents items as a percentage of (*assets/sales*).

8. Financial leverage (*decreases/increases*) the riskiness of the rate of return on equity.

9. The debt ratio (*excludes/includes*) the value of leases.

10. The times interest ratio uses interest payments in the (*denominator/numerator*).

11. In the cash coverage ratio, _____ _____ is added to the earnings before interest and taxes.

12. Liquidity refers to the ability to convert (*assets/liabilities*) to cash quickly and at low cost.

13. The difference between current assets and current liabilities is known as _____ _____ _____.

14. The quick or acid test ratio (*excludes/includes*) inventory.

15. The most liquid assets are cash and marketable _____.

16. The _____ measure indicates how many days a firm can pay its bills using only its cash and other liquid assets.

17. If a firm is operating at close to full capacity it likely will have a relatively (*high/low*) asset turnover ratio.

18. The inventory turnover ratio uses (*cost of goods sold/sales*) in the numerator.

19. The days' sales in inventory is the reciprocal of the inventory turnover ratio (*divided/multiplied*) by 365.

20. The average accounts receivable divided by the average daily sales is called the average _____ _____.

21. The net profit margin equals earnings before (*interest/taxes*) divided by sales.

22. In order to measure returns on all assets, interest is (*added to/subtracted from*) net profits.

23. If earnings are highly variable, the firm will likely have a (*high/low*) target payout ratio.

24. The proportion of earnings that are reinvested in the firm is called the _____ ratio.

25. Shareholders' equity grows faster if (*less/more*) dividends are paid.

26. A high price/earnings ratio for a company indicates that investors expect (*high/low*) growth rate of dividends.

27. A high dividend yield indicates that investors expect (*high/low*) dividend growth or that they require a (*high/low*) return.

28. Book value equals the amount common stockholders have invested in the firm (*minus/plus*) amounts that have been invested on their behalf.

29. The adjusted return on asset argues that interest tax shields should be (*added/subtracted*) in the numerator.

30. The Du Pont system of financial analysis links (*liquidity/profitability*) with (*efficiency/market value*) ratios.

31. Competition usually results in trade-offs between (*profitability/turnover*) and (*plowback/profitability*).

32. Incorporating a (*leverage/liquidity*) ratio in the Du Pont system allows one to analyze how financing choices affect returns to shareholders.

33. A company that has acquired another firm by paying more than book value will have goodwill on the (*balance sheet/income statement*).

34. In analyzing financial statements for a company, it is important to compare the ratios calculated with averages for the same (*industry/size*).

35. Studies have shown historical earnings are (*reliable/unreliable*) predictors of future earnings.

36. In the fixed-charge coverage ratio, fixed payments are made from (*before/after*)-tax earnings.

PROBLEMS

For problems 1–9 use the financial statements for Jennifer's Jai Alai and Jicama Corporation (JJAJC) as shown below:

BALANCE SHEET
(Millions of dollars)

Account	End of year	Start of year
Current Assets		
Cash	2	6
Accounts receivable	14	12
Inventory	21	17
Fixed Assets		
Plant and equipment	63	48
Accumulated depreciation	(10)	(8)
Total	90	75

	End of year	Start of year
Liabilities and shareholders' equity		
Current liabilities		
Debt due for repayments	10	6
Accounts payable	14	9
Other current liabilities	4	2
Long-term debt	5	2
Common stock (10 million shares)	24	18
Retained earnings	33	38
Total	90	75

INCOME STATEMENT
(Millions of dollars)

Net sales	100
Cost of goods sold	44
Depreciation & amortization	2
Other operating expenses	43
Earnings before interest and taxes (EBIT)	11
Net interest expense	1
Taxable income	10
Income taxes	5
Net income	5
Common dividends	1

1. Calculate the following ratios for JJAJC:
   a. Times interest earned
   b. Long-term debt ratio
   c. Total debt ratio
   d. Cash coverage ratio
   e. Current ratio
   f. Quick ratio
   g. Net profit margin
   h. Inventory turnover
   i. Days in inventory
   j. Average collection period
   k. Return on equity
   l. Return on assets
   m. Payout ratio

2. If JJAJC shut down operations, how many days could it pay its bills?

3. What must have been the investment in new plant and equipment during the latest year?

4. If the market value of the stock was $84 million at the end of the latest year, what was the price-to-book ratio?

5. What were JJAJC's earnings per share?

6.   What is the price-to-earnings ratio?

7.   What must have been the price of JJAJC's common stock at year-end?

8.   What were the dividends paid per share?

9.   What was the dividend yield on the common stock?

10.   A partial analysis of Paul Thomas Meats, Inc. reveals the following ratios:

Current	2.5
Quick	2.0
Inventory turnover	4.0
Operating profit margin	.10

       If the current liabilities were $6 million and operating expenses were $15 million, what must have been the cost of goods sold if we ignore taxes?

11.   What were PTM's sales for that year ignoring taxes?

ANSWERS TO COMPLETION QUESTIONS

1.   is
2.   leverage, liquidity, efficiency, profitability, market value
3.   Liquidity
4.   balance sheet
5.   employees
6.   excludes
7.   assets
8.   increases
9.   includes
10.   denominator
11.   depreciation & amortization
12.   assets
13.   net working capital
14.   excludes
15.   securities
16.   interval
17.   high
18.   cost of goods sold
19.   multiplied
20.   collection period
21.   interest
22.   added to

23. low
24. plowback
25. less
26. high
27. low, high
28. plus
29. subtracted
30. profitability, efficiency
31. turnover, profitability
32. leverage
33. balance sheet
34. industry
35. unreliable
36. after

SOLUTIONS TO PROBLEMS

1.   a. Times interest earned = EBIT/interest = $11/$1
        = 11

    b. Long-term debt ratio = long-term debt + value of leases/(long-term debt + value of leases + equity)
$$= \$5/(\$5 + \$57)$$
$$= 0.081$$

    c. Total debt ratio = total liabilities/total assets
$$= \$33/\$90$$
$$= 0.367$$

    d. Cash coverage ratio = EBIT + depreciation & amortization/interest payments
$$= (\$11 + \$2)/\$1$$
$$= 13$$

    e. Current ratio = current assets/current liabilities
$$= \$37/\$28$$
$$= 1.32$$

    f. Quick ratio = (current assets – inventories)/ current liabilities = $\dfrac{\text{cash + marketable securities & receivables}}{\text{current liabilities}}$

$$= (\$37 - \$21)/\$28$$
$$= 0.571$$

    g. Net profit margin = (net income + interest)/sales
$$= (\$5 + \$1)/\$100$$
$$= 0.06$$

h. Inventory turnover = cost of goods sold/average inventory

$$= \$44 \div [(\$21 - \$17)/2]$$
$$= 2.32$$

i. Days in inventory = average inventory/cost of goods sold per day

$$= \$19 \div (\$44/365)$$
$$= 158 \text{ days}$$

j. Average collection period = average accounts receivable/sales per day

$$= \frac{(\$14 + \$12)}{2} \div \$100/365$$
$$= 47.5 \text{ days}$$

k. Return on equity = net income/average equity

$$= \$5 \div [(\$57 + \$56)/2]$$
$$= 0.088$$

l. Return on assets = net income + interest/average assets

$$= (\$5 + \$1) \div [(\$90 + \$75)/2]$$
$$= 0.0727$$

m. Payout ratio = dividends/net income

$$= \$1/\$5$$
$$= 0.20$$

2.   The interval measure is the cash on hand plus accounts receivable divided by the total cash expenses per day. The cash expenses equal the cost of goods sold plus the other expenses. In this case the interval measure is

$$= (\$2 + \$14) \div [(\$44 + \$45)/365]$$
$$= 65.6 \text{ days}$$

3.   The new investment in plant and equipment must have been the increase in plant and equipment during the year. If only net plant and equipment was shown on the balance sheet, depreciation and amortization would be added to the change in the net amount during the year. In this case new investment = $63 – $48 or $15 million + $2 million = $17 million.

4.   The book value of the stock at year end was $57 million which, if divided into the market value of the stock outstanding of $84 million yields a price to book ratio of 1.47.

5.   Earnings per share equals net income divided by the number of shares outstanding. For JJAJC it is $5 million/10 million shares or $0.50 per share.

6.   The price-to-earnings ratio is the market value divided by the net income. This is:

$$= \$84/\$5$$
$$= 16.8$$

7. The stock price would be the market value divided by the number of shares outstanding. For JJAJC it would be $84/10 or $8.40 per share.

8. The total dividends paid were $1 million on the 10 million shares so the dividends per share would be $1/10 or $0.10.

9. The dividend yield would be $0.10/$8.40 = 0.012 or 1.2 percent.

10. The key to this problem is to write various ratios to solve for the missing amounts. For example, we know:

   current ratio = current assets/current liabilities

   2.5 = current assets /$6

   current assets = 2.5 × $6 = $15 million.

   Next we can find the inventory by remembering that the quick ratio equals current assets less inventories divided by current liabilities. This yields:

   2.0 = ($15 – inventory)/$6

   inventory = $15 – ($6 × 2) = $3 million

   In the last step we use the inventory turnover ratio as being the cost of goods sold divided by the inventory. For PTM it is:

   4 = cost of goods sold/$3

   cost of goods sold = 4 × $3 = $12 million

11. Sales can be found from the answer to problem 10 and by knowing that the operating profit margin without taxes equals sales less total expenses divided by the sales. The total expenses are the sum of the cost of goods sold and the operating expenses or $12 + $15 = $27 million.

   The operating profit margin = 0.10 = (sales – $27)/sales. Sales = $30 million.

CHAPTER 18

FINANCIAL PLANNING

INTRODUCTION

This second of three working capital management chapters focuses on the concepts of financial planning. Beginning with an assumption of volume (sales, production), the financial planning process, top-down or down-up, focuses all estimates and iterations in financial terms to a certain point in the future (balance sheet) or during the period (income statement or statement of cash flows). Every business person becomes involved in the planning process, formally or informally, so the financial planning concepts covered here have considerable value to students of all majors. Just like other chapters, the concepts of this chapter are easily applied to your own personal financial planning.

After an introduction to the planning process, the authors use the percentage of sales financial planning model to demonstrate the general framework of a financial plan. The general assumption is that specific asset levels are directly related to the level of sales. Given sales, asset needs for the future can be estimated. Some current liabilities, such as accounts payables, are directly related to inventory levels and increase with increased inventories. The difference between assets needed at some future point and financing provided, including any new retained earnings, is the funds needed or plug amount of financing that the financial manager must provide.

Estimating the amount of funds needed and when funds are needed are valuable inputs for the financial manager. The key issue in financial planning is not the single right estimate of what will exactly take place (that seldom occurs), but reviewing and understanding a series of likely scenarios is the real value of planning for the financial manager. Being ready, financially, for whatever happens in the sales and production areas is the crucial function of the financial manager.

The last section of the chapter interrelates investment policy, debt policy, dividend policy, and growth policy into a financial planning format. The concepts of internal growth rate (maximum sales or asset growth rate without external financing) and the sustainable growth rate (maximum growth rate within specific debt and dividend policy) are valuable concepts that tie several important financial policy areas together.

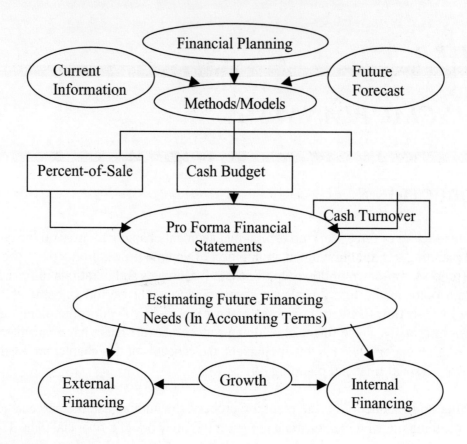

LEARNING CHECKLIST

After studying this chapter you should be able to:

____1. Describe the steps involved in preparing a financial plan.
____2. Construct a simple financial planning model.
____3. Estimate the effect of growth (sales and assets) on the need for external financing.

SOURCES OF BUSINESS INFORMATION

Finding Out the Practical Savings Plans: If you are self-employed, your earnings will be erratic. The traditional automatic monthly savings plans may not work out. You need another method to save money. Having said that, nobody can tell you how to do it except yourself. However, there are several issues deserving attention. First, as your income fluctuates, only do your planning for a short duration. Monitor income and expenses accordingly. Keep the surplus in the cash pool. Always be prepared for the tough times by putting off your luxuries until the growth is solid. TD Canada Trust has a Web site, "Planning for Your Future" at www.tdcanadatrust.com/planning, providing advice on saving strategies over the life span.

Starting Up a Business: Do you want to be an entrepreneur starting your own business? The Canada Business Service Centres at www.bsa.cbsc.org is an excellent source providing reliable information. The Web site is organized by geographical location. Depending on which province or territory you set up your business, you can find various topics about starting a business such as name and structure selection, business proposal, market research, financing, taxation, employees hiring, and much more. In addition, online tools such as Interactive Business Planner (IBP) and Interactive Export Planner offer software products designed to assist entrepreneurs in preparing business plans for their new or existing ventures.

CHAPTER OUTLINE, KEY CONCEPTS, AND TERMS

I.   **WHAT IS FINANCIAL PLANNING?**

    A.   **Financial Planning is a process consisting of:**
        1.   Analyzing the investment and financing choices available to the business.
        2.   Projecting the future consequences of current decisions under varying scenarios.
        3.   Deciding which alternative to undertake.
        4.   Later, measuring performance or results with the goals of the financial plan — the planning and control cycle.

    B.   **Planning Horizon** — The time line of financial planning includes both short-term planning, perhaps the next 12 months with a focus on cash flow timing, and long-term financial planning where the **planning horizon** or time associated with the plan is around 5 years or longer.

    C.   **Financial Planning Focuses on the Big Picture**
        1.   Financial plans include the strategic plan of the business or a "big picture" perspective, rather than the implications of individual investments and other decisions.
        2.   Alternative business plans might consider 3 scenarios relating to *best case, normal growth,* or *worst case* or *retrenchment.*
        3.   Planning may consider a variety of alternative opportunities or future options.
        4.   Financial plans often interrelate a level of activity such as sales to the level of assets needed, which in turn determines the amount of funds needed to finance the added investment.
        5.   Added sales increases the need for current assets, increases some current liabilities (accounts payable) or *netting* the two determines an added level of net working capital needed to fund asset growth.
        6.   Dividend policy is a factor in a financial plan, for the dividend/retention decision affects the level of earnings paid out or retained in the business to finance new assets needed.

7.   A firm has financial slack if the level of expected financing is greater than the funds needed for a period. Debt may be repaid, dividends increased, or stock repurchased when long-term financial slack exists.

8.   Businesses estimating rapid sales and asset growth beyond the funding ability of earnings, must prepare to raise external capital from banks, bonds, or common stock issues.

D.   **Financial Planning Is Not Just Forecasting**

1.   Forecasting attempts to estimate the most likely future outcome, such as a level of sales.

2.   Financial planning considers a variety of future outcomes and prepares for each should they occur.

3.   "What if" analysis is a major part of financial planning from changing a single variable in a plan (sensitivity analysis) and noting the effect on funds needed, to scenario analysis, where a situation involving a number of variables (recession) is analyzed to estimate the ability to serve customers and earn expected returns to equity should the scenario develop.

E.   **Three Requirements for Effective Planning**

1.   The *three* requirements for effective planning include forecasting, the process of choosing the best or optimal plan and watching the plan unfold, and comparing actual to the plan and addressing variances.

2.   Forecasting focuses on the most likely outcome and is not financial planning. However, a good forecast always is a good start for the financial plan. Anticipating competitive responses should be considered in the plan.

3.   After considering several scenarios, the financial manager must choose a plan which will direct the efforts of the business. Financial plans are often in accounting terms, not shareholders, such as total return. Shareholder interests should be represented in decisions and strategy, not accounting performance indicators.

4.   Financial plans are dated with the short passage of time, so a plan must be easily adapted as events and opportunities occur. Plans may serve a standard to compare experience.

II.   **FINANCIAL PLANNING MODELS**

A.   A financial planning model establishes relationships between economic activity (sales), business policies, such as a credit policy, and the resulting resources needed, including assets, employees, or financial capital.

B.   The equations or relationships in the financial model may be derived from past relationships (correlations) or expected relationships based on forecasts.

C.   Financial models using spreadsheet programs enable the planner to study a wide range of possible outcomes and prepare the firm to handle *what will occur*.

D.   **Components of a Financial Planning Model**

    1.   Financial plans include *three* components: inputs, the planning model, and outputs.

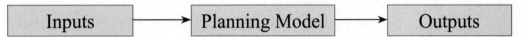

    2.   The inputs include current financial statements and forecasts. In most financial plans, expected sales is the major independent variable that drives the plan. Other variables, such as assets (inventories) are related to expected sales.

    3.   The planning model, with the established relationships between sales and assets, etc., calculates the estimated levels of resources needed, the expected amount of financing needed, and the expected profit and cash flow.

    4.   The output of the financial plans includes estimated financial statements based on the assumptions and relationships of the plan, called **pro forma** financial statements, such as income statements, balance sheets, and cash flow statements. Financial ratios, based on the pro forma financial statements, are usually calculated.

	Income Statement	
Sales		$1,200
Costs		1,000
Net Income		200

	Balance	*Sheet*		
Assets	$2,000		Debt	$ 800
			Equity	1,200
Total	$2,000		Total	$2,000

253

E. **An Example of a Planning Model**

1. The **percentage of sales model** is a financial planning model in which the future level of asset investment, and subsequent financing needs, is a function of forecasted sales. The assumption is that sales drives assets, which drives the financing needed. See Tables 18.1–18.3 in the textbook.

2. A simple percentage of sales model assumes no spare capacity in the asset (production) structure, so increased sales will require added current assets, fixed assets, perhaps some spontaneous financing from current liabilities, and added equity financing via retained earnings (net income minus dividends).

3. The pro forma balance sheet associated with the percentage of sales financial planning model uses any one of a number of ledger accounts as a variable to "balance" the balance sheet with a fixed debt-equity ratio. Dividends paid, a financing decision, may be the **balancing item** as might the debt/equity ratio, bank financing, or a generic "funds needed" liability account.

PRO FORMA INCOME STATEMENT	
Sales	$1,320
Costs	1,100
Net income	$ 220

PRO FORMA BALANCE SHEET			
Assets	$2,200	Debt	$ 880
		Equity	1,320
Total	$2,200	Total	$2,200

NEW PRO FORMA BALANCE SHEET			
Assets	$2,200	Debt	$ 960
		Equity	1,240
Total	$2,200	Total	$2,200

F. **An Improved Model**

1. The Executive Fruit Company pro forma example, Tables 18.4–18.9 in the textbook is a good example of the percentage of sales financial planning model.

2. Some balance sheet and income statement items vary directly with sales, but some do not. The relationship between sales and specific variables must be established before planning starts.

3. With 100% operating capacity, all asset accounts and spontaneous liabilities are tied directly to sales. Retained earnings also vary with sales, but not proportionally.

4. As sales drives the level of assets needed and the estimated required external financing needed, projecting sales for coming periods is the first critical step.

5. External funds needed are calculated according to the firm's growth forecasts and its dividend policy. The amount required equals to the

increase in assets netting out spontaneous increase in liabilities taking away increase in retained earnings.

6.   Cash flow forecast with pro forma statement alerts the firm to future cash needs or surplus available.

7.   Since plans derived from growth projections do not indicate the best financing mix, firms must still focus on the debt/equity mix and all possible financing sources.

8.   Given varied sales estimates, alternative forecasts of financing needed provide different scenarios that management has to face.

III.   PLANNERS BEWARE

A.   Pitfalls in Model Design

1.   Will a more sophisticated financial planning model give the financial manager an improved forecast of funds needed in the future? Is having "the" right forecast the real purpose of financial planning, or is financial planning really about estimating the range of possible outcomes?

2.   The value of the financial plan is to prepare for a variety of outcomes, not build the ultimate, realistic financial planning model.

B.   Shortcomings of Percentage of Sales Models

1.   Though a good "rough" first estimate for financial planning, the percentage of sales model is limited in that many estimated variables, such as assets, are not or are not always proportional to sales.

2.   Fixed assets are not easily added in small amounts, but are more economically added in large investments. Thus, the firm must plan based on expected production utilization rates. Asset investment is not usually proportional to sales in a shorter time span, and is better related over a longer planning horizon.

C.   There Is No Finance in Financial Planning Models

1.   Financial planning models estimate accounting statements, and do not focus on financial decision tools such as incremental cash flows, time value, market risk, etc.

2.   Financial planning models are not focused on financial decisions that would increase market value, though the debt/equity standards of the firm and the dividend policy of the business are built into financial planning.

IV. EXTERNAL FINANCING AND GROWTH

> Required external financing = new investment – addition to retained earnings
>
> = (growth rate × assets) – addition to retained earnings

A. Financial planning produces consistency between growth, investment, and financing goals of the business, for all are included in the plan. This section studies the relationships between growth objectives and requirements for external financing.

B. The general idea is that the faster the firm grows, the more financing, and probably more external financing, will be needed. The extent of external financing will be related to the asset intensity of the firm, the profitability of the firm and the debt/equity and dividend policies of the firm.

C. Sales growth drives asset growth drives funds needed. The higher the sales growth, the more assets/sales needed, the lower the profitability of the firm, the higher the dividend payout, the *greater* the more likely external funds (debt or equity) will be needed.

D. The **internal growth rate** of the firm is the maximum rate of growth *without* external financing. Where the upward sloping (slope related to profitability and dividend policy) line intersects the horizontal line (growth rate scale) is the internal growth rate, or the maximum growth rate at which the firm can grow and finance all its needs from internal sources (equity). The internal growth rate is the ratio of addition to retained earnings divided by assets. The higher the historic contribution of retained earnings to finance assets, the higher the growth rate the firm can maintain without external capital.

$$\text{Internal growth rate} = \frac{\text{addition to retained earnings}}{\text{assets}}$$

$$= \frac{\text{addition to retained earnings}}{\text{net income}} \times \frac{\text{net income}}{\text{equity}} \times \frac{\text{equity}}{\text{assets}}$$

E. The internal growth rate is the product of the plowback ratio times the ROE times the leverage ratio.

The higher the plowback ratio (lower dividend payout), the higher the profitability (ROE) and the higher the proportion of assets financed by equity, the greater the internal growth rate.

F. The **sustainable growth rate** is the maximum growth rate (sales or assets) the firm can maintain without changing the debt/equity ratio and without any external equity financing (sale of stock). While the internal growth rate is the maximum growth rate without *any external financing* (debt or equity), the sustainable growth rate is the maximum growth rate sustainable without *any external equity financing*.

> Sustainable growth rate = plowback ratio × return on equity

G. The sustainable growth rate will be greater than the internal growth rate for the former considers added debt financing along with added equity financing provided by additional earnings retained (not paid in dividends) in the period.

H. The sustainable growth rate is the product of the plowback ratio (proportion of net income retained in the firm) times the return on equity (ROE).

COMPLETION QUESTIONS

1. Financial planning is a process designed to (*minimize/take appropriate*) risks.

2. The planning horizon is (*short- and long-/long-*) term.

3. Often separate plans are submitted for the best case, normal growth, and (*exceptional growth/retrenchment*).

4. Sensitivity analysis and scenario analysis are used for (*how-to/what-if*) questions.

5. Forecasting is (*a part of/the same as*) planning.

6. When forecasts come from different areas of the company it (*is/is not*) important to have consistent assumptions for influencing variables such as inflation and economic growth.

7. The optimal financial plan typically (*is/is not*) developed by setting a goal of profit margin.

8. Long-term plans (*should/should not*) be revised periodically.

9. The three parts of all financial plans are inputs, outputs and (*cash flows/planning models*).

10. Projected or forecasted financial statements are called _____ _____ statements.

11. The planning model in which sales forecasts are the driving variables is called the _____ of sales model.

12. A variable that is adjusted to maintain consistency in a pro forma statement is called a balancing item or _____.

13. A firm that forecasts the need for an additional $100 of assets to support an increase in sales which are expected to generate total profits of $60 will need to acquire new financing of _____.

14. In the early steps of financial planning the (*amount/mix*) of financing is determined.

15. In estimating future financing requirements, amounts for depreciation of fixed assets (*add to/subtract from*) the projected needs.

16. The percentage of sales models of forecasting are (*less/more*) accurate because many variables are not proportional to sales.

17. Financial planning models (*do/do not*) emphasize tools of financial analysis.

18. The internal growth rate is the (*maximum/minimum*) rate of growth without external financing.

19. The sustainable growth rate is the maximum growth rate that a firm can maintain without (*decreasing/increasing*) leverage.

20. Unless a company does not borrow money, its internal growth rate will be (*less/more*) than the sustainable growth rate.

PROBLEMS

1. Why do businesses make financial plans?

2. Why are individual investment projects usually not considered separately in a financial plan?

3. How is uncertainty about the future incorporated into financial planning?

4. Discuss how inconsistencies may affect financial planning?

5. Matthew Tyler Stamps, Ltd. (MTSL) expects sales next year to be $10 million. Past experience indicates that the cost of goods sold will be 70 percent of sales, that

operating expenses will be 10 percent of sales, that interest expense will be $0.4 million, and that the income tax rate will be 40 percent. Develop the pro forma income statement for the coming year.

6. If the total assets for MTSL are projected to be $25 million next year and liabilities and equity are predicted to be $20 million, what is the estimated amount of funds required?

7. Suppose MTSL needs a minimum cash balance of $1 million. How would this affect the amount of financing required as determined in problem 6?

8. Suppose MTSL's assets, excluding cash, has been $3 million less than the total of predicted liabilities and equity. What would this mean?

ANSWERS TO COMPLETION QUESTIONS

1. take appropriate
2. short- and long-
3. retrenchment
4. what-if
5. a part of
6. is
7. is not
8. should
9. planning models
10. pro forma
11. percentage
12. plug
13. $40
14. amount
15. subtract from
16. less
17. do not
18. maximum
19. increasing
20. less

SOLUTIONS TO PROBLEMS

1. A major reason for financial planning is as an aid in anticipating the financial future of a company. By developing a sense of financial requirements in advance of their occurrence, more alternatives will likely be available. Financial problem solving in a crisis is not a remedy for long-term viability. Banks do not like surprises from their lending customers. They react by either reducing the loan amounts, raising the interest rate, adding restriction on the firm, or not even making the loans at all. Bottlenecks can be recognized early while there is still time to make adjustments. Another reason for planning is to establish some benchmarks to measure progress.

2. The nature of financial planning is to not show too much detail. This is why projects are often grouped into categories. The emphasis is on aggregate accounts. Unless a specific project is exceptionally large, its cash flows are best incorporated with others of a similar nature. Also as the time horizon is extended the precision of individual and small projections becomes blurred.

3. Typical ways of allowing for an uncertain future are to develop several forecasts and accompanying financial plans. For example, a conservative case, a most likely case, and a strong growth case may be prepared. This is the basis for scenario analysis. It provides a range of possible outcomes and alerts management to difficulties that can arise if the best-guess case does not happen.

4. Financial planning is a complex exercise involving many different people. A major concern is problems that arise because each person providing input to the process may not be using the same set of assumptions about key variables that affect the projections being made. For example, one division was expecting a downturn in the economy that would most likely influence the size of their forecasts. Another part of the firm could be highly optimistic about the future and base their projections on strong growth of the market. Other differences in the important variables are found in the expected changes in the cost of living, labour costs, prices of raw materials etc. This is why most financial plans are developed using a set of common assumptions about critical variables that affect the major lines of business of a firm.

5.   Pro Forma Income Statement for Matthew Tyler Stamps, Ltd.:

	(Millions of dollars)
Sales	10.0
Cost of goods sold (70% of sales)	7.0
EBIT	3.0
Operating expenses (10% of sales)	1.0
Interest expense	.40
Earnings before taxes	1.60
Corporate taxes (@40%)	.64
Net income	.96

6.   The plug or balancing account is determined by subtracting the liabilities and equity from assets. That is, $25 million – $20 million = $5 million. Since projected asset needs exceed the projected financing sources, the firm must raise the difference to support the projected level of sales.

7.   The amount of financing required must include a working cash balance. The information given does not specify what MTSL has initially so we must assume that the $1 million for the cash account must be added on to the fund needs making the total requirement as $6 million.

8.   In this case the predicted cash balance would be $3 million. If this is too much, the excess could be used to pay off liabilities, to pay more dividends, to buy more plant, to invest in marketable securities, etc. The point is that the financial manager will be able to provide top management with some pleasant alternatives.

CHAPTER 19

WORKING CAPITAL MANAGEMENT AND SHORT-TERM PLANNING

INTRODUCTION

The early part of the text is focused on the value creating aspects of business: investment, debt policy, and maybe, dividend policy. While value building is not generally associated with working capital management today, value may be negatively impacted by working capital inefficiencies, illiquidity, and policies adversely affecting customer relationships. This chapter opens with a general discussion of working capital, the net working capital concept, followed by the flow concept of the working capital and cash conversion cycles. The time line is used to discuss these concepts. Instead of a point-in-time, balance sheet perspective, the time line presentation of the cash conversion cycle, etc., puts working capital management into a "flow" perspective. Money flows through the firm and the financial manager must keep it flowing. When the time line lengthens, the balance sheet levels increase, reducing profitability and more financing. Think of a business as a "flow," or in a dynamic sense, rather than from a static, balance sheet perspective.

The second section of the chapter studies the short-term versus long-term financing tradeoffs. Presented with a seasonal variation in asset needs or a long-term trend, how should working capital (current assets) be financed? Short-term financing rates average well below long-term rates, but must be rolled over or refinanced frequently if one is financing permanent working capital needs. Long-term financing costs more but fewer trips to the market are necessary. Three alternative financing strategies are discussed.

The third section of the chapter is directed toward short-term planning using the sources and uses of cash and cash budget formats. Note that the cash budget includes only cash flows. Given a time period, such as a month, cash inflows and outflows are assumed to occur proportionally throughout the month. As we both know, cash inflows and outflows are not even throughout the month. One must shorten the time period considered, such as a week, to plan more specific cash flows.

The last section of the chapter centres on the financing of working capital. From negotiated loans from banks and finance companies to issuing commercial paper in direct financial markets, firms have several options and several "effective rates," for each financing option selected.

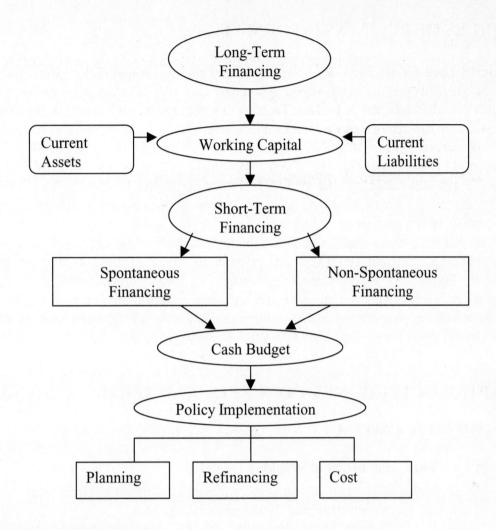

LEARNING CHECKLIST

After preparing this chapter you should be able to:

____1. Understand why a business must invest in working capital and how net working capital finances current assets.

____2. Show how long-term financing policy affects short-term financing requirements.

____3. Trace a business's sources and uses of cash and evaluate its need for short-term borrowing.

____4. Develop a short-term financing plan for future cash needs.

SOURCES OF BUSINESS INFORMATION

The Best Credit Card: There are hundreds of credit cards on the market. How to choose a credit card that fits you the best? Although you may find a lot of information online, most is a sales pitch. Fortunately, the "education" section at www.college-visa.com/css-1html from the United College Marketing Service offers some helpful advice. Usually, you should consider the following factors: (1) annual fee, (2) grace period, (3) interest rate charged on the unpaid balance, and (4) additional features. If you always make full payments by the due dates, your best bet is a no-fee card since the interest rate does not matter much. The longer the grace period, the more the time for making payment. Of course, you want a card with an extended grace period. If you always carry balances, a card with a lower rate is the sensible choice. However, you still have to check out how the interest is calculated for late payments. Cards with airline mileage sound great. But if you need to spend a lot to get the benefits, they are not worth the trouble. Particularly, if you have a large outstanding amount on your card, interest charges will easily wipe out any gains. Once you have a general understanding of credit cards, you can begin to search for your dream-card by visiting the Web sites of different organizations. Try MasterCard at www.mastercard.com, and VISA at www.visa.com.

CHAPTER OUTLINE, KEY CONCEPTS, AND TERMS

I.   **WORKING CAPITAL**

    A.   **The Components of Working Capital**

        1.   Short-term current assets, invested to support long-term fixed assets, and current liabilities are called working capital.

        2.   Current assets, composed of cash accounts, marketable securities, accounts receivables, and inventories represent an important level of asset investment for business that must be financed. See Table 19.1.

        3.   There are advantages of having plenty of current assets, such as having plenty of ready cash, promoting sales with generous credit terms (accounts receivable), and large amounts of inventories.

        4.   There are disadvantages of having too much invested in working capital. The profitability of assets is lowered if too much of cash assets are idle, too generous credit terms may bring losses, and inventory investments are unable to earn their opportunity rate of return.

        5.   Current liabilities are short-term obligations to pay suppliers (accounts payable), employees and borrowed funds (accrued expenses), and short-term lenders such as commercial banks.

    B.   **Working Capital and the Cash Conversion Cycle**

        1.   The difference between current assets and current liabilities is called **net working capital** (NWC). The term NWC is often used interchangeably

with working capital discussed above. NWC is the extent that the circulating current asset pool exceeds the current liabilities and is often thought of as the net liquidity of the business.

2. NWC is also the extent to which current assets is financed by long-term, noncurrent liabilities, sources of financing.

3. Working capital needs fluctuate with changes in sales, changes in credit policies, changes in production techniques, types of products produced, desired finished goods stocks desired, the credit terms of suppliers, the pay periods of employees, and many other variables that are related to business policies, type of business, and external operating environment.

4. Four key dates in the production cycle affect the level of investment in working capital. The longer the periods, the larger the investment. See Figure 19.1 in the textbook.

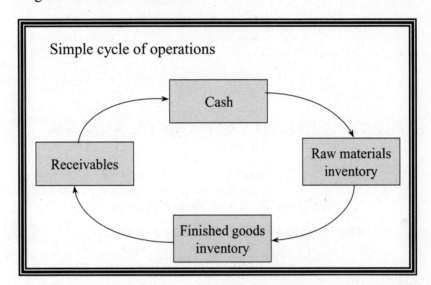

5. The first time period is the accounts payable period, the length of time the firm has between purchasing materials and the payment date for the materials. The longer the period, the larger the accounts payable balance and the shorter the cash conversion cycle.

6. The second key period is the inventory period, the time between the purchase of raw materials and the sale of the finished goods. The longer the time period, the greater the investment in inventory.

7. The third key period is the accounts receivable period, the time period from the sale of the goods (on credit) to when the cash is collected from the customer. Again, the longer the period, the larger the investment in accounts receivable.

8. The fourth key period is the **cash conversion cycle** or the time between the payment for raw materials and the collection of cash from the customer. Note that the accounts payable period, or the credit offered by suppliers, provides some financing for the working capital cycle, but the

longer the cash conversion cycle, the larger the investment in working capital. Cash conversion cycle:

= (inventory period + receivables period) – accounts payable period

9. The length of the inventory period is the average inventory divided by the daily cost of sales (CGS/365). The accounts receivable period is the average accounts receivables divided by the daily sales rate (sales/365). The accounts payables period is the average accounts payables divided by the daily cost of goods sold or purchases (CGS/365).

Cash Conversion Cycle

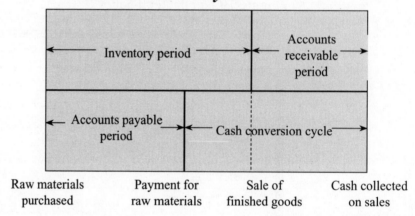

| Raw materials purchased | Payment for raw materials | Sale of finished goods | Cash collected on sales |

C. The Working Capital Trade-Off

1. The cash conversion cycle is influenced by management policies, such as credit policy, levels of inventory, and credit policies of suppliers.
2. The higher the level of working capital, the *greater* the **carrying costs** or the costs of maintaining current assets, including the opportunity cost of capital to finance the current assets.
3. The lower the level of working capital, the *greater* the **shortage costs** or the costs incurred from shortages in current assets, such as inventory stock outs and lost sales from a restrictive credit policy.
4. The financial manager must attempt to minimize the total opposing carrying and shortage costs. See Figure 19.3 in the textbook.

II.   LINKS BETWEEN LONG-TERM AND SHORT-TERM FINANCING

A.   The cost of total assets in the firm is called the total capital requirement. The total capital requirements change over time, increasing steadily in a growing company, varying seasonally as in lawn and garden stores, and decreasing as a firm is slowly liquidated. See Figure 19.4 in the textbook.

B.   The financial manager has a choice of financing the total capital requirement with debt or equity (discussed earlier) or short-term or long-term financing. *Three* variations of short/long financing are studied here. There is a risk/return tradeoff between the extremes. See Figure 19.5 in the textbook.

C.   The "relaxed strategy" is a conservative, mostly long-term financing with few payoff requirements in the short run. This strategy has considerable cash assets at times and emphasizes liquidity. The current ratio and level of net working capital would be very high, but the return on assets will likely be lower, because this strategy favours liquidity over profitability.

D.   The "restrictive strategy" uses the matched maturity approach and finances long-term assets with long-term financing and short-term assets with short-term financing. At times there will be a high level of short-term financing providing funds for a seasonal increase in inventory and accounts receivable. The current ratio will fluctuate considerably with the seasonal fluctuation in current assets and current liabilities, as will profitability as interest financing rates move up and down. This strategy is more profitability focused, but also more risky. Short-term financing may not always be affordable or available.

E.   The "middle-of-the-road" policy recognizes that a certain minimum level of current asset investment is always present or is permanent. Using the matching policy, the firm would finance the permanent portion of current asset investment with long-term financing and the short-term current asset needs with short-term financing. There are times in the seasonal cycle when the firm will borrow short-term, and there are times when idle funds will be invested in marketable securities waiting for the next seasonal cycle. In this case the firm will use the liquidity from *both* marketable securities and short-term financing.

III.   TRACING CHANGES IN CASH AND WORKING CAPITAL

A.   Comparing two balance sheets (points in time) enables the financial manager to see the changes or flows that occurred in the period between the two balance sheets.

Assets	2000	2001	Liabilities and Shareholders' Equity	2000	2001
Current assets			Current liabilities		
Cash	$ 4	$ 5	Bank loans	$ 5	$ 0
Marketable securities	0	5	Accounts payable	20	27
Inventory	26	25	Total current liabilities	$25	$ 27
Accounts receivable	25	30	Long-term debt	5	12
Total current assets	$55	$ 65	Net worth (equity and retained earnings)	65	76
Fixed assets			Total liabilities and owners' equity	$95	$115
Gross investment	$56	$ 70			
Less depreciation	16	20			
Net fixed assets	$40	$50			
Total assets	$95	$115			

B.   The sources and uses of cash statement (Table 19.5 in the textbook) are constructed by first noting the change in each of the balance sheet accounts (Table 19.3 in the textbook) and several items from the income statement.

Sources	
Issued long-term debt	$ 7
Reduced inventories	1
Increased accounts payable	7
Cash from operations	
Net income	12
Depreciation	4
Total sources	$31
Uses	
Repaid short-term bank loan	$ 5
Invested in fixed assets	14
Purchased marketable securities	5
Increased accounts receivable	5
Dividend	1
Total uses	$30
Increase in cash balance	$ 1

C.   Sources of funds are indicated by the cash flows from operations, decreases in assets, and increases in liability and equity accounts.

D.   Uses of funds are indicated by the increases in assets and decreases in liabilities and equity, including dividends paid.

IV. CASH BUDGETING

A. The cash budget estimates sources and uses of funds in future periods and provides information related to future cash needs and a plan for future cash flows.

B. **Cash Inflows**

   1. A sales forecast is the primary independent variable behind a cash budget.
   2. Cash inflows are derived primarily from the collections of accounts receivable that are related to the credit terms, the payment practices of customers, the collection efforts of the firms, and the level of credit sales. An estimate of the collections lag behind sales is an important estimate. See Table 19.6 in the textbook.
   3. Other cash inflows are added to each period considered, which could be weekly, monthly, or here, quarterly.

C. **Cash Outflows**

   1. Cash outflow estimates in the coming periods include payments of accounts payables, labour and administrative costs and other expenses, capital expenditures, taxes, interest, principal payments on loans, and dividends.

Example - Dynamic Mattress Company

Dynamic collections on AR

	Qtr			
	1st	2nd	3rd	4th
1. Beginning receivables	30.0	32.5	30.7	38.2
2. Sales	87.5	78.5	116.0	131.0
3. Collections				
· Sales in current Qtr (80%)	70	62.8	92.8	104.8
· Sales in previous Qtr (20%)	15.0	17.5	15.7	23.2
Total collections	85.0	80.3	108.5	128.0
4. Receivables at end of period				
.(4 = 1 + 2 − 3)	$32.5	$30.7	$38.2	$41.2

2.   Delaying payment or stretching payables offers the benefit of saving cash but the cost of discounts missed and possible termination of the supplier relationship.

D.   **The Cash Balance**

1.   The cash budget is usually comprised of a starting cash position in each period, followed by the net cash flow in the period giving the cash at the end of the period.

2.   A minimum cash balance is assumed and a cumulative cash surplus or shortage (borrowing needed) balance is estimated. The changes in the cumulative account is caused by the net cash flow in each period adjusted for borrowing and lending. See Table 19.8 in the textbook.

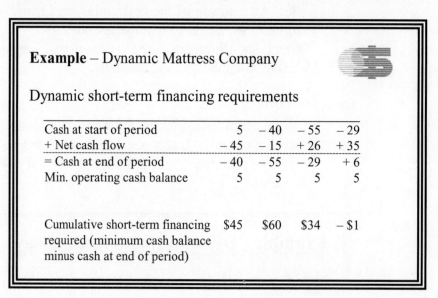

Example – Dynamic Mattress Company

Dynamic short-term financing requirements

Cash at start of period	5	– 40	– 55	– 29
+ Net cash flow	– 45	– 15	+ 26	+ 35
= Cash at end of period	– 40	– 55	– 29	+ 6
Min. operating cash balance	5	5	5	5
Cumulative short-term financing required (minimum cash balance minus cash at end of period)	$45	$60	$34	– $1

V.   A SHORT-TERM FINANCING PLAN

A.   The options for short-term financing include trade credit (accounts payable), accruals (delay in the receipt of services such as labour before payment), and negotiated, short-term borrowing.

B.   Stretching payables is costly if discounts are missed, but must be compared with taking the discounts and financing the early payments at the bank.

VI. SOURCES OF SHORT-TERM FINANCING

A. Bank Loans

1. A business interested in bank financing should establish a **line of credit** with the bank, an agreement by a bank that a company may borrow at any time up to an established limit.

Example –

Dynamic

Mattress

Company –

Financing Plan

	Qtr			
	1st	2nd	3rd	4th
Cash requirement				
1. Cash for operations	45	15	– 26	– 35
2. Interest on bank loan	0	.8	.8	.6
3. Interest on stretched payables	0	0	.8	0
4. Total cash required	45	15.8	– 24.4	– 34.4
Cash Raised				
5. Bank loan	40	0	0	0
6. Stretched payables	0	15.8	0	0
7. Securities sold	5	0	0	0
8. Total cash raised	45	15.8	0	0
Repayments				
9. Of stretched payables	0	0	15.8	0
10. Of line of credit	0	0	8.6	31.4
Increase in cash balances				
11. Addition to cash balances	0	0	0	3
Line of Credit				
12. Beginning of quarter	0	40	40	31.4
13. End of quarter	40	40	31.4	0

2. A revolving credit arrangement is a line of credit that establishes, for a commitment fee to the bank, a level of credit that the business may borrow at any time during the period.
3. Lines of credit may be associated with a minimum deposit balance requirement for the business called a compensating balance. Compensating balances, because they force the business to borrow more or use less of the loan, may increase the effective cost of the loan.

B. Commercial Paper

1. A larger business with a high quality credit rating may issue short-term, unsecured notes, called **commercial paper**, in financial markets.
2. The credit quality of commercial paper is enhanced by backup lines of credit from commercial banks, which would provide loans to the borrowing business to pay-off the commercial paper if credit problems arose and new commercial paper could not be sold to the market.
3. Credit ratings for commercial paper issues are available. Higher rated (R-1) issues carry lower yields than lower rated ones (R-3).

C. **Bankers' Acceptance**

    1.   This instrument is a firm's time draft (i.e., a post-dated cheque) endorsed by a bank.

    2.   With the bank guarantee of paying the stated amount on the draft when it is due, such an unsecured note can still be traded among investors in the market.

    3.   This time-honoured way of short-term financing helps the issuing firm to improve its cash flows.

D. **Secured Loans**

    1.   Current assets such as inventory and accounts receivables are often used as security for business loans.

    2.   Accounts receivables may be pledged or assigned as security for a loan or sold or factored to shorten the cash conversion cycle. Sale of the accounts receivable at a discount for funds is called factoring.

    3.   Standardized, identifiable inventory, such as autos, make excellent collateral for loans, whereas perishable low value items are less likely to serve as security for a loan.

    4.   A lender must establish some control over inventory pledge for a loan. The lender may have a general lien on inventory, hold title as with autos, store in a warehouse away from the business, or set certain inventory items aside in a field warehouse to limit access by the borrower.

VII.   THE COST OF BANK LOANS

A. **Bank Loan Terms**

    1.   The loan rate may be fixed or constant during the loan term, or

    2.   The loan rate may vary (variable) based on changes in a specific market rate or rate index.

Simple Interest

$$\text{Amount of loan} \times \frac{\text{annual interest rate}}{\text{number of periods in the year}}$$

Effective annual rate

$$\left(1 + \frac{\text{quoted annual interest rate}}{m}\right)^{m} - 1$$

B. **Interest Rate Calculations**

1. Interest charged and paid at the end of each interest period is called simple interest and is calculated as principal × periodic rate (annual rate/number of interest periods in a year) × time.

2. Compound interest involves monthly interest not paid each month being added to the principal and charged interest the next month. The effective rate of interest is higher than the simple rate because of the compounding of interest on interest. The effective rate is $(1 + \text{periodic rate})^m - 1$. M is the number of periods in a year. A stated simple rate of 12 percent compounded monthly (paid at end of year) would have an effective rate of $(1 + .12/12)^{12} - 1$ or 12.68 percent.

3. Loans with discount interest terms means the lender subtracts the entire interest amount at the beginning, lessening the amount of borrowed principal received or requiring the borrower to borrow more to net the amount needed. The effective rate on a discounted loan is higher than a non-discounted loan.

C. **Interest With Compensating Balances**

1. Compensating balances represent added deposits in the bank as requirements for the loan.

2. Compensating balances increase the amount borrowed (increase idle funds in a deposit account) and the effective rate of borrowing because it increases the amount of interest paid each period per the amount of usable funds, or:

Effective Rate (Comp. Balances) =

$$[(1 + \text{actual interest paid} \div \text{borrowed funds available})^m - 1]$$

COMPLETION QUESTIONS

1. Capital budgeting and capital structure are (*long-/short-*) term financial decisions that (*are/are not*) easily reversed.

2. Short-term assets and liabilities are called _____ _____.

3. Trade credit and/or consumer credit extended by a firm is reflected in its accounts (*payable/receivable*).

4. The cash conversion cycle is equal to the inventory period (*minus/plus*) the receivables period (*minus/plus*) the accounts payable period.

5. The inventory period is also called the (*days'/years'*) sales in inventory.

6. Costs of maintaining current assets, including opportunity costs, are called _____ costs.

7. Shortage costs are incurred when the levels of different current assets are too (*high/low*).

8. Assets like plant and equipment are usually financed with (*long/short*) -term sources.

9. In an extension of the matching principle, most firms finance (*permanent/temporary*) working capital requirements with long-term sources.

10. An increase in accounts (*payable/receivable*) is a source of funds.

11. When a firm uses cash to buy inventory, net working capital will (*decrease/increase/stay the same*).

12. Cash inflows come from (*collections of accounts receivable/credit sales*).

13. Stretching payables or delaying payment is a (*source/use*) of financing.

14. If suppliers offer discounts for prompt payment it is likely that stretching payables due to these vendors will be a very (*cheap/expensive*) financing source.

15. The simplest and most common source of short-term financing is (*secured/unsecured*) bank loans.

16. An agreement by a bank to permit a company to borrow at any time up to an established limit is called a (*line of/trade*) credit.

17. A revolving line of credit is usually for a (*longer/shorter*) time period compared to a line of credit.

18. A compensating balance requirement will (*lower/raise*) the effective cost to the borrower.

19. Commercial paper is issued (*by large, safe, and well-known firms/in bath rooms*).

20. A firm may raise funds by selling its accounts receivable to a financial institution known as a _____.

21. A field warehouse is an arrangement used in (*inventory/unsecured*) financing.

22. Banker's acceptance is a (*short/long*) -term time draft for which a (*bank/firm*) promises to pay the holder the face amount at maturity.

PROBLEMS

1. Indicate how each of the following transactions will affect cash and net working capital by using + for an increase, – for a decrease, or 0 for no change:
   a. Federal income tax due for the previous year is paid.
   b. A fixed asset is sold for less than book value.
   c. Merchandise is sold on credit.
   d. Short-term notes receivable are sold to pay off short-term notes payable.

2. Musselman Kennels had sales for the months of January through April of $150, $100, $120, and $200, respectively. The firm receives cash payments of 10 percent in the month of sale, 60 percent one month later, and the remaining 30 percent two months after the sale. What will be the cash inflows for April?

3. Tell how each of the following transactions will affect the current ratio (CR) and the net profits (NP) by using + for an increase, – for a decrease, and 0 for no change. Assume the current ratio is above 1 before each transaction.
   a. A fixed asset is sold for more than book value.
   b. Payment is made to trade creditors for previous purchases.
   c. Cash is obtained through short-term bank loans.
   d. Advances are made to employees.

4. Refer to the balance sheet and income statements used at the beginning of the problems for Chapter 18 of this Study Guide and prepare a Sources and Uses of Funds statement for JJAJC.

5. Rosenfeld, Inc. has a line of credit at 12 percent and a compensating balance requirement of 20 percent. How much will it need to borrow on the credit line if it needs $100,000?

6. Suppose another bank makes an offer to Rosenfeld for a line of credit without a compensating balance requirement. However, the interest rate would be 14 percent. Which bank is offering the best interest rate?

7. What is the cash conversion cycle? What is the purpose of this concept in working capital management?

8. Explain what the effect of each of the following actions would likely be on the cash conversion cycle:
   a. Implementation of just-in-time techniques in the production process.
   b. Addition of staff to the accounts receivable department who will focus their attention on managing the collection process.
   c. Obtain agreement from major suppliers that allows 45 days' payment instead of 30 days as has been the practice.

9. David's Computer Graphic's, Inc. had sales of $100,000 last year. The cost of goods sold was $60,000. The firm's average inventory, receivables, and payables during the year were $5,000, $10,000, and $9,000, respectively. What was David's cash conversion cycle?

10. Austin's firm pays its suppliers on the 15th day after receiving the invoice. What share of purchases will be paid:
    a. In the current quarter?
    b. In the following quarter?

ANSWERS TO COMPLETION QUESTIONS

1. long, are not
2. working capital
3. receivable
4. plus, minus
5. days'
6. carrying
7. low
8. long
9. permanent
10. payable
11. stay the same
12. collections of accounts receivable
13. source
14. expensive
15. unsecured
16. line of
17. longer
18. raise
19. by large, safe, and well-known firms
20. factor
21. inventory
22. short, bank

SOLUTIONS TO PROBLEMS

1. This problem will test knowledge of accounting. The answers below show the sign for change in the cash balance and the net working capital (NWC), respectively.

   a. – cash and 0 NWC. Federal income tax due is a current liability. It will drop by the same amount as the cash paid out.

   b. + cash and + NWC. Cash will increase from the sale and liabilities are unchanged.

   c. 0 cash and + NWC. Assuming this is a profitable company, they will sell items for above cost. The latter amount is the inventory value so the accounts receivable will increase by more than the decline in inventory. Cash and liabilities are not affected.

   d. 0 cash and 0 NWC. The notes receivable will decline by the same amount as the notes payable.

2. In April, 10 percent of that month's sales or $20 will be collected. Also 60 percent of the March sales or $72 will be received in cash. The other cash inflow will be 30 percent of February sales which is $30. The total for April will be $20 + $72 + $30 or $122.

3. a. + CR and + NP. Cash is the only current account to be affected and by definition, the transaction was profitable.

   b. + CR and 0 NP. Cash and accounts payable will decrease by the same amount but the ratio of current assets to current liabilities will increase. This is difficult to see without assuming amounts for the cash account and the accounts payable before and after the transaction. As the problem states, the beginning current ratio was above 1 so the end ratio will increase.

   c. – CR and 0 NP. This transaction has the opposite effect on the current ratio by the same logic as described in part (b). above. Again profits are not impacted by the transaction.

   d. 0 CR and 0 NP. Cash will decrease by the same amount that the other current asset account (advances to employees) increases. Nothing else is affected.

4. Decreases in assets and increases in liabilities and/or equity are sources of funds. Increases in assets and decreases in liabilities and/or equity are uses of funds. From these relationships the following statement can be prepared:

Sources and Uses of Funds for JJAJC
(Millions of dollars)

Sources of funds

Decrease in cash	4
Increase in accumulated depreciation	2
Increase in accounts payable	5
Increase in notes payable	4
Increase in other current liabilities	2
Increase in bonds	3
Increase in common stock	6
Total	26

Uses of funds

Increase in accounts receivable	2
Increase in inventory	4
Increase in plant and equipment	15
Decrease in retained earnings	4
Total	26

5. Since the firm can use only 80 percent of the amount borrowed it will need to arrange for a loan that is higher. Let X = the amount needed. Then:

$$0.8X = \$100,000$$
$$X = \$125,000$$

6. The effective interest rate offered by the bank with the compensating balance requirement is 12/.8 or 15 percent. Rosenfeld should choose the bank without the compensating balance requirement since the interest rate is only 14 percent.

7. The cash conversion cycle represents the time and amount of funds tied up in inventory and receivables less the time funds are provided by suppliers. It equals the days in inventory plus the days in accounts receivable minus the days in account payable. Focusing attention on the cash conversion cycle helps the financial manager to identify ways of shortening the time it takes for cash to make the cycle from purchases of materials to collections from sales of the finished goods.

8. a. Just-in-time is an important technique that involves having suppliers of raw materials deliver those items at the same time they are needed in the production process. The goal of passing the goods through the production process with minimal waiting time cuts the investment in inventory and thereby reduces the cash conversion cycle.

    b. The additional personnel will speed up collections which will reduce the investment in accounts receivable. This will also shorten the cash conversion cycle.

    c. Stretching out the time when accounts payable must be paid has the effect of securing additional financing from suppliers. This helps to reduce the cash conversion cycle.

9. The cash conversion cycle is computed from the accounts receivable period, the inventory period, and the accounts payable period.

    Accounts receivable period = ($10,000/$100,000) × 365
    = 36.5 days

    Inventory period = ($5,000/$60,000) × 365
    = 30.4 days

    Accounts payable period = ($9,000/$60,000) × 365
    = 54.8 days

    The cash conversion cycle = (36.5 + 30.4) − 54.8
    = 12.1 days

10. a. The 15-day period is 1/6 of a quarter so 5/6 or 83.3 percent will be paid in the current quarter.

    b. The remaining 1/6 or 16.7 percent will be paid in the following quarter.

CHAPTER 20

CASH AND INVENTORY MANAGEMENT

INTRODUCTION

This is the first chapter of a two-part section entitled "Short-Term Financial Decisions." Cash and inventory investment considerations are discussed here; accounts receivables are covered in the next chapter. The level of cash and inventories are investment decisions that are approached in similar ways. Financial managers are seeking returns on added investment that exceed the opportunity cost of capital. The optimal cash level provides liquidity and operational support. Too little cash and securities selling or borrowing costs are incurred. Too much cash in the bank or in the mail and profitability ratios (ROA) are adversely affected. Inventory levels, whether related to raw material, work in progress, or finished goods are approached in the same way. Too little and stock outs (opportunity cost of lost margins) and production down-time increases. Too much and efficiency is hindered.

The opposing cost decision models discussed here are similar for cash and inventory. The optimal point is that level that minimizes the sum of the two opposing costs.

Working capital balances have a tendency to increase quickly to control limits. Sales managers want ready inventory and generous credit, production managers want to avoid down-time. As the cash cycle time increases, so does the level of investment and the eventual conflict between the financial manager or credit manager and production and sales.

The "flow" concepts developed in the last chapter relating to working capital management are extended here. The business is a constant flow of values and managers must work to shorten and reduce the time line (reduce the level) needed to serve the capital assets.

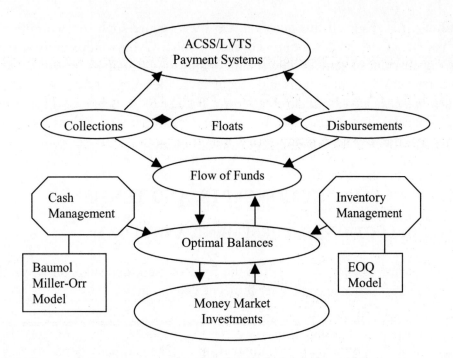

LEARNING CHECKLIST

After studying this chapter you should be able to:

_____1. Define the various types of float, how it arises, and how it can be controlled.
_____2. Calculate the value of changes in float.
_____3. Understand the costs and benefits of holding inventories.
_____4. List the costs and benefits of holding cash balances.
_____5. Understand how cost minimizing models are applied to both inventory and cash investments.

SOURCES OF BUSINESS INFORMATION

Can Anyone Open a Bank Account? As you start to check around, you will discover that financial institutions have managed to dream up all kinds of names for bank accounts that offer many different options and capabilities. Most banks levy some sort of fee against your account, from a per transaction amount to a monthly charge for an unlimited number of transactions. Also, there are various accounts that are designed for special purposes, for example, senior accounts, joint accounts, and foreign dollar accounts, etc. Visit TD Canada Trust's "Account Selector" at www.tdcanadatrust.com to help you make the best decision.

Online Banking: Ask yourself this question: Do I want more sophisticated online banking services? If you belong to the age group between 18 and 34, you would surely answer yes to having a banking machine at home. While you may enjoy the 24-hour services of home banking, you have to carry out your transactions and account activities on your own. As a smaller staff is needed, bank branches have begun to close down. The use of PC banking will forever reshape the way the financial industry works. Go to the Department of Finance's Web site at www.fin.gc.ca and find out the recent reforms.

CHAPTER OUTLINE, KEY CONCEPTS, AND TERMS

I. **CASH COLLECTION, DISBURSEMENT, AND FLOAT**

 A. Businesses keep their cash in the form of bank deposits and pay and receive funds via cheques and other forms of value transfer.

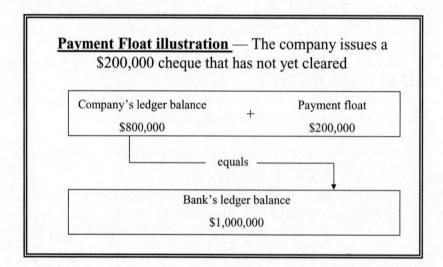

Payment Float illustration — The company issues a $200,000 cheque that has not yet cleared

| Company's ledger balance | + | Payment float |
| $800,000 | | $200,000 |

equals

Bank's ledger balance
$1,000,000

 B. Because cheques must be physically presented to the bank for payment, there are lags or delays in the movement of cheques through a business, through the mail, and through the bank clearing system.

 C. **Float**
 1. The lag or delay in the cheque delivery and clearing system is called float.
 2. When a company has written a cheque on its bank account and mailed the payment, it deducts the balance from its chequing ledger. **Payment float** is the time lag between the time the cheque was sent to when it is presented against (debited) the chequing account. The bank account balance (recorded by the bank) is the sum of the business' ledger balance plus the float, or the float is the difference between the bank's balance and the cheque book's balance.

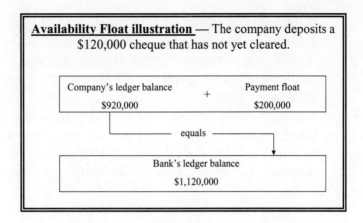

Availability Float illustration — The company deposits a $120,000 cheque that has not yet cleared.

Company's ledger balance	+	Payment float
$920,000		$200,000

equals

Bank's ledger balance
$1,120,000

3.   When cheques are deposited, the funds are often not immediately available. This lag or time delay is called **availability float**. The bank delays the availability because its funds availability is delayed when it sends the cheque to the Bank of Canada and the Canadian Payments Association for clearing. The company's bank balance is the sum of what is available plus what is deferred for a time (availability float).

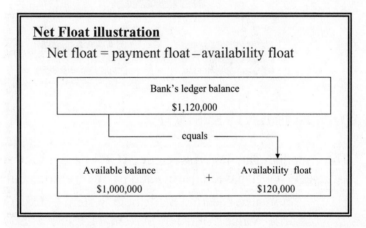

Net Float illustration

Net float = payment float − availability float

Bank's ledger balance
$1,120,000

equals

Available balance	+	Availability float
$1,000,000		$120,000

The **net float** for a business is the payment float less the availability float or the funds the firm has paid but has not cleared less the funds due the business but deferred by the bank.

D.   **Valuing Float**

1.   Float has a value because of the opportunity cost of funds. Money due the firm cannot be invested until "available," and cheques sent to suppliers but still "floating" may be used or invested until the cheque is presented at the bank.

2.   Payment float results from the delay between writing a cheque and the reduction in the chequing account. The level of payment float is related to the *size* of the average check and the *length* (days) of the float. The payment float is the product of the average daily cheques written times the number of days float. The benefit of the payment float to the business

is the total float times the opportunity rate of return for the period. The availability float is a cost to the receiving firm and the cost is the total float (average deposits delayed times the number of days delayed) times the opportunity rate of return. A business may have a net payment or net availability float.

3. Reducing the float provides (availability float) or reduces (payment float) the net float saving (costing) the business a *one time* amount of funds available or lost for investment. The present value of a permanent reduction in net availability float is the amount by which the float is reduced.

Managing Float

II. CANADA'S PAYMENTS SYSTEM

A. The Canadian Payment Association (**CPA**) provides Canada with an efficient, same-day, paper-based clearing and payment settlement system.

1. Automated Clearing Settlement System (**ACSS**) eliminates transit float.
2. Large Value Transfer System (**LVTS**) allows large domestic and international payments to be settled in real time.
3. A **direct clearer** is a member of the CPA who also has a clearing account with the Bank of Canada.

III. MANAGING FLOAT

A. Several kinds of delays or floats occur in the cheque payment system: mail, processing, and clearing as depicted in Figure 20.1 in the textbook.

B. The sum of the three floats above are associated with receiving a payment: the mailing time, the company processing time to get the cheque to the bank, and the clearing (availability) delays of the banking system.

C. Efforts to speed up collections are usually countered by efforts by payers to delay disbursements, but the ACSS/LVTS by the Canadian Payments Association is dedicated to reducing clearing float.

D. **Speeding Up Collections**

1. **Concentration banking**, a system of regional collection centres that transfers balances to one bank, is one method of speeding up collections and reducing mail, processing, and clearing float.

2. Concentration banking reduces mail float and clearing float, because the depository bank is located close to the paying customer.

3. Consolidating many balances in a single bank for possible overnight investment is a good cash management technique.

4. Balances may be transferred via the costly bank wire system or through the use of depository transfer cheques, which is a slower but cheaper method.

5. A **lock-box system** directs the customer to make payments to a post office box, the bank picks up the mail, quickly processes the cheque into the clearing system, and the customer posting is finished last.

6. A lock-box system reduces float, increases investable funds that may now earn a rate of return, but is profitable only if the annual added rate of return exceeds the annual cost of the lock-box.

E. **Controlling Disbursements**

1. Controlling disbursements is a process for lengthening the payment float or time it takes a mailed cheque to a supplier to reach the payer's bank.

2. Remote disbursement, or mailing cheques from a location distant from the supplier lengthens the mail float portion of the payment float. The clearing float may be lengthened by writing cheques on banks in remote geographic areas far away from larger clearing banks. As the Canadian payment system can settle cheques on the same day, remote disbursement has no practical value.

3. A **zero-balance account**, or account to which a paying business keeps only the daily amount of cheques presented, may be a part of the remote disbursement system.

F. **Electronic Funds Transfer**

1. Computerized automation has enhanced our ability to manage cash. Since funds can be transferred electronically from one account to another, many new issues arise. Each issue is good, or bad, depending on what side of the transaction you assume.

2. Table 20.1 in the textbook shows the ever-increasing electronic usage for transferring funds. While a paperless transfer can occur, there is no implication that transactions are more difficult to trace. Record keeping

is done electronically with the growing practice of the Electronic Data Interchange (EDI) process.

3. As electronic transfers can be completed almost instantly, floats are drastically reduced. However, some firms still rely on the snail pace of normal cash transfers and cheque clearing.

4. The cost of an electronic transfer is also much lower than traditional methods. As smaller staff is required, labour costs may be reduced. Unfortunately, banks often charge more for these cheaper and more efficient transactions.

IV. INVENTORIES AND CASH BALANCES

A. Cash and inventory are similar, i.e., to have them costs money and to not have enough of them costs money. Excess working capital reduces the return on assets; too little working capital loses sales, slows production, and chances illiquidity. The same analytical techniques used to assess the "right" balance that minimizes the total cost may be used with both inventory and cash management.

B. Cash management is a tradeoff of having too little cash and possibly incurring cost of selling interest-bearing securities, paying commissions, and taking losses, to having too much cash in an idle, non-earning account.

C. Inventory management has similar tradeoffs. Too little inventory minimizes carrying costs but customer service and missed sales hurt the business. Too much investment in inventory maximizes sales, but requires added capital and incurs carrying costs.

D. **Managing Inventories**

1. Carrying costs increase as inventory investment increases; ordering costs decrease as fewer orders are made during a period of time.

2. The **economic order quantity** is a cost minimization model that computes the EOQ, which minimizes total inventory costs, the sum of carrying and ordering costs. The EOQ is the square root of the product of 2 times the total inventory used in a period (sales) times the cost per order divided by the carrying cost.

$$\text{Economic Order Quantity} = \sqrt{\frac{2 \times \text{annual sales} \times \text{cost per order}}{\text{carrying cost}}}$$

3. Just-in-time inventory management, built on the stable production process of delivering materials to firms when needed, may reduce the inventory level.

E. **Managing Inventories of Cash: The Baumol Model**

1. The Baumol model applies the EOQ model to cash management and determines the amount of securities to be sold at one time to replenish cash accounts. The business is assumed to have its cash resources in either non-earning cash (chequing account) or short-term securities. At an assumed rate of cash usage, an assumed interest rate on the securities, and a cost of selling the securities (note opposing costs of earning and selling), there is a level of securities one must sell each time to minimize the total costs of cash versus securities.

2. The Baumol model calculates the optimum amount of securities to be sold as the square root of 2 times the annual cash disbursements times the cost per sale of securities divided by the earning interest rate on securities. The total costs of trading securities versus the opportunity costs of having cash and not securities are minimized at the Q^*.

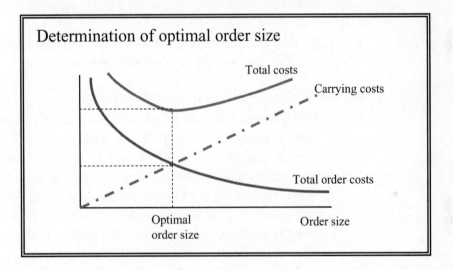

Determination of optimal order size

F. **Uncertain Cash Flows: The Miller-Orr Model**

1. The Baumol model assumes a certain, steady cash outflow without any random variations. The Miller-Orr model considers cash inflows and outflows with random, unpredictable changes.

2. The Miller-Orr model establishes a permissible range of cash balances and actions (buy/sell securities) that only occur if an upper/lower balance is reached. The range between the upper and lower limits is established by three factors: daily variance of cash flows, cost of buying or selling securities, and the rate of interest on the securities.

3. When the daily variation in cash flow is small, the cost of buying/selling low, or the interest rate high, the upper/lower limits should be narrow. With the variation low, it will seldom hit the limits. With the trading cost low, it will not cost much to buy (upper limit) or sell (lower limit).

Finally, with interest rates high the cost of high cash balances encourages a narrow range.

4.   The return point (replenished cash level) in the Miller-Orr model is one-third of the range up from the lower limit (point where one would sell securities), making it more likely to hit the lower limit.

5.   The Miller-Orr model return point minimizes the sum of transaction costs and opportunity interest costs (money not made by being in cash).

G.   **Cash Management in the Largest Corporations**

1.   For large balances normally associated with large businesses, the cost of selling securities to replenish cash is a very low proportional cost, so the average cash balance should normally be quite low.

2.   Large firms do hold cash balances as compensating balances for banking services and, with many decentralized plants and divisions operating around the country, each with a bank account, the balances sum to a rather large amount.

3.   Efficient cash management implies that centralization of balances for efficient investment or allocation is necessary.

H.   **Investing Idle Cash: The Money Market**

1.   When excess cash is present, securities are purchased. When funds are needed, securities are sold. The securities normally used for temporary investments are usually purchased in the **money market** where short-term, high quality, marketable securities are traded.

2.   When cash needs are known, securities of specific short-term maturity may be selected. If cash is needed, money market securities may be sold quickly, and because there is little price variability if market interest rates change, the cost of selling the securities is kept at a minimum.

3.   One choice of short-term, high quality investment is commercial paper, the unsecured short-term notes (maturities usually less than 270 days) issued by well-established industrial and financial corporations. The drawback is its low marketability.

4.   Certificates of deposits (CDs) are short-term notes issued by commercial banks, usually in denominations greater than $100,000.

5.   Repurchase agreements (repos), the purchase of securities under agreement to resell (at a higher price), are issued by commercial banks with minimum denominations of $100,000. The maturities range from a few days to overnight.

COMPLETION QUESTIONS

1. In principle, companies want to hold cash balances up to the point where the value of additional liquidity is equal to the value of interest (*earned/foregone*).

2. The amount of funds represented by cheques written that (*have/have not*) cleared is called payment float.

3. Cheques deposited that have not cleared is called _____ float.

4. When payment float exceeds availability float a firm will have a (*negative/positive*) net float.

5. To minimize having too much cash on hand the financial manager should maximize (*availability/payment*) float.

6. A principle of cash management is to (*slow down/speed up*) collections and to (*slow down/speed up*) payments.

7. Retail stores can reduce delays from receiving payments by encouraging customers to use (*credit/debit*) cards.

8. Preauthorized payments with customers are arrangements used by companies to (*decrease/increase*) float.

9. A system that has customers make payments to a bank in the customers' geographic area and then has the bank transfer the funds to one of that firm's principal banks is called (*concentration/investment*) banking.

10. Preprinted depository transfer cheques are (*faster/slower*) than wire transfers.

11. A system that has customers sending payments to a local post office box so that a local bank can process the cheques is called a _____-_____.

12. Remote disbursement is a method of (*decreasing/increasing*) payment float.

13. In a zero-balance account, funds flow (*from/to*) the firm's concentration account (*from/to*) its disbursement account.

14. Inventory management is similar to cash management in that there is a _____ between costs and benefits from holding a balance.

15. Total costs of inventory are equal to carrying costs (*minus/plus*) order costs.

16. The order size that minimizes total inventory costs is called the _____ _____ quantity.

17. The time that it takes to place an order and have it delivered should be incorporated into the (*economic order quantity/reorder point*).

18. Just-in-time inventory management systems involve (*almost no/substantial*) safety stocks.

19. According to the Baumol model for determining optimal cash balances, higher interest rates available on liquid investments will (*lower/raise*) the optimal level cash balances.

20. In the Miller and Orr model of cash management, the cash balance is allowed to vary within certain limits. When it reaches the maximum, securities are (*bought/sold*) to bring the cash level to its return point.

21. According to the Miller and Orr model, spread between upper and lower limits is (*directly/inversely*) proportional to transaction costs and uncertainty of the cash flow pattern and (*directly/inversely*) related to the level of interest rates on liquid securities.

22. If the cost of borrowing is high relative to the return on liquid investments, firms should borrow relatively (*less/more*).

23. Large firms should favour (*centralized/decentralized*) bank accounts.

24. The market for fixed income securities with maturities of less than one year is called the (*capital/money*) market.

25. Appropriate investments for amounts of temporary, idle cash are (*long/short*) -term securities because they have little interest rate risk and are issued by organizations having (*considerable/little*) financial strength.

26. _____ agreements are in effect loans that are collateralized with Treasury bills.

27. Automated Clearing Settlement System (ACSS) operated by the Canadian Payments Association is the mechanism by which the payer accounts are debited for (*same day/two days*).

28. A (*debit/credit*) card is one example of an electronic funds transfer.

PROBLEMS

1. DRD Corp. has a ledger balance of $80,000 in its bank chequing account at the end of the day; has written and mailed three cheques today totalling $35,000; and yesterday deposited two cheques totalling $15,000. The bank will credit DRD Corp.'s account for the deposits tomorrow.
    a. What is the current chequing account ledger balance of DRD?
    b. What is DRD Corp.'s current bank balance according to the bank?
    c. What is the payment float of DRD Corp.?
    d. What is the availability float of DRD Corp.?
    e. What is the current net float of DRD Corp.?

2. ATM Corp. has just called the bank and was told that their current bank balance was $54,000. The current ledger balance of their account is $42,000 and $15,000 in cheques were recently mailed. No other cheques are outstanding. No other deposits have been made recently. What is the likely amount of yesterday's deposit that has not yet been made available at the bank? What is the net float of ATM Corp.?

3. Zoo Corp. has a chequing account ledger balance of $41,000, and after calling the bank, found that the bank balance was $47,000. A deposit of $5,000 was made this morning and has not yet been credited by the bank. What explains the difference between the bank balance of Zoo Corp. and their ledger balance?

4. In an attempt to reduce mail, processing, and availability float, AU Corp. is considering a lock-box arrangement with First National Bank. With a current annual rate of investment return of 6 percent available on any funds made available from the lock-box system, a cost $25 per day on currently used depository transfer cheques, AU Corp. estimates that it can reduce its float by two days with the lock-box system. The bank charges $10 per day for the lock-box system. What is the break-even amount of collections per day that would equate the new lock-box system with the current depository transfer cheque system? (**Hint**: The break-even amount made available for investment at a daily rate (365 day year) that would equal the $25 cost of the current depository transfer system.)

5. With reference to the question above, if AU Corp. has a daily receipts amount of $125,000, should they adopt the new lock-box system?

6. Heather is reviewing a lock-box proposal just presented to her by a local bank. The lock-box system is designed to reduce the mail, cheque processing, and availability float of the 95 checks received daily by Heather's firm, Dolls, Inc. The average invoice is $800, the current annual rate on invested funds is 10 percent, and it estimated that the lock-box system will save three days float for Dolls, Inc. The bank charges $.30 per cheque processing fee for the service. What is the estimated daily savings with the new lock-

box system? What should Heather recommend? (**Hint**: One must compare the added return on the cash made available compared to the bank charges for the new system.)

7.   In the question above, what is the minimum reduction in float time to collect and process the cheques of Heather's business that is needed to justify the adoption of the new lock-box system?

8.   One year ago, Allstar, Inc. began disbursing cheques to suppliers from a small bank in Montana. The annual amount of disbursements was $20 million with 10,000 cheques. Assuming an annual investment rate of 8 percent on investable funds made available, an extension of Allstar's float by six days, and a cost of the cheque disbursement system of $7,000 per year plus $.15 per cheque processed, has this been a profitable venture by Allstar? Assume a 205-business day year.

9.   In the question above, what is the value of the increase in float if the benefits are expected to be permanent? Are there any other costs of this system that Allstar should consider?

10. Jason's Computer center uses 515 boxes of paper every year, but has limited space and some pilferage so the carrying costs per box is estimated at $2 per box. The average cost per order each time new paper is ordered is estimated to be $15.03.
     a. What is the economic order quantity (EOQ) that minimizes total ordering and carrying costs?
     b. How many orders should the computer centre place per year?
     c. What is the average inventory of paper in the computer centre?
     d. As order costs, carrying costs, and total usage increases, what is the effect on the EOQ?

11. Financial Corp. has an erratic cash flow pattern that offers an opportunity to invest in money market securities, and once in a while, a need to sell the money market securities to meet obligations. The current investment rate in money market securities is 6 percent and the cost of selling securities is currently $34.70 per sale. The firm pays out cash at the rate of $2,000,000 per month. Using the Baumol Model, what is the optimal amount of securities that should be sold each time to minimize the cost of investing cash?

12. With reference to the question above, as interest rates and security transaction charges increase, what is the impact on the optimal level of securities to sell each time cash is needed? What are the assumptions of the Baumol Model?

13. With reference to the Financial Corp. above, and now including an assumed variability of cash inflows and outflows (Miller/Orr Model), if the standard deviation of cash flows is $8,000 and the minimum cash balance is $150,000,
     a. Calculate the spread between the upper and lower cash balance limits.

b. Calculate the upper limit where securities would be purchased (upper) and the lower limits where securities would be sold. (**Hint**: Assume a 365-day year.)

14. With reference to the question above, what is the impact of lower interest rates, increased variability of cash flows, and a decrease in securities transaction costs on Financial Corp.'s cash balance.

15. The cost of keeping cash balances is the interest opportunity cost of securities, now 6 percent. If the bank borrowing cost, should cash be needed, is 10 percent, the cash balances should be adjusted to a level so that the probability of borrowing from the bank is what?

ANSWERS TO COMPLETION QUESTIONS

1. foregone
2. have not
3. availability
4. positive
5. payment
6. speed up, slow down
7. debit
8. decrease
9. concentration
10. slower
11. lock-box
12. increasing
13. from, to
14. tradeoff
15. plus
16. economic order
17. reorder point
18. almost no
19. lower
20. bought
21. directly, inversely
22. less
23. centralized
24. money
25. short, considerable
26. Repurchase
27. same day
28. debit

SOLUTIONS TO PROBLEMS

1. The cheque book ledger balance (an asset account) of DRD Corp. differs from its bank balance by the net float (amount of outstanding cheques and deposits not yet credited to the bank balance). DRD has debited (added) the amount of its deposits and has credited (subtracted) the amount of cheques written to determine its ledger balance.
    a. DRD Corp.'s ledger balance is its current cheque book balance of $80,000.
    b. The bank balance equals DRD ledger balance minus deposits not yet credited by the bank plus cheques written, not yet cleared.

    Bank Balance = $80,000 – $15,000 + $35,000 = $100,000

    c. The payment float represents cheques written by DRD Corp. that have not cleared or $35,000.
    d. The availability float or cheques already deposited that have not yet been posted to the account is $15,000.
    e. The net float is the payment float (outstanding cheques) less the availability floats (unavailable deposits) or $35,000 less $15,000 or $20,000. When positive net float is a net payment float (ledger < bank); if negative, a net availability float (ledger > bank).

2. The amount of yesterday's deposit was $3,000. The difference between ATM's ledger (cheque book) balance and bank balance is the net float, which is the difference between the payment float and the availability float (the deposit).

    Bank – Ledger = Net Float = Payment Float – Availability Float

    $54,000 – $42,000 = $12,000 = $15,000 – Availability Float (Deposit)

    Availability Float (Deposit) = $3,000

    Another way?   Use the standard cheque book reconciliation method:

$54,000	Bank balance
+$3,000	Deposit made, not credited by bank
$57,000	Bank balance before outstanding cheques
–$15,000	Cheques written, not cleared
$42,000	ATM ledger (cheque book) balance

3. The difference between Zoo Corp.'s ledger (cheque book) balance and the balance recorded by the bank is the net float, the net amount of cheques written by Zoo (deducted from their ledger account), but not yet back to the bank, and the deposit

made by Zoo (and added to their cheque book amount), but not yet credited to their account by the bank. The difference between the bank balance and ledger balance, $6,000, is not explained by the $5,000 deposit. Zoo has cheques outstanding or payment float of $11,000 which has been deducted from their ledger account and a $5,000 deposit which they have added to their account. The net difference, $6,000, is the difference between the bank and ledger balances.

$$\text{Bank} - \text{Ledger} = \text{Net Float} = \text{Payment Float} - \text{Availability Float}$$

$$\$47,000 - \$41,000 = \$6,000 = \text{Payment Float} - \$5,000$$

$$\text{Payment Float} = \$11,000$$

4. The daily interest savings (rate × time × amount?) on some amount of funds made available by the new lock-box system must cover the daily cost of the lock-box system and equal the $25 current charge of the depository transfer cheque system.

Break-even = net cost of lock-box = cost of depository cheques
If "X" equals the size of daily cash transfers;

$$(.06/365)\ (2\ \text{days})\ (X) - \$10.00 = \$25.00$$

$$.0001644\ (2)\ (X) = \$35.00$$

$$X = \$106,458$$

The break-even daily cash flow made available and invested for two days plus $10 necessary to match the cost of the current payment process is $106,458.

5. With any average cash disbursement above $106,458 the new lock-box system should be adopted. The added investment return ($125,000 × 2 days × .06/365)

$$\$125,000 \times 2 \times .06/365 - \$10.00 = \$31.09 \text{ net daily return}$$

The $31.10 added daily profit exceeds the $25 daily cost of the prior depository transfer cheque by $56.10. The new lock-box system is advantageous. The bank could charge up to $16.09 per day for the lock-box system before AU Corp. would go back to its current system.

$$\$125,000(2)(.06/365) - X = \$25.00$$

$$X = \$16.09$$

6. Average number of daily payments to lock-box = 95

    Average size of payment   = $800

    Rate of interest/day = .10/365   = .0002739

    Float savings with new system   = 3 days

    The daily savings is the added interest return on the funds available less the cost of the lock-box system.

    95 items/day × $800/item × 3 days = $228,000 funds available for investment.

    $228,000 × .0002739 = $62.45 investment return/day

    The daily cost of the lock-box system proposed is 95 items/day × $.30/cheque charge = $28.50. The daily earnings from the cash made available, $62.47, exceeds the daily cost of the proposed lock-box system. The new system should be adopted.

7. The break-even point float time saved is the number of days float saved that just equals the daily cost of the system or $28.50.

    Solve for the unknown, Days

    95 items/day × $800/item × Days × .0002739 = $28.50

    20.8219 Days = $28.50

    Days = 1.37

    A float reduction of 1.4 days or 33 hours will cover the charges for the lock-box system.

8. The analysis compares the investment return on the invested cash emanating from delayed disbursement to the cost of the delayed-disbursement system.

    Daily Disbursement = $20 mil. per year/205 = $97,561

    $97,561 daily disbursements × 6 days × .08 = $46,829 added investment return

    $10,000 cheques/year × $.25 + $7,000 = $9,500 cost of system

    The delayed disbursement program has saved Allstar $46,829 − $9,500 = $37,329 per year.

9. The value of the float increase is, assuming a perpetuity:

$97,561 daily disbursement × 6 days = $585,366 cash saved and available or,

PV = $46,829 added invested return/.08 = $585,366

While speeding cash returns to a firm is the "white-knight," positive aspect of cash management systems, remote disbursements is a "black-knight," negative side, that many firms play without discussion. Suppliers are most likely to feel the impact of delayed payments. Supplier credit terms may be changed or other sanctions applied unless, of course, Allstar is a valuable customer!

10. a. The EOQ for the computer centre is:

$$Q^* = \sqrt{\frac{2 \times \text{unit sales} \times \text{cost per order}}{\text{unit carrying cost}}}$$

$$= (2 \times 515 \times 15.03/2)^{.5} = 88$$

b. The number of orders per year is 440/88 = 5
c. The average inventory is the EOQ/2 = 88/2 = 44 boxes
d. As order costs increase, the EOQ increases and the computer centre will place fewer orders and hold a larger inventory of paper. As carrying costs increase, more orders will be placed or less inventory will be on hand at any time. As total usage increases, the EOQ increases.

11. The value of short-term securities sold, Q^*, each time the cash balance is replenished is:

$$Q^* = \sqrt{\frac{2 \times \text{annual cash disbursements} \times \text{cost per sale}}{\text{interest rate}}}$$

$$= [2 \times (\$2 \text{ million} \times 12 \text{ months}) \times \$34.70/.06]^{.5}$$

$$= \$166,613$$

The amount of T-bills sold each time, ($2 million/$166,613) = 12 or once per month with an average cash balance (inventory) of $166,613/2 = $83,307.

12. The level of T-bills to sell each time cash is needed is directly related to the annual cash disbursement level and the cost of selling securities and inversely related to the T-bill interest rate. Selling $167,000 in securities minimizes the transaction cost of selling securities and the opportunity cost of selling securities (interest given up by selling securities). The Baumol model assumes steady use of cash with little variability of cash flows. Thus we study the Miller-Orr model for more practical problems of cash flow variability.

13. a. The spread between the upper and lower cash balance limits is:

$$\text{spread} = 3^{.33} \sqrt{\frac{.75 \times \text{transaction costs} \times \text{variance}}{\text{interest rate}}}$$

$$= 3[.75(\$34.70 \times 8000^2)/.06]^{.33}$$

$$= \$8,384$$

Upper limit = lower limit ($150,000) + $9,084 = $159,084

Return point = lower limit + spread/3

$= \$150,000 + \$9,084/3$

$= \$153,028$

Lower limit = $150,000 minimum cash balance

b. If the cash balance reaches $159,084, then $6,056 in securities ($159,084 – $153,028) will be purchased, bringing the cash balance to the return point of $153,028. If the cash balance drops to the minimum level, $3,028 in securities ($153,028 – $150,000) will be sold to bring the balance to the return level of $153,028.

14. The lower the interest rates, the higher is the allowable spread between the upper and lower limits. This is so because the opportunity cost of cash is lower. Cash flow variability and transaction costs are directly related to the spread. As transaction costs and variability increases, so does the cash/securities adjustment.

15. Cost of cash balances/Cost of borrowing
    = 6/10 = 0.6

    The best cash balance depends upon the cost of borrowing and the extent of uncertainty about future cash flow. If the cost of borrowing (denominator) is high relative to the opportunity cost of cash balances (numerator), the probability of borrowing the high cost funds should be low.

CHAPTER 21

CREDIT MANAGEMENT AND COLLECTION

INTRODUCTION

In this third working capital management chapter, credit management is the focal point. Accounts receivable represents a significant investment for many businesses. Why give credit? Credit is a competitive necessity, and combined with the product or service, is a major factor influencing sales. Like investment in capital assets, working capital investments should, at the margin, provide returns in excess of the firm's minimum required rate of return. This investment level is affected by who receives credit, the level of sales, the terms of sales, and the paying practices and/or collection efforts of the firm.

This chapter provides many of you with your first and only look at credit management concepts. While most of you will not work in the credit-granting area of a business, almost all of you working in business must work with the credit operation and that of other businesses during your career.

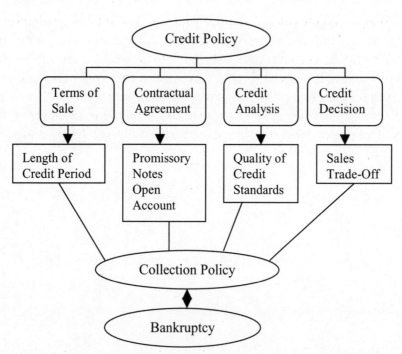

LEARNING CHECKLIST

After studying this chapter you should be able to:

____1. Measure the implicit interest rate charged for credit.
____2. Understand the range of credit and IOU arrangements that a business and customer might have.
____3. Understand the process by which a credit applicant's credit record is assessed.
____4. Summarize the bankruptcy procedures available to debtors and creditors.

SOURCES OF BUSINESS INFORMATION

How To Fix a Credit Problem? You will find two types of credit resources online. There are companies who promise to improve your poor credit record. In most cases, these credit repair services are scams taking money from your pocket to theirs. Read the report prepared by the Federal Trade Commission at www.webcom.com. The second resource is the reputable organizations providing practical plans you can really follow. Legitimate credit counselling may be found on the Internet by using a search engine such as www.yahoo.com. Avoid the high-fee counsellors. Both VISA at www.visa.com and MetLife at www.metlife.com have excellent overviews of dealing with credit problems. You may find helpful information when you are in trouble.

Prepare for the Worst: When you go through your life, you may have already experienced financial difficulty. For example, you need to borrow money whether for your studies or a new car. Most financial institutions provide good information online about loans. However, there are several issues involved such as collateral requirements, and co-signer mandates, etc. Check out Scotiabank's "Personal Lending Centre" at www.scotiabank.com. Usually, banks have assessed your repaying ability to determine how much they can safely lend to you. The Office of the Superintendent of Bankruptcy at www.osb-bsf.gc.ca will give you relevant bankruptcy acts and laws.

CHAPTER OUTLINE, KEY CONCEPTS, AND TERMS

I. TERMS OF SALE

A. Credit **terms of sale** vary between industries and are directly related to the credit rating of the customer, the size of the account, the durability of the product, and the length of time it takes the customer to sell the product.

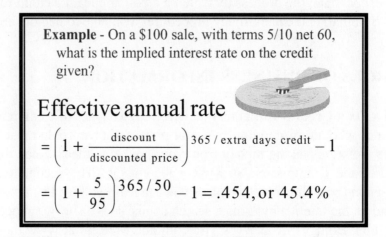

Example - On a $100 sale, with terms 5/10 net 60, what is the implied interest rate on the credit given?

Effective annual rate

$$= \left(1 + \frac{\text{discount}}{\text{discounted price}}\right)^{365 \, / \, \text{extra days credit}} - 1$$

$$= \left(1 + \frac{5}{95}\right)^{365 \, / \, 50} - 1 = .454, \text{or } 45.4\%$$

B. Credit terms range from cash before delivery (CBD), cash on delivery (COD), net terms without trade discounts and with trade discounts for early, or timely payments. End of the month (EOM) billing and terms is common with continuous purchase/shipment activity.

C. Trade credit terms of 2/10, net 30 allow a 2 percent discount if paid within 10 days of the invoice, with the net due in 30 days.

D. The effective annual cost of passing the discount on the tenth day and paying 20 days later is 1 + (discount rate/1 – discount rate) raised to the power of 365/n minus 1, where "n" is the number of days "borrowed" by not paying on the tenth. In the above example, if the discount is passed on the tenth for the added 20 days, the effective rate is:

$$44.6\% = [1 + 0.02/(1 - 0.02)]^{365/20} - 1 = 1.4459 - 1$$

E. The cost of discounts missed is usually much higher than commercial bank lending rates. Business should, if needed, borrow on the tenth, pay the discount, and lower their costs of discounts missed.

F. High effective rates for discounts missed penalizes firms that stretch their payables.

II. CREDIT AGREEMENTS (NATURE OF THE CONTRACT)

A. Credit agreements between supplier and customer vary from very informal to formal IOUs.

B. An **open account** is a trade credit agreement without any formal debt contract. A promissory note formalizes the obligation, as does an accepted commercial draft called a trade acceptance, which is an acknowledgment of payments due on receipt of goods (sight draft) or later (time draft). If the customer's bank accepts the customer's obligation as their own, the trade acceptance becomes a banker's acceptance.

C. A conditional sales agreement maintains title to goods until payment is made.

III. CREDIT ANALYSIS

A. The procedure to determine if the customer is likely to pay for goods shipped or services rendered is called **credit analysis**.

B. Prior payment practices, high ratings from credit analysis firms such as Dun and Bradstreet, rating agencies such as Dominion Bond Rating Services, and credit bureaus help discriminate payers from non-payers.

C. **Financial Ratio Analysis**
   1. A supplier providing trade credit may assess the ability and willingness to pay by performing their own financial analyses with their customers' financial data.
   2. With reference to Chapter 17, the liquidity, debt capacity, and long-term profitability of a customer is assessed.

D. **Numerical Credit Scoring**
   1. The scope of a financial analysis includes an assessment of the customer with regard to the "five Cs of credit": character, capacity to pay, capital, collateral, and conditions.
   2. Numerical credit scoring models are developed and used to discriminate between characteristics of those who pay as agreed and those customers who do not. See Example 21.2 in the textbook.
   3. The credit scoring model is an effective screening device for low-risk and high-risk customers, with the latter undergoing substantial credit analysis.

4. Considerable research effort, including classic research by E. I. Altman and the *Z score* has been devoted to this area.

Multiple Discriminant Analysis - A technique used to develop a measurement of solvency, sometimes called a *Z Score*. Edward Altman developed a Z Score formula that was able to identify bankrupt firms approximately 95% of the time.

Altman Z Score formula

$$Z = 3.3 \frac{EBIT}{total\ assets} + 1.0 \frac{sales}{total\ assets} + .6 \frac{market\ value\ of\ equity}{total\ book\ debt}$$

$$+ 1.4 \frac{retained\ earnings}{total\ assets} + 1.2 \frac{working\ capital}{total\ assets}$$

E. **When to Stop Looking for Clues**

1. Credit analysis costs money and there are two general rules as to when to stop.
2. The two rules are 1) do not undertake a full credit analysis unless the order is large enough to justify it, and 2) undertake a full credit analysis for the doubtful or higher risk customers only.

IV.   THE CREDIT DECISION

A. **Credit policy** establishes standards determining the amount and type of credit terms to extend to customers. The review of the credit decision process is shown in Figure 21.1 in the textbook.

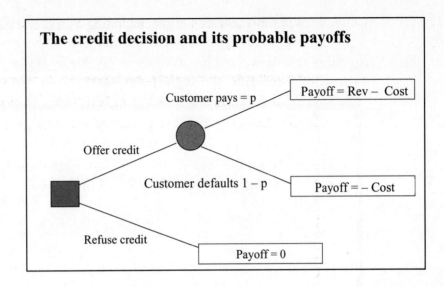

The credit decision and its probable payoffs

Customer pays = p

Payoff = Rev − Cost

Offer credit

Customer defaults 1 − p

Payoff = − Cost

Refuse credit

Payoff = 0

B.   Credit should be extended if the expected profit from the credit sale is greater than the expected profit from refusing credit. If paid as agreed, the profit margin will be realized on the sale; if payment is not received, the firm loses the cost of sales. Refusing credit makes no profit.

C.   **Credit Decisions with Repeat Orders** — The chance of repeat orders and future profits from a credit customer increases the expected value of granting credit and encourages credit extension.

D.   **Some General Principles**
   1.   The job of the credit manager is to maximize profits, not minimize losses. Tight credit terms turn away good repeat customers, so some losses are expected.
   2.   Concentrate efforts on large order, high-risk accounts.
   3.   Consider a new account as a possible long-term customer. Offer small amounts of credit to high-risk customers until a good payment record is established.

V.   **COLLECTIONS POLICY**

A.   Slow payers impose two costs on a business: collection expenses and a greater investment in working capital, specifically accounts receivable.

B.   The investment in accounts receivables is the product of the daily sales rate times the average collection period. As the collection period is extended by slow payers or no payers, the investment increases and required opportunity cost of capital is incurred.

C.   **Collections policy** includes the procedures to collect and monitor receivables.

D.   An **aging schedule** classifies accounts receivable by the length of time they are outstanding. See Table 21.1 in the textbook.

Sample aging schedule for accounts receivable

Customer's Name	Less than 1 month	1 – 2 months	2 – 3 months	More than 3 months	Total Owed
A	10,000	0	0	0	10,000
B	8,000	3,000	0	0	11,000
*	*	*	*	*	*
*	*	*	*	*	*
*	*	*	*	*	*
Z	5,000	4,000	6,000	15,000	30,000
Total	$200,000	$40,000	$15,000	$43,000	$298,000

E.   Collections efforts range from friendly reminders to collection agency and court actions.

F.   There is always a conflict of interest between sales, who desire generous credit terms, and the collections department who "remind" good-customer deadbeats of their payment practices or the financial manager who must control the level of accounts receivable investment in order to maximize value.

VI.   BANKRUPTCY

A.   **Bankruptcy** is the court-directed procedure whereby a failing business is reorganized or liquidated.

B.   **Bankruptcy Procedures**
1.   A problem business and their creditors have a range of options before bankruptcy, including extension of time for payment, or a possible composition of obligations that reduces the amount to be paid by some proportion.
2.   These informal arrangements above, taken before bankruptcy, are referred to as a **workout**.

3.   Bankruptcy results in either a **liquidation** or sale of a business' assets to generate money for claimants, or a **reorganization**, which restructures the financial claims on a business in an attempt to keep it operating.
4.   In a bankruptcy liquidation, there is an official order of claimants.
5.   During bankruptcy, the creditor claims and individual efforts to collect are suspended and the operation of the business, through management or a court appointed trustee, are monitored by the bankruptcy court.
6.   A reorganization plan evaluates and selects the higher of the value of the business as liquidated or as a reorganized business.
7.   A reorganization plan must be approved by creditors and confirmed by the bankruptcy court.

C.   **The Choice between Liquidation and Reorganization**
1.   In theory, the liquidation/reorganization decision should be based on which produces the higher value.
2.   Other factors, including tax considerations, cash flow considerations of reorganization, and time delays, are variables in the court decisions.
3.   To support all reorganizations, two major issues must be addressed, namely the fairness handling claims in the order of their legal and contractual priority; and the feasibility concerning an adequate operating income to cover fixed charges.
4.   Federal Bankruptcy and Insolvency Acts provide reorganization for and liquidation of insolvent firms. The legislation lists separate laws, which are necessary pre-condition to legal action. While the law provides safeguards against fraud by the debtor, it also establishes an equitable distribution of the firm's asset.

COMPLETION QUESTIONS

1.   The credit, discount, and payment terms are called the _____ _____ _____ .

2.   Manufacturers sometimes delay dating invoices for products sold unevenly during the year in a practice known as _____ _____.

3.   The longer the period after the discount period lapses, the (*higher/lower*) is the cost of using trade credit.

4.   Open account sales are an agreement whereby sales are made with (*a/no*) formal debt contract.

5.   A _____ draft requires payment immediately.

6. A trade acceptance is signed by the (*bank/purchaser*).

7. _____ acceptances are often used in international trade.

8. The procedure to determine the likelihood that a customer will pay its bills is known as a (*cash flow/credit*) analysis.

9. The 5 Cs of credit are _____, _____, _____, _____, and _____.

10. In numerical credit scoring systems, the applicant's sex and race (*may/may not*) be used.

11. Credit scoring systems favour large (*families/incomes*).

12. An important indicator of potential bankruptcy for a firm is a (*high/low*) EBIT to total asset ratio.

13. More intensive analysis is recommended for (*large/small*) orders and (*strong/weak*) customers.

14. Credit decisions are based on expected (*collections/profits*).

15. When considering long-run sales to a customer, the higher discount rates will favour (*higher/lower*) break-even probabilities.

16. An aging schedule is helpful when establishing a (*collection/payment*) policy.

17. The situation in which a firm that cannot pay its debts is reorganized or liquidated is called _____ .

18. In a workout, the troubled firm (*avoids/declares*) bankruptcy.

19. An extension or a composition are arrangements negotiated (*prior to/during*) bankruptcy.

20. The restructuring of financial claims to keep a firm operating occurs in a _____.

21. Shareholders and junior creditors usually have strong reasons for preferring (*liquidation/reorganization*).

22. High profit margin goods are usually given with more (*liberal/strict*) credit terms.

PROBLEMS

1. Company A sells on terms of 2/10, net 45 basis. Debi buys goods with an invoice of $10,000.
   a. How much will Debi pay if she pays by the 10th day of the month?
   b. How many extra days can Debi receive if she gives up the discount and pays according to terms?
   c. If Debi passes the discount, what is the effective annual rate of interest paid her if she pays on the net date?

2. With reference to Question 1 above, if Customer B is able to finance the purchase at an effective annual rate of 14 percent, how much will they pay ($) for the financing?

3. Which of the following credit terms has the highest effective annual rate (cost) of discounts missed?
   a. 2/10, net 30
   b. 1/5, net 60
   c. 3/20, net 45

4. With reference to Question 2 above, if customers had opportunities to finance at a bank at an effective rate of 12 percent, under what credit terms above are businesses likely to borrow and pay the invoice on the discount date?

5. Jordan Inc. purchases $60,000 worth of goods from Wall's Inc. every month. Wall's has recently changed its credit terms from 2.5/10, net 30 to 2/10, net 45. Jordan Inc. has always paid on the 10th, but now is asking you for your opinion?

6. Kellen Corp. has recently changed its credit terms from 1/10, net 60 to 2/10, net 40. What has this action done to the effective cost of discounts missed for its customers and the likely impact upon its level of accounts receivables?

7. Greg's Golfing Store that has always sold its merchandise for cash is considering adopting a net 30, EOM policy, in line with larger competitors. The business feels that, while its merchandise is superior to that of competitors, it is losing sales because of its "cash basis" policy. It is estimated that sales/month would increase 10 percent from the current level of $2000/month. The price per unit is $130 and the cost (in present value terms) is $65. The current interest rate is 9 percent per year. Should the new credit policy be adopted?

8. With reference to Question 7 above, if it is estimated that 1 percent of all customers will not pay, should the new credit policy be adopted?

9. Econopools sells portable swimming pools to retailers for $1000. Each pool costs $500 to make. With credit terms of net 30 and estimates of bad debts of 4 percent, should Econopools accept a one-time order on credit? The current interest rate is 1 percent per month.

10. In the above Question 9, what is the break-even probability of collection?

11. With reference to Econopools in Question 9 above:
    a. If after paying for its first pool order, the customer places an identical order each month forever. With little chance of default, should credit be extended for these additional orders?
    b. What is the break-even probability of collection with this repeat-sale customer?

12. Microven, Inc. manufactures a miniature microwave oven for reheating coffee. It costs $50 to produce and sells for $80. The bad debt proportion is estimated to be 5 percent and the firm offers terms of net 30. An order from Wallpark for 2000 units has just arrived. Assuming interest rates of 9 percent annually, should Microven, Inc. take this one-time order? Assume the customer will pay the invoice or nothing at all.

13. With reference to the Microven, Inc. problem above, what is the break-even probability of collections?

14. Youth Bouncebeds, Inc. has been selling trampoline beds for "active" children for many years. It is currently studying a proposal to tighten credit policy in an attempt to reduce its bad debt expense ratio, now 5 percent to 3 percent. Sales are estimated to decline by 10 percent. The cost of sales is 80 percent of the selling price. Should the company adopt this new credit policy?

15. Reemay sells $50,000 of product to Gardner's Fair each month. Gardner's Fair has always borrowed and paid on the 10th day of the month in response to Reemay's 1.5/10, net 30, and Gardner's Fair is now considering payment on the net date. What do you advise? Gardner's Fair has an investment in money market securities earning 5 percent.

ANSWERS TO COMPLETION QUESTIONS

1. terms of sale
2. seasonal dating
3. lower
4. no
5. sight
6. purchaser
7. Banker's

8.   credit
9.   character, capacity, capital, collateral, conditions
10. may not
11. incomes
12. low
13. small, weak
14. profits
15. higher
16. collection
17. bankruptcy
18. avoids
19. prior to
20. reorganization
21. reorganization
22. liberal

SOLUTIONS TO PROBLEMS

1. a. If the invoice is postmarked by the 10th, Debi will receive a 2 percent discount or .02 x $10,000 = $200, and will pay $9,800.

    b. For $200, Debi can delay payment for 35 days (45 – 10).

    c. If the discount is passed, the effective annual rate of discounts missed is:

    $(1 + \$200/\$9,800)^{365/35} - 1 = (1.0204)^{365/35} - 1 = 23.5\%$

2. If Debi passes the discount, it will cost them $200 for 35 days at an effective cost of 23.5 percent. (See Problem 1 above.) An effective borrowing rate of 14 percent is $(1.14)^{35/365} - 1$ or 1.264 percent times ($9,800 cost of invoice on 10th) = $123.91 interest cost for 35 days. The $123.91 interest cost is less than the $200 offered by Company A for 35 days. Debi should borrow and pay the invoice by the 10th.

3. The effective annual rate of discounts missed are:
    a. 2/10, net 30

    One gives up 2 percent for 30 – 10 = 20 days added time to finance 100 – 2 = 98 percent of any invoice amount on an annualized basis.

    $(1 + 2/98)^{365/20} - 1 = (1.020408)^{18.25} - 1 = 44.6$ percent

b. 1/5, net 60

$$(1 + 1/99)^{365/55} - 1 = (1.0101)^{6.636} - 1 = 6.9 \text{ percent}$$

c. 3/20, net 45

$$(1 + 3/97)^{365/25} - 1 = (1.03092)^{2.6} - 1 = 8.24 \text{ percent}$$

The 2/10, net 30 is the most punitive if the discount is passed.

4. With a 12 percent borrowing rate available, borrowing on the 10th and paying the invoice for the 2/10, net 30 terms would save considerable amounts of money. It is cheaper to pay on the net date for "b" and "c."

5. The effective annual rate of discounts missed has changed from:
   a. 2.5/10, net 30

$$(1 + 2.5/97.5)^{365/20} - 1 = (1.02564)^{18.25} - 1 = 58.7\%$$

   b. 2/5, net 60

$$(1 + 2/98)^{365/55} - 1 = (1.0204)^{6.64} - 1 = 14.3\%$$

The prior terms with an effective cost of missing the discount of 58.7 percent, meant that Jordan's Inc. was likely to pay on the 10th each month. The new terms warrant an analysis. If the bank charges an effective rate of 14.3 percent or more, borrow and take the discount. If the bank rate is greater than 14.3 percent, pass the discount and pay on the net date. Under the new terms the discount of ($60,000 × .02) = $1200 buys 55 days. If the bank had a 14.3 percent rate, Jordan Inc. would pay $1184 for the 55 days of borrowing $(1.143475)^{55/365} - 1 = .020408(\$58,000) = \$1184$ in interest, approximating the $1200 discount ($60,000 × .02).

6. When Kellen changed its credit terms from 1/10, net 60 to 2/10, net 40, the cost of discounts missed changed.

Cost of discounts missed:

1/10, net 60

$$(1 + 1/99)^{365/50} - 1 = 7.6 \text{ percent}$$

2/10, net 40

$$(1 + 2/98)^{365/30} - 1 = 27.9 \text{ percent}$$

This policy change was intended to encourage customers to take the discount and pay by the 10th of every month. The policy change should reduce accounts receivables by about 50 days and free up capital to be invested elsewhere, at a cost of 1 percent of their margin. Customers, on the other hand, now face a shift from net terms (60) to borrowing and taking the discount on the 10th. Their accounts payable should decline by 50 days and borrowing costs increase somewhat (difference between 7.6 percent effective cost of merchandise before to whatever the bank rate might be, most likely under 27.9 percent).

7. The current value of a cash sale is the units sold times the profit/unit or:

$$2000 \text{ units} \times (\$130 - 65) = \$130,000 \text{ current value of sales}$$

If one month (30 days) credit is given, the present value of revenue falls from its current value of $130 (cash received now) to $130/1.0075 = \$129.03$ per unit ($130 discounted one month — $.09/12 = .0075$).

If both existing and new customers now take the net credit terms, the value of the sales, now 10 percent higher, is:

$$2000 \ (1.10) \ (\$129.03 - \$65) = \$140,866$$

Adopting the new credit terms would increase the value of sales. The new credit policy should be adopted.

8. If in the question above, we now add a 1 percent bad debt expense to the issue, the expected value (probability times dollars) of the sales is now:

$$2200 \ [.99 \ (\$129.03 - \$65) - .01(\$65)] =$$

$$2200 \ (\$63.3897 - .\$65) = \$138,027$$

The 1 percent bad debt expense associated with the new credit policy still adds to the value of sales, compared to the $130,000 value before the credit policy change. What bad debt expense ratio, "X," would hold the value of sales at $130,000. Hint: Let "X" equal bad debt loss rate and $(1 - X)$ be the probability of a paid sale.

$$2200[(1 - X)(\$129.03 - \$65) - X \ (\$65)] = \$130,000$$

9.   The present value of cost is $500.

The present value of revenue (PV of revenue collected in one month) is $1000/1.01 = $990.10.

The value of a sale of one unit is $450.50.

.96($990.10 − $500) − .04($500) = $470.50 − $20 = $450.50

The new credit terms have a positive value and should be adopted.

10.   The break-even probability of a collection is the point where the expected value equals zero.

Let X = probability of collections
$1 − X$ = probability of default

$X(\$990.10 − \$500) − (1 − X)500 = 0$
$\$490.10X − \$500 + 500X = 0$
$\$990.10X = \$500$
$X = 50.5$ percent
$1 − X = 49.5$ percent

Econopools, with a good profit margin, could lose up to $1 − .505 = .495$ or 49.5 percent of its sales before the value of sales would fall below zero.

11.   a.   A paying customer is a cash flow profit stream forever per month of ($990.10 − $500) = $490.10). The PV of this $490.10 perpetuity is $490.10/.01 = $49,010. The PV of a sale, given a 4 percent loss rate is:

.96($49,010) − .04($500) = $47,050 − $20 = $47,030

It clearly makes sense to make the repeat sale on credit. The PV, $47,030, is greater than zero.

b.   The break-even probability of collection, p, is found by solving for:

$p(\$49,010) − (1 − p)\$500 = 0$
$\$49,010p − 500 + 500p = 0$
$\$49,510p = \$500$
$p = .01$

The probability of collections need only be 1 percent for the credit policy to break even.

314

12. The present value per unit of revenue is $80/1.0075 = $79.40, where the one month discount rate is .09/12 = .0075. The cost is $50.

The value of the sale is:

$$.95(\$79.40 - \$50) - .05(\$50) = (\$28.025 - \$2.50) =$$

$25.525 per unit or $51,050 value of the 2000 unit order.

13. The break-even probability of collection for Microven, Inc. is:

$$p(\$79.40 - \$50.00) - (1 - p)\$50.00 = 0$$
$$\$29.40p - \$50.00 + 50p = 0$$
$$\$79.40p = \$50.00$$
$$p = .63$$

The probability of collection must be approximately 63 percent for the sale to break even.

14. The expected profit margin under the existing and the new, tighter credit policy is outlined below:

	Present	New
Sales	100.00	90.00
– Bad debt exp.	5.00	2.70 (.03 × 90)
– cost of sales	80.00	72.00 (.8 × 90)
Profit	15.00	15.30

The new policy increases expected profits and should be adopted.

15. Under the current terms the annualized cost of discounts missed is:

$$(1 + 1.5/97.5)^{365/20} - 1 = 32 \text{ percent}$$

It is obvious that Gardner's Fair would always borrow and take the discount on the 10th of every month. Now with .5/10, net 30, the effective annualized cost of discounts missed is:

$$(1 + .5/99.5)^{365/20} - 1 = 9.6 \text{ percent}$$

Paying on the net date increases the cost of the merchandise by $250 from a discount-assuming base of $49,750 for 20 days, a cost of $(1 + 250/49,750)^{365/20} - 1 = 9.6$ percent.

As long as the bank's annualized effective rate is **above** 9.6 percent, Gardner's Fair should pay on the net date. If bank rates are less than 9.6 percent, they should borrow on the 10th of every month and take the discount. With liquid securities available for sale, the cost of taking the discount on the 10th is only 5 percent, the opportunity cost of securities.

CHAPTER 22

LEASING

INTRODUCTION

The central focus of this chapter is the valuation of a lease to determine whether, and to what extent, it tends to enhance the value of the firm. Financial leases are leases that cover most of an asset's estimated economic life. These leases are non-cancellable by the lessee or cancellable only if the lessor is reimbursed for expected losses arising from forgone income. Financial leases are essentially considered as substitutes for buying the asset and financing the same by borrowing the money required. A continuing comparison between leasing and borrowing is made as financing alternatives. The decision rule that emerges is: a financial lease is superior to buying and borrowing if the financing provided by the lease exceeds the present value of the liability it creates.

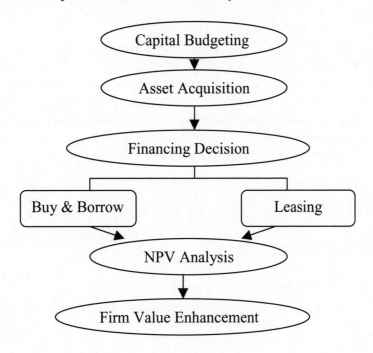

LEARNING CHECKLIST

After studying this chapter, you should be able to:

____ 1. Understand different types of leases and why they are being used.
____ 2. Assess the net present value of a long-term lease.
____ 3. Know how leasing is an alternative to debt financing.

SOURCES OF BUSINESS INFORMATION

Apples to Apples: Instead of purchasing equipment, you are thinking of leasing. Before you process your leasing application, you want to know more about the leasing industry. There are Web sites providing useful information such as www.gecapital.com from GE Capital who is a large Canadian lessor, and www.cfla-acfl.ca from the Canadian Finance and Leasing Association. For a nominal fee, you should be able to find some leasing specialists who can customize a leasing contract to suit your business. A good start is to talk to the leasing officer in a bank such as www.scotiabank.com. Since leases are created differently, you need to carefully compare things like rates, timing of payments, fees, term, and security deposits, etc.

Too Good to Be True: Leasing certainly makes good business sense in terms of flexibility and the PST & GST payment deferral. Often enough, leasing is promoted as the best alternative to preserve your cash. Don't be fooled! As you know from the accounting theory, the claim is not valid. Setting your money free is nothing more than a marketing gimmick. So, look for something in your leasing package with substance such as seasonal payment options or asset financing lines. For curiosity, visit the Web site from an independent leasing company at www.LeaseLinx.com and see how they operate their businesses.

CHAPTER OUTLINE, KEY CONCEPTS, AND TERMS

I.   **WHAT IS A LEASE?**

    A.   **Basics of Leasing**
        1.   A lease is a legal contract between two parties, the lessor, who owns the assets, and the lessee, who uses the assets. The ability of using the asset is more important than the ownership.
        2.   The lessor allows the lessee to use the leased property for a specific period of time that is known as the lease period.
        3.   The lessee buys the right to use the property by making a series of periodic payments called lease payments.
        4.   Besides the payment and the term, a lease contract also contains provisions for renewal or purchase of the asset by the lessee,

conditions for cancellation, and responsibilities of repair and maintenance.

5.   Lessors and lessees can be people or companies. Equipment manufacturers (e.g., Xerox), banks and independent leasing company (e.g., GE Capital) are major lessors in today's market.

B.   **Types of Leasing Arrangements**

1.   Operating leases provide for temporary use and have shorter terms than the life of the asset. These leases are cancellable at the option of the lessee.

2.   Financial leases are long-term and non-cancellable. The asset is usually fully amortized.

3.   Since the lessor does not provide maintenance, insurance and taxes for most financial leases, they are known as net leases. If the lessor pays these expenses, the leases are said to be the full-service or rental leases.

4.   In a sale and leaseback arrangement, the owner of an asset sells the property to another company and simultaneously leases it back for a specific period at specific terms. Even the original owner now becomes the lessee, this setup allows a firm to raise capital and still retain use of the asset.

5.   With a sale-leaseback, the equipment has been used. With a direct lease, new equipment is purchased by the lessor from a manufacturer rather than from the lessee.

6.   Leveraged leasing involves a third part called the lender from whom the lessor borrows a large amount to finance the leased asset using the lease contract as security.

C.   From the view of a lessee, leasing is a flexible source of financing and permits better timing of more permanent investments. A financial lease contract indeed is a substitute for borrowing.

II.   WHY LEASE?

A.   **Sensible Reasons for Leasing**

1.   Lease can reduce taxes. Lessors benefit from the CCA deduction and save taxes. By leasing, the lease payments from lessee are tax deductible.

2.   Lease can reduce uncertainty and strengthen the value of the firm. The lessee passes the risk of obsolescence (the risk that the equipment becomes outdated) to the lessor with the cancellation options.

3.   Transaction costs can be lower for a lease contract than for an outright purchase. If a firm needs an asset for only a short period of time, a

full-service lease is convenient. With standardization, specialty lessor may achieve the economies of scale.

B. **Some Dubious Reasons for Leasing**

1. Leasing avoids capital expenditure controls. Leases are not subject to a number of restrictive covenants. Applications for lease are usually approved faster, and with relaxed standard, than those for purchasing.

2. Leasing preserves capital. Although leasing companies provide the full cost of the property, the lessee cannot really save the cash for other things. Whether the firm leases or borrows-to-buy, it ends up with the same liability. But, in case of an initial payment required by the lessor, the 100% financing claim breaks.

3. Lease may be off-balance-sheet financing. Lease can make a firm's book income and balance sheet look stronger than they actually are. However, investors will not be fooled in an efficient capital market.

C. **Off-Balance-Sheet Financing**

1. Using leasing financing rather than buy-and-borrow can affect the firm's balance sheet. Particularly, the leverage ratios are lower for firms who lease compared to the ones who borrow to purchase the assets. However, the fixed charge ratios representing the financial risk of a firm are higher under leasing than under buy-and-borrow.

2. Countries such as Germany refer to leasing as "off-balance-sheet" financing because neither assets nor lease liabilities appear on the firm's balance sheets. This practice does not make sense due to the potential financial leverage distortion.

3. The CICA Handbook requires firms to "capitalize" certain financial leases by reporting the present value of future lease payments as a liability and a corresponding leased properties must be posted under fixed assets that can be amortized over the life of the lease like purchased assets.

4. The CICA Handbook requires its disclosure as a footnote for an operating lease. Capitalization of operating leases is recently proposed. Indeed, to properly assess a firm, both major and minor lease obligations must be recognized.

5. The distinction between operating and financial leases is somewhat arbitrary. The conditions under which a lease is taken as a financial lease if (1) the lessee gets property ownership when the lease expires; or (2) the lease period goes beyond 75 percent of the asset's economic life; or (3) the present value of the lease payments covers 90 percent of the asset cost.

III.   VALUING LEASES

A.   Lease analysis begins only after the firm has committed to having the asset. Therefore, the lease decision is a financing decision, not a capital budgeting decision. Leases must be evaluated by both the lessee and the lessor.

B.   **Operating Leases**
1.   Compare the equivalent annual cost of buying the asset with the annual lease payment charged by the lessor.
2.   For the lessee, if the cost of leasing is less than the cost of owning, the asset should be leased.
3.   The value of cancellation option embedded in an operating lease is difficult to measure.

C.   **Financial Leases**

1.   Valuation of a financial lease is similar to valuing any set of cash flows. Identify all the cash flows involved and calculate the present values at the appropriate discount rates.
2.   Add up the present values to find the NPV. Accept the lease if the NPV is positive.
3.   Usually, the decision of leasing versus borrowing-to-purchase is analyzed from the lessee's perspective.

D.   **Cash Flows of a Financial Lease**
1.   At the start (time 0), the lessee saves the cost of purchasing the asset that is viewed as a cash inflow.
2.   During the lease period, the lessee promises to pay regular lease payments that are tax-deductible. Most likely, those payments start at time 0.
3.   Since lessee is not the owner, the tax shields from CCA are not available. Treat this loss of tax privilege as a cost for the lessee. For the same token, at the end of the lease, record the loss of salvage value from not owning the asset, if any.
4.   There may be other cash flows such as maintenance cost to be accounted for.
5.   The approach is to find the present value of the above cash flows and sum them up. See Table 22.1 in the textbook. The only issue is the discount rate to be used. The common practice is to use the after-tax cost of debt to discount all the cash flows, except the salvage value that is discounted at the cost of capital.

E.   **Who Really Owns the Leased Asset?**

1.   The lessor is clearly the legal owner of the property, however, the user is the real owner from an economic point of view.

2.   Although a financial lease is equivalent to a secured loan, complications arise when the asset user gets into financial trouble.

F.   **Leasing and Canada Customs and Revenue Agency (CCRA)**

1.   The lessor, as legal owner, uses the CCA tax shield, but must report the lease payment as taxable rental income.

2.   For the lessee, lease payments are legitimate deductible expenses for income tax purposes unless the CCRA is suspicious about the lease being an instalment sale.

3.   Whether a contract is a lease or a sale depends on the legal relationship created by the details of the arrangement. There is no hard-and-fast rule to follow.

G.   **Equivalent Loan**

1.   Since leasing is analogous to debt financing, the equivalent loan is the loan that exactly matches the lease liability at each point in time. Simply, equivalent loan is the present value of the lease cash outflows discounted at the after-tax cost of borrowing. See Table 22.2 in the textbook.

2.   Compare the financing by the lease with the financing provided by the equivalent loan and accept the lease if the value of the lease is positive.

3.   Net value of lease = cash flows from leasing – value of equivalent loan

4.   Cash flow from leasing is also known as the initial financing provided, which equals the cost of the leased asset minus any immediate lease payment.

5.   The two approaches of evaluating a financial lease would give exactly the same answer.

IV.   WHEN DO FINANCIAL LEASES PAY?

A.   If all the factors are identical for the lessee and the lessor, then the values of the lease to the lessee and lessor would be equal (but of opposite sign).

B.   It is impossible to have a mutually beneficial lease transaction if the lessee and the lessor have the same tax rates, the same cost of asset and the same discount rate.

C.   Thus, a lease would fly only if the lessee and the lessor have different tax rates. Of course, the lease may also make sense when the cost or the discount rate varies, but then this is not a reason for leasing.

D.   There may exist a case where the government incurs a loss on the lease and the other two parties gain.

COMPLETION QUESTIONS

1.   The user of a leased asset is called the ____, whereas the owner of a leased asset is called the ____.

2.   Leases which are short-term and cancellable during the contract period at the option of the (*lesse/lessor*) are called ____ leases.

3.   Leases that are long-term or extend over the economic life of the asset and that cannot be cancelled or can be cancelled only if the (*lessee/lessor*) is reimbursed for losses are called ____ lease.

4.   A (*full-service/ full-payout*) lease is taken out when the lessor promises to maintain and insure the leased assets and pays property taxes on it.

5.   Currently, banks (*can/cannot*) provide consumer car leasing.

6.   When the (*lessee/lessor*) agrees to maintain the leased asset, insure it and pay property taxes due on it, the lease is known as a net lease.

7.   We may regard the lease alternative as a commitment to finance the asset with (*0/100*) percent.

8.   The choice of leasing or owning should depend on the (*future/present*) value of the (*after/before*) tax cash flows to the users of the asset.

9.   A (*direct/leveraged*) lease is a type of financial lease in which the lessor issues equity in the financial markets and uses the funds acquired to purchase the asset.

10.   Generally accepted accounting principles (GAAP) (*does/does not*) allow off-balance-sheet financing in Canada.

11.   Lease payments of (*financial/operating*) leases must be capitalized, which is to say that the present value of the lease payments must be estimated and shown as debt on the right-hand side of the balance sheet.

12. Other things being equal, the potential gains to lessor and lessee are (*highest/lowest*) when the lessor's tax rate is substantially higher than the lessee's.

PROBLEMS

1. What are three benefits that accrue to a lessor and represent opportunity losses for a lessee?

2. How do we modify the decision rule if we apply the IRR method instead of the NPV approach to decide whether to purchase or lease?

3. What is the major difference between leveraged leases and sale-leaseback arrangements?

4. The ABC Co. decides to lease additional computer equipment for the next 5 years. The deal requires annual lease payments of $66,000 commencing on the day the contract is signed. Had the equipment been purchased, it would have cost $320,000. Suppose that the computer can be sold for a salvage value of $20,000 at the end of year 5. A straight-line depreciation is used for simplicity. The company's combined marginal tax bracket is 35 percent, and its long-term borrowing rate is 10 percent. The overall cost of capital is 15 percent. Calculate the net present value of the lease.

5. The ABC Co.'s treasurer suddenly realizes that the company does not need to pay taxes in the next five years. How does this affect the NPV of the lease in Problem 4?

6. The XYZ Inc. has an after-tax cost of borrowing of 10 percent and is subject to a 35 percent combined tax rate. The company is considering the purchase of a machine for $100,000. With the heavy use, there is no salvage value left. The straight-line method is used for depreciation. The company wants to lease out the machine for 5 years at a required return of 15 percent. Calculate the net cost of the annual lease payments XYZ will charge a lessee. The first lease payment starts once the contract is signed.

ANSWERS TO COMPLETION QUESTIONS

1. lessee, lessor
2. lessee, operating
3. lessor, financial
4. full-service
5. cannot
6. lessee
7. 100

8. present, after
9. direct
10. does not
11. financial
12. highest

SOLUTIONS TO PROBLEMS

1. Three benefits to the lessor and the corresponding opportunity cost losses to a lessee are (1) tax shield from CCA, (2) tax credits from asset investment, and (3) salvage value.

2. Although the NPV is often recommended for determining whether to lease or buy and borrow, the IRR method can be employed to make the decision. Either method should serve the purpose. Always go for the option that yields the lowest cost (in present value terms). Remember in the NPV method, we are dealing with net cash flows. The comparison is basically done between the costs of leasing and buying. The decision rule is simple. If PV(lease) < PV (buy and borrow), then lease; otherwise, buy. However, return from cash flows is what the IRR method focuses. The decision needs modification. If IRR (lease) < after-tax cost of debt, then lease; otherwise, buy.

3. A leveraged lease involves a lessor and a lender. Both put up part of the cash to cover the purchase of an asset. The lender is a creditor who has claim on the asset and receives a return from part of the lease payments. The lessor also receives a portion of the rentals that should provide a given rate of return. However, the return to the lessor is higher because of the leverage involved. For the lessee, whether a lease is leveraged or not will not be a concern at all. Sale-leaseback arrangements call for the owner (a firm) of an asset to sell the asset to another firm who then becomes the lessor and leases the asset back to the original owner of the asset. The main accomplishment is to help the original owner raise capital. In some cases, at the termination of the lease contract, the asset reverts back to the original owner. An adequate compensation to the lessor is expected.

4. The analysis is provided in the table below. Since the NPV is positive ($26,680), accept the lease.

Cash Flow Analysis of the Lease (in $000s)

	Year 0	Year 1	Year 2	Year 3	Year 4	Year 5
Cost of computer	320					
Lost depreciation tax shield		−21.00	−21.00	−21.00	−21.00	−21.00
Lease payment	−66.00	−66.00	−66.00	−66.00	−66.00	
Tax shield from lease payment		23.10	23.10	23.10	23.10	23.10
Lost of salvage value						−20.00
Cash flow of lease	254.00	−63.90	−63.90	−63.90	−63.90	−17.90
PV@6.5%	254.00	−60.00	−56.34	−52.90	−49.67	−8.41
NPV	26.68					

Note: Borrowing cost is 10 percent. With tax rate 35 percent, the after-tax rate is 6.5 percent. Following the usual practice, we assume that the computer is purchased in year 1. Hence, the first depreciation would occur in year 1, which is slightly different from the setup in the textbook. Furthermore, in practice, we know that the lease payment tax shield occurs with a time lag. The lease end cash flow should be handled with care. Particularly, discount the $20,000 at 15 percent.

5. There are some adjustments needed for the case of no tax. Given a zero tax rate, the after-tax rate is the same as the borrowing cost at 10 percent. While there is no lost depreciation tax savings, lease payment tax savings is unavailable now. The analysis of the lease is given as below while we keep all the previous assumptions.

Cash Flow Analysis of the Lease (in $000s)

	Year 0	Year 1	Year 2	Year 3	Year 4	Year 5
Cost of computer	320					
Lost depreciation tax shield		0.00	0.00	0.00	0.00	0.00
Lease payment	−66.00	−66.00	−66.00	−66.00	−66.00	
Tax shield from lease payment		0.00	0.00	0.00	0.00	0.00
Lost of salvage value			−20.00			
Cash flow of lease	254.00	−66.00	−66.00	−66.00	−66.00	−20.00
PV@10%	254.00	−60.00	−54.55	−49.59	−45.08	−9.94
NPV	34.84					

The NPV of the lease is $34,840. The zero tax rate now makes the lease even more attractive.

6. With an annual depreciation = $100,000 / 5 = $20,000, the depreciation tax shield over the lease period becomes ($20,000)(0.35) × PVIFA(10%, 5) = $26,535.60. The net cost of machine is $100,000 − $26,535.60 = $73,464.40 that is also the after-tax amount the lessor has to recover from the lease payments. With a required return of 15 percent, let the required net annual lease payment be $X. Since $73,464.40 = [X × PVIFA(15%, 5)](1.15), solving for X, we have X = $19,056.76. With the 35 percent tax rate, the company must ask the lessee to pay $19,056.76 / (1 − 0.35) = $29,318 per year.

CHAPTER 23

MERGERS, ACQUISITIONS, AND CORPORATE CONTROL

INTRODUCTION

Just as there are markets for securities and commodities, so is there a market for corporate control, the buying and selling of controlling influence over business. The transactions are mergers, acquisitions, leveraged buy-outs, and other similar terms. The deals are carried out in smoke-filled rooms, annual meetings, in the mail for proxies, and in large expensive ads in The Globe and Mail. This chapter provides the terminology and concepts related to the market for corporate control. It is an extensive, intuitive chapter centering on one of the two exciting activities of financial management. The other is going public, covered in an earlier chapter. There is always a good proxy fight occurring in the newspapers during each semester to provide a good current event discussion and assignment.

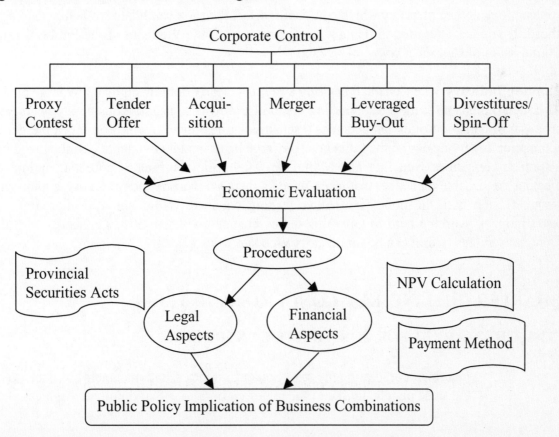

LEARNING CHECKLIST

After studying this chapter you should be able to:

____1. Describe ways that companies change their ownership or management.
____2. Explain the motivations for merger. What are the gains from merger?
____3. Describe how the gains from merger are divided among the sellers and buyers.
____4. Describe several takeover defences.
____5. Summarize the evidence related to whether mergers enhance efficiency.

SOURCES OF BUSINESS INFORMATION

Career Planning: Have you thought about the type of business or industry in which you would like to spend your life? Just as families and relationships vary in tempo, stress, etc., so do business. There are a number of references and periodicals that frequently list the best companies to work for. "Job Postings" is one of the student employment magazines in Canada. It is published seven times during the school year with issue dates in September, October, November, January, March, April, and May. Although positions listed are full-time entry level and aim for university and college fresh graduates, you may find information about co-ops/internships as well. Organized by the field of study at their Web site www.jobpostings.ca, you can look at the criteria by which companies select their job candidates to help you to plan ahead. If you are interested in being a civil servant, visit the Web site of the Public Service Commission of Canada at www.jobs.gc.ca.

Banking Industry: The Canadian banking system is clearly dominated by a few large banks. Although there is no evidence supporting the industry owns substantial business powers, any proposal of bank consolidation becomes a sensitive issue. Government prohibits a merger or acquisition involving one of the Canada's five large banks and its two large demutualized life insurance companies, Sun Life and ManuLife. This policy eliminates potential options to meeting the sizeable challenges that face Canada's financial industry today and in the future and is out of step with the policies of other leading countries. Now, the Canadian Bankers Association is working hard to have this policy changed. Other industry concerns with the financial services reform can be found at its Web site www.cba.ca.

CHAPTER OUTLINE, KEY CONCEPTS, AND TERMS

I.   THE MARKET FOR CORPORATE CONTROL

A.   In a small corporation the stockholders, directors, and managers are likely to be the same people, unlike in the major corporations that dominate business.

B. Shareholders elect the board of directors who in turn appoint management. Control of the business is vested in management, with the board left to an oversight role.

C. Ownership and control of businesses change. The market place where this exchange takes place is called the market for corporate control.

D. There are four ways that the management of a corporation can change: proxy contest, merger, leveraged buy-out, and divestiture.

E. In any business transaction, including mergers, one must distinguish between what is purchased, what is used for payment and how much is paid for it, and how or who will manage the assets/business in the future.

F. **Proxy Contests**
    1. Existing management may be changed or replaced by the board of directors, or failing that, by changing the board of directors who are elected by the shareholders.
    2. A **proxy contest** is an attempt to replace the board, and later management, by an outsider group or owners or other interested parties. Shareholders may delegate or "proxy" their vote on issues to others. A group may wage a proxy fight to elect directors. Control is decided by shareholders by how they vote or to whom they proxy their vote.
    3. Most proxy fights by outsiders fail for existing managers have the advantages of company funding and inertia.

G. **Mergers and Acquisitions**
    1. Corporate control is more likely to be changed through acquisition via three ways. Something is purchased and something is given in consideration.
    2. **Merger**, the combination of two firms into one, is the first method of acquisition with the purchases assuming the assets and liabilities of the target firm. The acquired firm ceases to exist and the former shareholders are given cash or securities, perhaps in the acquiring firm. In Canada, mergers are statutory amalgamation where the assets and liabilities of two companies are combined into one and both original firms may disappear.

Year	Buying Company	Selling Company	Value (in millions)
2000	Vivendi (France)	Seagram	$41,650
2000	Nortel Networks Corp.	Alteon WebSystems Inc.	11,523
2000	Alcatel SA	Newbridge Networks Corp.	10,800
2001	Sun Life Financial Services	Clarica Life Insurance	6,800
2001	Conoco Inc.	Gulf Canada Resources	6,700
2000	BCE Inc.	Teleglobe Inc.	6,400
2000	Shire Pharmaceuticals Group	BioChem Pharma	5,900
2000	Abitibi-Consolidated	Donohue	5,600
2001	Duke Energy Corp.	Westcoast Energy Inc.	5,500
2001	Newmont Mining Corp.	Franco-Nevada Mining Corp. and Normandy Mining	5,281
2000	Nortel Networks Corp.	Xros	4,750
2001	Investors Group Inc.	Mackenzie Financial Corp.	4,149
2000	Telus	Clearnet Communications	4,091
2000	CanWest Global Communications	Hollingers (newspapers)	3,200
2000	PMC-Sierra	Quantum Effect Devices	3,170

3. Another means by which a firm is acquired is by the purchase of the target company's stock. Cash or securities is paid, stockholders change places, and change is affected via board and management changes. A **tender offer** is where an unwanted acquirer invites shareholders to offer or tender their shares at a specified price to the acquirer.

4. The third way to acquire control over a company's assets is to purchase the assets directly from the selling company. Again cash and/or securities are the likely consideration.

H. **Leveraged Buy-Outs**

1. When a firm's assets or stock is purchased by a private group using borrowed funds, the change in corporate control is called a **leveraged buy-out (LBO)**.

2. When the buyers are current or former managers, the term **management buy-out (MBO)** is used.

I. **Divestitures and Spin-Offs** — Divisions, subsidiary corporations, and assets may be sold to other businesses (divestiture) or sold or spun-off to the general public or new owner group.

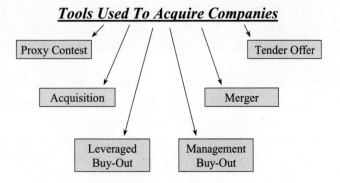

Tools Used To Acquire Companies

Proxy Contest   Tender Offer

Acquisition   Merger

Leveraged Buy-Out   Management Buy-Out

II.   SENSIBLE MOTIVES FOR MERGERS

A.   Mergers are categorized as horizontal, vertical, or conglomerate, depending upon the nature of the business acquired.

B.   If a firm in a similar line of business is acquired, the merger is called a horizontal merger. The acquisition of Canadian Airlines by Air Canada is an example. If a supplier or a customer is acquired (vertical in the supply chain), it is a vertical merger. For example, Pepsi owns Burger King. A conglomerate merger is the acquisition of an unrelated line of business, for example, Daewoo.

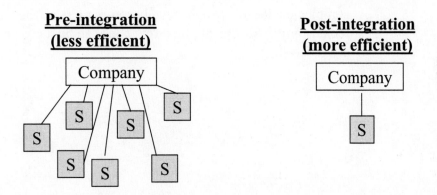

Pre-integration (less efficient)

Post-integration (more efficient)

C.   The motives for acquiring another business or its assets include the desire to replace existing management, and to improve efficiency or to produce synergies. The synergies or the value added by combining businesses may be explained by the following six areas.

D.   **Increased Revenues**

1.   When one firm combines with another firm in the same business, they are likely to abuse the market to raise revenues.

2.   For the protection of consumers and competitors, mergers must follow the anti-combines laws. However, merger proposals are seldom disapproved based on anti-competitive concerns in Canada.

E.   **Economies of Scale**

1.   The ability to derive reduced cost efficiencies through larger operations is an often quoted benefit of mergers.

2.   Horizontal mergers, in the same line of business, and from centralizing such functions as finance and accounting is likely to produce economies of scale.

F.   **Economies of Vertical Integration**

1.   Efficiencies related to controlling raw material supplies and final customer contact benefit some industries.

2.   Benefits in this area are often questionable. Note that gains should be realized through better coordination of production, not from the suppressed price paid to the back-end supplier.

3.   Nowadays, vertical integration becomes less important due to the efficient outsourcing and the just-in-time inventory systems.

G.   **Combining Complementary Resources**

1.   Some mergers involve firms where each has valuable assets which complement the other so the total becomes more efficient or better serves the customer. As a result, total revenues can be increased or total costs are reduced.

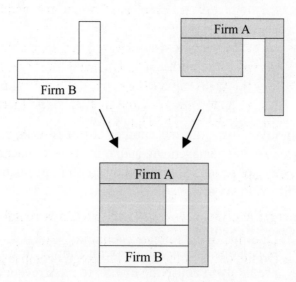

H.   **Merging to Reduce Taxes**

  1.   Firms having significant tax deductions and/or operating loss carry-forward, but expecting to have low income, become targets for mergers.

  2.   When merging is solely for using operating losses, the CCRA usually does not accept such tax deductions.

  3.   Ideally, the acquirer can take advantage of the unused debt capacity from the target by generating more interest tax savings to reduce taxes.

I.   **Mergers as a Use of Surplus Funds**

  1.   The presence of free cash flow in a mature firm often motivates managers to purchase other firms.

  2.   Unless the merger contributes positive NPVs, increased dividends or stock repurchase via downsizing is the better option for shareholders. Taxes on dividends and repurchases should be considered.

III.   **DUBIOUS REASONS FOR MERGERS**

A.   **Diversification**

  1.   It is easier for shareholders to diversify than businesses via asset investment.

  2.   Diversification by itself is a poor reason for mergers, unless the merger is likely to produce value added (positive NPVs).

B.   **The Bootstrap Game**

  1.   The bootstrap effect is the arithmetical result of a higher post-merger earnings per share created when the acquiring firm has a higher price/earnings ratio.

  2.   Bootstrapping merger-oriented firms are able to produce high earnings growth rates, attract added demand for shares and increased stock prices, and maintain higher P/Es that continues until the market assesses the actual added value of the mergers. The market usually is able to see through the "smoke and mirrors."

IV.   **EVALUATING MERGERS**

A.   All merger analysis centres around two fundamental questions.

  1.   Does the merger create economic gain?

  2.   Do the terms of the merger make my company's shareholders better off?

B.   If given a simple answer to each, there would be no magic in the analysis of a merger. Unfortunately, the answers are usually less than obvious.

$$
\begin{aligned}
\text{Economic Gain} &= \text{PV(increased earnings)} \\[2ex]
&= \frac{\text{New cash flows from synergies}}{\text{discount rate}}
\end{aligned}
$$

C.   **Estimating the Gain**

1.   Economic gain from merger occurs only if the two firms are worth more together than apart. Estimating and evaluating the economic gain is the central focus of merger analysis.

2.   The economic gain is shared between the selling shareholders and the purchasing shareholders with the share to each determined by the price paid or negotiated.

3.   The focus of a merger evaluation is the estimated amount of economic gain produced by the merger and the sharing of the gain between seller and buyer.

4.   The cost of a merger is the share of economic gain given to the selling shareholders. The sellers' gain is the buyers' cost.

D.   **Mergers Financed By Cash**

1.   The merger should be effected by the acquirer if the economic gain (the added value of the combination) exceeds the cost (the share of the gain given to the selling shareholders). The cost of the merger is often difficult to assess.

2.   When the compensation for selling shareholders is cash, the distribution of the gain is thought to be easily determined versus the difficult problem of assessing the value of securities used as payment.

3.   When cash is used as compensation to the selling shareholders, the cost is not affected by the actual economic gain from the merger. It is fixed, for the good or bad of it.

E.   **Mergers Financed By Stock**

1.   The cost (gain given up by the buyer) is difficult to determine because the price of the selling stock may include some of the estimated premium (cost) paid by the buyer.

2.   When securities are used as compensation to the selling shareholders, the value of securities given are related to the economic gain to be derived. Thus, the cost is related to the future economic gain derived, because the economic gains that occur will be included in the share prices.

F.   **Warnings**
       1.   The key to successful mergers is the estimation of the gain and the negotiation of the share of the gain.
       2.   When evaluating the economic gain, instead of estimating the target firm's future cash flows, the analyst should estimate the current value of the target firm and adjust this value by the estimated changes in future cash flows after the merger.
       3.   Incremental economic gain from the merger will be derived from the value added (positive NPVs from added cash flows) produced after the merger.
       4.   The market evaluates all mergers, the estimated gain and the sharing of the gain.

G.   **A Note On Tax Complications**
       1.   A taxable acquisition occurs if the selling shareholders receive cash for their shares. Alternatively, the selling shareholders are given shares having ownership of the merged company. As long as there is no capital gain realized, the acquisition is tax-free.
       2.   For the buyer, the taxable acquisition calls for larger CCA deductions leading to less tax payable in the future.
       3.   In a tax-free acquisition, no incremental tax savings are generated for the firms.

V.   **MERGER TACTICS**

A.   **Takeover Defences**
       1.   Takeover defences are commonly approved by shareholders or legislated by various provincial securities acts to "protect" their businesses (managers) from unwanted takeovers. The Ontario Securities Commission (OSC) is the leader setting the rules.
       2.   Two takeover defences are generally used. The first common practice in Canada is called **shark repellent** where shareholders approve amendments to the charter and bylaws that require a supermajority of shareholders to approve a merger, or make changes in the number of directors and/or how directors are elected. In Canada, most mergers require a 2/3 majority by law.
       3.   The second takeover defence is called **shareholders' rights plan** or **poison pill** and it involves contingency plans of selling large numbers of common stock only to existing shareholders at a low price if the bidder acquires a substantial holding. The purpose is to dilute the relevant shareholding, and hereby to increase the cost of a takeover.

4. In Canada, shareholders' rights plans are rarely observed because they are often killed by the OSC at the request of the bidder. As a result, the target company extends the bidding time giving other bidders time to make offers.

5. A **white knight** is often used to fend off an undesired takeover. The white knight is defined as a takeover, but with a friendly face. While it is still a takeover, the terms are usually much more generous to existing management.

B. **Who Gets the Gains?**

1. Who benefits from mergers or who receives the economic gain, if any, from a merger?

2. Research indicates that target or selling shareholders have taken the larger share of the "gain."

3. Acquiring shareholders have received the smaller share of the gains or seem to break even.

4. Sellers receive the larger share because of competitor bidding. A firm receiving an unwanted takeover bid often invites other firms to bid, or uses legal and other defences to force the bid higher. "Professionals" such as accountants, lawyers, etc., seem to get their share of the gain, as do speculators and insiders who buy/sell on anticipation of merger activity.

VI. LEVERAGED BUY-OUTS

A. An acquisition in which the majority of the compensation to selling shareholder is borrowed by the takeover group is called a leveraged buy-out.

B. Publicly owned (large number of shareholders) corporations are taken "private" when managers (management buy-out or MBO) borrow and buy the outstanding shares of the company. They become owner/managers with large obligations over their heads. They work harder, cut costs, and compete more effectively.

C. The RJR Nabisco LBO by KKR was a more notorious LBO case where entrenched management was outbid in their LBO attempt by an outside investor group. Recently, the use of LBO to acquire unwanted divisions, rather than entire companies has become frequent.

D. **RJR Nabisco**

1. KKR expected to repay the enormous debt incurred to buy the RJR Nabisco stock and realize economic gains with the expected interest tax shields, favourable financing rates, availability in the junk bond market,

reduced capital expenditure (free cash flow theory) and operating expenses, and the sale of some parts of RJR Nabisco.

2. The decline in the available high-risk bond market and in the increased cost of borrowing at the time forced KKR to add equity to the deal.

E. **Barbarians at the Gate?**

1. The LBO activity of the late 1980s had considerable negative press but has some redeeming features.

2. Sellers seem to have received most of the economic gain, not the buyers or raiders.

3. LBO activities were driven by the relatively cheap and available junk bond markets.

4. While an LBO generates more borrowing or debt, the benefits of LBOs seem to come from benefits other than tax benefits and leverage benefits.

5. Bondholders seemed to lose at the expense of selling stockholders in the LBO period. High rated bonds became junk as massive debt levels were added to finance the repurchase of stock.

6. LBOs provide considerable incentives to the owner/manager to improve economic efficiency.

7. The presence of free cash flows in mature industries was a major, but not the only, incentive for LBO activity.

VII. MERGERS AND THE ECONOMY

A. **Merger Waves**

1. Merger activity has occurred in cycles in this century, coinciding with periods of increased stock prices.

2. Are mergers driven by economic opportunity or cheap financing? Probably both.

B. **Do Mergers Generate Net Benefits?**

1. Mergers tend to benefit selling shareholders.

2. Mergers tend to improve real productivity.

3. While mergers may reward selling stockholders, the LBO movement of the 1980s tended to reward these selling stockholders and "professionals" at the expense of bondholders, CCRA tax revenues, and perhaps employees at takeover firms.

4. The possibility of takeovers provides incentives for firm managers to manage efficiently, but are there other incentives for business productivity?

COMPLETION QUESTIONS

1. In a _____ contest, outsiders compete with management for shareholders' votes.

2. Institutional investors have (*decreased/increased*) managerial accountability.

3. A combination of two firms into one with the acquiring company assuming all of the assets and liabilities of the other is known as a _____.

4. In a leveraged buy-out a group takes the firm (*private/public*).

5. When a firm sells a part of its business it is a _____; when it distributes stock in a part of its business it is a _____.

6. The acquisition of one computer firm by another computer firm is called a _____.

7. The acquisition of a wood door manufacturer by a company with sawmills is an example of a _____ merger.

8. A _____ merger occurs when a movie firm buys an oil company.

9. Economies from larger operations, vertical integration, and combinations of complementary resources are sources of _____.

10. Diversification is easier and cheaper for (*companies/shareholders*).

11. The incentive for firms selling at high price earnings ratios to acquire firms with low price earnings ratios is called the _____ game.

12. When the present value of a combined firm is worth more than the present value of each separate firm, the result is (*capital/economic*) gain.

13. The NPV of a merger is equal to the gain from the merger (*minus/plus*) the portion of the gain paid to the acquired firm's owners.

14. When stock is offered to purchase another firm, the (*pre/post*) -merger share price of the acquiring company should be used in figuring the cost of the acquired firm.

15. A friendly potential acquirer sought by a target company threatened by an unwelcome suitor is called a _____ _____.

16. Amendments made to a firm's charter to forestall takeover attempts are termed _____ _____.

17. A provision offering selected shareholders a discount on the purchase of new shares when a bidder acquires a significant holding in the company is an example of a _____ _____.

18. Gains from mergers normally go mainly to the (*buying/selling*) firm.

19. Often times unwanted divisions of large firms are sold through a _____ buy-out.

20. The junk bond market (*enhances/inhibits*) leveraged buy-outs.

21. High merger activity is related to (*highs/lows*) in the stock market.

22. Merger activity tends to result in (*decreased/increased*) operating efficiency.

23. A (*taxable/tax-free*) acquisition leads to stepping up the asset pool.

PROBLEMS

1. Daytime, Inc., wants to acquire Nitetime, Ltd., because it feels the "whole can be worth more than the sum of the parts." Savings from the merger are estimated to be a one-time after-tax benefit of $100 million. Nitetime has 5 million shares outstanding at a current market price of $60 per share. What is the maximum cash price per share that could be paid for Nitetime stock?

2. Hot Foods, which has 1 million shares outstanding, wishes to merge with Cold Drinks with 2 million shares outstanding. The market prices for HF and CD are $40 and $15 per share, respectively. The merger could create an estimated savings of $600,000 annually for the indefinite future. If HF were willing to pay $20 per share for CD, and the appropriate cost of capital is 12 percent, what would be the:
   a. Present value of the merger benefit?
   b. Net cost of the cash offer?
   c. The net present value of the offer?

3. What is the major argument against seeking mergers as a strategy for diversifying to reduce risk?

4. Briefly identify the most valid reasons for mergers.

5. Tell why and how a proxy contest occurs.

6.	What are LBOs?

7.	Define the following terms:
	a.	Poison pill.
	b.	Shark repellent.
	c.	White knight

8.	East, Inc., is considering acquiring all of West's 1 million shares because it believes its methods of operation could increase West's compound annual growth rate of earnings and dividends from 10 percent to 12 percent. The market capitalization (share price × the number of shares outstanding) for East and West is currently $50 million and $20 million, respectively. If West is expected to pay $1 per share dividends in the coming year, what would be the estimated gain from the merger using the dividend growth model to value West?

ANSWERS TO COMPLETION QUESTIONS

1.	proxy
2.	increased
3.	merger
4.	private
5.	divestiture, spin-off
6.	horizontal
7.	vertical
8.	conglomerate
9.	synergy
10.	shareholders
11.	bootstrap
12.	economic
13.	minus
14.	post
15.	white knight
16.	shark repellent
17.	poison pill or shareholders' rights plan
18.	selling
19.	management
20.	enhances
21.	highs
22.	increased
23.	taxable

SOLUTIONS TO PROBLEMS

1. The market value of Nitetime is $60 per share × 5 million shares or $300 million. The $100 million one-time benefit would be added to this making the value of Nitetime $400 million ÷ 5 million or $80 per share. If any more were paid the value of the combined entity would decline.

2. a. The gain from the merger would be the present value of the $600,000 annual savings. Because these are estimated to occur each year for the indefinite future they would be valued like a perpetuity as $600,000 ÷ 0.12 or $5,000,000.
    b. The offer for Cold Drinks would cost $20 per share × 2 million shares or $40 million. This is above the market value of $15 per share × 2 million shares or $30 million. The net cost would be $40 – $30 or $10 million.
    c. The net present value of the acquisition would be the outlay of $10 million less the $5 million NPV of the savings. The *negative* NPV of $5 million indicates too much is being paid for CD.

3. There is no doubt that volatility can be reduced by operating in businesses that act differently as the economy moves through expansion and contraction phases. However, it is easier and usually cheaper for individual investors to buy stocks in firms representing a wide range of business activities. This type of diversification results in a less risky portfolio because the returns will vary less than those received when the investment is concentrated in a few business sectors. It also allows investors to pick well-managed companies rather than to expect one firm to be able to excel in very different industries.

4. The basic idea behind mergers is the benefits of synergy. This is the notion that two firms can be worth more together than they are separately. The reasons for this include economies gained from: having larger scale operations; being vertically or horizontally integrated; capitalizing on unique strengths of each firm through the use of complementary resources; and the opportunity to better deploy cash being generated by a successful but mature firm.

5. When a group of investors becomes dissatisfied with the way a company is being run they can either sell their stock or they can try to effect a change in management. In the latter case they can seek to gain control of the firm by electing new directors. This is accomplished by convincing a sufficient number of shareholders to vote for the proposed slate of directors. Since shareholders vote using a proxy, a contest is created between the dissatisfied investors and the current board of directors. If the dissidents are successful in soliciting enough proxy votes in favour of their candidates, a new board will be elected, new policies established, and new management will be chosen to implement the board's wishes.

6. An LBO, or leveraged buy-out, is the process of converting a public company into a private one. Before this happens, the shares are freely traded; after, they are held by a small number of investors. The financing for this to occur comes from debt. The relatively small group of investors borrow sufficient funds to buy all the stock held by the general public. Because this uses so much leverage, the debt is usually low grade (junk bonds). If the investors seeking the takeover are officers of the firm it is called a management buy-out.

7. a. A poison pill is a measure designed to prevent an unwanted takeover from occurring. For example, the shareholders may pass a resolution that allows them the right to purchase additional shares at a substantial discount *if* an outside party acquires a substantial amount of the stock. The unfriendly bidder is not entitled to this privilege. When the new shares are issued, the bidder is further away from gaining control.
   b. Shark repellent is another advance step that discourages unwanted takeovers. For example, a provision could be passed by shareholders that requires a supermajority of votes to approve a merger.
   c. A white knight is a friendly acquirer that is sought when a firm is being threatened for takeover by an unfriendly suitor. When an unwanted bid is received, the target company seeks someone else (white knight) to buy it.

8. The current market price of West is $20 million ÷ 1 million shares or $20 per share. Using this figure and the dividend growth model, we can solve for the return (r) West investors are expecting on the shares that are growing at 10 percent and will pay $1 per share in dividends. This relationship is:

$$\$1 \div (r - 0.10) = \$20$$
$$r = 0.15 \text{ or } 15 \text{ percent.}$$

With the new growth rate of 12 percent the shares would be valued at:

$$\$1 \div (0.15 - 0.12) \text{ or } \$33.33$$

The gain from the merger would be:

$$(\$33.33 - \$20.00) \times 1 \text{ million shares } \$13.33 \text{ million.}$$

CHAPTER 24

INTERNATIONAL FINANCIAL MANAGEMENT

INTRODUCTION

When considering international cash and investment flows, foreign exchange rates and political risks are an added dimension for the financial manager. These risks are covered thoroughly in this chapter. Starting with a discussion of foreign exchange rates using the exchange rate table from <u>The Globe and Mail</u>, a discussion of why spot and forward rates differ is presented. This section, featuring Figure 24.1, is a very effective method for explaining the interrelationship of spot and forward exchange rates, interest rates, and inflation rates. You will not find a better presentation on this topic and will use this reference for years to come.

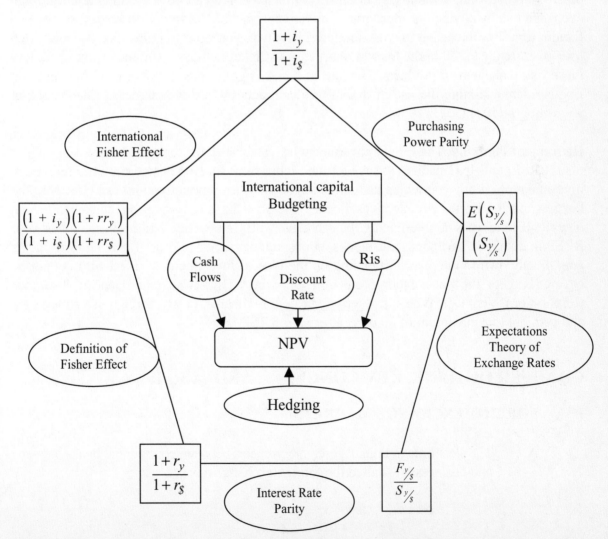

LEARNING CHECKLIST

After studying this chapter you should be able to:

_____1. Understand why spot and forward exchange rates differ.
_____2. Understand the basic relationships between spot exchange rates, forward exchange rates, interest rates, and inflation rates.
_____3. Describe simple strategies or procedures by which a business can protect itself against exchange rate risk.
_____4. Perform an NPV analysis for projects with cash flows in foreign currencies.

SOURCES OF BUSINESS INFORMATION

Foreign Exchange Risk: When investing in another country, you first convert your Canadian dollar into a foreign currency. Then, when your foreign investment is done, the process must be reversed. In essence, two investments are made. One investment is in the foreign assets, and the other is in that foreign country's currency. Fortunately, you can do something about foreign exchange risk by buying the appropriate forward contract on the foreign currency to lock in a fixed return. For the hedge to work properly, however, you need to know exactly how much foreign currency to sell in the forward market. As a finance student, you may want to explore those risk management products. The site of the AIB group has intuitive examples in plain English demonstrating the use of derivatives contracts by currency traders. Take a look at www.aibgroup.com.

Retirement Planning: The federal government has established the registered retirement savings plan (RRSP) to help Canadians to save for their retirement. An RRSP is essentially a retirement investment providing you with a tax deduction equal to the amount you invest. However, the law restricts RRSPs to "eligible investments." The Scotiabank at www.scotiabank.ca offers an overview of the types of investments you can make with your RRSP. While you can invest your RRSP in cash, you may contribute stocks, bonds, mutual funds, or other financial instruments you already own to the plan. Depending on the type of investment, your RRSP may not be covered except the ones under protection with the CDIC (Canadian Deposit Insurance Corporation). Visit their Web site at www.cdic.com for details. Lastly, foreign investments are allowed, but to a maximum of 30 percent of your RRSP.

CHAPTER OUTLINE, KEY CONCEPTS, AND TERMS

I. FOREIGN EXCHANGE MARKETS

A.   The electronic trading of foreign currencies between commercial banks, dealers, and businesses is called the foreign exchange market.

B. The foreign exchange markets have no central marketplace, and participants trade via sophisticated communications systems.

C. The amount of one currency needed to purchase one unit of another currency is called the exchange rate.

D. Foreign exchange rates are expressed in two ways. The **direct quote** shows that the amount of Canadian dollars is required for one unit of foreign currency. That is,

$$S = \text{(foreign currency)} / \text{(domestic currency)} = SF_r / C\$.$$

With such a definition, an increase in S means a depreciation of Canadian dollars.

E. The other alternative (used throughout the text) is the **indirect quote** that is the reciprocal of the direct quote listing the amount of foreign currency that it takes to purchase one Canadian dollar. That is,

$$S = \text{(domestic currency)} / \text{(foreign currency)} = C\$ / SF_r.$$

An increase in S indicates that the domestic currency (C$) appreciates.

F. The spot exchange rate is a quote for an immediate transaction, whereas a forward exchange rate is the price, determined today, of foreign currency delivered at some future date. The forward exchange rates may trade at a premium or discount relative to the spot rate. Using indirect exchange rate quotes, a spot/forward differential is equal to the spot minus the forward divided by the forward and annualized. When the forward rates buy less Canadian, as in the text case of the yen, the differential is quoted at a yen forward premium (expected to appreciate against the $) and the dollar is at a forward discount (expected to depreciate against the yen). The sign (+ or –) of the foreign currency forward differential indicates a premium (+) or discount (–) or the expected direction of the value of the foreign currency.

$$\frac{\text{Forward Price} - \text{Spot Price}}{\text{Spot Price}} = \text{Premium or } (- \text{Discount) if direct quotes are used}$$

G. Foreign exchange futures contracts are traded on futures exchanges and are available for hedging foreign exchange risk.

II. SOME BASIC RELATIONSHIPS

A. There are several basic relationships between spot rates, forward rates, expected relative country inflation rates, and country interest rates that are fundamental to international financial management.

B. The spot/forward differential reflects market expectations of relative country inflation rates. Interest rates differential reflects the spot/forward differential that reflects the expected relative country inflation rate. Investors are seeking a real, inflation adjusted, exchange rate adjusted, after-tax return, and price spot/forward differential to provide that return.

$$\frac{1 + r_{foreign}}{1 + r_{\$}} \quad \text{equals} \quad \frac{1 + i_{foreign}}{1 + i_{\$}}$$

equals   equals

$$\frac{f_{foreign/\$}}{S_{foreign/\$}} \quad \text{equals} \quad \frac{E(s_{foreign/\$})}{S_{foreign/\$}}$$

C. **Exchange Rates and Inflation**
1. The economic **law of one price** theory states that the prices of goods in all countries should be equal when translated to a common currency.
2. Inflation is the decline in purchasing power of a currency (or an increase in the price level in a currency).
3. For the law of one price to hold, exchange rates must vary with inflation to provide similar values for currencies or **purchasing power parity (PPP)** across countries. See Figure 24.2 in the textbook.
4. Estimated future spot exchange rates (forward rates) closely reflect estimated relative inflation rates between countries.

D. **Inflation and Interest Rates**
1. Investors' real, nominal adjusted for inflation, return is the one that counts.
2. The **international Fisher effect** is a theory that says that real interest rates in all countries should be equal, with the differences in nominal rates reflecting differences in expected inflation.
3. Countries with high inflation rates tend to have high subsequent interest rates. See Figure 24.3 in the textbook.

346

E.   **Interest Rates and Exchange Rates**

1.   International lending (investing) and borrowing entail transferring balances between currencies when lending and borrowing occurs. This concern of future exchange rate levels when the investment is complete or when returns/payments are made forces most to buy forward exchange contracts for adverse exchange rate movements. Capital tends to flow to its highest real, risk adjusted rate of return.

2.   Market forces and capital flows tend to provide **interest rate parity** among countries in that spot/forward foreign exchange rate differentials tend to offset interest rate differences between countries and tend toward offering investors nearly the same exchange rate adjusted, rate of return in all countries.

F.   **The Forward Rate and the Expected Spot Rate**

1.   Forward rates are expected future spot rates.

2.   The percentage spot/forward differential (premium or discount) reflects the exchange markets' estimate of the percentage change in the exchange rate between two countries, and is called the expectations theory of exchange rates.

3.   While forward rates are not good predictors of actual future spot rates, *on average* the forward rate is equal to the future spot rate.

G.   **Some Implications**

1.   The above four relationships are long run, "tending toward" relationships that tend to hold over the years.

2.   International financial decision makers should implant those relationships and be wary when betting against them.

III.   **HEDGING EXCHANGE RATE RISK**

A.   Foreign exchange risk is the variability in returns and cash flows (gains and losses) that occurs when one must transfer values from one currency to another.

B.   There are two types of foreign exchange risk. Contractual risk is the variability of outcomes occurring when a specified currency exchange must be made on a given date. Noncontractual risk includes the general business impact of changing exchange rates on importers and exporters, investors, etc.

C.   One may assume foreign exchange risk and take the loss/gain consequences of changing foreign exchange rates or remove the impact of varying exchange rates by hedging.

D.   One may hedge foreign exchange risk by trading in forward foreign exchange contracts, foreign exchange futures contracts, or financial futures option contracts. See the Enterprise Oil example in Table 24.4 in the textbook.

E.   The cost of the hedge is the difference between the forward rate and the expected spot rate when payments are made.

F.   Hedging foreign exchange risk makes sense for it focuses the business manager on "business" and not exchange rate forecasting and does not cost much.

IV.   **INTERNATIONAL CAPITAL BUDGETING**

A.   **Net Present Value Analysis**
      1.   The decision-making rules in international investments and currencies are essentially the same process as with domestic projects. If NPVs are positive, make the investment.
      2.   The exchange rate risk consideration may be handled two ways. First, the estimated foreign cash flows are converted to dollars at the projected exchange rates and discounted at the dollar cost of capital. Second, in order to avoid making estimates of future exchange rates, calculate the future foreign denominated cash flows and discount at the foreign cost of capital. The foreign currency NPVs are then converted to domestic currency at the current spot rate.
      3.   Under the assumptions developed above both evaluation methods should give the same investment decisions.
      4.   The key point is not to make investments dependent upon specific, estimated future exchange rate movements. Select the investment based on the NPV and hedge the foreign exchange rate.

B.   **The Cost of Capital for Foreign Investment**
      1.   An international investment is an additional investment to the total portfolio, so the relevant risk of the added investment is its effect on the total portfolio risk.
      2.   The discount rate on international investments should reflect this incremental risk effect on the total investment portfolio.

C.   **Political Risk**
      1.   The term is used to describe the possibility of the expropriation of assets, changes in tax policy, the enforcement of restrictions on the exchange of foreign currency for domestic currency, and the repatriation of profits or other changes in the business climate of a country.

2. Organizations such as PRS Group rank countries for investment according to their political risk based on regime stability, financial transfer, and turmoil. See Table 24.5 in the textbook.

D. **Avoiding Fudge Factors**
   1. The usual international risk adjustment practice is adding an increment to the discount rate to cover the risks of expropriation, foreign exchange restrictions, and tax changes.
   2. A better method is to specify the international risks and their likely impact on cash flows and reduce the expected future cash flows.

COMPLETION QUESTIONS

1. The amount of currency needed to purchase one unit of another currency is called the _____ _____.

2. The _____ exchange rate is the price of currency for immediate delivery.

3. The _____ exchange rate is the price of currency delivery at some time in the future.

4. The theory that prices of goods in all countries should be equal when translated into a common currency is the law of _____ _____.

5. The theory that the cost of living in different countries is equal and exchange rates adjust to offset different exchange rates across countries is _____ _____ _____.

6. Countries with high inflation rates will tend to have their currencies (*appreciate/depreciate*).

7. The international Fisher effect is a theory that says real interest rates in all countries should be equal with any differences in nominal rates reflecting differences in _____.

8. The theory that says the interest rate differential must equal the differential between forward and spot exchange rates is called _____ _____ parity.

9. When you receive fewer forward yen for a dollar compared to the amount when buying spot yen, the yen is selling at a forward (*discount/premium*).

10. It is easier to hedge (*contractual/non-contractual*) exchange rate risk.

11. The hedge of a future dollar obligation can be accomplished by either borrowing in the foreign currency and lending dollars or by buying (*forward/spot*) dollars.

12. When calculating net present values for capital budgeting a multinational firm (*should/should not*) make currency forecasts.

13. The general principle of NPV calculations for international firms is to match the (*discount/inflation*) rate with the specific cash flows in the corresponding currency.

14. The authors of the text recommend incorporating uncertainty by adjusting the (*discount rate/expected cash flows*) for multinational capital budgeting.

15. One way of minimizing harmful changes in foreign government policies is for the domestic parent company to invest in the (*debt/equity*) of its foreign subsidiary.

PROBLEMS

1. Refer to Table 24.1 of the textbook to determine:
   a. The number of Hong Kong dollars per Canadian dollar.
   b. The cost in C$ of a plastic replica of the Toronto CN Tower selling in Hong Kong HK$60.
   c. If the 12-month forward exchange rate for the HK$ is 0.2. Is there a premium or discount relative to the Canadian dollar?
   d. The annual percentage of the premium or discount specified in part (c) above.
   e. The implied 1-year interest rate in Hong Kong if the comparable rate in Canada is 3.55 percent.
   f. What is the expected spot rate for the HK$ in 12 months time according to the expectations theory of exchange rates?
   g. What is the expected difference in the rate of inflation in Hong Kong and Canada according to purchasing power parity.

2. Marlene returned from a trip abroad with 30 Australian dollars, 45 Swiss francs, 350 Greek drachmas, 2500 Japanese yen, and 20 Swedish kronas. How much does this total in C$?

3. From Table 24.2 of the textbook you can see the cost of a Big Mac in US$ varies from $3.65 in Switzerland to $1.37 in Hong Kong. Does this variation refute the law of one price?

4. Ivan's Imports sells Mexican pottery. His next order will be for a 1-year supply and he wants to lock-in the price now. His source in Mexico has agreed to a price in pesos today but does not require payment until the goods are shipped in 3 months' time. What should Ivan do if he wants to avoid the risk of the peso appreciating against the dollar?

5.   Megan's Exports, Inc., sells gold jewellry in Germany. Her prices are quoted in Euros. How can Megan reduce her exposure to currency risk?

6.   Suppose a U.S. firm expects to receive payment in Canadian dollars for a project it will complete there in 4 years. If its bankers do not want to offer an attractive forward contract that far into the future, how could the company hedge against a depreciation in the value of the Canadian dollar?

7.   Consider the capital budgeting process for a multinational firm based in Canada. If the potential investments are reviewed in Canadian dollars, which inflation and interest rates are relevant in the decision-making process?

8.   Suppose you purchased 100 shares of an British company last year for 12.50 pounds per share when the exchange rate was 0.865 pounds per Canadian dollar. What is your percentage return using the British currency if the current stock price is 14.80 pounds per share?

9.   What is the percentage return for the investment made in problem 8 if you calculate it in U.S. dollars and if the current exchange rate is 0.7022 pounds per dollar?

10.   Refer to Table 24.1 of the textbook and calculate:
      a. The number of Swiss francs you could buy with 100 British pounds.
      b. The spot rate of Swiss francs in terms of Singapore dollars.

ANSWERS TO COMPLETION QUESTIONS

1.   exchange rate
2.   spot
3.   forward
4.   one price
5.   purchasing power parity
6.   depreciate
7.   inflation
8.   interest rate
9.   premium
10.   contractual
11.   forward
12.   should
13.   discount
14.   expected cash flows
15.   debt

SOLUTIONS TO PROBLEMS

1. a. You will receive HK\$4.9677=1/0.2013 in exchange for each Canadian dollar.
    b. HK\$60/4.9677 = C\$12.08
    c. The 12-month forward exchange rate is C\$0.2 per Hong Kong dollar. In other words, you will receive HK\$5 = 1/0.2 per Canadian dollar. As you get more Hong Kong dollars in the future, they are said to be selling at a discount relative to C\$.
    d. Use the direct quote, forward premium is given by (forward rate – spot rate) / spot rate = (0.2 – 0.2013) / 0.2013 = -0.0013 or –0.13% where the minus sign represents a discount.
    e. The ratio of the forward to the spot exchange rates is equal to the ratio of the interest rates in the two countries. In this case,

$$\frac{1+r_{HK}}{1+r_C} = \frac{5}{4.9677} \Rightarrow X = \frac{(5)(1.0355)}{4.9677} \Rightarrow X = 1.04223 \text{ where } X = 1 + \text{the one-year}$$

   interest rate in Hong Kong. The required interest rate is 4.22% in Hong Kong.
    f. The expected spot rate in 12 months' time is HK\$5 per C\$.
    g. According to the purchasing power parity, the ratio of the growth in prices in different countries is equal to the ratio of the forward to the spot exchange rate.

   Since $\dfrac{1+i_{HK}}{1+i_C} = \dfrac{f_{HK\$/C\$}}{s_{HK\$/C\$}} = \dfrac{5}{4.9677} = 1.0065$, then the expected rate of inflation in

   Hong Kong over the next 12 months is 0.65% higher than the inflation rate in Canada.

2.
	Foreign currency per unit in Canadian Dollars	C\$
30 Australian \$	0.7749	23.25
45 Swiss francs	0.9867	44.40
350 Greek drachmas	0.004269	1.49
2500 Japanese yen	0.01355	33.88
20 Swedish kronas	0.1485	2.97
		105.99

3. The law of one price states that, in theory, the same item should cost the same in all countries when the prices are translated into a common currency. The fact that the dollar cost of a Big Mac is different in every country shown in Table 24.2 would seem to refute this theory. This is because it is theoretically possible to buy Big Macs where the price is cheap as in Hong Kong and sell them in Switzerland where they would sell for more than 2.6 times as much. Of course this doesn't happen because the transport costs more than offset the potential gain. The law of one price works much better for commodities such as gold where the transportation costs are small relative to the value of the item. Services such as taxi rides and medical operations are not transportable at

all and indeed their prices expressed in dollars do vary considerably. In summary, the law of one price explains the tendency for prices to be similar even though they will not be equal around the world. Each item is unique and price variations will exist due to specific circumstances in each country and in the nature of the particular good or service.

4. Ivan should buy forward pesos for delivery in 3 months. In so doing he will fix, today, the number of dollars he pays for the imports. No matter which way the peso moves, relative to the dollar, Ivan's outlay is a set and known figure.

5. If the dollar falls relative to the Euro, Ellen will lose money because the Euro she receives from sales in Germany will buy fewer dollars when she converts the Euro into dollars. In theory she could simply raise prices in Germany to offset this loss but that would have a negative impact on her business. One way to minimize the currency problem would be to sell Euro forward so she could be assured of receiving a known amount of dollars for her jewellery.

6. The U.S. firm could arrange a 4-year loan in Canada for the present value of its future payment in Canadian dollars. Then it would sell, on the spot market, the proceeds for U.S. dollars. These dollars would be invested in the U.S. debt market for four years. The Canadian dollar loan would be repaid in 4 years when the U.S. firm's Canadian customer paid its obligation. At the same time, the U.S. firm would have the proceeds from the sale of its debt investment in the U.S. Throughout this entire process the U.S. firm has been insulated against foreign exchange movements which was the purpose of the transactions.

7. To prepare cash flows from foreign projects, the estimates of future inflation rates in the foreign country and future exchange rates with that country are needed. In addition, current interest rates in Canada are required to help determine the domestic cost of capital.

8. In British pounds (L) the return is $(L1480 - L1250) \div L1250 = .184$ or 18.4 percent.

9. The cost of the 100 shares was 1250 pounds $\div$ 0.865 pounds per US\$ = \$1445. The value today is 1480 pounds $\div$ 0.7022 pounds per US\$ = \$2108. This makes the return:
$$= (\$2108 - \$1445) \div \$1445$$
$$= 0.459 \text{ or } 45.9 \text{ percent.}$$

10. a. The table does not show the Swiss francs to British pound conversion factor but the translation can be accomplished by converting the pounds into Canadian dollars and then the Canadian dollars into francs as follows:

   100 pounds × C$2.3017 per pound = C$230.17

   C$230.17 × 1.0134 Swiss francs per C$ = 233.27 Swiss francs.

   Note: with a direct quote of 0.9867 = C$ /SF$_r$, the indirect quote becomes SF$_r$ / C$ = 1/0.9867 = 1.0134 Swiss francs per Canadian dollar.

   b. $\dfrac{SF_r}{S\$} = \dfrac{SF_r}{C\$} \times \dfrac{C\$}{S\$} = 1.0134 \times 0.9045 = 0.9166$ Swiss francs per Singapore dollar.

CHAPTER 25

OPTIONS

INTRODUCTION

The growth of financial derivative securities for hedging and speculating has been dramatic. With lenient margin requirements, the speculator is provided an exciting place to play. For the risk manager, hedging with derivatives, the subject of the next chapter, has provided the opportunity to decide what risks to accept in the business and which to hedge.

In this first of two chapters associated with risk management, options, from traded exchanged-based to contract options in securities to imbedded options in real assets, are discussed. The "Financial Alchemy with Options" is an excellent section, along with Figures 25.4–25.6 in the textbook, for discussing investor payoff positioning. The discussion of option value factors provides insight as to what makes an option valuable.

Traditionally, financial management texts espoused financial flexibility. What were they talking about? Options, at some cost, provide the financial manager choices for the future. This chapter comes at the end of the textbook, but today represents the most dramatic and sophisticated aspect of finance. The recent losses in derivative positions by various corporations (they were speculating) has now let the public know what we now know, that risk shows its ugly side about as often as the high returns associated with the risk.

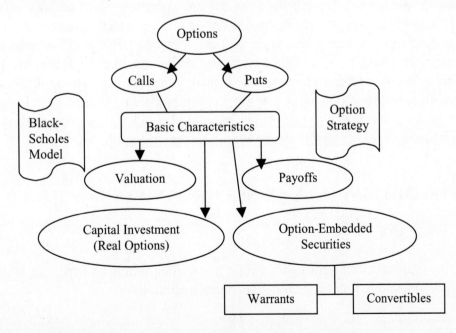

LEARNING CHECKLIST

After studying this chapter you should be able to:

____1. Calculate the payoff to buyers and sellers of call and put options.
____2. Understand the determinants of option values.
____3. Recognize options in capital investment projects (real assets).
____4. Identify options that are provided in financial securities.
____5. Use the Black-Scholes Model to determine the value of an option.

SOURCES OF BUSINESS INFORMATION

Options For Everybody? Options offer another way to play the investment game, but are not for the faint of heart. Option trading is generally linked to stocks, but you can also use stock indexes, futures, bonds, and currencies, some of which your broker may not offer. As you notice, not all stocks have options on them. Indeed, while many stocks in the U.S. market have options, few in Canada do, e.g., Royal Bank (RY), Petro Canada (PCA), Placer Dome (PDG), and Barrick Gold (ABX). While option trading provides tremendous opportunities for profits, you must have significant investing experience and a strong risk tolerance to win the battle. To help you to understand the terminology used in the industry, visit the Web site run by the Options Industry Council at www.optionscentral.com. This educational site gives out free books, computer software, videos, and seminars in the U.S. and Canada.

Real Options: You probably are already familiar with call options to buy stocks and put options to sell stocks. You may also know that convertible bonds and preferred stocks have embedded call options. Or you even realize that warrants and stock purchase rights are special types of call options. However, options are not restricted only to the financial investments, you will be amused to find options nearly everywhere. For example, think about a natural resource investment, whereby the firm can delay extraction until economic conditions are favourable. This flexibility needs to be considered when evaluating the proposal. The application of option pricing models to such real options is a rapidly expanding field of finance. Check out the visual discussion of real options at www.puc-rio.br/macro.ind/faqs.html . A good reading list in this area can be found at www.realoptions-software.com/articles.html.

CHAPTER OUTLINE, KEY CONCEPTS, AND TERMS

I. **CALLS AND PUTS**

A. Options, the right to act within a specified period of time, are widespread in business, financing, and investment operations.

B.   Options have value because they specify the ability to take action whether buying, selling, expanding, or doing nothing.

C.   Standardized option contracts on a variety of commodities and financial assets began trading on the Chicago Board Options Exchange (CBOE) in 1973. Nowadays, options on stock indexes and foreign currencies exist. Investors and businesses trade options to speculate and, more importantly for businesses and investors, to hedge price risk, the risk of unfavourable price movements in their business or portfolio. In Canada, options on stocks and bonds are traded on the Bourse de Montreal, home of the Canadian Derivatives Exchange.

D.   A **call option** gives the owner the right to buy an asset at a specified price on or before a specified date called the exercise date. A buyer of a call option may exercise the option in the option period or let it expire. In the case of the Celestica options, the owner of the call would exercise the call (right to buy Celestica at $14.50) if the price of Celestica exceeded $14.50. If the price remains below $14.50, the call will not likely be exercised. See Figure 25.1 in the textbook.

E.   A **put option** is a right to sell an asset at a specified exercise price on or before the exercise date. A buyer of a put would exercise if Celestica fell below $14.50 by buying Celestica below $14.50 and selling it for $14.50. If the price remains above $14.50, the put will not be exercised.

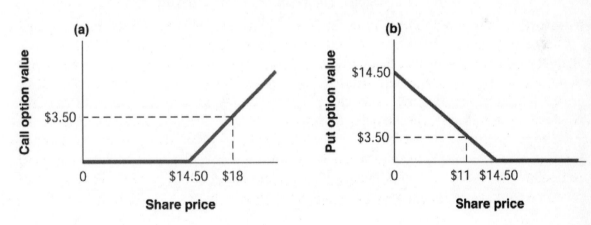

F. The quotations from Figure 25.2 in the textbook illustrate many of the terms and definitions described previously using Bombardier as an example. Calls/puts are worth more when the exercise price is lower/higher.

Stock Series		Close Bid	Ask	Last	Total Vol	Op. Int.	Stock Series		Close Bid	Ask	Last	Total Vol	Op. Int.
BmbrB		$12.94			1315	49501		$20.00p	7.00	7.25	6.00	10	521
Oct 01	$12.50	1.00	1.25	1.20	107	154		$22.50	0.05	0.25	0.25	14	1495
	$12.50p	0.55	0.80	0.60	185	185		$22.50p	9.65	10.05	9.40	10	722
	$15.00	0.35	0.50	0.40	60	487		$25.00		0.25	0.20	25	3349
	$15.00p	2.30	2.55	2.45	10	35		$27.50p	14.70	15.20	15.15	9	88
	$22.50P	9.55	9.95	9.70	25	438	Apr 02	$12.50	1.70	2.75	1.95	92	319
	$25.00		0.05	0.04	5	4547		$12.50p	1.20	1.45	1.15	15	45
Jan 02	$10.50	2.60	2.85	3.60	10	148		$15.00	1.00	1.15	1.20	83	177
	$10.50p	0.25	0.50	0.45	20	54		$15.00p	2.85	3.10	2.80	5	40
	$11.50	1.85	2.10	2.05	15	501		$17.50	0.50	0.70	0.75	10	251
	$11.50P	0.40	0.65	0.65	5	66		$22.50	0.05	0.30	0.25	3	278
	$12.50	1.35	1.50	1.50	112	626	Jan 03	$15.00	1.80	2.20	2.25	13	20
	$12.50P	1.05	1.10	1.05	28	160		$17.50	1.85	1.90	2.20	25	979
	$13.50	0.90	1.05	1.05	144	4034		$20.00	1.30	1.35	1.20	4	1526
	$13.50p	1.35	1.60	1.45	30	220	Jan 04	$12.50	5.00	5.30	5.50	22	30
	$14.50	0.70	0.85	0.65	108	394		$22.50p	9.55	10.05	9.20	2	49
	$14.50p	2.05	2.30	2.10	5	86		$25.00	0.90	1.20	1.70	5	110
	$15.50	0.50	0.65	0.65	52	902		$25.00p	12.00	12.50	12.05	7	54
	$17.50	0.20	0.35	0.35	40	728							

G. **Selling Calls and Puts**

1. Traded options on exchanges are issued by the call and put writers, usually investors. The positive/negative payoff of a call/put buyer is matched by call/put writers or option sellers. See Figure 25.3 in the textbook.

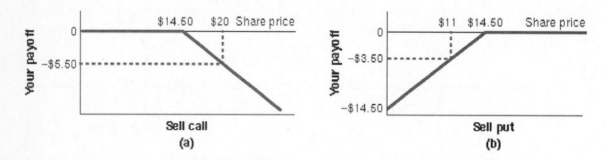

2. The buyer of calls and puts has a limit on the negative payoff equal to the cost of the option paid to the writer. The writer's negative payoff potential may be very high, especially if the writer does not own the underlying asset (Celestica stock). This is so-called uncovered or naked option writing.

H. Financial Alchemy with Options

1. Options can be mixed to alter the risk features of a portfolio as desired.

2. A **protective put** strategy involving the purchase of stock combined with a put option on the same stock guarantees minimum proceeds equal to the exercise price of the put. This practice is not free because the investor has to pay the cost for the option that should be viewed as the insurance premium.

3. However, the ultimate cost of such "**stock price insurance**" will be affected by the investor's degree of bearishness that further determines what exercise price and expiration month to use.

4. Once the position is established, the investor has upside price opportunity and downside protection. If the stock price falls, the gain from the option may offset the decline in the stock value.

5. To keep a stable price range ($10 to $15, say) from volatility, the owner of Bombardier stock can simultaneously buy a put option with exercise price of $10 and sell a call with exercise price of $15. If the stock price falls below $10, the call will expire valueless, but the put will allow the stock to be sold at $10. Hence, this strategy offers protection against the stock price falling below the lower limit. If the stock price rises above $15, the put will be worth nothing and the call will be exercised against the seller who must deliver the stock for an exercise price of $15. Thus, the maximum value under this situation will be $15. The purpose is to take a sure position in the stock regardless of the price movement in either direction. Of course, the call sold must balance the cost of the put bought.

6. If an investor does not own Bombardier but wants to profit from its increased volatility, s/he should establish a **straddle** position, buying both a put and a call each with the same exercise price and expiration date. If the stock is volatile enough to cover the cost of the options, the investor wins.

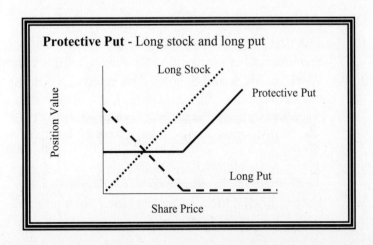

359

II.   WHAT DETERMINES OPTION VALUES?

A.   Upper and Lower Limits on Option Values

1.   While an option is worthless when expired, why does an option have a positive value before expiration?

2.   The upper boundary on the value of a call option is the share price value, while the lower boundary on the value of a call is the payoff if exercised immediately.

3.   The value is related to the stock price. The call is always worth more than its value if exercised now (lower bound) and never worth more than the stock price itself (upper bound). See Figure 25.7 in the textbook.

4.   The value of the option lays between the upper and lower bounds. The market value will lay on the curved upward sloping line in Figure 25.7 in the textbook.

B.   The Determinants of Option Value

1.   Given the exercise price, the value of a call option increases as the stock price increases.

2.   Three key points on the option value curve, Figure 25.7 in the textbook, are important reference points.

3.   At Point A, when the stock is worthless, the option is worthless. At Point B, when the stock price becomes very high, the option price approaches the stock price less the PV of the exercise price. The value of a call increases directly with increases in the rate of interest and the time to expiration. And at Point C, the option price always exceeds its minimum value, except when the stock price is zero. There is always a chance that the stock price will advance to the exercise price.

4.   The value of an option is directly related to the stock price volatility. The greater the volatility, the greater the chance that the stock will move above the exercise price.

C.   Option-Valuation Models

1.   The best method for estimating the value of an option is to find a best combination of borrowing and making an investment in the stock.

2.   Work by Black and Scholes developed this options value theory.

Black-Scholes Option Pricing Model

$$O_C = P_s[N(d_1)] - S[N(d_2)]e^{-rt}$$

---

3.   Value of call option = [current stock price × delta] – [bank loan].

III. SPOTTING THE OPTION

A. Options, either explicit or implicit, are present everywhere in business and investments.

B. The challenge is to identify the option present and to consider the value of the option.

C. **Options on Real Assets**
1. **Real options** or the implicit (implied with ownership) options on real assets such as plant, land, etc., are present in any business setting.
2. The first real option is the option to expand an investment, such as a production facility, at a future date. This call option, option to buy more production facilities, is often called flexibility.
3. The business also has the option to abandon an investment. This option to sell (put) or quit is valuable, especially when the value of the underlying asset is volatile.
4. All aspects of project management from expansion, contraction, delay, or abandonment contain real options.

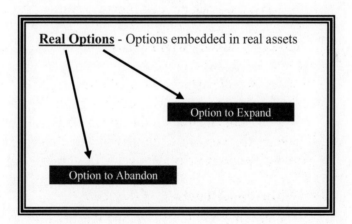

D. **Options on Financial Assets**
1. Options to participate in the common stock are often attached to debt securities. A **warrant** is a right to buy (call) shares from a company at a stipulated price before a set date.
2. The right to participate in the equity is valuable to the bondholder and the market. Warrants may be detachable and trade separate from the bonds.
3. A **convertible bond** is a bond that may be exchanged for a specified number of common shares. The convertible bond has a call option on a

number of common shares. A conversion ratio of 26.7 shares on a $1000 bond has a conversion price of $37.45 (1000/26.7).

4. The value of a convertible bond is driven by the bond value when the stock price is low and becomes related to the stock value when the stock price approaches and passes the conversion price. The bond value establishes a floor or minimum price for the convertible bond; the upper bound is unlimited, dependent upon the value of the common stock. The value of the call option is equal to the difference between the convertible selling price and its bond value.

5. **Callable bonds** include a call option held by the borrower or issuer to repurchase or refund the bond before maturity at a specified call price.

6. Lenders are likely to lose their high rate callable bonds if interest rates decline, so they demand a higher rate of return. The value of the call option is the yield on the callable bond less the yield on a noncallable, similar bond.

Appendix: The Black-Scholes Option Valuation Model

A.   **Notations**

O_c = the value of the call option

P = the current stock price

EX = the exercise price; PV(EX) is calculated by discounting at the risk-free interest rate, r_f.

t = time to expiration

σ = the stock's standard deviation

ln( ) = the natural logarithm

N(d) = the probability from a standard normal distribution that a variable will be less than or equal d

B.   **The Model**

$$O_c = \left[N(d_1) \times P \right] - \left[N(d_2) \times PV(EX) \right]$$

$$\text{where } d_1 = \frac{\ln\left[\dfrac{P}{PV(EX)}\right]}{\sigma\sqrt{t}} + \frac{\sigma\sqrt{t}}{2} \quad \text{and} \quad d_2 = d_1 - \sigma\sqrt{t}$$

1.   Calculate d_1 and d_2.

2.   Look up the values for $N(d_1)$ and $N(d_2)$ in Table 25A.1 in the textbook.

3.   Using $N(d_1)$ and $N(d_2)$, compute the value of the call option, O_c.

C.   **Key Assumptions in the Black-Scholes Option Pricing Model**

1.   The stock market operates continually.

2.   The stock price is continuous and there is no sudden jump in price.

3.   The option can only be exercised at expiration.

4.   The perfect world exists.

D.   Despite the unrealistic assumptions, the Black-Scholes model is a good predictor of actual option prices.

COMPLETION QUESTIONS

1.   A call option gives the owner the right to (*buy/sell*) stock at a fixed exercise price on or before a specified exercise date.

2.   The value of a call option will be _____ if the stock price is less than the exercise price when the option expires.

3. An investor in put options is expecting share prices to (*fall/rise*).

4. Traded options (*are/are not*) sold by the companies themselves.

5. If you own a stock you can achieve portfolio insurance by buying a (*call/put*) for that same stock.

6. By (*buying/selling*) two puts in a stock you own you can create a situation of making a gross profit no matter which way the stock moves.

7. In the case of the situation described in question 6, you must (*add/deduct*) the cost of the call option premiums to compute the net profit.

8. If you sell two calls in a stock you own you will (*gain/lose*) from any stock price volatility.

9. The value of a call option (*decreases/increases*) as the stock price rises.

10. When the stock price is well (*above/below*) the call exercise price, buying that call is equivalent to buying the stock now with deferred payment and delivery.

11. The value of a call option will (*decrease/increase*) as interest rates increase and be (*higher/lower*) for longer as opposed to shorter times to expiration.

12. The greater the expected volatility in the stock price the (*greater/less*) will be the value of a call option.

13. As the exercise price increases, the value of a call option (*decreases/increases*).

14. It is possible to replicate the purchase of a call option by a bank (*deposit/loan*) and the purchase of the stock.

15. In capital budgeting, the projects being considered for investment are similar in concept to buying a (*call/put*) option.

16. The possibility of abandoning an existing project may be thought of as a (*call/put*) option.

17. A warrant is a long-term (*call/put*) option.

18. A _____ bond is a straight bond with a call option.

19. If the stock price in the case of a convertible bond is (*above/below*) the conversion price, that convertible bond will always sell for more than its bond value.

20. A callable bond is like a combination of a non-callable bond and a call option held by the (*investor/issuer*).

21. (*Risky/Safe*) bonds are those where the asset value of the firm is less than the amount of debt outstanding.

22. An individual thinking of investing in an option pays the ask price when (*buying/selling*) and receives the bid price when (*buying/selling*).

23. All other things equal, compared to equivalent non-callable bonds, callable bonds are sold for (*lower/higher*) prices.

PROBLEMS

1. Suppose you own 100 shares of Neverfail, Inc. The firm is working on a project, which if successful, would result in a huge profit. However, if the project does not work out, the company could go bankrupt. Explain:
   a. How you could use an option to protect against loss.
   b. How the cost of insuring against the loss is related to the option price.

2. What is the incentive for someone to write a put or a call option?

3. If you bought a call option for $4 that had an exercise price of $70 per share, what would be the value of that option at its expiration if the stock was trading at:
   a. $70
   b. $75
   c. $65

4. If you owned 100 shares of Slone Stoneworks, Inc., and then bought a put on that stock with an exercise price of $24, what would be the value of your holding if you closed out your position at the expiration date of the put and if the stock was trading at:
   a. $20
   b. $28

5. How much would be the payoff at the expiration date if you owned 100 shares of a stock and 2 puts for that stock with exercise prices of $46 when the market price for the shares are:
   a. $40
   b. $46
   c. $52

6. Discuss the major factors that influence the value of a call option.

7.   What is the maximum potential loss if you buy a:
        a. put option?
        b. call option?

8.   What is the maximum potential loss if you write a
        a. put option?
        b. call option?

9.   Is the conversion feature on a convertible bond like a put or a call option?

10.   What type of option is related to the case of a computer firm that forms a strategic alliance with a software developer by agreeing to advance $10 million for the rights to freely use a software program that is currently being written?

11.   If a call option is selling for $5 and has an exercise price of $50, what will be the net profit if you buy it and then exercise it when the stock price is $60?

12.   A stock is selling for $16 and has a return variance of 16 percent per year. If a call option with an exercise price of $20 expires in 6 months, find its value using the Black-Scholes formula. Assume that the annual risk-free rate is 12 percent. How much is the bank loan? How many shares do you need to purchase?

ANSWERS TO COMPLETION QUESTIONS

1.   buy
2.   zero
3.   fall
4.   are not
5.   put
6.   buying
7.   deduct
8.   lose
9.   increases
10.   above
11.   increase, higher
12.   greater
13.   decreases
14.   loan
15.   call
16.   put
17.   call
18.   convertible

19. above
20. issuer
21. Risky
22. buying, selling
23. lower

SOLUTIONS TO PROBLEMS

1. a. To protect against the loss that would result if the stock price fell below the current market price, a put option could be purchased. This would allow the owner of the option to sell the stock at the exercise price on or before the exercise date. If the stock declined the investor would exercise the option and sell the 100 shares owned. This establishes a minimum value for the stock. On the other hand, if the stock price increased the owner would sell the stock at the higher price and realize a gain. The put option would be allowed to expire without being used since with a stock price rise, the investor would receive more by selling the stock in the open market as compared to selling it through the put option.

   b. The cost of insuring that a decline in the stock price will not hurt the owner of the 100 shares is the cost of buying the put option. This is similar to insuring a home or a car against a loss. You pay an insurance premium for that protection. In the case of the stockholder, the insurance premium is the price paid for the put option.

2. The incentive to be an option writer is much like the incentive to write insurance. You expect that the premiums received will cover the costs of claims, etc., and provide a profit. In other words, the insurance companies expect to be compensated for bearing the risk of loss. Option writers receive the premiums and hope those amounts will more than offset the losses they incur as a result of price moves in the wrong direction resulting in the writer having to pay more than the going market price when a put is exercised or to sell at the below the market price when the call they wrote is exercised.

3. a. The value of the call is equal to the exercise price minus the market price for the stock. With the stock selling at $70 the call option value is:
$$= \$70 - \$70$$
$$= \text{zero}$$

   b. With the stock selling at $75 the call option value is:
$$= \$70 - \$75$$
$$= -\$5.$$

   However, the option value will never be negative so the value in this case is zero.

c. With the stock selling at $65 the call option value is:
$$= \$70 - \$65$$
$$= \$5$$

4. a. You would exercise the put and receive $100 \times \$24$ or $2,400.

b. You would let the put go unused and sell the stock for $100 \times \$28$ or $2,800. Notice that if your stock falls below the exercise price you receive the exercise price as the minimum or floor price. If the stock rises you participate in the appreciation.

5. a. The puts would have a positive value whenever the stock is below the exercise price. In this case you could sell your shares with one of the puts and receive $100 \times \$46$ or $4,600. The other put could be sold in the market for its value of ($46 – $40) $\times$ 100 or $600. Your total value would be $4,600 + $600 or $5,200.

b. At a market price of $46 for the stock, the puts would have zero value so the shares would be worth $100 \times \$46$ or $4,600.

c. At $52, the puts would have zero value but the stock would be worth $100 \times \$52$ or $5,200. So the value of the portfolio with 2 puts is at the minimum when the stock is trading at the exercise price. Whenever the stock goes up or down from that price the portfolio value will increase.

6. The major factors that influence a call option's price are:
a. Exercise price—the lower this is, the higher the value of the call.
b. Stock price—the lower this is, the higher the value of the call.
c. Expiration date—the longer this is, the higher the value of the call.
d. Volatility of the stock—the more volatile the stock, the higher the value of the call.

7. a. The maximum loss you could incur if you purchased a put option would be the price paid for that option.

b. The maximum potential loss to the owner of a call option is the price paid for that option.

8. a. The maximum loss that could occur to the writer of a put option would be the exercise price for that option if the stock went to zero before the expiration date. Since options are written for 100 shares the maximum loss would be 100 times the exercise price.

b. The maximum potential loss to the writer of a call option would be unlimited in theory because the writer would have to deliver the stock if the call were exercised. This unlimited exposure is true only if the writer does not own the shares. That would be an uncovered position and would be very risky. Most writers of call options do so on shares they have in their portfolio. The loss they incur if the stock rises substantially is an opportunity loss since they could have sold their shares at the higher market price.

9. In the case of a convertible bond, the owner has a call option because the bond can be exchanged for common stock at a predetermined price. In other words the convertible bond can exercise the right to "buy" common stock using the par value of the bond as the purchasing medium.

10. By investing the $10 million now the computer company is fixing the price it will pay for the software program. This is similar to what an investor does when buying a call option.

11. Net profit = $P - EX - O_C = \$60 - 50 - 5 = \$5$

12. $$d_1 = \frac{\ln\left[\dfrac{p}{PV(EX)}\right]}{\sigma\sqrt{t}} + \frac{\sigma\sqrt{t}}{2} = \frac{\ln\left[\dfrac{16}{20/(1.12)^{0.5}}\right]}{(0.4)\sqrt{6/12}} + \frac{0.4\sqrt{0.5}}{2} = -0.447$$

$$d_2 = d_1 - \sigma\sqrt{t} = -0.447 - (0.4)\sqrt{0.5} = -0.447 - 0.283 = -0.73$$

From Table 25A.1, $N(d_1) = 1 - 0.6736 = 0.3264$, $N(d_2) = 1 - 0.7673 = 0.2327$

$$O_C = [N(d_1) \times P] - \left[N(d_2) \times PV(EX)\right] = \left[(0.3264)(\$16)\right] - \left[(0.2327)(\$18.898)\right] = \$0.82$$

The amount of bank loan is given by $[N(d_2) \times PV(EX)] = \$4.3976$. The number of shares purchased is given by $N(d_1) = 0.3264$.

CHAPTER 26

RISK MANAGEMENT

INTRODUCTION

The business and financial risks faced by financial managers today are considerable, especially with the globalization of businesses and as competition increases. Today a manager must recognize what risks are faced, the range of outcomes, and the type and extent to which, and at what cost, the risks might be shifted to others, reduced, or accepted. The management of risk has always been a key financial manager function, but the orientation until recently was focused only on the pure risk faced by the business. Pure risk is the risk of loss on real assets from fire, theft, loss of use of assets, etc. A risk management approach to all business pure and financial risks is developing. This chapter is one of the first on the subject to appear in a financial management text. Soon the topic will be integrated throughout the chapters.

The financial manager that wishes to control the level of specific risks so identified may eliminate them by avoiding the risk, remove by contract, such as with contractual options, or hedge where cost justified and available, by using "off-balance sheet" or "off business" hedging tools such as futures, forwards, or SWAPS. Such hedging contracts are either exchange-based or are, as with forwards, negotiated with other parties with a mirror image risk to hedge or via a hedge dealer who will contract between parties as with SWAPS.

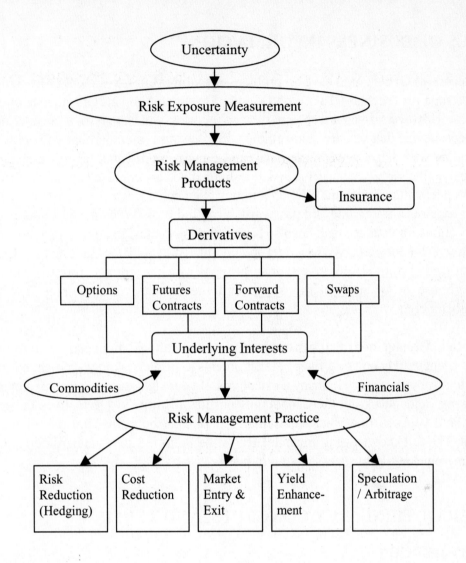

LEARNING CHECKLIST

After preparing this chapter you should be able to:

____ 1. Understand why companies hedge to reduce risk.
____ 2. Use options, futures, and forward contracts to devise simple hedging strategies.
____ 3. Explain how companies can use SWAPs to change the risk of securities that they have issued.

SOURCES OF BUSINESS INFORMATION

Place a Successful Order: You have no problem executing your investment order with a full-service brokerage firm such as CIBC Wood Gundy. Be sure to shop around since commissions can vary a lot. However, if you are an experienced investor, you can go for a cheaper discount broker. Select the one that you are comfortable with. Always remember that you get what you pay for. Dealing with a discounter sometimes can be annoying. If you trade by phone, you will unlikely speak to the same person again. Ask questions if you are confused about any jargon and demand for clarification. In the meantime, you may even consider the least expensive Internet trading that requires a user name and password. You find most Web sites not only accepting online applications for your account, but also having trading demos. Examples include the Royal Bank Action Direct at www.actiondirect.com, the CIBC Investor's Edge at www.investorsedge.com, HSBC InvestDirect at www.hsbcinvestdirect.com, the TD Canada Trust Waterhouse at www.tdwaterhouse.ca, and the ScotiaMcLeod Direct Investing at www.scotiabank.com.

Financial Risk Management Professional: While corporations, financial institutions, and government agencies rely on using financial instruments to hedge, risk management has become an independent subject of study in many curriculums. If your sights are set on an exciting career in this growing field, check out the Canadian Securities Institute's "Derivatives Program" at www.csi.ca and you will find what requirements it takes to be a financial risk management professional. The full knowledge of financial derivatives, plus the high standard of conduct and ethics ensure your long-term success in the industry.

CHAPTER OUTLINE, KEY CONCEPTS, AND TERMS

I. **WHY HEDGE?**

    A. Hedging involves incurring a cost to reduce the risk of adverse price movements.

    B. Hedging makes financial planning easier and allows the manager to focus on internal, controllable production efficiency rather than external, noncontrollable price speculation.

    C. One tool for hedging involves contracting in financial derivatives, contracts whose value is derived from the value of other financial or real assets.

    D. Hedging involves contracting to gain in a derivative contract if a loss or an opportunity loss should occur in the business, real assets, or securities. If the hedge is properly in place, any adverse business price changes will be offset by a gain in the hedging contract, whether it is a futures contract, option on futures contract, swap, etc.

II. REDUCING RISK WITH OPTIONS

A.   Hedging with options provides adverse side price protection for a large number of real and financial assets from wheat and oil to Treasury bonds.

B.   The hedger selects the option exchange contract that is best associated with the price risk (risk of adverse price movements) at hand. There is also a large volume of option contracts written off of the exchanges between hedgers, who have price risk in a commodity or financial asset and a speculator, who has no cash, current, or spot position in the asset.

C.   Hedging is performed by taking a position in the option contract, or other hedging contract, so that adverse price movements in the business (raw material costs increasing) is offset by gains in the hedging contract. It is assumed that the business or investor will continue their business by buying/selling in the spot or cash market.

D.   If a business will be adversely affected by rising prices, such as a processor of agricultural goods, a call option will offer one side price protection for a price, the price of the call. If raw prices rise for the business, they will rise to and above the strike price, providing option contract gains to offset business losses (opportunity costs of buying at a higher price). If prices fall, the call option holder will let the option expire.

E.   If a business, such as a farmer or manufacturer, has the risk of falling prices for its production, it may purchase put options or options to sell. If corn prices fall between planting and harvest, the economic loss in the business is offset by the gains in the put contract. The farmer is selling corn at a specified price when the puts are purchased. If prices fall, the option contract is in the money, offsetting the reduced margins in the business. If prices rise, the put option is never exercised. The cost of the option is the insurance premium spent to avoid adverse price movements.

F.   Option contracts may protect holders of financial assets. A Treasury bond investor may be worried about the Bank of Canada raising interest rates. If rates rise, bond prices will fall. How can an investor hedge the risk of interest rate increases or falling bond prices? Yes! Buying T-bond puts provides the downside protection. Focus on the direction of the adverse price movement and protect with a counter position in the option contract.

G.   Unlike futures contracts and forward contracts, hedging with options provides one-way insurance protection against adverse price movements. The option holder has a choice whether or not to carry out the contract.

III.   FUTURES CONTRACTS

A.   **Futures contracts**, exchanged-traded contracts to buy or sell a standard amount of an asset at a specified price at a specific date, are frequently used to hedge price risk.

1.   While **long contract** means buy assets at future date, **short contract** means sell assets at future date. The purpose is to lock in future prices to reduce price risk.

2.   Profit to buyer = ultimate market price – initial futures price

3.   Profit to seller = initial futures price – ultimate market price

Future	Principal Exchange
Government of Canada Bonds	ME
Standard & Poor's Canada 60 Index	ME
U.S. Treasury notes	CBT
U.S. Treasury bonds	CBT
Eurodollar deposits	IMM
Standard & Poor's Index	IMM
Euro	IMM
Yen	IMM
German government bonds (Bunds)	Eurex

B.   Futures contracts are marked to market to avoid default risk. No money changes hands when contracts are initiated. Instead, each party is required to set up a margin account.

1.   For a small cost and a margin deposit, a farmer can protect against price declines by selling corn futures with total contracts approximating production. With a choice of possible delivery date, the maturity selected should be slightly longer than the period of price risk.

2.   If corn prices fall, the daily **mark-to-market** procedure of future exchanges will add deposits to the farmer's account. Otherwise, the farmer needs to put up money into the account.

3.   Unlike option contracts, if prices for corn increase, the gain in the business is offset by losses on the sale (short position) of corn futures.

C.   **The Mechanics of Futures Trading**

1.   Due to the standardization, the futures contract with the exchange is highly liquid and can be easily traded again in the market.

2.   Although futures contract specifies delivery of type of assets at future date, it allows substitutes for possible delivery to prevent corner.

3.   An organized futures exchange acts as a middleman and has a clearing corporation to execute the margin accounts and to arrange deliveries as required.

4. At expiration date, the futures contract becomes a spot contract with immediate delivery and the price of the futures contract equals to the price of the underlying asset delivered.

5. Futures contracts usually do not have to deliver because of the offsetting positions taken. Only the net long and short position matters.

6. A financial manager, worried about higher interest rates during a heavy borrowed period, can hedge higher rates and lock in today's rates by selling T-bill or Eurodollar futures contracts. If rates rise, the business will pay more interest, but rising rates are associated with falling financial futures contract prices. As rates rise, the exchange will credit the manager's account. The manager is gaining for s/he has sold a contract that can be reversed later at a lower price, or s/he has locked in the cost of funds when the futures contract was sold and current rates are now higher.

D. **Commodity and Financial Futures**

1. Commodity and financial futures exist in areas where there is extreme price variability. Futures began first in commodity markets, and became very popular later in the 1970s as interest rates became extremely volatile. Futures lock in prices today, avoiding *both* adverse and favourable future price movements.

IV. FORWARD CONTRACTS

A. **Forward contracts** are agreements to buy or sell an asset in the future at an agreed price. Forward contracts are designed specifically for the risk, amount, and period, whereas futures contracts are standardized contracts as to amount, time, and specific commodity or financial asset.

B. Forward contracts entail delivery; futures seldom entail delivery. Forwards are not marked to market daily like futures, but are settled at maturity which greatly increases the risk of default.

C. In general, it is hard to find a counter party for forward contracts.

V. SWAPS

A. A **SWAP** is an arrangement between two traders to exchange a series of future payments on different terms.

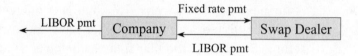

B. A SWAP hedge entails trading a possible adverse price movement for known cash flows with a party that has the opposite need. In the chapter example, Computer Parts was able to improve the terms of its loan for its foreign subsidiary and reduce foreign exchange risk by borrowing in Canada at favourable rates and swapping the dollar loan commitment for a series of annual Swiss francs.

C. SWAPS are often used to trade variable and fixed interest cash flows in the future. Like options and futures and other derivatives, they can be used to hedge business risk or to speculate on future price or interest rate movements. Lack of liquidity is the major disadvantage. However, advantages of swaps include risk reduction, no change in balance sheet, and longer term than futures or options.

D. Is "Derivative" A Four-Letter Word?
1. Derivatives have become infamous to the general public due to the headlines created when investors lost money speculating.
2. The vast majority of investors and businesses use derivatives to hedge the variety of risks they face. Alas, this information does not make splashy headlines.

COMPLETION QUESTIONS

1. _____ is the practice of taking off-setting risks.

2. A producer may wish to purchase a (*call/put*) option to hedge against a price decline.

3. A futures contract involves (*a binding promise/an optional choice*).

4. Use of futures contracts enables a producer to eliminate (*price/quantity*) risk.

5. When trading futures contracts the margin is the (*borrowed/down payment*) amount.

6. The requirement for futures contracts to pay for any loss or receive credit for any profit on a daily basis is called _____ to _____.

7. The ability to manage risks of changing interest rates, exchange rates, and security prices involves the use of _____ futures.

8. A (*hedger/speculator*) in futures markets takes on risk to provide others with insurance.

9. An agreement to buy or sell an asset in the future at an agreed price but without the marked to market requirement is called a _____ contract.

10. An agreement between two traders to exchange a series of future payments on different terms is called a _____.

11. The majority of firms borrowing in the (*domestic/international*) bond market use currency and interest rate SWAPs.

12. The (*Bourse de Montreal/ Winnipeg Commodity Exchange*) trades financial futures.

13. Interest rate swaps are (*more/less*) liquid than futures contracts.

14. The (*fixed/floating*) rate on a swap corresponds to the coupon rate on a discount bond of equivalent maturity.

PROBLEMS

1. What is the general principle of insurance?

2. What are the most frequent types of insurance used by businesses?

3. The chief financial officer of a firm wishes to refinance a long-term bond issue that her company has outstanding because interest rates have declined since the bonds were sold. However, since rates are still falling she thinks it is best to wait and thereby save more money. If she is wrong and interest rates increase she will have to pay more than she would have by refinancing now. How could she use Treasury bond futures contracts to hedge against a possible rise in interest rates?

4. Suppose Megan had a supply of silver that you planned to sell in 6 months. Today's price is $5 per ounce but she wants to be protected against a price decline. The price of silver for 6-months-ahead delivery is $5.25 per ounce. What be her strategy?

5. Could you have used a put or a call option instead of entering into a futures contract as described in problem 4?

6.   What is the difference between a currency swap and an interest rate swap?

7.   What is the difference between a futures contract for foreign exchange and an option to buy or sell foreign exchange?

8.   Discuss how a maker of bread and a wheat farmer could use commodity markets to lessen risk?

9.   What are the disadvantages of holding a commodity instead of selling it through the futures market?

ANSWERS TO COMPLETION QUESTIONS

1.   Hedging
2.   put
3.   a binding promise
4.   price
5.   down payment
6.   marked, market
7.   financial
8.   speculator
9.   forward
10.   swap
11.   international
12.   Bourse de Montreal
13.   less
14.   floating

SOLUTIONS TO PROBLEMS

1.   The general principle of insurance is to protect against a loss by paying a relatively small amount of money. This cost will reduce profitability but it will prevent a much larger disappointment if certain events happen. The key is to think not only in terms of traditional forms of protection offered by insurance companies but to consider a wide variety of business activities that can be protected by the use of certain financial instruments.

2.   Businesses use insurance for protection of property damage due to fire, flood, wind, earthquake, theft, vandalism, war, etc. They insure against various liabilities and court judgements. This chapter considers the use of various financial instruments to help

hedge against movements of commodity prices and financial related variables such as interest rates, foreign currencies' and stock prices.

3. The CFO could sell long-term bond futures with a delivery date of some months into the future. If interest rates increased the value of the bond futures would decline and create a profit, as measured by the difference between the original price received from selling the bond futures and the lower market price paid when covering the earlier sale. This profit would offset the opportunity loss by not refinancing the bonds at the current interest rate which turns out to be lower than the higher rate later. If interest rates had fallen, there would be a loss on the futures contract but this would be offset by the increased savings the company would realize by refinancing at the lower rate.

4. Megan should sell a 6-month futures contract at the $5.25 per ounce price. If she sold her inventory today she would receive the spot price of $5 per ounce. With the futures contract she will receive $5.25 but she will have incurred costs of storage and experienced the opportunity loss of not being able to invest the money if she had sold today.

5. If you purchased a put option, you would pay some amount based on the exercise price, the volatility of silver prices, expected direction for those price movements, etc. This would be a cost of insurance. If silver increased above the exercise price your put would be worthless. If silver declined, you would make a profit from the option. The option gain or loss would offset most of the change in silver prices in comparison to the spot price.

6. With a currency swap, two companies agree to exchange a specific amount of one currency for a specific amount of another at specific dates in the future. A physical transfer of foreign exchanges occurs at the beginning and the end of the contract. Interest rate swap does not involve the switch of any principals. Those two kinds of swaps are very similar.

7. An individual who expects that prices for foreign exchange will rise is said to take a long position. By contrast, someone who expects foreign exchange prices to fall is said to take a short position. Hedging takes place through the purchase of a futures contract for foreign exchange, which specifies today both the delivery date and the price at which the foreign exchange will be acquired. Therefore, it involves taking one position in the cash market and an opposite one in the futures market. Unless the individual has taken another offsetting position, delivery must be carried out when the time is due. The option to buy or sell foreign exchange may not have the delivery unless it is profitable to do so.

8. Both the wheat farmer and the bread maker are exposed to wheat price fluctuations, but any fluctuations have opposite effects for the two parties. If these two parties get together, then much of the risk can be eliminated. The wheat farmer and the bread

maker can simply agree that, at set dates in the future, the wheat farmer will deliver a certain quantity of wheat, and the bread maker will pay a set price. Once the agreement is signed, both parties will have locked in the price of wheat for as long as the contract is in effect, and both of their risk profiles with regard to wheat prices will be completely flat during that time. Note that the wheat farmer does not actually know what the size of the crop will be ahead of time. If the crop is larger than expected, then some portion of the crop will be unhedged. If the crop is small, then the farmer will have to buy more to fulfil the contract and will thereby be exposed to the risk of price changes. Either way, there is some exposure to wheat price fluctuations. But, by hedging, exposure is sharply reduced.

9.   Individuals who are risk-averse wish to avoid risk. Many derivatives products can be used to serve the purposes. Holding a commodity is subject to price fluctuation that is considered to be the major disadvantage. Selling the commodity through the futures market is a hedging process protecting one self against future price changes by shifting some or all of the risk to someone else. Since the individual already owns the commodity, s/he has a position to protect. Unlike a speculator taking no position, s/he cannot bet on price changes in the hope of making a profit.